Peter Zoellner, Robert Halm, Daniela Schapler, Karen Schulze

EWM with SAP S/4HANA®: Architecture and Programming

T0075998

Rheinwerk
Publishing

Editor Meagan White
Acquisitions Editor Hareem Shafi
Copyeditor Melinda Rankin
Cover Design Graham Geary
Photo Credit iStockphoto: 1431499957/© jpgfactory
Layout Design Vera Brauner
Production Graham Geary
Typesetting III-satz, Germany
Printed and bound in Canada, on paper from sustainable sources

ISBN 978-1-4932-2399-2
© 2023 by Rheinwerk Publishing, Inc., Boston (MA)
2nd edition 2023

Library of Congress Cataloging-in-Publication Control Number: 2023019416

All rights reserved. Neither this publication nor any part of it may be copied or reproduced in any form or by any means or translated into another language, without the prior consent of Rheinwerk Publishing, 2 Heritage Drive, Suite 305, Quincy, MA 02171.

Rheinwerk Publishing makes no warranties or representations with respect to the content hereof and specifically disclaims any implied warranties of merchantability or fitness for any particular purpose. Rheinwerk Publishing assumes no responsibility for any errors that may appear in this publication.

"Rheinwerk Publishing" and the Rheinwerk Publishing logo are registered trademarks of Rheinwerk Verlag GmbH, Bonn, Germany. SAP PRESS is an imprint of Rheinwerk Verlag GmbH and Rheinwerk Publishing, Inc.

All of the screenshots and graphics reproduced in this book are subject to copyright © SAP SE, Dietmar-Hopp-Allee 16, 69190 Walldorf, Germany.

SAP, ABAP, ASAP, Concur Hipmunk, Duet, Duet Enterprise, Expenselt, SAP ActiveAttention, SAP Adaptive Server Enterprise, SAP Advantage Database Server, SAP ArchiveLink, SAP Ariba, SAP Business ByDesign, SAP Business Explorer (SAP BEx), SAP BusinessObjects, SAP BusinessObjects Explorer, SAP BusinessObjects Web Intelligence, SAP Business One, SAP Business Workflow, SAP BW/4HANA, SAP C/4HANA, SAP Concur, SAP Crystal Reports, SAP EarlyWatch, SAP Fieldglass, SAP Fiori, SAP Global Trade Services (SAP GTS), SAP GoingLive, SAP HANA, SAP Jam, SAP Leonardo, SAP Lumira, SAP MaxDB, SAP NetWeaver, SAP PartnerEdge, SAPPHIRE NOW, SAP PowerBuilder, SAP PowerDesigner, SAP R/2, SAP R/3, SAP Replication Server, SAP Roambi, SAP S/4HANA, SAP S/4HANA Cloud, SAP SQL Anywhere, SAP Strategic Enterprise Management (SAP SEM), SAP SuccessFactors, SAP Vora, TripIt, and Qualtrics are registered or unregistered trademarks of SAP SE, Walldorf, Germany.

All other products mentioned in this book are registered or unregistered trademarks of their respective companies.

Contents at a Glance

Dear Reader,

Everyone has unique warehousing needs, whether you're a multimillion-dollar corporation with warehouses on three continents—or you're just trying to figure out how and where to store your Christmas decorations when they're not in use. First, you consider the "standard" workflow: most people only need to retrieve their decorations once a year in December, so up into the attic they go, helpfully placed behind the camping equipment you only use in the summer.

But wait! What if you're a decorating fiend who reuses lights and wreaths for multiple holidays? You like to decorate for Valentine's Day, Easter, St. Patrick's Day, Fourth of July, International Talk Like a Pirate Day—the list goes on. Well, in that case, you have unique-to-you warehousing needs and need a solution that goes beyond just the standard workflow.

Enter *EWM with SAP S/4HANA: Architecture and Programming*. While it might be a bit too much to run an entire implementation just to store your holiday decorations, it's probably just right for your complex enterprise warehouse!

What did you think about our new second edition? Your comments and suggestions are the most useful tools to help us make our books the best they can be. Please feel free to contact me and share any praise or criticism you may have.

Thank you for purchasing a book from SAP PRESS!

Meagan White
Editor, SAP PRESS

meaganw@rheinwerk-publishing.com
www.sap-press.com
Rheinwerk Publishing · Boston, MA

Contents

3   Frameworks and Development Tools in Extended Warehouse Management

147

4   Enhancing SAP Best Practices for Embedded EWM

5   Function Modules, Methods, and APIs for Extended Warehouse Management

6 Useful Business Add-Ins within Extended Warehouse Management

Appendices

Foreword

Today, more than 2,500 companies from various industries already use SAP Extended Warehouse Management (SAP EWM) for their warehouse sites located in more than 65 countries. Current global disruptions make companies even more aware of the fact that a functional supply chain is an essential driver for their business success. Hence, they further invest in their supply chains.

SAP EWM is a best-of-breed warehouse management solution that is integral to building an intelligent supply chain operation, covering a broad range, from small to high-end automated storage facilities acting as production supply warehouses, distribution centers, and transit hubs. The application is capable of optimizing core warehouse processes, simplifying and automating complex process steps, eliminating redundancy, and enhancing the visibility of warehouse operations and the stock situation. This is mainly achieved through tight integration with other applications, such as SAP Transportation Management (SAP TM) and SAP Manufacturing Execution, or global track-and-trace software. Such integration increases both user engagement and productivity by integrating wearables, mobile devices, and modern radio-frequency identification (RFID) technology.

Starting with SAP S/4HANA 1909, SAP bridged the feature gaps between decentralized SAP EWM based on SAP S/4HANA and the standalone SAP EWM 9.5. As SAP EWM is the official successor to Warehouse Management, they put major effort into simplification, such as with synchronous postings of goods movements.

In addition, having identified software integration as an important key to business success, SAP has greatly extended the involvement of SAP EWM in plant maintenance and production processes. In this area, SAP has provided just-in-time (JIT), Kanban, and work-in-progress (WIP) handling, plus dynamic production staging capabilities. SAP has also enabled further scenarios in the area of integration with quality management. However, the biggest change was made in the integration between SAP TM and SAP EWM based on a common object—the freight order—which is called *advanced shipping and receiving*.

Last but not least, as a shortage in labor is further driving the need for automation in different areas of the warehouse, SAP has recently made available an out-of-the-box integration of SAP EWM with SAP Warehouse Robotics.

No warehouse site is identical to another, and each business or company has its own functional requirements, so there will always be a need for individual adjustments and enhancements of warehouse management software, either through configuration or custom development. Based on the new SAP S/4HANA technologies following the market expectation to make a software product easy to extend, SAP has further invested into application programming interfaces (APIs) based on Open Data Protocol (OData).

These APIs allow SAP to expose core SAP EWM functionalities to the outer world. Via such APIs, SAP can allow its users to simplify the way they enrich existing SAP EWM functionalities. Other technologies SAP has invested into include the commonly available ABAP RESTful application programming model and ABAP core data services (CDS views). Finally, SAP also continuously strives to help its users to ensure good quality of their custom developments by adding SAP EWM–specific checks to the ABAP Test Cockpit.

These are just a few examples of how SAP is innovative in its strategic warehouse management solution. The company will continue to invest in more innovative warehouse capabilities, such as camera recognition and dedicated mobile applications. For the future, SAP intends to further focus on improving the user experience by investing in role-based SAP Fiori transactions.

This book will help you become acquainted with the basic principles of the SAP EWM architecture so that you can improve development decisions for your own SAP EWM implementation. You should pay special attention to the quality and performance of custom code, staying close to the standard way of processing to ensure that your enhancements support your supply chain sustainably and efficiently and that you can benefit from future innovations that are already planned.

The authors of this book share with you their valuable knowledge gained through many years of practical experience in the implementation support, development, and optimization of embedded and decentralized SAP EWM. I hope you enjoy reading this book and wish you many more successful implementations of SAP EWM in SAP S/4HANA.

Florian Kuchta
Head of Product Management, SAP Extended Warehouse Management, SAP SE

Preface

SAP Extended Warehouse Management (SAP EWM) is SAP's strategic software solution for warehousing and was introduced to the market in 2006. Now embedded in SAP S/4HANA, EWM largely surpasses SAP S/4HANA's stock room management solution regarding functionality, deployment, usability, throughput, and scalability. It can thereby more effectively support the advanced requirements for the operation of large distribution, production, and transit or hub warehouses.

> **Note**
>
> Throughout this book, the term *EWM* always refers to EWM in SAP S/4HANA, both the decentralized and embedded deployment options. Where differentiation by deployment option is required, we will use *decentralized EWM* to refer to the official decentralized EWM *based on* SAP S/4HANA, and *embedded EWM* for embedded EWM *in* SAP S/4HANA.

Both technical and functional improvements in EWM increase the flexibility of the software, but they also require an appropriate understanding of the software's implementation and operation. In order to be able to implement and use EWM successfully, a solid understanding of its working principles and functionalities is essential—a challenging task in a complex application such as EWM.

Compared to other business software applications, warehouse management solutions often require a higher proportion of custom-specific enhancements; hardly any warehouse is completely run on standard functionality due to the fact that industry and site-specific requirements vary widely. From a higher-level perspective, core warehousing process flows may seem identical, but differences are likely to be identified when going into the details. SAP has well considered this variance with its many years of experience in the design of warehouse management software. The design and development of EWM have resulted in a plurality of configuration and enhancement options. The high number of customizing transactions, Business Add-Ins (BadIs), and enhancement frameworks available in EWM clearly prove this thought and allow for a customized implementation of the system without modification of the source code—thus being release stable.

As long-time developers and consultants for SAP warehouse management software— specifically for EWM—we have decided to write a second edition of this book to continuously give you everything you need to have your project benefit from EWM's enhancement options, while demonstrating numerous examples of practical implementations for your reference. The time seems appropriate, as with growing product maturity, customers from various industries seeking an extendable and actively developed warehousing solution for their global operations are frequently implementing EWM.

Who Should Read This Book?

We've written this book for all who wish to deepen their architectural and technical understanding of EWM in SAP S/4HANA. This may include consultants and developers planning or working on EWM projects. It can also serve as a guide for solution architects aligning customer requirements and solution design to the standard functionality provided, identifying functional gaps, and seeking extendibility options.

Implementation projects of business applications are frequently run by separating functional and technical roles and responsibilities. This behavior is usually less pronounced in warehousing solution implementations, and this is why the book claims to jointly present process and technology knowledge while still focusing on technical features of EWM. The target group, and thus the content of the book, is less separated by functionality or technology than is often the case in the SAP environment.

Structure and Content

The first three chapters of this book will give you the basic knowledge that you will require in order to properly plan, design, and implement custom developments in EWM. Their content is therefore more theoretical but may in some cases include coding examples to explain the use of fundamental programming logic and frameworks in EWM:

- **Chapter 1** talks about the need for flexibility in software solutions for warehouse management and provides an overview of the extensibility of EWM.
- **Chapter 2** describes the main components of EWM with regard to their data objects, functions, and integration with other EWM software modules. Graphical representations of data models support the explanations. You will gain the basic architectural knowledge that should enable you to identify the right spot for an enhancement and plan out its design, which essentially describes the work of a solution architect.
- **Chapter 3** introduces the main frameworks that are used in EWM and shows their use in each module of the software. Where applicable, explicit enhancement options for each framework are described. Their handling is explained in detail as most extensions will be implemented using the frameworks. This chapter provides the necessary basic knowledge for additional programming with these frameworks and thus is especially useful for developers.
- **Chapter 4** builds on the first three chapters. It presents the basic enhancement concepts by giving examples and hence provides more practical knowledge. The SAP Best Practices content for embedded EWM forms the underlying organizational and procedural solution setup for these example enhancements. We introduce this solution setup in the first section of the chapter.

In the second section, we present two process scenarios for goods receipts. The third section of the chapter again deals with the two process scenarios of outbound-oriented operations and goods issue. Finally, the last section of the chapter presents the periodic physical inventory process scenario. Within a selection of five processes that are a part of the SAP Best Practices for embedded EWM, we describe many potential enhancements in detail alongside coding examples.

Although all the functionality of the EWM solution may not be covered within the processes run by SAP Best Practices, the basic functionality of warehouse logistics is still contained in therein. In this book, we sensibly restrict the presentation of EWM to the functional scope of SAP Best Practices so as to keep focus on, and allow for reenactment of, the developments of enhancements.

- **Chapter 5** describes a selection of core functions in warehouse logistics. We focus on central and frequently used functions and offer a quick overview of their uses. A full presentation of all functions available for warehouse logistics alone would most certainly go beyond the scope of this book.

- **Chapter 6** presents a listing and descriptions of central BAdIs of the core EWM applications. Again, as there are more than 800 BAdIs available in the core EWM applications alone, we are concentrating on frequently used BAdIs in the functional areas of delivery processing, wave management, and warehouse task/order processing, as well as exception handling.

- In **Appendix A**, you'll find a collection of programming guidelines that you can use as a reference when enhancing EWM.

- In **Appendix B**, we conclude with some thoughts on the migration of SAP EWM to EWM in SAP S/4HANA, introducing potential strategies and procedures tied to that topic.

Prerequisites

Before you plan and implement additional developments for EWM, you should ensure that the functional requirement isn't already covered by standard provided functionality. Therefore, readers of this book should already hold fundamental knowledge of EWM processes and customizing as it is, for example, offered in EWM training curriculums or presented within the book *Warehouse Management with SAP S/4HANA* (Namita Sachan and Aman Jain, SAP PRESS, 2022) and *Warehouse Management with SAP EWM* (Balaji Kannapan, Hari Tripathy, and Vinay Krishna, SAP PRESS, 2016). This book builds on that knowledge.

All coding presented in this book has been well documented; however, we still assume basic knowledge of ABAP Objects programming. We have made most of the coding examples contained in this book publicly available in the GitHub repositories for user EWMDEV (SAP S/4HANA EWM Architecture and Programming). You can find these at *https://github.com/ewmdev*. The repositories are structured by and named for the chapters of this book in which the code is presented. They can be viewed, downloaded, and implemented for trial and referencing purposes in a sandbox environment. Make sure to have the latest build of the open-source GIT client for ABAP (abapGit) installed on the system in which you would like to implement the code. This client comfortably connects your SAP system with the GitHub platform. You can find it at *https://abap-git.org* along with further documentation.

It is not our aim to teach you programming in ABAP but to make it easier for you to plan and implement development enhancements in EWM. Ideally, you have an SAP system at your disposal in which you can activate the SAP Best Practices for embedded EWM. This will enable you to reenact the examples given in the second part of the book, which will certainly be optimal for your learning.

Throughout the book, icons will alert you to special tips, notes, and examples, as follows:

Note

This icon helps expand on a topic, either by presenting you with extra information or by providing you with links to additional resources.

Hints and Tips

This icon highlights tips that will make your work easier. It also alerts you to additional information on the topic in question.

Examples

This icon explains and gives more information on a current topic based on practical examples.

Acknowledgments

The author team would like to thank everyone who supported and inspired us during the writing of this book—especially the EWM product development team at SAP, and Meagan, Hareem, and everyone at Rheinwerk Publishing.

Very special thanks to Florian for taking his valuable time to write this edition's foreword.

We also thank our consulting and support colleagues at SAP, prismat, and abat.

Chapter 1

Flexible Warehouse Management with Extended Warehouse Management

No warehouse is like any other; the diversity of stored goods and warehouse sites make for some challenges when it comes to warehouse management with standardized software. This chapter discusses how EWM offers the flexibility to meet specific warehousing requirements.

In addition to the general configurability of SAP software, organizations frequently make use of its extensibility. This is why a variety of software and consulting firms specialize in the enhancement of SAP software and organizations also maintain in-house development departments.

Every day, thousands of people exchange information within SAP's own public platform for SAP professionals, SAP Community (*https://community.sap.com/*), regarding tips and tricks, and not only for developing with SAP software. In this book, we support companies running SAP, consultants, and developers in enhancing EWM because our project experience shows us that SAP software extensibility is heavily used in implementation projects of warehouse management solutions.

[+]

EWM on the SAP Community

Again, there is a specific topic on EWM available at SAP Community, which you can find at *https://community.sap.com/topics/extended-warehouse-management*. You can use this as your entry point to valuable information about new functionality, the product roadmap, and training.

In the following sections, we examine the reasons for this extensibility usage and give an overview of the extensibility of EWM. Next to the various deployment options for EWM in the system landscape, integration with other SAP and non-SAP software products, and configuration of the warehouse organizational structure and process flows, it is the especially high enhancement capability of EWM that ensures software flexibility and adaptability during implementation and operation.

Throughout this book, the term *EWM* always refers to EWM in SAP S/4HANA, both the decentralized and embedded deployment options. Where differentiation by deployment option is required, we will use *decentralized EWM* to refer to the official decentralized EWM *based on* SAP S/4HANA and *embedded EWM* for embedded EWM *in* SAP S/4HANA.

1.1   Warehouse Management with Standardized Software: Deployment, Configuration, and Enhancement

Using standardized software when it comes to managing a warehouse with a large functional scope will depend on the adaptability of the application simply because no warehouse is identical to another in regard to physical layout and operation. The need for deployment options and configurability of the software mainly stems from the uniqueness of warehouses in the following areas:

- Physical layout
- Availability of storage space: capacity utilization
- Nature of products: storage concepts
- Degree of automation (e.g., automation equipment and robots)
- Degree of system availability (e.g., performance requirements and planned downtime)

It should be noted that storage and system availability requirements may frequently change over a warehouse's lifetime. These changes might occur with the introduction of new products or automation equipment, as well as strategic realignment of supply chains, all of which may result in new creation or conversion of storage areas. As a change to the physical layout may be costly, be time-consuming, and lead to a temporary loss of storage space, change capabilities of a warehousing software application are often called for, not only to adapt to new physical conditions but also to avoid physical adaptation efforts.

Such detailed customer requirements are difficult to predict and can no longer be anticipated in the context of configurability. This is where the focus turns from configuration to the enhancement options of the application.

Under these conditions, the architect of standard software needs to identify the basic requirements and functionality. Keeping track of potential variations is a key element of standard software design, as is incorporating corresponding configuration and enhancement options.

Regarding the flexibility of the software, we understand the capability of the application to adapt to customer requirements. Ultimately, this flexibility might be measured by the number of existing deployment, configuration, and enhancement options. In the next section, we'll talk about these options for EWM.

1.2   Flexibility of Extended Warehouse Management

So, what is SAP's answer to the previously identified need for flexibility in software solutions for warehouse management? In this section, we highlight some examples of the deployment options, configurability, and extensibility of EWM. Let's start with the deployment options that have become available with EWM in SAP S/4HANA.

With SAP S/4HANA, two deployment options for EWM are available: embedded EWM, since version 1610, and decentralized EWM, since version 1809 FPS 02. Embedded EWM represents a new offering for warehouse management directly included in SAP S/4HANA (to date, licensed in a basic or advanced option), where SAP EWM based on SAP NetWeaver had only been available as a standalone system from its first release onward. Although embedded and decentralized EWM share the same code base, functional differences exist mainly due to the nature of a decentralized system following different integration architecture principles: while *embedded EWM* follows the SAP S/4HANA simplification approach, focusing on the elimination of redundant transactional and master data, *decentralized EWM* further relies on relevant data objects to be available in its own system so to ensure operation while the backend ERP system might not be available. Such functional differences should be considered next to strategic, operational risk, and cost criteria when choosing the right deployment option.

[«]

SAP EWM Deployment Options Best Practices

SAP Note 1606493 contains valuable information on EWM deployment. You should also find other highly informative support SAP Notes referenced or referencing this note. Consider this the starting point for an evaluation of a discussion about the deployment of your EWM implementation. We also recommend studying the release information and restrictions for EWM in the latest available SAP S/4HANA versions.

Now turning to configuration and enhancement options, we chose the following examples because we wanted to highlight two new functionalities of EWM that were not available in SAP ERP Warehouse Management or WM in SAP S/4HANA (and neither are in its SAP S/4HANA successor, stock room management). First, we'll look at activity areas as new elements of the warehouse organizational structure; second, we'll turn toward the modeling of multistep warehouse processes by means of storage control.

1.2.1   Activity Areas: Flexible Assignment of Storage Bins to Work Areas

EWM allows for the grouping of storage bins for a particular activity, such as putaway or picking. Such groups are called *activity areas*. The grouping of storage bins into activity areas can be done regardless of the bins' storage types or storage area assignments and is also not limited to other storage bin characteristics.

After completing the activity area setup and bin assignment, the bins belonging to certain activity areas are sorted by configurable criteria. This bin sorting will be applied for the sequencing of warehouse tasks within a warehouse order.

The available customization of activity areas includes configuration options for relevant parameters of the warehouse operation, as follows:

- Activities (definition and determination)
- Activity areas (definition and assignment of bins)
- Sort sequences (bin sorting rule within an activity area)

Figure 1.1 shows the available Customizing transactions for the configuration of activity areas.

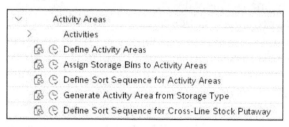

Figure 1.1 Customizing of Activity Areas

The sorting of storage bins within an activity area is of great importance: it ultimately controls the paths and distances that need to be traveled by the operators in the warehouse while executing movement activities, as well as the utilization of storage bins. EWM provides configuration options for the sorting logic that controls the sort order, as shown in Figure 1.2.

Figure 1.2 Customizing of Sort Sequences

The available configuration options should already perfectly meet the sorting requirements of many warehouses. But should they still be insufficient, a program for uploading sorting data from external sources and a BAdI by which a custom sorting logic can be implemented are also available. You can find the BAdI in the Implementation Guide (IMG) under the path **Business Add-Ins (BAdIs) for Extended Warehouse Management • Master Data • Activity Areas • BAdI: Define Sort Sequence of Activity Areas**. The BAdI allows you to change the bin sorting that has been determined according to the configuration parameters. The sorting is made available as a data input parameter of the BAdI method and allows for being adapted inside the BAdI. This way you can flexibly enhance or overrule the configuration options provided by implementing and activating the BAdI.

1.2.2 Storage Control: Modeling Multistep Warehouse Processes

The second example to illustrate EWM's flexibility in configuration and enhancement takes us to the storage control functionality. This can be differentiated into layout-oriented or process-oriented storage control, and both can be used simultaneously. By using storage control, you can, for example, define the additional activities that should be carried out for certain products or movements before putting away the stock. This activity can be modeled as a work step and be determined as part of a warehouse process flow.

When configured as such, EWM will create a warehouse task to move the stock from the receiving zone into the work center at the time that the goods receipt has been completed. The confirmation of this task will automatically generate the follow-up warehouse task for putaway. For this to work, the stock must actually be contained in a handling unit as the handling unit keeps track of the progress within the process flow by holding the current process step. The respective steps in the process can be modeled in a flexible way and be combined with layout-oriented routing.

As an example, you can configure things so that, on the way from the receiving zone to the work center, stock has to be handed over between resources of different resource types. This way you can have the system control the warehouse activities to a great extent and increase the visibility of inventory at any time. Similarly, as in the example of the activity areas, the storage control functionality can be set up via configuration options. Figure 1.3 and Figure 1.4 show the respective Customizing transactions for layout-oriented and process-oriented storage control, which allow for a high degree of flexibility even when configuring more complex process flows.

But it may happen that you have a requirement that can't be covered by means of configuration alone. Let's say you want to suspend an intermediate location of the layout-oriented setup or skip a process-oriented step in certain situations or for certain products. For this purpose, once again, BAdIs are available that allow you to individually tailor solution logic to the particular requirements of storage control, as shown in Figure 1.5.

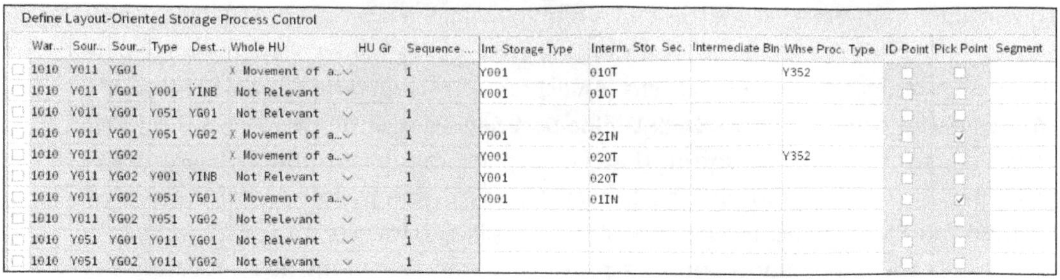

Define Layout-Oriented Storage Process Control

War...	Sour...	Sour...	Type	Dest...	Whole HU	HU Gr	Sequence ...	Int. Storage Type	Interm. Stor. Sec.	Intermediate Bin	Whse Proc. Type	ID Point	Pick Point	Segment
1010	Y011	YG01			X Movement of a...		1	Y001	010T		Y352	☐	☐	
1010	Y011	YG01	Y001	YINB	Not Relevant		1	Y001	010T			☐	☐	
1010	Y011	YG01	Y051	YG01	Not Relevant		1					☐	☐	
1010	Y011	YG01	Y051	YG02	X Movement of a...		1	Y001	02IN			☐	☑	
1010	Y011	YG02			X Movement of a...		1	Y001	020T		Y352	☐	☐	
1010	Y011	YG02	Y001	YINB	Not Relevant		1	Y001	020T			☐	☐	
1010	Y011	YG02	Y051	YG01	X Movement of a...		1	Y001	01IN			☐	☑	
1010	Y011	YG02	Y051	YG02	Not Relevant		1					☐	☐	
1010	Y051	YG01	Y011	YG01	Not Relevant		1					☐	☐	
1010	Y051	YG02	Y011	YG02	Not Relevant		1					☐	☐	

Figure 1.3 Configuration of Layout-Oriented Storage Control

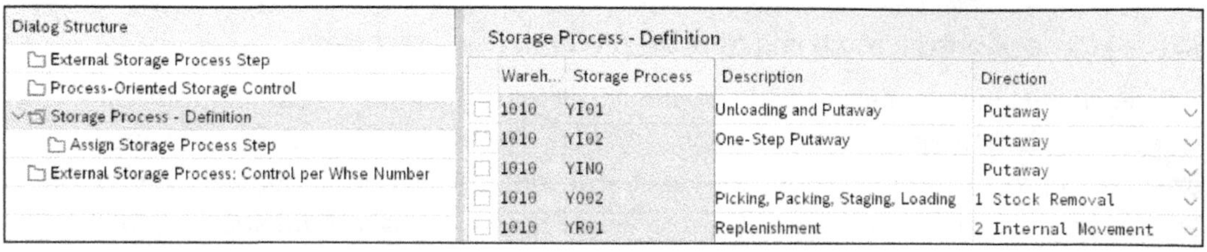

Wareh...	Storage Process	Description	Direction
1010	YI01	Unloading and Putaway	Putaway
1010	YI02	One-Step Putaway	Putaway
1010	YINQ		Putaway
1010	YO02	Picking, Packing, Staging, Loading	1 Stock Removal
1010	YR01	Replenishment	2 Internal Movement

Figure 1.4 Configuration of Process-Oriented Storage Control

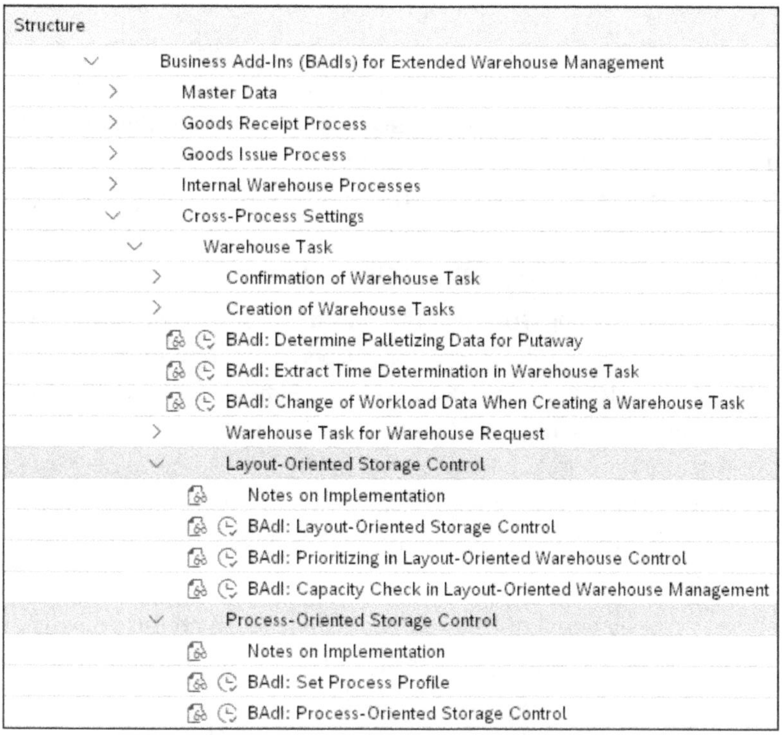

Figure 1.5 Enhancement Options for Storage Control

1.3   Summary

EWM indeed offers a huge variety of configurable and expandable functionality in both available deployment options. Ultimately, there are more than 800 Customizing tables and 800 BAdIs available in the latest release of EWM in SAP S/4HANA for the warehouse logistics module alone, which can be seen as the core module of EWM.

EWM thus can be called a highly flexible warehouse management solution. Numerous requirements of medium complexity can already be met by the vast functional scope and configurability of the standard-provided software application. If enhancements are necessary, they can often be achieved through BAdI implementations or by using specialized frameworks to realize adaptations and enhancements of, for example, mobile transactions or monitor applications. Using these, you can create release stable enhancements. Experience teaches us that such enhancement options are commonly used in EWM implementation projects, especially for the implementation of highly customer-specific requirements. You'll learn how to use the enhancement tools in Chapter 3, but first, let's look at EWM's architecture in the next chapter in order to grow your understanding of the solution from a technical point of view.

Chapter 2
Architecture

In order to program in EWM, we must first understand the software's individual components. This chapter describes the main components in terms of their function and objects and concludes by discussing their integration with the SAP ERP or SAP S/4HANA system.

The architecture of extended warehouse management (EWM) in SAP S/4HANA is characterized by a variety of application components and objects that exhibit the rich functionality of the system itself. Some of these components will be discussed in detail with respect to their function and their properties in the following sections of this chapter:

- **Delivery processing (see Section 2.1)**
  Delivery processing receives requests for inbound storage and outbound retrieval, as well as for the transfer of stock, which mainly result from the order management applications of the SAP ERP or SAP S/4HANA system. It is therefore closely linked to the SAP ERP or SAP S/4HANA system's materials management, sales and distribution, logistics execution, and production planning functionalities as well as most of its own components.

- **Warehouse logistics (see Section 2.2)**
  Warehouse logistics, also considered the *core*, provides a multiplicity of functions that are necessary for the planning and execution of activities within the warehouse, predominantly using warehouse tasks and warehouse orders.

- **Inventory management (see Section 2.3)**
  Inventory management allows for the management of stock in different spatial and physical states to the level of the storage bin, resource, and transportation unit. It is closely linked with inventory management within materials management.

- **Quality inspection (see Section 2.4)**
  For quality control of inbound and stocked goods, EWM provides a close link to inbound delivery processing and inventory management. Decentralized EWM relies on the Quality Inspection Engine, while embedded EWM eliminates the Quality Inspection Engine and directly connects to SAP ERP or SAP S/4HANA's quality management functionality.

- **Integration with ERP systems (see Section 2.5)**
  Integration with ERP systems can be considered a cross-sectional component of EWM as most of the previously mentioned functional areas natively interface with the SAP ERP or SAP S/4HANA system. This section presents numerous interfaces for

the interaction between SAP ERP or SAP S/4HANA and EWM, again emphasizing differences of decentralized and embedded EWM along with integration options for non–SAP ERP systems.

Other components of EWM such as labor management, material flow system, exception handling, value-added services, EWM's own master data, and integration with other SAP and non-SAP systems, to only name a few, are not considered in this chapter, but discussion of them may rudimentarily be dotted throughout the other chapters. Instead, we try to focus on what we consider the most frequently used components of EWM.

2.1 Delivery Processing

The EWM *delivery* in its various forms, also often more technically referred to as a *warehouse request*, is one of the key objects in EWM. In this section, we explain how this rather complex data object is constructed. Here, we will stick to the name *delivery*.

Business inventory inflows and outflows are usually booked into and out of EWM based on inbound deliveries and outbound deliveries. Once the SAP ERP or SAP S/4HANA system is integrated with EWM, such deliveries will usually be created in EWM with reference to a corresponding SAP ERP or SAP S/4HANA document, such as an SAP ERP or SAP S/4HANA delivery resulting from a purchase order or sales order.

The delivery in EWM is modeled in several different documents. Depending on function and processing phases, different types of documents may be used that will be categorized by predefined document categories. In decentralized EWM, you can distinguish between *notifications or requests* (copies of the preceding SAP ERP or SAP S/4HANA document), which in a decentralized environment are essential from the perspective of communication with SAP ERP or SAP S/4HANA or other *legacy*, meaning non–SAP, ERP systems, and *deliveries or delivery orders* (processing documents), which are mainly worked with and updated alongside the warehouse operation. Apart from this, embedded EWM makes use of these processing documents only to eliminate redundancies in a same-system environment.

Table 2.1 provides an overview of all document categories in the delivery processing used in EWM and mentions the central transaction for each of them as well as their availability in SAP S/4HANA.

Document Category	Description	EWM Transaction	Available in SAP S/4HANA
IDR	Inbound delivery notification	/SCWM/IDN	■ Embedded: no ■ Decentralized: optional
ODR	Outbound delivery request	/SCWM/ODR	■ Embedded: no ■ Decentralized: optional

Table 2.1 Overview of Document Categories and Associated /SCWM/ UI Transactions

Document Category	Description	EWM Transaction	Available in SAP S/4HANA
POR	Posting change request	/SCWM/IM_DR	■ Embedded: no ■ Decentralized: optional
GRN	Expected goods receipt notification	/SCWM/GRN	■ Embedded: no ■ Decentralized: optional
PDI	Inbound delivery	/SCWM/PRDI	■ Embedded: yes ■ Decentralized: yes
PDO	Outbound delivery order	/SCWM/PRDO	■ Embedded: yes ■ Decentralized: yes
SPC	Posting change	/SCWM/IM_PC	■ Embedded: yes ■ Decentralized: yes
EGR	Expected goods receipt	/SCWM/GRPE /SCWM/GRPI	■ Embedded: no ■ Decentralized: yes
WMR	Stock transfer	/SCWM/IM_ST	■ Embedded: yes ■ Decentralized: yes
FDO	Outbound delivery	/SCWM/FD	■ Embedded: yes ■ Decentralized: yes
PWR	Production material request	/SCWM/PMR	■ Embedded: yes ■ Decentralized: yes

Table 2.1 Overview of Document Categories and Associated /SCWM/ UI Transactions (Cont.)

In the following sections, we describe how deliveries are arranged in the logistics overall flow and give an overview of the key technical objects.

[«]

Production Material Request

The *production material request* was introduced as part of the *advanced production integration* functionality of EWM. The production material request originates from the production or process order in SAP ERP or SAP S/4HANA. However, the distribution of this object does not use the delivery interfaces; furthermore, the strict update restrictions for deliveries from SAP ERP or SAP S/4HANA to EWM do not apply.

2.1.1   Function of Delivery Processing

Delivery processing provides a number of functions to perform various logistical activities in the warehouse. In particular, it has the task of handling inbound, outbound, and internal transfer and posting change operations of stock and triggering the feedback to the respective SAP ERP or SAP S/4HANA system.

The component uses documents that are tailor-made for each particular business context. We will elaborate on these different documents in this section.

When distributing SAP ERP or SAP S/4HANA deliveries to decentralized EWM, notifications or requests may be created, from which in turn EWM deliveries are produced using the transfer service class /SCDL/CL_TS_MANAGEMENT (method TRANSFER_OBJ). The preceding documents can be seen as content templates for the creation of the later deliveries. That is, based on the data of the preceding document, the EWM-specific information from Customizing (e.g., document categories, item categories, warehouse process types) and master data (e.g., warehouse product, storage bin, batch) will be read in order to enrich the warehouse request accordingly. Activities that were carried out by operators within the system during the warehouse request processing are updated in these documents. Thus, you always find an overview of the current processing progress of the relevant document in the system, mainly by means of document flow and status management.

For a schematic overview of the relationship between notifications and deliveries in decentralized EWM, see Figure 2.1; it shows what delivery objects from an SAP ERP or SAP S/4HANA system finally produce which EWM deliveries according to the logistical process.

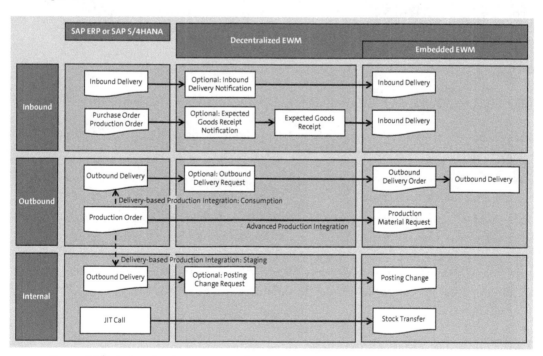

Figure 2.1 Relationship between Notifications and Deliveries Regarding Deployment Options

Regarding the technical document architecture, however, there is no difference between notifications and deliveries. Technically, all documents in the delivery

2

processing are built and modeled identically using a common underlying framework, which we will introduce shortly.

Delivery Processing of EWM in SAP S/4HANA

For more functional information about supported processes of delivery processing in EWM in SAP S/4HANA and references to configuration options, see the application documentation within the SAP Help Portal (*http://help.sap.com/*). From the start page, follow this path: **SAP S/4HANA • Product Assistance • Enterprise Business Applications • Supply Chain • Warehousing • Extended Warehouse Management • Delivery Processing**.

2.1.2   Object EWM Delivery and Data Model

In EWM, deliveries are modeled based on ABAP Objects. By reading deliveries, object instances are created that represent the respective documents. These object instances may then be accessed for updates of certain object aspects on either the document header or item level, for example, of delivery dates.

In addition to pure reading of database data, more automatic processes occur in background during the reading or creation of such object instances; among other functions, determinations and validations are performed on the object instances to evaluate and set dynamic data—for example, aggregated quantities, statuses, and so on.

In the following sections, we will go into more detail about the modeling of the delivery object in EWM, starting with the modeling framework and going into the key aspects of the object and object data access.

Business Object Processing Framework

In this context, we briefly explain the Business Object Processing Framework (BOPF) and the way determinations, validations, and actions are performed on EWM delivery objects. BOPF is in its present form a framework for the implementation of business objects, following the principles of a service-oriented architecture (SOA).

It contains the necessary functions for the implementation of enterprise document objects and supports a uniformly usable modeling standard. The SOA concept is mainly based on enterprise services, which underlie a strict governance process to ensure the necessary uniform business semantics of existing applications and beyond. The enterprise services delivered by SAP are structured along business process lines and can be assembled into an automated processing flow.

BOPF controls the business logic of the application and covers the deployment, buffering, and storage of data. Hence, business logic and data management are strictly separated, as well as modification of and checking the data managed. From the software application platform layer perspective, today's BOPF, as it is used in various SAP products (e.g., SAP Transportation Management), is no longer compatible with the EWM

BOPF; however, the basics are still recognizable in EWM delivery processing. Via Transaction /BOPF/CONF_UI, an insight into the clearly structured modeling of the various document categories of EWM delivery processing is provided (see Figure 2.2).

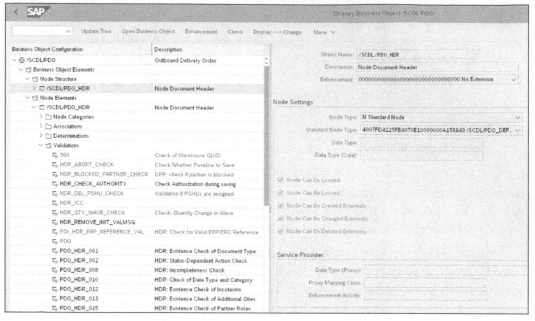

Figure 2.2 BOPF UI to Object /SCDL/PDO

Construction of the EWM Delivery Object

An EWM delivery object always consists of a header and at least one item. The technical relationship is produced by the key holding the DOCID (globally unique internal header identification) and the ITEMID (globally unique internal item identification). In addition, the following other properties, called *aspects*, are assigned by default as well:

- Status
- Dates
- Reference documents
- Aggregated quantities
- Locations
- Business partners
- Document flow

Additional data objects that you can use optionally, such as handling units, transportation units, and so on, are also linked from the corresponding applications to the delivery. Figure 2.3 roughly shows the construction of the warehouse request or delivery object.

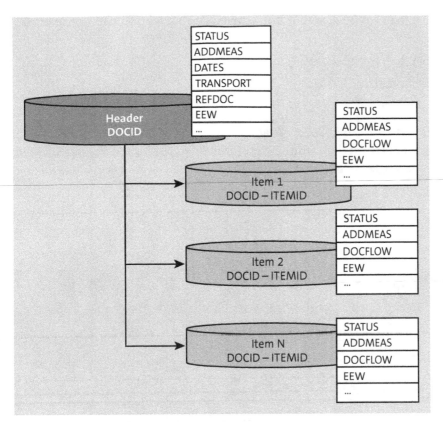

Figure 2.3 Construction of Delivery Object in EWM

A delivery object is represented by document categories at the header level (refer back to Table 2.1) and item categories at the item level. These header and item categories form the basis on which the business properties of each document are categorized.

The following item categories exist in EWM as of the SAP S/4HANA 2022 release for document categories:

- DLV: Standard delivery item (PDI and PDO)
- PAC: Packing item (PDI and PDO)
- RET: Returns item (PDI and PDO)
- TXT: Text item (PDI and PDO)
- CGO: Transit item (PDI and PDO)
- WIP: Work in progress (PDI)
- VAL: Value item (PDO)
- CMP: Component (PWR)
- OCP: Outbound component (PWR)

In addition, at the item level, among others, the following hierarchy elements are distinguished:

- Main item (DSP)
- Batch split item (BSP)
- Delivery split item (FSD)

The split items can occur in EWM, for example, when you post the goods issue only for a specific item and not for the entire delivery (delivery split) or when you pick different batches for one single main item (batch split). Split items are always in a fixed hierarchy from the main item.

Table 2.2 shows the database tables for document header and item data in delivery processing. For more database tables for the objects mentioned, you can check the dictionary objects included in package /SCDL/DATA_MODEL.

Database Table	Description
/SCDL/DB_REQH	Inbound Delivery Notification/Outbound Delivery Request: Header
/SCDL/DB_REQI	Inbound Delivery Notification/Outbound Delivery Request: Item
/SCDL/DB_PROCH_I	Inbound Delivery: Header
/SCDL/DB_PROCI_I	Inbound Delivery: Item
/SCDL/DB_PROCH_O	Outbound Delivery Order: Header
/SCDL/DB_PROCI_O	Outbound Delivery Order: Item
/SCDL/DB_DLVH_O	Outbound Delivery: Header
/SCDL/DB_DLVI_O	Outbound Delivery: Item
/SCDL/DB_PROCH_P	Production Material Request: Header
/SCDL/DB_PROCI_P	Production Material Request: Item

Table 2.2 Database Tables of Delivery Header and Item

The structure and the concept of the delivery object in EWM allows you to access individual items and extrapolate them without locking the entire delivery. This has, in practice, the great advantage of allowing different items of a delivery to be worked on in parallel—for example, during picking—without evoking any locking conflicts.

From a performance point of view, this also results in a further advantage: processes using delivery data can work at the item level and may therefore load the respective item data only, without needing to load all of the other items of the relevant delivery document in the memory.

Service Providers and Aspects

To allow all applications in EWM to access a delivery object via a central interface, service providers are used. These service providers consist of interfaces and their respective methods that enable the applications to read, write, and execute actions for a specific business object. Also, the service providers serve to return the requested data from the business object, well prepared in the respective structures of the calling application. This architecture allows a generic use of the business object, tailored to the specific requirements of each EWM application.

There are two central service providers in EWM:

- **/SCDL/CL_SP**
  /SCDL/ service provider layer

- **/SCWM/CL_SP**
  /SCWM/ service provider layer of the user interface (UI)

These abstract classes, with their interfaces, build the foundation for the special use cases within the delivery processing component of EWM. Here the main difference between /SCDL/CL_SP and /SCWM/CL_SP is that the service providers of the UI—depending on the particular transaction—hide diverse fields or properties of the business object and perform additional checks before updating the object. Furthermore, the object data will also be enriched by short descriptions through the UI service provider. The various uses of the delivery service providers are shown graphically in Figure 2.4.

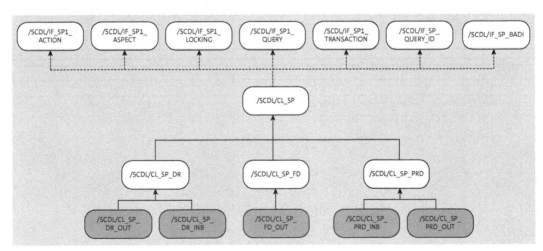

Figure 2.4 Architecture of Service Provider /SCDL/CL_SP

The structures by which the service providers communicate with the application programs are called *aspects*. An aspect represents a specific attribute of the business object. There is, for example, an aspect for date data at the header level (/SCDL/S_SP_A_HEAD_DATE) and an aspect for date data at the item level (/SCDL/S_SP_A_ITEM_DATE).

In the architecture of an enterprise service, we distinguish between *key aspects* and *aspects*. Here, the key aspect always contains the semantic key of an object (similar to a primary key). All aspects must be assigned to a key aspect to be clearly identifiable.

There are no specific repository objects for the respective aspects. To accommodate for the highly dynamic approach of this architecture, the caller has to ensure that the desired context will be passed when calling the service provider methods. The appropriate definitions can be found as constants within the /SCDL/IF_SP_C and /SCWM/IF_SP_C interfaces. The coding example in Listing 2.1 will give you an example of how to use the most important aspects and service provider methods. First, you create object instances with reference to the /SCDL/CL_SP_PRD_OUT (outbound delivery request) and /SCDL/CL_SP_MESSAGE_BOX (collector for messages during delivery processing) classes. You use class /SCDL/CL_SP_PRD_OUT here because you will select an outbound delivery. The message box will be needed to capture any messages—for example, in case of errors.

> [»]
>
> **Example Report for Delivery Processing**
> The code presented in the following listings in this chapter forms part of an example report that you can copy over into your own system to get acquainted with warehouse request processing. Just copy the code snippets one after the other. You can also simply pull the code from the GitHub platform at *https://github.com/* if you have installed the abapGit client, which allows you to interact with GitHub straight from your SAP system. The code can be found in GitHub repository ewmdevbook_2.1.

```
*&---------------------------------------------------------------------*
*& Report ZEWMDEVBOOK_21
*&---------------------------------------------------------------------*
*& Example Report for Delivery Processing
*&---------------------------------------------------------------------*
REPORT zewmdevbook_21.

PARAMETERS: p_lgnum  TYPE /scwm/lgnum     OBLIGATORY,
            p_docno  TYPE /scdl/dl_docno  OBLIGATORY,
            p_itemno TYPE /scdl/dl_itemno OBLIGATORY,
            p_wt_fm  RADIOBUTTON GROUP wtcr,
            p_wt_api RADIOBUTTON GROUP wtcr.

"2.1 Object Instances /SCDL/ Service Provider
BREAK-POINT ID zewmdevbook_21.
TRY.
    DATA(lo_message_box) = NEW /scdl/cl_sp_message_box( ).
    DATA(lo_sp)          = NEW /scdl/cl_sp_prd_out(
      io_message_box = lo_message_box
```

```
      iv_doccat      = /scdl/if_dl_doc_c=>sc_doccat_out_prd
      iv_mode        = /scdl/cl_sp=>sc_mode_classic ).
  CATCH /scdl/cx_delivery.
ENDTRY.
```

Listing 2.1 Example Report Parameters and Creation of Required Object Instances

Now select an ITEM aspect using an SAP ERP or SAP S/4HANA delivery number and the item number. We illustrate how this works in Listing 2.2. In the following section, we explain what is happening with the complex selection criteria.

```
"2.2 /SCDL/ Service Provider-based Delivery Query
DATA: lt_bopf_items TYPE /scdl/t_sp_a_item.

lo_sp->query(
  EXPORTING
    query      = /scdl/if_sp_c=>sc_qry_item
    selections = VALUE /scdl/t_sp_selection(
    ( fieldname = /scdl/if_dl_logfname_c=>sc_docno_h
      sign       = wmegc_sign_inclusive
      option     = wmegc_option_eq
      low        = |{ p_docno ALPHA = IN }| )
    ( fieldname = /scdl/if_dl_logfname_c=>sc_itemno_i
      sign       = wmegc_sign_inclusive
      option     = wmegc_option_eq
      low        = |{ p_itemno ALPHA = IN }| ) )
  IMPORTING
    outrecords = lt_bopf_items
    rejected   = DATA(lv_rejected) ).
IF lv_rejected = abap_true.
  DATA(lt_messages) = lo_message_box->get_messages( ).
  CALL METHOD /scwm/cl_tm=>cleanup( ).
  EXIT.
ENDIF.
```

Listing 2.2 Sample Call of /SCDL/IF_SP1_QUERY~EXECUTE

The returning lt_bopf_items parameter contains both the DOCID and the ITEMID fields, the GUIDs for document and item. Both values are needed to continue using the key aspect, /scdl/t_sp_k_item. Next, you can select the aspect for your item, which includes the delivery terms (see Listing 2.3).

```
"2.3 /SCDL/ Service Provider-based Delivery Aspect Selection
DATA: lt_a_item_delterms TYPE /scdl/t_sp_a_item_delterm.

lo_sp->select(
```

```
    EXPORTING
      inkeys      = CORRESPONDING /scdl/t_sp_k_item( lt_bopf_items )
      aspect      = /scdl/if_sp_c=>sc_asp_item_delterm
    IMPORTING
      outrecords  = lt_a_item_delterms
      rejected    = lv_rejected
      return_codes = DATA(lt_return_codes) ).

IF lv_rejected = abap_true.
  lt_messages = lo_message_box->get_messages( ).
  CALL METHOD /scwm/cl_tm=>cleanup( ).
  EXIT.
ELSEIF line_exists( lt_return_codes[ failed = abap_true ] ).
  lt_messages = lo_message_box->get_messages( ).
  CALL METHOD /scwm/cl_tm=>cleanup( ).
  EXIT.
ENDIF.
```

Listing 2.3 Sample Call of /SCDL/IF_SP1_ASPECT~SELECT

If you have extended the warehouse request item with customer own fields and would like to read or update these fields, you use the SC_ASP_ITEM_EEW_PRD aspect instead of SC_ASP_ITEM_DELTERM. If you do not want to provide a specific item for the delivery or if you first want to determine the corresponding items, you could use the call in Listing 2.4.

```
"2.4 /SCDL/ Service Provider-based Delivery Aspect Selection by Relation
lo_sp->select_by_relation(
    EXPORTING
      relation  = /scdl/if_sp_c=>sc_rel_head_to_item
      inrecords = CORRESPONDING /scdl/t_sp_k_head( lt_bopf_items )
      aspect    = /scdl/if_sp_c=>sc_asp_head
    IMPORTING
      outrecords  = lt_bopf_items
      rejected    = lv_rejected
      return_codes = lt_return_codes ).

SORT lt_bopf_items ASCENDING.
DELETE ADJACENT DUPLICATES FROM lt_bopf_items.
LOOP AT lt_bopf_items ASSIGNING FIELD-SYMBOL(<bopf_item>).
  WRITE: / 'SCDL',
           <bopf_item>-itemno,
           <bopf_item>-itemcat,
           <bopf_item>-itemtype.
ENDLOOP.
```

Listing 2.4 Sample Call of /SCDL/IF_SP1_ASPECT~SELECT_BY_RELATION

We recommend using aspects only if you have to select certain pieces of information from a warehouse request object or if you want to update certain customer fields. You should have these features override standard values only in exceptional cases and only if you are absolutely sure what effect this will have; otherwise, data inconsistencies may occur.

In general, however, a warehouse request object needs various information from various aspects. To this end, there are other functions, which we will explain in the next section.

Using the EWM Delivery Query

To select delivery documents or warehouse requests without having to use individual aspects directly, SAP provides the QUERY method. This method is one of the main classes of the /SCWM/CL_DLV_MANAGEMENT object manager. Depending on the document category you want to select, you will need to use the designated class. Inbound delivery notifications, for example, are read with a different class than inbound deliveries. Table 2.3 shows the class references you should use to select the objects according to each document category using the QUERY method.

Document Category	Class
IDR	/SCWM/CL_DLV_MANAGEMENT_DR
ODR	/SCWM/CL_DLV_MANAGEMENT_DR
POR	/SCWM/CL_DLV_MANAGEMENT_DR
EGR	/SCWM/CL_DLV_MANAGEMENT_DR
PDI	/SCWM/CL_DLV_MANAGEMENT_PRD
PDO	/SCWM/CL_DLV_MANAGEMENT_PRD
SPC	/SCWM/CL_DLV_MANAGEMENT_PRD
WMR	/SCWM/CL_DLV_MANAGEMENT_PRD
FDO	/SCWM/CL_DLV_MANAGEMENT_FD
PWR	/SCWM/CL_DLV_MANAGEMENT_PRD

Table 2.3 Document Categories and Associated Query Classes

The coding example in Listing 2.5 will help you understand how to use the delivery query to read the header and item information of an outbound delivery order for an SAP ERP or SAP S/4HANA delivery number on complex selection criteria (for exporting parameter IT_SELECTION).

```
"2.5 Service Methods-based Delivery Query
BREAK-POINT ID zewmdevbook_21.
"Get instance of service method class
DATA(lo_delivery) = NEW /scwm/cl_dlv_management_prd( ).
"Call query method of service method class
TRY.
    CALL METHOD lo_delivery->query
      EXPORTING
        iv_doccat        = /scdl/if_dl_c=>sc_doccat_out_prd
        it_selection     = VALUE /scwm/dlv_selection_tab(
            ( fieldname = /scdl/if_dl_logfname_c=>sc_docno_h
              sign      = wmegc_sign_inclusive
              option    = wmegc_option_eq
              low       = |{ p_docno ALPHA = IN }| ) )
        is_read_options  = VALUE #(
data_retrival_only       = abap_true
mix_in_object_instances  = /scwm/if_dl_c=>sc_mix_in_load_instance )
      IMPORTING
        et_headers       = DATA(lt_srv_headers)
        et_items         = DATA(lt_srv_items)
        eo_message       = DATA(lo_message).
    IF lo_message IS BOUND.
      DATA(lt_message) = lo_message->get_messages( ).
    ENDIF.
  CATCH /scdl/cx_delivery INTO DATA(lx_delivery).
    IF lx_delivery->mo_message IS BOUND.
      lo_message->add( lx_delivery->mo_message ).
    ENDIF.
ENDTRY.

LOOP AT lt_srv_headers ASSIGNING FIELD-SYMBOL(<srv_header>).
  WRITE: / 'SRV ',
           <srv_header>-docno,
           <srv_header>-doccat,
           <srv_header>-doctype.
ENDLOOP.
```

Listing 2.5 Sample Call of EWM Service Method-based Delivery Query

If you want to use more complex selection criteria, you must know the association between the corresponding database fields—in our example, the SAP ERP or SAP S/4HANA delivery number—and the logical field names. For this mapping, see the IMG, under **EWM • Cross-Process Settings • Delivery Processing • Extend Delivery Processing • Define Logical Field Names.**

Alternatively, the constants for the logical field names can be found in the following interfaces:

- /SCDL/IF_DL_LOGFNAME_C
- /SCWM/IF_DL_LOGFNAME_C

As a result, the system provides even further delivery-related information next to the header or item data. Depending on the class used, this can include, for example, assigned handling units or transportation units.

The selection of delivery objects can have a strong impact on the performance of a process in certain circumstances. That depends not only on how many documents and items there are to be read but also on what states or values from the database information must be calculated at runtime. Special header and item information—for example, status values and quantity roles—are dynamic (transient state) and have to be calculated at runtime based on other static values (persistent state). You can find an overview of the characteristics of a status in the IMG under **EWM • Cross-Process Settings • Delivery Processing • Status Management • Define Status Profiles**.

Note that there could be different configurations for a status at the header and item levels. For example, for outbound delivery orders, the DPI status (Picking) at the item level is persistent. But at the header level, it is calculated at runtime from the status of the items and therefore is transient.

To control the selection behavior of the delivery query for the specific needs, SAP delivers the following structures as import parameters:

- IS_READ_OPTIONS controls the selection behavior.
- IS_INCLUDE_DATA includes certain aspects.
- IS_EXCLUDE_DATA excludes certain aspects.

The IS_EXCLUDE_DATA parameter, however, is obsolete and only mentioned here to provide comprehensive information. You should not use it in your implementations.

In your programming, you should closely examine in each context exactly what you need the delivery object for (read or write accesses). In addition, check if the data in the selection results are really necessary.

[Ex]

Query Control during Data Selection

In an evaluation for special deliveries, you want to determine for which of these documents the goods issue has already been posted. The status to check for at the item level is called DGI and is persistent. You would therefore call the delivery query for a read-only access and you need only ET_ITEMS as a return parameter. Creation of an object instance and the calculation of dynamic values are not necessary. Accordingly, you can use the DATA_RETRIEVAL_ONLY indicator in the IS_READ_OPTIONS structure and set the IS_INCLUDE_DATA-ITEM_STATUS structural value.

A detailed description of how to use the special reading options can be found in the documentation of the QUERY method in the /SCWM/CL_DLV_MANAGEMENT_PRD class. In any case, you should always set the appropriate reading options before every call of the delivery query for performance reasons.

Another fundamental part of deliveries is the respective item quantities. EWM provides various functions for editing delivery items, which the status management cannot solely manage. For example, imagine you would like to know exactly what quantity has not yet been posted by the system during a partial goods receipt—which means what quantity is still open to receive. This aspect will be displayed using single quantity roles.

You can find the current quantities of a delivery item in the delivery UI under the **ADDL QUANTITIES** table tab. Similar to the status management, the quantity offsetting also contains persistent and transient values. For example, the W1 quantity role (Picking Planned) will be calculated from the document flow of an item at runtime.

The delivery document flow is technically a separate framework, which is why we will not go into it in greater detail at this point. Basically, it represents node relationships that contain information on specific actions to a delivery item.

For an overview of the properties of all quantity roles as well as their determination, see the IMG under **EWM • Cross-Process Settings • Delivery Processing • Quantity Offsetting**.

The example in Listing 2.6 shows how to evaluate the item hierarchy, status, and quantity roles. We use the already selected table of items, lt_srv_items, and first examine whether any delivery split items exist.

```
"2.6 Service Methods-based Delivery Hierarchy reading
LOOP AT lt_srv_items ASSIGNING FIELD-SYMBOL(<srv_item>).
  "Check hierarchy
  DATA(lo_corr) = /scwm/cl_dlv_correlation=>get_instance( ).
  LOOP AT <srv_item>-hierarchy ASSIGNING FIELD-SYMBOL(<srv_item_hierarchy>).
    TRY.
        CALL METHOD lo_corr->get_hier_cat
          EXPORTING
            iv_hierarchy_type = <srv_item_hierarchy>-hierarchy_type
          IMPORTING
            ev_hierarchy_cat  = DATA(lv_cat).
      CATCH /bopf/cx_frw .
    ENDTRY.
    "Skip split items
    IF  lv_cat = /scdl/if_dl_hierarchy_c=>sc_cat_ssp
    AND <srv_item_hierarchy>-parent_object IS NOT INITIAL.
      DATA(lv_skip) = abap_true.
      EXIT.
```

```
    ENDIF.
  ENDLOOP.
  IF lv_skip = abap_true.
    DELETE lt_srv_items.
    CONTINUE.
  ENDIF.
```

Listing 2.6 Evaluate Delivery Item Hierarchy

Delivery service classes as used for hierarchy determination are grouped under /SCWM/ CL_DLV* in the /SCWM/DELIVERY package. It is in this package that the core functions of the delivery processing are developed.

Now we will look at the DPI status (Picking) to evaluate the items that have not yet been completely picked, assuming they are at all relevant for picking (see Listing 2.7).

```
"2.7 Delivery Item Status-based checks
TRY.
      DATA(ls_status) = <srv_item>-status[
        status_type = /scdl/if_dl_status_c=>sc_t_picking ].

      IF ls_status-status_value = /scdl/if_dl_status_c=>sc_v_not_relevant.
        DELETE lt_srv_items.
        CONTINUE.
      ELSEIF ls_status-status_value NE /scdl/if_dl_status_c=>sc_v_finished.
        "Item & not yet completely picked.
        MESSAGE i001(zewmdevbook_21) WITH <srv_item>-itemno.
        CONTINUE.
      ENDIF.
    CATCH cx_sy_itab_line_not_found.
      "Item & not relevant for picking.
      MESSAGE i003(zewmdevbook_21) WITH <srv_item>-itemno.
  ENDTRY.
```

Listing 2.7 Evaluate Delivery Item Status

Finally, we check the PA quantity role (Pack) for items that have not yet been completely packed after picking, again considering whether they are at all relevant for packing (see Listing 2.8).

```
"2.8 Delivery Item Quantity-based checks
TRY.
      DATA(ls_addmeas) = <srv_item>-addmeas[
        qty_role = /scdl/if_dl_addmeas_c=>sc_qtyrole_pack
        qty_category = /scdl/if_dl_addmeas_c=>sc_qtycat_open ].
      IF ls_addmeas-qty NE 0.
        "Item & not yet completely packed.
```

```
        MESSAGE i002(zewmdevbook_21) WITH <srv_item>-itemno.
      ENDIF.
    CATCH cx_sy_itab_line_not_found.
      "Item & not relevant for packing.
      MESSAGE i004(zewmdevbook_21) WITH <srv_item>-itemno.
  ENDTRY.
ENDLOOP.
```

Listing 2.8 Evaluate Delivery Item Quantity Role

Alternative approaches for working with EWM data object APIs have been available within SAP S/4HANA. These were partly introduced with the rise of warehouse management functionality in SAP S/4HANA Cloud. Several SAPUI5-based transactions were created to be used in such an environment alongside new OData services. The APIs can be seen as a wrapping layer around the classical function modules and allow for object-oriented programming and external access. Listing 2.9 shows an example of how to use such APIs for a delivery query for the earlier provided document number. It is generally recommended to work with available APIs before turning to methods at the /SCDL/ service provider level because they allow for easier parameter handling.

```
"2.9 API based Delivery Query
BREAK-POINT ID zewmdevbook_21.
"Set warehouse request of type Outbound Delivery Order
DATA: lo_whr_api_outb TYPE REF TO /scwm/if_api_whr_outbound.
TRY.
    /scwm/cl_api_factory=>get_service( IMPORTING eo_api = lo_whr_api_outb ).
    "Set warehouse number obligatory for API
    /scwm/cl_tm=>set_lgnum( p_lgnum ).
    "Map business keys to warehouse request keys and read ODOs
    lo_whr_api_outb->/scwm/if_api_warehouse_request~get_keys_for_bus_keys(
        EXPORTING
          it_whr_bus_keys = VALUE /scwm/if_api_warehouse_request=>yt_whr_bus_
key(
            ( docno = |{ p_docno ALPHA = IN }| ) )
        IMPORTING
          et_whr_keymap   = DATA(et_keys_map) ).

    lo_whr_api_outb->read_outbound_dlv_order(
      EXPORTING
        it_whr_key      = CORRESPONDING #( et_keys_map )
        is_include      = VALUE #( head_refdoc = abap_true )
        is_read_options = VALUE #( fast_for_display = abap_true
                                   include_deleted  = abap_true )
        is_locking      = VALUE #( lock_result = abap_false )
      IMPORTING
```

```
         et_headers       = DATA(lt_whr_api_headers) ).
    CATCH /scwm/cx_api_faulty_call.
ENDTRY.

LOOP AT lt_whr_api_headers ASSIGNING FIELD-SYMBOL(<whr_api_header>).
    WRITE: / 'API ',
              <whr_api_header>-docno,
              <whr_api_header>-doccat,
              <whr_api_header>-doctype.
ENDLOOP.
```

Listing 2.9 Sample Call of API-Based Warehouse Request Query

We create an object instance for an outbound delivery order alongside the service initiation using the /scwm/cl_api_factory=>get_service static API factory method. Before mapping the technical warehouse request GUIDs for the external (SAP ERP or SAP S/4HANA) delivery document number, we need to set the warehouse number for the transaction manager using method set_lgnum. Having mapped out the GUIDs, we can easily move on to reading the warehouse request data, applying the earlier-mentioned input parameters is_include and is_read_options. Looping over the returned delivery document headers will finally simply output some of its data on the screen.

2.1.3 Integration with Other EWM Components

In Section 2.1.1, we outlined the central functionality of the delivery processing, and in Section 2.1.2 we described how service providers of the respective /SCWM/ application programs manage and update the warehouse request objects. The most important of these EWM components in this context is the warehouse task processing for deliveries or warehouse requests. Through this component, the special warehouse tasks for putaway and picking will be created with reference to a warehouse request. In contrast to that, there are also warehouse tasks not related to warehouse requests. But for these non-delivery-related warehouse tasks, we use other functions of the warehouse task processing.

The coding example in Listing 2.10 shows how easy it is to use the /SCWM/TO_CREATE_WHR function module to create the warehouse tasks for deliveries or warehouse requests. Again, we use the already selected table lt_srv_items as a reference. Because we work in the field of /SCWM/ components, we also need to pass the appropriate warehouse number, to be found in parameter p_lgnum.

```
"2.10 Delivery-based Warehouse Task Creation by Function Module DATA: lt_create_
whr TYPE /scwm/tt_to_prep_whr_int,
        lt_ltap_vb    TYPE /scwm/tt_ltap_vb,
        lt_bapiret    TYPE bapirettab,
        lv_severity   TYPE bapi_mtype.
```

```
BREAK-POINT ID zewmdevbook_21.
IF p_wt_fm = abap_true.
  "Call Central Cleanup
  /scwm/cl_tm=>cleanup( EXPORTING iv_lgnum = p_lgnum ).
  "Transfer DLV Keys
  LOOP AT lt_srv_items ASSIGNING <srv_item>.
    DATA(ls_create_whr) = VALUE /scwm/s_to_prepare_whr_int(
      rdocid  = <srv_item>-docid
      ritmid  = <srv_item>-itemid
      rdoccat = <srv_item>-doccat ).
    APPEND ls_create_whr TO lt_create_whr.
    CLEAR ls_create_whr.
  ENDLOOP.
  "Trigger Warehouse Task Creation for Warehouse Request per Function Module
  CALL FUNCTION '/SCWM/TO_CREATE_WHR'
    EXPORTING
      iv_lgnum       = p_lgnum
      iv_bname       = sy-uname
      it_create_whr  = lt_create_whr
      iv_update_task = abap_false
      iv_commit_work = abap_true
    IMPORTING
      et_ltap_vb     = lt_ltap_vb
      et_bapiret     = lt_bapiret
      ev_severity    = lv_severity.
```

Listing 2.10 Sample Call of /SCWM/TO_CREATE_WHR

The lt_ltap_vb return parameter provides the warehouse tasks that have been created. Table lt_bapiret and variable lv_severity contain the creation log, as well as the aggregated message type (E, I, etc.). If you want to implement your own UI transaction for this application in a project—for example, because the end user needs to see the created warehouse tasks before saving—use function module /SCWM/TO_PREP_WHR_UI_INT instead of /SCWM/TO_CREATE_WHR. The program logic is basically identical. The difference is that in the case of /SCWM/TO_PREP_WHR_UI_INT, the warehouse tasks will initially be created only within the SAP memory (internally) and then, depending on the action of the user, either be published and saved or deleted via rollback. If you are using function module /SCWM/TO_PREP_WHR_UI_INT, you are completely responsible for the entire update (commit) control. To guide you to the appropriate logic, take a look at function module /SCWM/TO_CREATE_WHR. Here the /SCWM/TO_PREP_WHR_INT function module takes care of both the internal warehouse task creation and, afterward, depending on the reported result, the update logic.

> **Transfer Parameters of the /SCWM/TO_CREATE_WHR Function Module**   [«]
>
> The /SCWM/TO_CREATE_WHR function module has various parameters that are all well documented in the function module itself. In the coding example (Listing 2.10), we only used the most important parameters.

Similar to working with deliveries, as shown previously, APIs have been made available in EWM in SAP S/4HANA for warehouse tasks and warehouse order processing. You may check Chapter 5 for more information on EWM APIs. Listing 2.11 shows an example of how method create_for_whr of the /scwm/if_api_whse_task API can be used to trigger warehouse task creation for delivery items.

```
"2.11 Delivery-based Warehouse Task Creation by API
DATA: lo_wt_api TYPE REF TO /scwm/if_api_whse_task.
ELSEIF p_wt_api = abap_true.
  TRY.
      /scwm/cl_api_factory=>get_service( IMPORTING eo_api = lo_wt_api ).
      "Trigger WT Creation for Warehouse Request per API
      lo_wt_api->create_for_whr(
          EXPORTING
            iv_whno        = p_lgnum
            it_create      = CORRESPONDING #( lt_srv_items )
          IMPORTING
            et_created_wht = DATA(lt_created_whr_wht)
            eo_message     = DATA(lo_error_msg) ).

    lo_error_msg->get_messages( IMPORTING et_message = DATA(lt_error_msg)
                                          et_bapiret = lt_bapiret ).
    CATCH /scwm/cx_api_whse_task.
  ENDTRY.
ENDIF.
WRITE: / 'Number of messages from WT creation:', lines( lt_bapiret ).
```

Listing 2.11 Sample Call of /SCWM/IF_API_WHSE_TASK

> **Availability of APIs for Extended Warehouse Management**   [«]
>
> Before embarking on using APIs for EWM, make sure to check SAP Note 3115182 to see which APIs are available for EWM as of which SAP S/4HANA release.

The following additional components of EWM also interact with delivery objects:

- EWM master data
- Packing
- Wave management

- Labor management
- Kitting
- Cross-docking
- Value-added services (VAS)
- Shipping and receiving
- Advanced shipping and receiving
- Transit warehousing
- Production integration
- Just-in-time processing (JIT)

In the other chapters in this book, we will provide you with some implementation examples in relation to delivery processing. For example, in Chapter 3, Section 3.6.6, we will describe how delivery processing integrates with special packaging features.

Delivery References in Inventory Management

A major advantage of EWM is the quant separation based on delivery reference. This allows you to, for example, move already picked goods back and forth easily within the warehouse without losing the reference to the delivery. The delivery reference of the stock will remain clearly identifiable throughout.

Furthermore, delivery processing includes interfaces for the integration of the following components:

- Quality Inspection Engine in decentralized EWM based on SAP S/4HANA
- Quality management in embedded EWM in SAP S/4HANA
- Post Processing Framework (PPF)
- Route determination (routing guide)
- SAP Global Trade Services (SAP GTS)
- SAP Transportation Management (SAP TM), including advanced shipping and receiving

In addition to the various interfaces and calling options for delivery objects, EWM also offers a number of BAdIs that allow you to carry out your own determinations and validations as well as handle your custom fields. SAP delivers sample implementations for various BAdIs of delivery processing to give you a programming template for orientation.

Further Sources of Technical Information on EWM Delivery Processing

For further technical information, we highly recommend checking out how-to guides on delivery processing like *How to Access "Delivery—Warehouse Request" Objects in EWM in SAP S/4HANA* and *How to Enhance an EWM Delivery with Own Coding in SAP S/4HANA.*

These can be found in the SAP Community wiki at *https://wiki.scn.sap.com/wiki/display/ SCM/How-To+Guides+for+SAP+EWM*.

2.2   Warehouse Logistics

The warehouse logistics component of EWM includes all goods movements—both within the warehouse complex and around the warehouse. EWM supports numerous processes such as the arrival of goods in the warehouse, goods receiving, and the put-away process. It also supports internal storage processes, such as inventory, quality control, supply, and reorganization.

The most important processes are often considered to be picking and shipping. As the basis for almost all follow-up logistics processes, warehouse logistics thereby serves the delivery demand. The processing delivery document for outbound flows, called an *outbound delivery order*, thus forms the basis for the warehouse on which planning and reporting take place. For this document, you can see the current processing status and document flow for all dependent documents.

For *shipping and receiving*, complete deliveries, respective items, or individual handling units are assigned to a transportation unit. You can again group transportation units by vehicles, where a vehicle may be assigned multiple transportation units. The central document in EWM is the warehouse task, in which activities within the warehouse are performed and documented. It serves the movement of stock and/or handling units according to the data specified in the delivery items. But it is also possible to create and process warehouse tasks without reference to a delivery, such as for internal warehouse processes like replenishment or rearrangement.

In addition to the warehouse task, more processes can be carried out, such as inbound quality checks (Section 2.4). Value-added services (VAS) can be integrated into the inbound and outbound delivery process. In the outbound process, the delivery items are grouped in waves. Warehouse tasks are created for a complete wave and bundled into warehouse orders according to customizable criteria—that is, the warehouse order creation rules.

2.2.1   Shipping and Receiving

An incoming transport, such as a truck, often contains more than one delivery. To illustrate this fact in the EWM system, we can create a separate object—the transportation unit—and assign deliveries, delivery items, or handling units to the transportation unit activity.

When you create a transportation unit, a transportation unit activity will always be created in the background alongside the transportation unit. This transportation unit activity itself is not editable. Such activities actually exist as well for other shipping and receiving objects, mainly vehicles and doors. They are always valid for a specific time frame, as defined in the activity. The transportation unit activity is defined as the external transportation unit number plus the carrier identification, and there may be several *planned* activities but only one *active* activity; an activity is activated by the arrival of the transportation unit at the checkpoint. Activities of one or more transportation units can be assigned to a vehicle.

The use of the object vehicle will only bring an added value when more than one transportation unit is used—for example, a truck with a trailer. If a delivery is distributed among multiple transportation units, this can be represented in the system by direct assignments of the delivery items or handling units to these transportation units. This takes place primarily in the goods issue process during loading, when the final outbound deliveries are not yet known, and processing again takes place on outbound delivery orders.

[»]

Yard Management in EWM

The *yard* is what we call the area outside of the warehouse complex, where the arriving and departing transportation units are handled. With yard management in EWM, you can not only register the incoming transportation units at the gate but also assign locations and move them within the yard. You can occupy parking spaces and create warehouse tasks for moving the transportation unit to its destination (mainly a door). This provides an opportunity for parking management and administration of additional transportation units—for example, swap bodies or trailers that must be moved with their own resources.

The doors of the warehouse, where transportation units are loaded and unloaded, must be assigned to a storage bin in the warehouse. These door bins are necessary to create warehouse tasks for the door. But this does not involve physically existing places where goods are actually stored. Working with yard management, the doors must also be assigned to a storage place outside of the warehouse—the place where the transportation unit is off target. The two bins assigned to a door (outside and inside) connect the yard to the warehouse complex.

The movement of a transportation unit with a warehouse task to a door automatically creates or activates a door activity for the transportation unit. Only one transportation unit can be docked at a door. For this reason, we recommend the use of yard management for timely postings only. Without yard management, you must create and activate door activities manually in a transportation unit transaction. Shipping and receiving works based on activating and deactivating transportation unit statuses with time stamps (current date and time).

The use of transportation units also provides the ability to post stock to the transportation unit location. You can therefore post goods receipts sooner without taking up storage space. Outbound process staging areas will be cleared not only from the goods issue but also by loading the transportation unit, so you can manage staging areas better. Of course, loading is possible without transportation units; in this case, stock is moved to the door bin. Stock transparency is thus no longer ensured as the door bin physically does not exist, and stock cannot be checked. Accordingly, it is not clear where in fact the goods are located.

The activity of a transportation unit contains information about when the transportation unit is expected in and at what time it will leave the warehouse again. The activity may provide additional information, such as the driver and means of transport (e.g., license plate), including other identifications and seal information. But above all, it includes status information.

The activity of a transportation unit is activated by the **Arrival at Checkpoint** user action, found in the menu. With yard management activated, the handling unit of the transportation unit is moved to the checkpoint bin. From that point on, the transportation unit can be moved with warehouse tasks within the yard to a door where it is unloaded or loaded. If no free door exists, it can be moved temporarily to a parking lot.

We will now take a deeper look at inbound and outbound operations and then at the underlying data model of the shipping and receiving functionality.

Receiving

In inbound processing, Customizing decides if the goods receipt is posted to the transportation unit location or door bin or to the staging area and thus if goods must be unloaded or not. Customizing for goods receipt posting can be found in the IMG for SCM at **Extended Warehouse Management • Cross-Process Settings • Shipping and Receiving • General Settings • Control of Goods Movements**. If a goods receipt is posted to a transportation unit or door bin, unloading is required with the help of a warehouse task. From the goods receipt bin to the staging area, no unloading is required, but this process is still supported with simple unloading. After unloading the transportation unit, it can leave the door and depart from the checkpoint, or it can be reused again for loading with an outbound transportation unit activity.

Status

Object transportation units and vehicles contain a number of statuses to document the current state of an activity—for example, *arrival at checkpoint*, *docked to door*, *begin loading*, and *loading end*. Existing for both the objects of delivery and transportation units, statuses may be synchronized between the two objects. The transportation unit informs the delivery upon arrival at checkpoint about its own status change, which sets the status to **In Yard** for the delivery. If the transportation unit is already planned for a door, the door information is also passed to the delivery in case no open warehouse task already exists for the delivery item. Staging area determination is called to find an optimized staging area for the door on the delivery item level. When changing the transportation unit, the synchronization between the transportation unit and the delivery will take place directly. For this reason, the deliveries will be blocked and must be changeable. Otherwise, the change is not possible for the transportation unit.

Status changes on the delivery, as with changes in loading or goods movement status, may lead to a recalculation of the corresponding status in the transportation unit activity. Changes in quantity and repacking eventually lead to a change in capacity of the transportation unit activity. Changes in the delivery, such as status or quantity changes that affect the transport, are not updated directly in the transportation unit, but they result in scheduling a PPF action that synchronizes the transportation unit (see Figure 2.5).

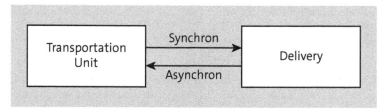

Figure 2.5 Synchronization between Delivery and Transportation Unit

[»]

Transportation Units Contain Only References

Transportation units do not contain their own quantity, product, or handling unit information, only references to the delivery number, respective item, and possibly to handling units.

For this reason, the UI of the transportation unit always shows the current state of the handling unit data. These data do not necessarily correspond with the data of the received handling units after unloading.

Shipping

For shipping, a transportation unit activity can arrive at a checkpoint that only picks up goods or a transportation unit can be reused that previously delivered incoming goods and is still active in the yard or at the door. For such a transportation unit, the shipping activity can be activated, and the system automatically closes the incoming activity. If the incoming activity is located at a door, a door activity is created and activated for the outgoing transportation unit activity as well. With active yard management, the location of the transportation unit does not change.

Because the transported objects, mainly handling units, need not necessarily be planned for transportation, they can be assigned to a transportation unit spontaneously by loading. As opposed to inbound processing and unloading, the loading completion is not automatically set by the system; it can, however, be proposed to the operator in case of assigned deliveries being completely loaded. Therefore, the **Loading Completed** status must always be set or at least confirmed manually; if loading has started, completion is a prerequisite before the transportation unit can depart from the checkpoint again.

Warehouse tasks are necessary for the unplanned loading of transportation units, which provide the assignment of handling units to transportation units.

Data Model

The shipping and receiving application component of EWM is part of the /SCWM/ namespace. Its responsibility is summarized in the SCM-EWM-SR technical component and its subcomponents. Beside the object's transportation unit, vehicles, and door, this application component also handles the functionality of staging and door determination, as well as all loading and unloading. Such functionality is also quite relevant for delivery processing, regardless of the use of transportation units.

The /SCWM/SHP_RCV package is divided into five subpackages. In addition, package /SCWM/YARD_MGMT is valid for the yard management functionality. Table 2.4 lists the packages that are relevant for shipping and receiving.

The processing of transactional data is done via classes, as shown in Figure 2.6.

Each activity will be managed by a separate instance of that particular class. The data can be found in the classes starting with /SCWM/CL_SR_DO.... The business logic is executed through the associated classes starting with /SCWM/CL_SR_BO..., which hold a reference to the current instance of data. The /SCWM/CL_SR_BOM property manager manages the instances of business objects named /SCWM/CL_SR_BO... and the like.

Package	Function
/SCWM/SHP_RCV_CORE	Processing of transportation unit, vehicle, door, and staging area determination
/SCWM/SHP_RCV_CUST	Customizing tables, maintenance views, functions for reading Customizing and F4 help
/SCWM/SHP_RCV_PPF	Implementing PPF
/SCWM/SHP_RCV_UI	Transactions for processing of transportation unit, vehicle, and door activities
/SCWM/ERP_TM_INTEGRATION	Customizing and IDocs for integration of SAP ERP or SAP S/4HANA shipments (logistics execution transport)
/SCWM/YARD_MGMT	Definition of checkpoints, transaction for check-in and check-out, yard moves

Table 2.4 Packages for Shipping and Receiving

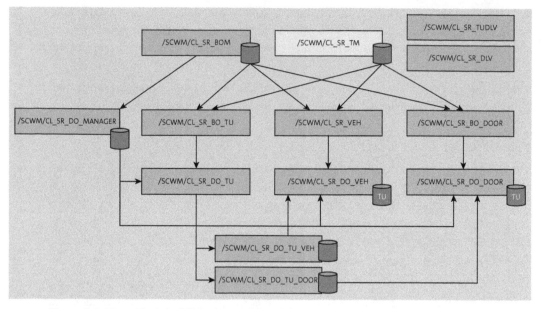

Figure 2.6 Class Model of Shipping and Receiving

The links between a transportation unit and vehicle or door are managed in their own classes, which are referenced in the /SCWM/CL_SR_DO_TU class. For performance reasons, keep the corresponding instances of door and vehicle keys with a table of the associated transportation units.

The link between transportation units and delivery is managed in class /SCWM/CL_SR_ TUDLV. This class is independent of the other classes and may also be used without them if no other information about the transportation unit or vehicle is required. Class /SCWM/CL_SR_DLV is the interface of the transportation unit for the delivery. It informs the delivery about changes in its assignment and status.

The /SCWM/CL_SR_DO_MANAGER class exists only for historical reasons and must not be used directly. Only the methods for reading/setup of all relevant objects will remain and must only be used by the business object manager class, /SCWM/CL_SR_BOM.

The three objects in shipping and receiving consist of the object header and any number of activities in this header. For an entry in table /SCWM/TUNIT or /SCWM/VEHICLE, at least one entry in its activity table /SCWM/TU_SR_ACT respective to /SCWM/VEH_SR_ACT must exist. All additional tables contain entries relevant to the activity. The tables of the objects are listed in Table 2.5.

The transportation unit and vehicle header are deleted if the last activity is deleted.

The door object has a special status because it is defined in Customizing. An entry must exist when creating an activity, and door activities cannot be created as standalone entities. They only exist with a reference to a transportation unit activity. This means that for any entry in table /SCWM/DOOR_SRACT, an entry in table /SCWM/TU_DOOR must exist.

Object	Table	Activity	Additional Table
Transport unit	/SCWM/TUNIT	/SCWM/TU_SR_ACT	/SCWM/TU_STATUS /SCWM/TU_IDENT /SCWM/TUNIT_SEAL /SCWM/TU_VEH /SCWM/TU_DOOR /SCWM/TU_DLV
Vehicle	/SCWM/VEHICLE	/SCWM/VEH_SR_ACT	/SCWM/VEH_STATUS /SCWM/VEH_IDENT
Door	/SCWM/TDOOR	/SCWM/DOOR_SRACT	

Table 2.5 Tables of Objects in Shipping and Receiving

For just about any action that can be performed for an activity, the /SCWM/EX_SR_ACTION_TU BAdI for transportation units, /SCWM/EX_SR_ACTION_VEH for vehicles, and /SCWM/EX_SR_ACTION_DOOR for doors are called. These BAdIs can be used for custom checks and trap implementations.

Because the three objects are independent of each other and some changes have an impact on more than one object, the consistency of the objects must be ensured when the data change occurs. For this reason, if any business object method of the /SCWM/CL_SR_BO_... class is performed, a copy of data object instance /SCWM/CL_SR_DO... is saved before the first data change. In addition, they inform the /SCWM/CL_SR_TM class that it has produced such a copy.

If an action is successful, the application that called the action—such as upon arrival at the checkpoint—calls class /SCWM/CL_SR_TM to initialize and inform all stored business object instances to delete the copy.

If an error is raised within an action in one of the objects, class /SCWM/CL_SR_TM is also called. It will inform all stored business object instances to discard the current data object reference and replace it with the copied one. Furthermore, it's ensured that if an error occurs, data will be the same on all objects as before the action started.

Integrating SAP Transportation Management without Using EWM Shipping and Receiving in SAP S/4HANA

Before closing this section, we would like to mention the advanced shipping and receiving feature in EWM as a new integration method of EWM and SAP TM that eliminates the transportation unit or vehicle as a redundant object in EWM. The SAP TM freight order acts as the sole transportation execution object in this scenario. This new feature is quite extensive in scope and still being extended. We recommend referring to SAP Help for both EWM and SAP TM. We also recommend information sources from SAP PRESS in this area, such as the *Integrated TM and EWM in SAP S/4HANA* E-Bite, to learn more (*https://www.sap-press.com/5315/*).

2.2.2   Warehouse Task and Warehouse Order

Goods movements within the warehouse are carried out using the warehouse task object. For goods movements, such as goods receipts, goods issues, and posting changes, the system generates completed warehouse tasks without a warehouse order for documentation. Other than that, warehouse tasks will usually be assigned to a warehouse order.

Rearrangements within the warehouse consist of scheduled and completed warehouse tasks. When creating a scheduled task, a warehouse order is automatically generated in accordance with the warehouse order creation rules defined in Customizing. The warehouse order can be assigned to a resource group and is used to update and confirm assigned warehouse tasks.

The purpose of a warehouse task can be identified by its warehouse process category (TRART). Available categories are listed in Table 2.6. The data available on the warehouse task depends on this process category. See Table 2.9 for further information.

Warehouse Process Category	Description
1	Putaway
2	Picking
3	Internal movement
4	Inventory
5	Goods receipt
6	Goods issue
7	Posting change

Table 2.6 Warehouse Process Categories in EWM

Storage and retrieval can be done in several steps. This can be due to the warehouse process (in this case, the process will be guided by process-oriented storage control) or warehouse layout (which is defined by layout-oriented storage control). The various storage process steps of the process-oriented storage control are usually optional, and some can be placed at any point in the process. Most can be defined as rule-based, which means they can be included in the process profile, but they are carried out only on the existence of a referenced document.

These steps are divided into two stages and must be completed manually after the transfer, while single-stage process steps are completed automatically with the confirmation of the warehouse task. At each process step, the system determines whether the completion of the process step leads automatically to the creation of a warehouse task of the next step or whether this takes place later on, such as at handling unit closing at a work center. To use process-oriented storage control, it is necessary to work with handling units, which serve as carriers of the storage control information.

In the following sections, data determination for storage and retrieval is discussed in more detail. We will start with warehouse inbound operations, touching on potential activities while receiving goods, followed by outbound operations while issuing goods. After taking a deeper look at the data models of the core objects of warehouse tasks and warehouse orders, we will finally describe the logic of putaway and removal strategies.

Warehouse Process Category 1 (Putaway)

The putaway storage process consists of handling unit and product warehouse tasks. The final putaway can be done with both types of warehouse tasks. This way, it is also possible to put away mixed handling units. Product warehouse tasks always contain an inbound delivery reference, whereas handling unit warehouse tasks only refer to a document if it is unique.

If warehouse tasks are created prior to goods receipt, then the source location is determined from the first delivery items within the tasks (handling unit). After goods receipt, the source location is determined by the location of handling units or stock that should be moved. Destination data comes from the storage process or putaway strategy (for the final putaway task).

In the goods receipt process, the last step is always final storage. However, the warehouse tasks for this process step can be created at any time during the storage process. This is done on the identification **PRODUCT/HU WT** in the assignment of the storage process step to a storage process in Customizing. In this case, the warehouse tasks are created with the **WAITING** status and assigned to a warehouse order. The following steps describe a multistage goods receipt process and explain the roles of the warehouse task and handling unit objects:

1. **Move transportation unit to door**
   Upon arrival of a transportation unit, it can be moved with active yard management using warehouse tasks in the yard. Such a warehouse task technically moves a handling unit named like the transportation unit. As a source location, the actual location of the transportation unit/handling unit is determined. It can either obtain its destination from the storage process type or by manual input. Confirmation of the warehouse task will dock the transportation unit to a door. If no yard management is used, then the process of door docking is carried out manually.

2. **Unloading**
   If the goods receipt of a delivery item is received in the staging area, unloading is not mandatory, but it can be done by so-called simple unloading. In the delivery, a document flow is generated by the unloaded amount and the **UNLOADED** status is set for the handling units.

   If the goods receipt of the delivery item is posted to the transportation unit or a door bin, then handling units or unpacked stock must be unloaded with warehouse tasks. Unloading is an integral part of the goods receipt process. There are basically two options for unloading:

- **Unloading without storage process**

  For unpacked goods, the system creates a warehouse task with the storage process type of the delivery item. In this case, the warehouse task represents unloading and putaway. This is also possible for handling units when creating the putaway warehouse task. Confirmation of the unloading will also confirm the putaway step if no manual interaction with a change of destination is performed. From the unloading UI, it's also possible to unload the handling unit to the staging bin of the delivery item.

- **Unloading with storage process**

  The first warehouse process step of the storage control in the handling unit must be the unloading step. If warehouse task creation is called for, this handling unit, the system automatically creates a handling unit warehouse task from the delivery item goods receipt location to the staging area of the inbound delivery.

For unloading, warehouse tasks using a warehouse order creation rule of the **Load/ Unload** type makes sense. You can create it by choosing the IMG path **Extended Warehouse Management • Cross Process Settings • Warehouse Order • Define Warehouse Order Creation Rule**. Use the **Load/Unload** creation type for the corresponding warehouse order creation rule (see Figure 2.7).

Warehouse Order Creation Rules			
Warehouse Number WO Cr. Rle		Description	Creat. Cat
☐ 1710	Y001	Full Pallet Picking	A Consolidation Group
☐ 1710	Y002	Picking for Multiple Cust.from Mezzanine	A Consolidation Group
☐ 1710	Y003	Picking for Single Cust.from NA Pick. A.	A Consolidation Group
☐ 1710	Y004	Repl.:NA to Mezzanine for Multiple Items	B Pick Path
☐ 1710	Y005	NA: Replenishment of Picking Area	B Pick Path
☐ 1710	Y006	Complete HU Withdrawal for UoM = PAL	A Consolidation Group
☐ 1710	Y007	Replenishment of Picking Area for Bulk B	B Pick Path
☐ 1710	Y008	Full Pallet Removal	B Pick Path
☐ 1710	Y009	Partial Stock Removal	B Pick Path
☐ 1710	YPAL	Max. 1 WT, no Filter, no Sorting	B Pick Path
☐ 1710	YPI1	WO for 20 Physical Inventory Items	H Physical Inventory
☐ 1710	YSC1	Scrapping of Full Pallets	B Pick Path
☐ 1710	YSC2	Scrapping of Loose Items	B Pick Path

Figure 2.7 Warehouse Order Creation Category within Warehouse Order Creation Rule

If the unloading warehouse tasks are created automatically by the system from PPF or manually for a complete delivery or transportation unit, then all warehouse tasks are created in parallel. In this case, all warehouse tasks are assigned to one warehouse order. Depending on the number of workers configured, additional warehouse orders without warehouse tasks are created to allow parallel unloading using radio frequency (RF) technology. Confirmation of an unloading warehouse task will reassign the warehouse task from the main warehouse order to the warehouse order of the worker. This means that multiple users can process the same worklist without a predefined unloading sequence. In the end, the identity of the user who unloaded the single handling unit is documented.

3. **Counting**

Counting may be included as a rule-based step in the storage controller. If a handling unit item is relevant for counting because of an existing counting document for the packed delivery item, then a handling unit warehouse task is created for a counting station. There the content of the handling unit is counted, and the step is then completed. If the counting step is not identified as rule-based, the handling unit is brought to the counting station regardless of the existence of a counting document.

For delivery items with a counting and quality step or a VAS, the counting step must be included in the storage control prior to those steps. For storage processes that contain only deconsolidation and putaway after unloading, counting may be completed implicitly by those warehouse tasks.

4. **Quality inspection**

A quality inspection may be included as another rule-based step in the storage process. If a quality inspection document/lot exists for the content of the handling unit, a warehouse task is created for the inspection bin determined by the inspection document (inspection rule). However, the handling unit is only moved to the quality work center of the first relevant quality inspection. If the handling unit contains several test-relevant items with different quality work centers, then the routing between them must be done manually. If no work center can be determined, then no handling unit warehouse task is created, and the step must be completed at the current bin.

After completion of the quality inspection, the handling unit must be marked **Completed**. The system does not check whether there is still noninspected stock in the handling unit.

5. **Value-added service**

The storage process step for VAS should be defined as rule-based also. This step is relevant if at least one item of the handling unit contains a VAS order. A handling unit warehouse task is created for a work center for VAS. After completion of VAS, the user must mark the handling unit as **Completed**.

Although the VAS step can be implemented at any point in the storage process, processing a product after a possible quality inspection makes the most sense.

6. **Deconsolidation**

Deconsolidation is an optional step in storage control that may be marked as rule-based. To use a deconsolidation step, it is mandatory to create putaway warehouse tasks in an earlier defined process step. Those putaway warehouse tasks are then created with status **Waiting**.

A handling unit is relevant for deconsolidation if there is more than one warehouse task for the content of the handling unit with a different consolidation group. The content of the handling unit has to be repacked so that the resulting handling unit can be used for putaway. The deconsolidation step must also be set to **Completed** manually.

7. **Putaway**

Putaway is always the last step in the goods receipt process. You can create the warehouse task for this step at any time in the process. In the putaway step, you create a putaway warehouse task or activate an already existing putaway warehouse task with the **Waiting** status.

Warehouse Process Category 2 (Picking)

The outbound process always starts with a product warehouse task with reference to the outbound delivery order, which is called *picking*. For this product warehouse task, the source stock determination is done by way of the warehouse process type from the delivery item and the picking strategy. The destination data comes from the outbound delivery order.

Upon creation of picking warehouse tasks, they are bundled to warehouse orders with warehouse order creation rules. In picking, the warehouse order creation provides the most opportunities for optimization and processing of different scenarios (see Table 2.7). For this reason, it makes sense to create as many warehouse tasks as possible together. For this, EWM offers *wave* functionality: with waves, delivery order items that are to be picked in a certain period are pooled, and with a wave release, the warehouse tasks for all items within this pool are created.

Creation Category	Description
Consolidation Group	If possible, all warehouse tasks for one consolidation group are picked together. This way, all products going to the same customer are held (packed) together at an early stage.
	The picking path is a bit longer, but you can possibly skip an additional repacking.
Pick Path	Warehouse tasks are sorted by pick path and then bundled so that the shortest paths are covered, and the pickers are working in different areas. But products have to be brought to a packing station to consolidate deliveries.
Pick Pack Pass—System	The warehouse tasks are bundled according to the consolidation group within an activity area. The order of the warehouse orders of a consolidation group is defined in Customizing, and only one warehouse order is active. Others are waiting. Confirming a warehouse order activates the next warehouse order of the same consolidation group in the next activity area. For this scenario, several activity areas must be assigned to the activity area for warehouse order creation.
Pick Pack Pass—User	In this scenario, the warehouse tasks are also bundled on consolidation group per activity area, but all warehouse orders are active.

Table 2.7 Warehouse Order Creation Categories for Picking

Process-Oriented Storage Control in Outbound Processing

In this section, a multistage outbound process is described, and the roles of the warehouse task and handling unit objects are explained. The five stages, in order, are as follows:

1. **Picking**
   Warehouse task creation for picking is completed, like the outbound delivery order item and picking strategies described earlier.

2. **Value-added services**
   The storage process step for VAS should be maintained as rule-based within the storage process. In this case, the step is only relevant if a VAS document exists for the outbound delivery order item. If VAS is the second step within the storage process, then picking warehouse tasks are already created to the VAS work center. On confirmation of picking warehouse tasks, picking handling units must be used. If VAS is not the second step within the storage process, an additional handling unit warehouse task is created for the VAS work center.

3. **Packing**
   If warehouse tasks are bundled by pick path, different pickers pick stock for one delivery. For shipping, that stock must be consolidated and packed at a packing work center. In this case, picking warehouse tasks are created directly for the packing work center. With the VAS step, the handling units are moved from the VAS work center to the pack station with a handling unit warehouse task if needed. The packing step in the storage process must be completed manually.

4. **Staging**
   In the staging step, the handling units are moved to the staging area.

5. **Loading**
   Loading creates handling unit warehouse tasks from the staging area to the door of the outbound delivery order item. Confirmation of any warehouse task to a door bin is defined as a loading warehouse task and creates a document flow entry in the delivery order items and a status for the handling unit in case of a handling unit move. If a transportation unit is docked to the door when confirming the warehouse task using RF, the destination of the warehouse task is changed directly to the transportation unit.

Data Model

The processing of warehouse tasks can be found in package /SCWM/CORE. Warehouse order creation is assigned to package /SCWM/WHO.

Planned warehouse tasks are stored in table /SCWM/ORDIM_O with an identical entry in table /SCWM/ORDIM_L. On confirming or canceling this planned warehouse task, the entry in table /SCWM/ORDIM_O is deleted, and a new entry is created in table /SCWM/ORDIM_C. This ensures that the table of open warehouse tasks is kept small and thus that accesses perform well. Warehouse tasks always reference a warehouse order in table /SCWM/WHO.

Table 2.8 lists the tables in which the data for warehouse task processing is stored.

Table	Usage
/SCWM/ORDIM_O	Planned warehouse tasks with status open or waiting
/SCWM/ORDIM_OS	Serial number for open warehouse tasks
/SCWM/ORDIM_L	Log table for planned warehouse tasks. This is a copy of the original entry in /SCWM/ORDIM_O, which documents the initial values. It is not updated at any point in time
/SCWM/ORDIM_LS	Serial numbers for log table
/SCWM/ORDIM_C	Completed warehouse tasks
/SCWM/ORDIM_CS	Serial numbers for completed warehouse tasks
/SCWM/ORDIM_H	Stock information for confirmed handling unit warehouse tasks with mixed stock
/SCWM/ORDIM_HS	Serial numbers on mixed handling unit warehouse tasks referencing /SCMW/ORDIM_H
/SCWM/ORDIM_E	Exception codes for completed warehouse tasks

Table 2.8 Tables of Warehouse Tasks

The amount to be moved with a warehouse task can be confirmed partially. This is called splitting the warehouse task. It creates a confirmed warehouse task entry with the confirmed partial quantity. This is necessary, for example, if the amount is divided between more than one destination (pick) handling unit or if the source handling unit is a nested handling unit and picking is done from part of a subhandling unit or from some complete subhandling units. The table keys of /SCWM/ORDIM_O and /SCWM/ORDIM_L are the warehouse number and warehouse task. Tables of confirmed warehouse tasks contain an additional item number.

The attributes of the warehouse task can be divided into the following groups:

- Organizational data like user name, creation date, resource, queue, confirmation date, and so on
- Stock attributes like product, quantity, batch, stock category, and so on
- A source location description of the location in the warehouse where the stock is currently placed, such as source storage bin, source handling unit, sources resource, or source transportation unit
- A destination location—that is, a description of the location in the warehouse where the stock must be put—such as a destination storage bin, destination handling unit, destination resource, or destination transportation unit

- Additional data, including more general attributes, such as FLGHUTO, which indicates the move of the complete source handling unit, or the HOMVE field, which signifies for the product warehouse tasks that the complete stock of the source handling unit should be moved and if the move of the complete handling unit is possible

Organizational data attributes are always filled. Stock attributes are only filled for product moves, stock changes, and handling unit moves with unique stock. Source and destination data depend on the type of warehouse task. What data is filled on which posting (process category and product or handling unit posting) can be found in Table 2.9. The process categories shown are defined in table /SCWM/T333A.

Type	TRART	Source	Destination	Stock	Additional Data
Product goods receipt	5		X	X	
Handling unit goods receipt	5		X	Optional	FLGHUTO
Product goods issue	6	X		X	
Handling unit goods issue	6	X		Optional	FLGHUTO
Posting change	7	X	X	X	
Product putaway, picking, internal move	1, 2, 3	X	X	X	HOMVE HUENT
Handling unit putaway, picking, internal move	1, 2, 3	X	X	Optional	FLGHUTO MOVEHU
Inventory of complete handling unit	4	X	X	Optional	FLGHUTO
Product inventory	4	X	X	X	

Table 2.9 Provided Data within Warehouse Tasks Depending on Type of Task

From and to data include the location and the handling unit. Besides the location, the affected GUID_HU is always filled. The handling unit identification remains for the initial dummy handling units, which makes it easy to see whether this is a real or a virtual handling unit. Flag FLGHUTO indicates whether the task was created as a handling unit posting. If destination storage type does not allow real handling units, only the content of the handling unit is moved, which can be identified via flag MOVEHU. If a product warehouse task for a complete handling unit is created, it is identified by flag HOMVE. In this case, the complete handling unit can be moved like a handling unit warehouse task, and flag HUENT is set to indicate the handling unit move.

Warehouse tasks can have different statuses (see Table 2.10).

Status	Usage
Open	Warehouse task waiting for processing
Waiting	Warehouse task that reserves source stock and capacity on destination but cannot be processed
Confirmed	Warehouse task was processed successfully
Canceled	Planning was canceled

Table 2.10 Status of Warehouse Tasks

Planned Warehouse Tasks Are Never Deleted

Planned warehouse tasks can only be canceled, not deleted. Confirmed warehouse tasks and stock postings cannot be canceled. They must be posted in the opposite direction with a new warehouse task.

Source Data Determination

For putaway warehouse tasks for inbound delivery items without goods receipt, the source bin is determined from the inbound delivery item's goods receipt location. After goods receipt, the source location is taken from stock with reference to this inbound delivery item. For manual product warehouse tasks (Transaction /SCWM/ADPROD) or handling unit warehouse tasks (Transaction /SCWM/ADHU), stock must be selected by the user to be able to create a warehouse task.

For pick warehouse tasks, source data is determined by available quantities (table /SCWM/AQUA) with a picking strategy and packaging specification for the product. An exception to this rule is the warehouse task creation for a cross-dock scenario. In this case, the outbound delivery order already contains information about the inbound delivery and warehouse task searches for inbound delivery stock reference (where putaway has not been completed). Source location determination is done in function group /SCWM/REM_BIN_DET.

Figure 2.8 shows the Customizing of the picking strategy.

The picking strategy defined in Customizing is used to determine the source storage bin for the source handling unit. If a quantity classification is defined in the source storage type, then the system calls the packaging specification determination with type OWHT and determines the relevant level for operations with the quantity classification of the storage type. Upon successful level determination, the operational unit of measure (UOM) is set by the level of the packaging specification. An optional rounding of the warehouse task quantity can be done (e.g., to ensure that only whole boxes are picked), or the quantity can be reduced to one unit of the operating unit (e.g., in a bulk storage where one warehouse task must be created per pallet).

Figure 2.8 Customizing for Picking Strategies

With the BAdIs listed in Figure 2.9, the picking strategy and thus the affected source location determination can be customized specific to the process. For example, the operational UOM can be set if stock is stored in a different UOM than in the standard storage type.

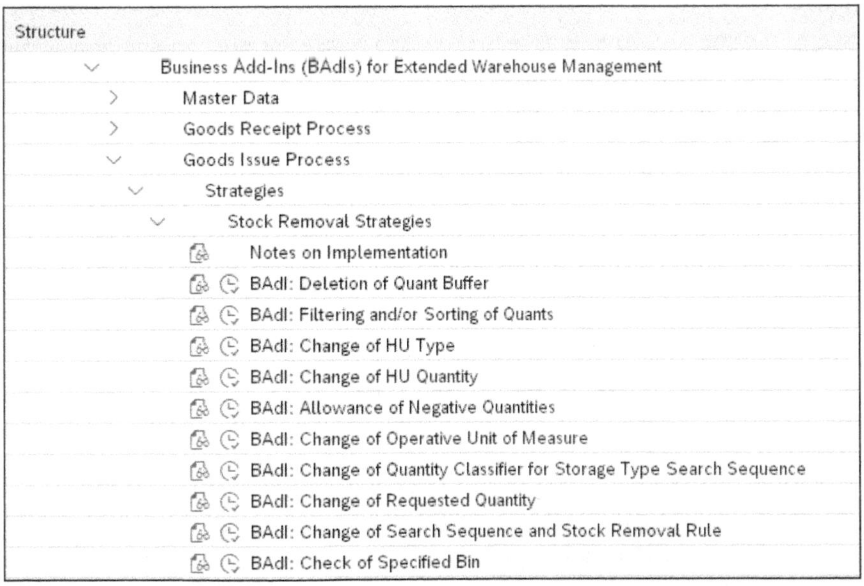

Figure 2.9 Business Add-Ins to Influence Picking Strategy and Source Location Determination

To allow parallel warehouse task creation, the source storage bin is locked with a shared enqueue. This allows any number of parallel processes to access this data. An exclusive lock is used for the quantity of the created warehouse task to ensure availability. For product warehouse tasks with a given source handling unit, the handling unit also receives a shared lock. This is also true for repacking at a work center. When moving a complete handling unit or repacking a complete handling unit, the handling unit gets an exclusive enqueue. Therefore, repacking stock must be saved prior to repacking or moving the handling unit.

Destination Data Determination

Destination data for final putaway is determined by the putaway strategy defined by the product. The definition of the putaway strategy is completed in the Customizing of the goods receipt process (see Figure 2.10). For other processes, destination data is taken from the delivery item or storage process step (e.g., work center) or is defined manually.

Structure
∨   SCM Extended Warehouse Management
∨   Extended Warehouse Management
Enable Decentralized EWM
>   Master Data
∨   Goods Receipt Process
Configure Availability Group for Putaway
Activate Parallel Processing for Inbound WT Creation
>   Slotting
∨   Strategies
Define Product Putaway Profile
Configure Deletion of Fixed Bin Assignments
Define Warehouse Number Parameters for Putaway
∨   Storage Type Search
∨   Definition of Groups
Define Storage Type Groups
Assign Storage Types to Storage Type Groups
Define Group for Stock Type
Define Group for Process Types
Define Storage Type Search Sequence for Putaway
Assign Storage Types to Storage Type Search Sequence
Define Putaway Control Indicator
Specify Storage Type Search Sequence for Putaway
Optimize Access Strategy for Storage Type Search: Putaway
>   Storage Section Search
>   Storage Bin Determination
>   Storage Bin Determination for Transit Warehouse
∨   Putaway Rules
>   Storage Behavior: Pallets
>   Storage Behavior: Bulk Storage
>   Storage Behavior: Flexible Bin
>   Sorting Near To Picking Bin

Figure 2.10 Customizing of Putaway Strategy

Examination of destination data is done in function group /SCWM/PUT_BIN_DET. Here, according to the settings for the storage type (see Figure 2.11), the mixed storage and capacity check is called. On moving a complete handling unit (handling unit warehouse task or product warehouse task for complete handling unit quantity), the capacity of the handling unit header is used for the capacity check. Mixed stock and capacity checks are performed in function group /SCWM/HUFUNC. Function module /SCWM/TO_HU_INT is called. The destination handling unit (so long as it's not a dummy; see Section 2.3.2) is locked exclusively by an enqueue. Destination bins are also locked if a mixed stock and capacity check must be done. Deactivation of a capacity check and capacity updates can be useful for work center and staging bins.

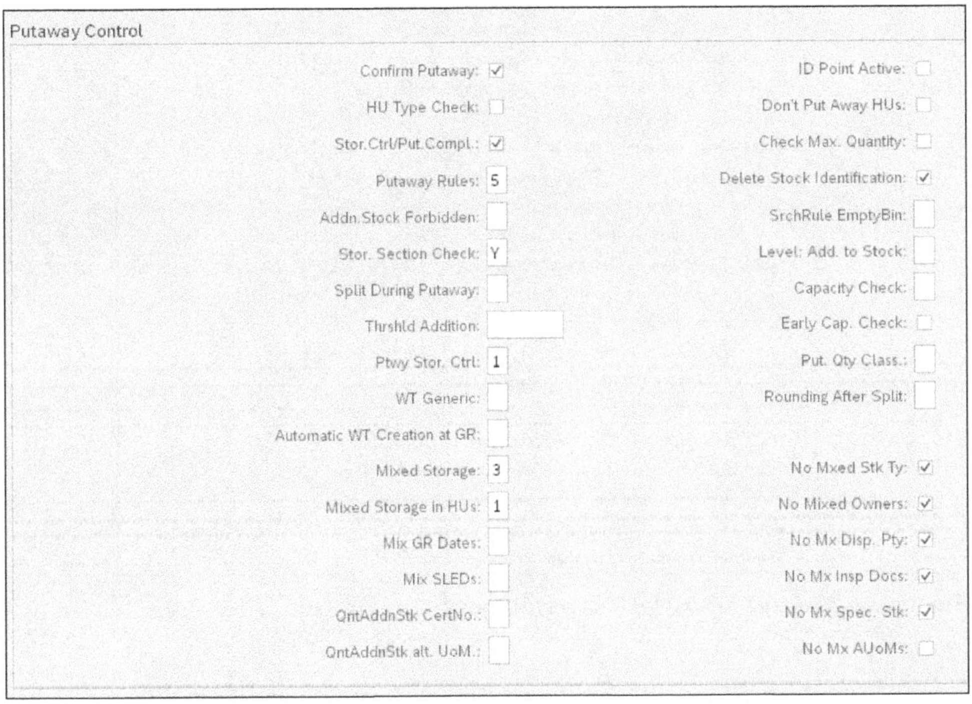

Figure 2.11 Setup for Mixed Storage and Capacity Check within Storage Type

Pure product warehouse tasks determine a packaging specification with condition type OWHT. Capacity information is determined up to the relevant level in the packaging specification, which is defined by the quantity classification for putaway (general quantity classification if no specific one is defined). Only handling unit–relevant levels are used. If you cannot find the packaging specification, use the capacity information if the product master of the base UOM is used. Products with a catch weight are the exception. In that case, the quantity of capacity–relevant UOM is used.

Influencing all parameters of the putaway strategy is possible via BAdI implementation. An overview of the available BAdIs is shown in Figure 2.12.

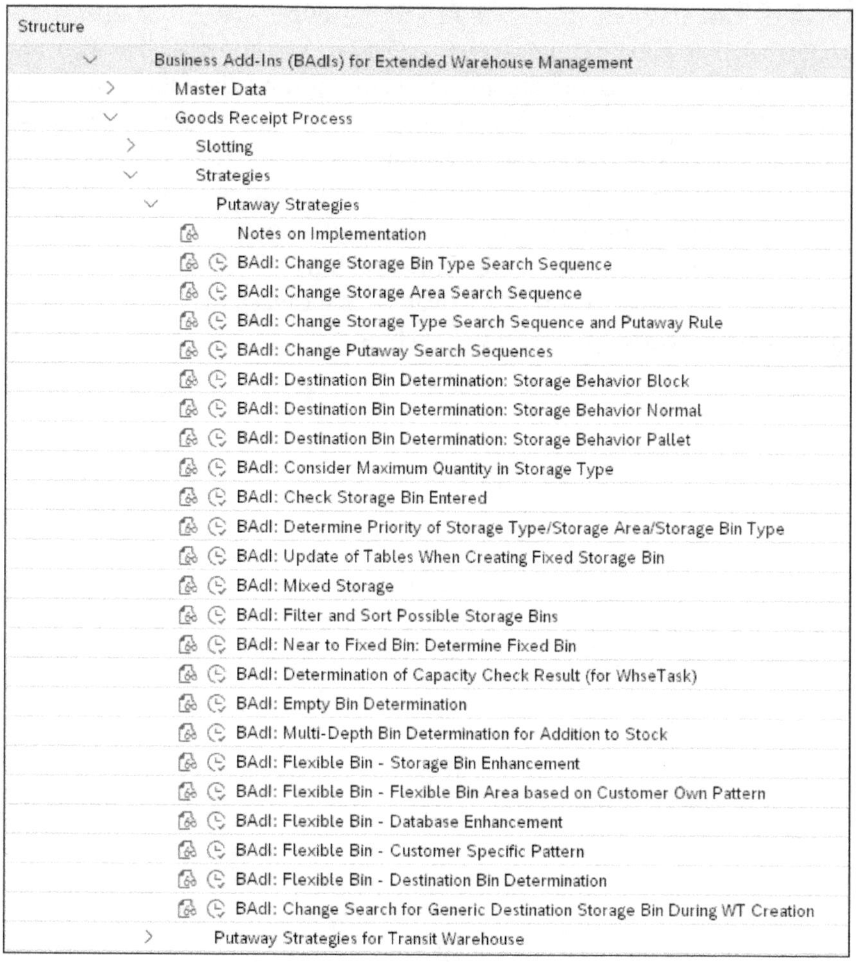

Figure 2.12 Business Add-Ins for Putaway Strategy

2.3   Inventory Management

Inventory data and hierarchies in EWM are stored in the logistics inventory management engine. The structure model of EWM and the logistics inventory management engine contains three object types:

- Location
- Handling unit
- Stock

The objects of these types form a hierarchy, with stock always stored in handling units. Handling units can contain other handling units, and a handling unit is always anchored on a location. An example is shown in Figure 2.13.

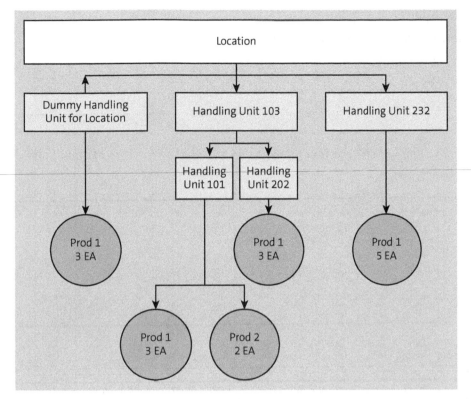

Figure 2.13 Example for Stocks and Hierarchies in Logistics Inventory Management Engine

Although the logistics inventory management engine can also manage stock in locations, the decision was made in EWM not to allow any direct stock in locations. Stock is only allowed in handling units in order to facilitate access by a single parent.

The logistics inventory management engine also offers the possibility of a hierarchy of locations. This option is not in use in EWM. A location can only contain handling units and is always the top level of a hierarchy.

As a generic engine, the logistics inventory management engine works only with the global unique identifier (GUID) within the hierarchies and stock. Table /LIME/NTREE is responsible for the hierarchy table, and tables /LIME/NQUAN and /LIME/NSERIAL are responsible for the stock table. In the index tables of the application (e.g., EWM), the business key is stored for a GUID.

All index tables of EWM start with the client and warehouse number. This data structure enables the core of the logistics inventory management engine: unified coding for all applications. For access via the index table's application, specific code generates the logistics inventory management engine with the allocation of the index tables.

In the following sections, we'll take a deeper look into aspects of inventory management in EWM. This will include locations, handling units, and stock.

2.3.1 Locations

In EWM, four types of locations exist for managing handling units and stock:

- Warehouse number
- Storage bins
- Resources
- Transportation units

In Table 2.11, you will find the four location index tables, their usages, keys, and linked master data.

Table	Usage	Key	Master Data
/SCWM/LOC_IW01	Bins (storage bins, work centers, doors, etc.)	LGNUM LGTYP LGPLA	/SCWM/LAGP
/SCWM/LOC_IW02	Resources	LGNUM RSRC	/SCWM/RSRC
/SCWM/LOC_IW03	Warehouse number (logical location)	LGNUM LGNUM_VIEW	
/SCWM/LOC_IW04	Transportation unit	LGNUM TU_NUM	/SCWM/TUNIT

Table 2.11 Location Index Tables

The location indexes (GUID_LOC) for a bin, resource, and transportation unit are created with the creation of corresponding master data. The location index for the warehouse number (table /SCWM/LOCK_IW03) is created with the definition of the warehouse number (as normally transported to a system) with first usage.

At the warehouse number level, virtual stock (e.g., planned handling units in the delivery) and difference quantities from inventory are stored. For reasons of transparency on different types of differences within a warehouse number, we use different locations. Currently these are as follows:

- Differences on valuation quantity (only when using catch weight functionality)
- To-be-compensated differences
- Quantities without storage space allocation

2.3.2 Handling Units

For each location, a handling unit with identical information exists and is used to store unpackaged stock. This handling unit is created with the master data and is not visible in the UI due to parameter VHI (virtual handling unit indicator), which is predefined by the logistics inventory management engine in the index. These dummy handling units are not visible in the UI, but they are used in the program run as normal handling units.

Each handling unit is defined by index table /SCWM/HU_IW01, the key for which is LGNUM HUIDENT VHI. The corresponding attributes can be found for active handling units in table /SCWM/HUHDR. If a handling unit contains delivery-related stock, the reference to the delivery header is also stored, for performance reasons, in table /SCWM/HUREF. Each handling unit can have multiple statuses via usage of a status object in table /SCWM/HUS-TOBJ and a status in /SCWM/HUSSTAT. In addition to the unique identification of a handling unit, the HUIDENT handling unit can still have several other identifications. These can be found in table /SCWM/HU_IDENT. The handling unit item is the stock, and EWM-specific inventory attributes can be found in table /SCWM/QUAN. Each goods receipt or goods issue creates an entry in table /SCWM/GMHUHDR, through which the attributes of the handling unit are stored at the time of goods movement. Also, for the other tables, there are corresponding /SCWM/GMHU* tables, which store quantity and hierarchy information.

The handling unit index table contains the VHI field, which serves to classify different types of handling units. The VHI field is also provided in table /SCWM/HUHDR as an attribute and can have the following values:

- <space>: Real handling units (physically exist)
- A: Dummy handling units for all types of locations
- B: Planned handling units (only possible in inbound delivery)
- E: Transportation unit
- C, P, U: Dummy handling units for different kinds of differences
- R: Dummy handling unit for rounding residuals
- W: Planned shipping handling unit

VHI allows the creation of different types of handling units with the same external identification. Handling units may exist with the same identification as a storage bin. Planned handling units are an exception, as their usage of VHI in the logistics inventory management engine would lead to a changed GUID during goods receipt. As this must not occur, the VHI of planned handling units only exist in table /SCWM/HUHDR and not in the logistics inventory management engine.

During the creation of transportation units, a new location is created and two handling units are allocated to it: one dummy handling unit with VHI = 'A', to store unpacked goods on loading or goods receipt, and an handling unit with VHI = 'E'. The latter handling unit is used with active yard management to move the transportation unit between bins and move it with warehouse tasks from checkpoints to parking lots and doors. Transportation units thus can be moved like normal handling units without special programming effort and with standard warehouse tasks. Furthermore, this handling unit has the advantage that it is always empty. It has no content in the logistics inventory management engine and therefore no performance problems occur when moving large transportation units in the yard. You can move a handling unit to the checkpoint bin during check-in and move it back to the transportation unit location upon checkout.

2.3.3 Stock

Locations and handling units have a simple local key, whereas stock has a large number of key fields, which leads to a separation of the stock. A record with individual characteristics is called a *quant*. The table key of a quant contains the handling unit index where the stock is located (GUID_PARENT) and the stock index (GUID_STOCK).

In the following sections, we'll take a more detailed look at aspects of stock, looking at field types, indexes, counters, and quantities.

Field Types

The logical (business) key can be distinguished in three different types of fields. We group them into types A, B, and C (see Table 2.12).

Field	Type	Description	Usage
LGNUM_STOCK	A	Warehouse number	Fixed key for all stock within a warehouse
MATID	A	Product	Master data of product that must exist in EWM
BATCHID	A	Batch	Master data for a batch must exist in EWM
CAT	A	Stock type	Possible usage of stock (e.g., free usage in putaway, blocked in putaway, available)
STOCK_USAGE	A	Stock usage	Initial, project stock, customer stock
OWNER OWNER_ROLE	A	Owner	EWM business partner who owns the stock from the financial point of view, represented in SAP ERP or SAP S/4HANA by the plant
ENTITLED ENTITLED_ROLE	A	Entitled	EWM business partner that makes decisions about stock; normally identical to the owner, differs for consignee stock

Table 2.12 Fields for Business Key of Stock

Field	Type	Description	Usage
STOCK_DOCCAT STOCK_DOCNO STOCK_ITMNO	A	Type of reference number item	Customer-owned stock with order number, item, or project stock with project number
DOCCAT DOCID ITEMID	B	Document reference	Normally references a warehouse request, but on differences it refers to an inventory document or a warehouse task
INSPTYP INSPID	B	Inspection	An inspection document or item awaiting quality inspection linked to stock
IDPLATE	B	Stock identification	Unique identification of the quant; can be used in the inbound and outbound process and deleted on final storage types
WDATU	C	Goods receipt date	Date of first goods movement in the warehouse
VFDAT	C	Shelf life expiration date	Date when usability of the product/batch ends
COO	C	Country of origin	Country where the product was produced
BRESTR	C	Batch status	Status of the batch (free/blocked)
STK_SEG_LONG	C	Stock segment	As of SAP S/4HANA 2022, used for stock segmentation

Table 2.12 Fields for Business Key of Stock (Cont.)

The following are the different types of fields described:

- **Type A**
  These are fields that classify the stock. They are used in the stock index of logistics inventory management engine as a key. Fields relate either to master data (e.g., the **Product** field) or a list of fixed values (e.g., the **Stock Type** field). The number of all possible combinations of A fields is therefore limited. Because it is likely that stock for a stock index (e.g., product A with stock type F2) exists several times, the reusability of the index entry is high. The fields are grouped together in structure /SCWM/S_STOCK.

- **Type B**
  This is reference data that is necessary for unambiguous processing and thus leads to different quants. Because the reference data is ongoing and continuous, these

fields are not suitable as a key for the stock index in the logistics inventory management engine. Often stock (e.g., product A with batch B) is temporarily and uniquely tied to a reference document, such as an inspection lot or a delivery. Because the reference data does not reoccur, it is not stored in the index of the logistics inventory management engine. The reference attributes are included in the structure /SCWM/S_QUAN_STOCK2.

- **Type C**
  These are stock attributes that do not lead to separate quants. During Customizing control, an addition to existing stock can be prevented. The stock attributes are grouped in structure /SCWM/S_QUAN_STOCK1.

Stock Index Tables

A stock index table contains a key part and a data part. Key fields of table /SCWM/STOCK_IW01 can be found in Table 2.13. The stock index, represented by GUID_STOCK, is available in the data part.

Field Name	Description
LGNUM	Warehouse number/warehouse complex
MATID	Product
CAT	Stock category
STOCK_USAGE	Stock usage
OWNER	Owner
OWNER_ROLE	Partner role of the owner (business partner)
ENTITLED	Entitled
ENTITLED_ROLE	Partner role of the entitled (business partner)
STOCK_CNT	Counter to allow different stock in B fields by a restricted number of indices

Table 2.13 Stock Index /SCWM/STOCK_IW01

Counter for Stock Separation

If stock differ only in type B fields, then these stock have the same stock index (GUID_STOCK). To deal with different references of type B in the same handling unit, a further technical key, the counter for the stock separation (STOCK_CNT), extends the stock index tables in the logistics inventory management engine. This is a numeric counter.

The first inventory in a handling unit is created with the index of the business key and the counter 0 in the index table. This is a second stock packed into the same handling unit with same business key in the A fields but with difference in a B field. Then another entry with the same business key and counter 1 is created. For each additional component with a different reference, another index with a higher count is applied.

For example, the same product (same stock) is picked for multiple delivery items and deployed in the same staging bin for shipping. Staging of the stock for the delivery item 4711 10 creates a quant with an index S0. In EWM, the quant references delivery item 4711 10. For another delivery item, 4713 10, the same product is picked and staged in the same bin. Because there is already a quant with the same business key, a new index is created with STOCK_CNT = '1', index S1. Stock with the same business key but a different stock reference creates additional indices with a higher STOCK_CNT.

If delivery 4711 is posted as a goods issue, the quant with stock index S0 is deleted. If a new quantity of the same business key is put in the bin, then index S0 will be reused. So the maximum number for STOCK_CNT is the maximum number of quants within one handling unit with an identical business key but different references.

In application table /SCWM/QUAN in the logistics inventory management engine index (GUID_STOCK), the index with STOCK_CNT = '0' is also stored (GUID_STOCK0). By placing the two logistics inventory management engine indexes, faster comparisons and queries are possible. For determining the available quantity or mixed stock check, the reference is irrelevant. Here we are working only with GUID_STOCK0.

Finally, we clarify why there is not just one EWM stock index table, but four. You can see them in Table 2.14.

To avoid empty key fields in the index tables, batch-managed products have their own index table, /SCWM/STOCK_IW02. Non-batch-managed products are listed in index /SCWM/ STOCK_IW01. Stock that is picked for a delivery is no longer available for other picks. For this reason, picked stock has its own index table (/SCWM/STOCK_IW03). The infrequent stock for project and sales order stock are managed in the fourth index table (/SCWM/ STOCK_IW04). In the logistics inventory management engine, inventory index tables are used in the short form, W01 to W04.

Table	Stock Description
/SCWM/STOCK_IW01	<ul><li>Non-batch-managed products</li><li>Normal stock</li><li>Vendor consignment</li><li>Additional packaging</li></ul>
/SCWM/STOCK_IW02	<ul><li>Batch-managed products</li><li>Normal stock</li><li>Vendor consignment</li><li>Additional packaging</li></ul>

Table 2.14 Four Stock Indexes in EWM

Table	Stock Description
/SCWM/STOCK_IW03	Products (with or without batches) that are assigned to a delivery, warehouse task, or inventory document
/SCWM/STOCK_IW04	Special stock (with or without batches) such as sales order stock and project stock

Table 2.14 Four Stock Indexes in EWM (Cont.)

When using batches or special stock with nonrecurring values, over time too many entries in the logistics inventory management engine index tables (e.g., after sale of a batch) become obsolete after a short usage period. Using report /LIME/BACKGROUND_ DELETE_EXEC, index entries are deleted for which there are no quantities left in EWM.

When posting EWM stock in the logistics inventory management engine, a BAdI implementation ensures that the posting is made through the EWM application. This means that a direct call of the logistics inventory management engine function modules in custom programs is not possible. Only read accesses are allowed.

Quantities

Fields of quantity table /LIME/NQUAN can be assigned to the key part or the data part. You can find the key parts of the fields in Table 2.15.

Field Name	Description
GUID_STOCK	Identification of stock index with index reference in the data part
GUID_PARENT	Identification of handling unit where stock is located
VSI	Virtual stock indicator
QUAN	Quantity
UNIT	UOM

Table 2.15 Key of /LIME/NQUAN

In the data part, the index identification of stock index table IDX_STOCK can be found where the business key of the GUID_STOCK is defined (e.g., W01 refers to table /SCWM/STOCK_ IW01). With the unit as part of the key, it is possible to store several quantities of one stock. EWM uses this feature to manage catch weight.

The virtual stock indicator allows for the storage of different types of stock. Virtual stock includes stock in planned handling units for inbound deliveries prior to goods receipt or quantities of kit headers, which are not stock-managed.

In addition to the physical quantities in the logistics inventory management engine, EWM stores the available quantities in table /SCWM/AQUA. The available quantity is an aggregated quantity within the highest-level handling unit, or on the bin level, minus the quantities for which open warehouse tasks exist. Storage bins are grouped in storage types that are defined in Customizing and structure the warehouse. At the storage type level, the decision is made if the available quantity is on the handling unit or bin level. For all location types other than bin level, the available quantity is defined on the handling unit level.

The level of the available quantity defines at what level automatic warehouse task creation takes place. If the available quantity is defined on the bin level (only recommended for bulk storage), a warehouse task is created only with the bin information. The warehouse worker has to enter the handling unit he removed or from which the stock has been removed at warehouse task confirmation. With the handling unit availability level, a source handling unit is already specified in the warehouse task to be used for picking.

If manual warehouse tasks are created from a handling unit lower than the availability level (lower-level handling unit or when the availability level is at the bin level), the system must know that quantity from this handling unit is not available for another warehouse task. The quantity will be reduced in the available quantity entry in /SCWM/AUQA and a reserved quantity is written to the handling unit used in the warehouse task. The reserved quantity is stored in the logistics inventory management engine as a quantity with a virtual stock indicator (R).

There are two possibilities to post stock in EWM:

- Quantity changes (goods receipt and goods issue, inventory posting, and differences) and changes to stock attributes (posting changes) are all triggered by different methods and function modules and post with function module /SCWM/GM_CREATE.

- Location changes are always processed with warehouse tasks. While entries in table /SCWM/QUAN are deleted if the quantity is 0, the entry in table /LIME/NQUAN remains as long as the handling unit exists. This way, entries in table /LIME/NQUAN are available also for empty bins (empty handling units).

2.4   Quality Inspection

Through early quality control of incoming goods, you can ensure that only proper goods are stored in the warehouse and finally paid to the supplier. Ad hoc inspection of stocked goods as well as recurring inspection will also allow you to keep a high level of stock quality throughout storage.

As we mentioned briefly in Chapter 1, with the introduction of embedded EWM, there has been a clear step taken toward reduction of redundancy in the area of quality inspection while making use of quality management in SAP S/4HANA rather than the Quality Inspection Engine, fostering the SAP S/4HANA promise to provide simplification. But an additional decision has been made to use the Quality Inspection Engine module in decentralized EWM. For this reason, we are dividing the following sections on quality inspection into embedded EWM and decentralized EWM, providing a short functional description of available inspection procedures and an overview of the technical implementation for both deployment options of EWM.

It might be interesting to note that EWM quality inspection relies on the *service adapter framework* to determine the correct classes to be used when evoking quality inspection–related functionality. This determination is based on the respective EWM deployment option, here also referred to as *context*. Table 2.16 depicts the service adapter framework–based services that have been defined for the respective quality inspection functionality, requiring differentiation between Quality Inspection Engine (decentralized EWM) and quality management (embedded EWM) handling.

Function	Service Adapter Framework Service Interface	(Sub)classes	Superclass
Q-inspection planning	■ /SCWM/IF_AF_QIN-SP_INT	■ /SCWM/CL_QDOC ■ /SCWM/CL_QLOT_S4	■ /SCWM/CL_QINSP_SUPER
Follow-up processing	■ /SCWM/IF_AF_QFU_INT	■ /SCWM/CL_QFU ■ /SCWM/CL_QFU_S4	■ /SCWM/CL_QFU_SUPER
Goods receipt control	■ /SCWM/IF_AF_QGR_CONTROL	■ /SCWM/CL_QGR_CONTROL_INSPDOC ■ /SCWM/CL_QGR_CONTROL_QLOT_S4	
Q-inspection planning production	■ /SCWM/IF_AF_QIN-SP_MFG	■ /SCWM/CL_QDOC_MFG ■ /SCWM/CL_QLOT_MFG_S4	
Q-inspection returns	■ /SCWM/IF_AF_QM_RETURNS_INT	■ /SCWM/CL_RETURNS_ITEM ■ /SCWM/CL_RETURNS_ITEM_S4	
Q-inspection setup	■ /SCWM/IF_AF_QSETUP_INT	■ /SCWM/CL_QSETUP ■ /SCWM/CL_QSETUP_S4	
Partial inspection	■ /SCWM/IF_AF_QUI_PINSP_INT	■ /SCWM/CL_QUI_INSPELM ■ /SCWM/CL_QUI_INSPPLOT_S4	■ /SCWM/CL_QUI_PINSP_SUPER

Table 2.16 Quality Inspection–Related Services of Service Adapter Framework

Function	Service Adapter Framework Service Interface	(Sub)classes	Superclass
Q-inspection stock handling	■ /SCWM/IF_AF_QUI_STOCK_INT	■ /SCWM/CL_QUI_INSP_STOCK ■ /SCWM/CL_QUI_INSP_STOCK_S4	■ /SCWM/CL_QUI_INSP_STOCK_SUPER
Q-inspection Customizing	■ /SCWM/IF_QCUST_SEL	■ /SCWM/CL_QCUST_SEL_INT ■ /SCWM/CL_QCUST_SEL_INT_S4	
Q-inspection rule UI—transaction manager	■ /SCWM/IF_QRS_TA_MANAGER	■ /SCWM/CL_QRS_TA_MANAGER ■ /SCWM/CL_QRS_TA_MANAGER_S4	■ /SCWM/CL_QRS_TA_MANAGER_SUPER

Table 2.16 Quality Inspection—Related Services of Service Adapter Framework (Cont.)

Within the service adapter framework, superclasses are usually applied if there is common functionality required between the individual contexts, with the superclass providing commonly usable methods. The subclasses, also referred to as *adapter classes*, then individually implement the service interface methods for the respective context and data objects further used. Classes for embedded EWM will usually contain the suffix S4.

In the following two sections, we address the individual aspects of quality inspection in the two main deployment options of EWM. We start with decentralized EWM because this is where quality inspection for EWM originated. Then we turn to embedded EWM, focusing on major differences compared to inspection in decentralized EWM. Thereafter we turn first to functions, then toward objects and data models, and then we close, for decentralized EWM, with integrational topics.

EWM Deployment Differences

SAP has published EWM deployment difference overviews for the latest versions of SAP S/4HANA, which contain information on functionality differences in embedded and decentralized EWM at times compared to the last SAP EWM release 9.5. We recommend going through such overview documents, which are attached to, for example, SAP Note 3218648 to gain an understanding of factors such as deployment differences in quality inspection processing within the various EWM versions. Similar SAP Notes should be available for lower SAP S/4HANA versions, so make sure you are considering your current system's version.

2.4.1   Quality Inspection in Decentralized EWM

In this section, we will focus on quality inspection in decentralized EWM. Specifically, we will discuss its functions, objects and data model, and integration.

Function

Now let's discuss inspection object types, inspection document creation, routing, inspection results, and follow-up handling.

Inspection Object Types

Different types of selected EWM objects that should be able to be inspected in the warehouse are defined by *inspection object types*. Inspection activities are planned and processed by *inspection documents,* which are created after evaluation of *inspection rules* with different determination attributes per inspection object type, referred to as *properties*. Inspection object types offer the opportunity to perform different inspection rule evaluations based on such properties. Inspection object types are stored in table QIE_IOBTYP.

Inspection rules again contain further aspects of the inspection to be performed, as defined by arguments. Inspection rules are stored in table QIE_IRULE.

Decentralized EWM uses Quality Inspection Engine to handle quality inspection requirements. This software component had been developed to provide a service-oriented solution for quality-based activities called by diverse consumer systems. It offers the flexibility to consider different EWM objects like deliveries, stocks, or handling units for quality inspection, in order to capture results and trigger follow-up actions. It also allows you to connect to external quality management systems to perform more detailed inspections or meet advanced requirements in the result captures.

The inspection object types in Quality Inspection Engine cannot be delivered out of the box. They must be generated per system (cross-client). Before generating the inspection object types, determination attributes, the previously mentioned properties, must be defined in Customizing. Changes to inspection object types result in a loss of all data created so far. This is why versions of an inspection object type exist in decentralized EWM. Already created inspection document data can indeed no longer be used for processing, but it can still be read. Existing inspection documents therefore still can be displayed. From the perspective of Quality Inspection Engine, the new inspection object type version is nevertheless regarded as a different inspection object type.

The inspection object types listed in Table 2.17 are offered by decentralized EWM.

Inspection Object Type	Description
1	Preliminary Inspection Inbound Delivery
2	Counting Inbound Delivery

Table 2.17 Available Inspection Object Types in Decentralized EWM

Inspection Object Type	Description
3	Q-Inspection Returns Delivery
4	Q-Inspection Product/Batch Inbound Delivery
5	Q-Inspection Product/Batch Warehouse-Internal
6	Preliminary Inspection HU

Table 2.17 Available Inspection Object Types in Decentralized EWM (Cont.)

Let's consider detailed descriptions of the inspection object types from Table 2.17:

- **Preliminary Inspection Inbound Delivery (IOT1)**
  This is a high-level initial check to see whether a delivery is accepted or rejected. Any logistical posting in EWM for this delivery will automatically confirm this inspection as accepted. An activity is only necessary in case of refusal, which will reject the delivery completely.

  The advantage of the preliminary inspection is a uniform reporting on the quality of the delivery of the forwarding agent or supplier because it is a superficial initial examination of the complete delivery.

- **Preliminary Inspection HU (IOT6)**
  This inspection is an inspection of the packages of a delivery for external damage; it takes place before the goods receipt. The inspection document is created for each inbound delivery. Handling unit inspection is implemented in an RF transaction and can only be created and processed there. Each handling unit must be scanned as good or bad. At the end, a product inspection document is created (if the inspection rule for the product inspection can be found) for all scanned goods handling units. All handling units are then posted with goods receipts, with the contents of bad handling units being posted in the *blocked stock* stock category.

- **Product Inspections (IOT2, IOT3, IOT4, and IOT5)**
  Product inspections allow you to test products on their product attributes and to evaluate and determine their future use. The following inspections are grouped as product inspections:

  - Counting in goods receipt (has no influence on stock attributes and therefore is not a follow-up action—only quantity corrections). This is possible in addition to other inspections (IOT3 and IOT4).
  - Quality inspection in inbound delivery.
  - Quality inspection in returns processing (applies to all return processes).
  - Warehouse internal quality inspection.

Unlike the preliminary inspections and counting, it is possible to use sampling inspection and distribution of the inspection to an external system for product inspections.

This allows more complex inspections, such as feature-based inspections in quality management in SAP ERP or SAP S/4HANA. Using IOT4, EWM also allows for separation of the sample quantity, calculated via the sampling procedure in SAP ERP or SAP S/4HANA, from the remaining quantity, only moving the sample quantity to the quality area. The remaining quantity can be moved to final putaway. Decentralized EWM stores the sample quantity in the **External Sample Size** field of the inspection document, while embedded EWM simply holds it in the inspection lot. The separation is achieved by posting the sample quantity to a different inspection ID type, 'S' (normally 'A' for IOT4). Both quants have the same inspection lot/document ID reference. In the following step, the sample quantity can be chosen, similar to a partial quantity decision.

An inspection rule defines everything about the inspection by its arguments: the type of inspection, determination of samples, possible findings, and the location of the inspection and system. Determination of an inspection rule is done by attributes that are defined prior to activating an inspection object type. EWM has a predefined set of inspection attributes that can be used for the determination by a given sort order. Performance of inspection rule determination is faster the fewer the attributes there are.

An inspection document is created if the inspection object type is activated in Customizing of the warehouse number, and an inspection rule can be found for given attributes. You can simulate and test inspection rule determination in Transaction /SCWM/QRSIM and on the inbound delivery item level in Transaction /SCWM/PRDI.

[»]

Values in Inspection Rule Determination

For the attributes of the inspection rule determination, note that the complete ANSI character set is valid. However, no special characters or signs must be used. In general, we advise you not to use special characters and signs in Customizing and master data.

Inspection rules can define a location-independent stock type for the inspection stock. Upon creation of a product inspection document, stock will be posted to the new stock category with reference to the inspection document (also for planned stock). This allows you to select the relevant stock when a decision is made based upon the inspection document. Likewise, you can evaluate and update the inspection document in accordance with a quality check at the inspection work center.

In addition, the inspection document reference in stock guarantees adequate routing in the putaway process. Stock-respective handling units are moved according to the configuration set up in the inspection rule's process step. Should a sample be movement-relevant in a sample inspection, the quality inspection module influences the routing of the sample only. The rest of the stock is put away regularly without any influence from the process step.

Inspection Document Creation

The quality inspection must be activated in the system for each warehouse number after generating an inspection object type. Here you need to define the attributes, such as the number range of the inspection document, items, samples, and time of inspection document creation. If you want to perform the inspection within an external system, you also need to maintain this information on the inspection object type level for each warehouse number. Only if this information is maintained will you be able to later specify the arguments for external inspection in the inspection rule.

Delivery-related inspection documents can be created with the activation of the inbound delivery. Alternatively, the **In Yard** status is another possible point in time for delivery-based inspection document creation. A product inspection document must be created before creation of a putaway warehouse task as the inspection may affect the stock and its routing.

The preliminary inspection inbound delivery (IOT1) and counting inspection (IOT2) are directly created as active documents. Product inspections in the inbound process (IOT3 and IOT4) are generally released at goods receipt, given that the processes of *acceptance sampling* (purchasing) or *presampling in production* (manufacturing) have not been defined in the inspection rule. These processes will allow or even demand a decision be made before any goods receipt is processed (e.g., using the functionality of *goods receipt control*). Upon the sampling inspection with stock-relevant samples, the assignment of the samples to the handling units is done during goods receipt.

Manually created ad hoc product inspections (IOT5) via the warehouse monitor are released automatically when the inspection document is created. Any potentially required move of the respective stocks to an inspection work center must be initiated by manual warehouse task creation.

Inspection documents are created in accordance with the definition of the inspection rule. An inspection document may contain one or more *elements*, which are either samples or items. Using a sample-drawing instruction that is associated with the inspection rule for the inspection document creation, samples will be generated for the inspection document. In Transaction /SCWM/QIDPR (Edit Product Inspection), manual elements of type item can be created—for example, on the handling unit level of the stock to be inspected. Decisions made in the inspection work center also generate elements of type item per (partially) decided stocks and results.

Routing

The quality inspection is defined as a dynamic step in the storage process, and the storage control checks if any inspection-relevant items are packed in the handling unit. These can be 100% inspections or a stock-relevant sample. If there is no destination bin given in the storage process step, the inspection rule is read and checks if it contains a storage process step that defines a destination bin. Figure 2.14 shows an example of what storage control may look like.

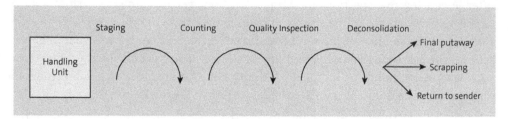

Figure 2.14 Quality Inspection Included in Putaway Process

After goods receipt and optional unloading, the handling unit is moved to a counting work center. After completion of counting, it is moved to the inspection work center, if required, and then moved to deconsolidation. Here the stocks are repacked according to their final destinations (final bin, scrapping, intermediate storage).

Counting must be done prior to quality inspection, and the processing of VAS only makes sense after quality inspection. Deconsolidation may happen at any time in the process. It makes sense prior to quality inspection if sampling is used to separate the samples from the rest of the stock and only bring the samples to the inspection work center while the remaining stock might already be put away inside the warehouse.

If no process-oriented storage control is active or the inbound delivery is not packed, the product warehouse tasks are always created for the quality inspection work center that is determined by the process step in the inspection rule. For a sample inspection, only the samples are moved to the work center. If no inspection work center can be determined, no warehouse task is created.

Inspection Results

Results capturing and decision-making for the inspection can be done in the inspection UI on an inspection work center, in an RF, or in an external system. The inspection document UI allows you to make decisions about the complete inspection document. For product-based inspection documents, samples or contents of complete handling units can be decided upon. Within the inspection work center transaction, the decision is therefore also available on the level of the stock. Here it is possible also to correct the quantity, product, and batch.

An inspection result consists of at least a decision and a follow-up action. In addition, findings (in standard errors and effort) may be captured and documentation (e.g., a photo) appended. Findings and documentation are optional and need not be used.

Decisions and follow-up actions can be recorded separately. For example, you can make a decision at the work center level and submit a follow-up action in the inspection document UI. In the inspection rule, you define a follow-up code group for the inspection rule, which is set up in Customizing for the decision, via menu path **Extended Warehouse Management • Cross-Process Settings • Quality Management • Results**. Here decision codes, errors, and follow-up actions are defined. First define possible decision codes and code groups, and then assign the decision to code groups (see Figure 2.15). When assigning decision codes to decision code groups, you specify which decision code is used in an automatic decision.

Dialog Structure	Decision Codes				
⮐ Decision Codes					
∨🗀 Code Group	Decision Code	Description	Valuation	QScore	Follow-Up Action
🗀 Codes	☐ S_0	Without Inspection Decision	∨		
	☐ S_A		A Accept ∨		
	☐ S_A0	Acceptance, Untested	A Accept ∨		
	☐ S_A1	Acceptance, Temporary	A Accept ∨		
	☐ S_AC001	Acceptance, Critical Character. Rejected	A Accept	∨ 1	
	☐ S_AC030	Acceptance, Major Character. A Rejected	A Accept	∨ 30	
	☐ S_AC060	Acceptance, Major Character. B Rejected	A Accept	∨ 60	
	☐ S_AC080	Acceptance, Secondary Character. A Rej.	A Accept	∨ 80	
	☐ S_AC090	Acceptance, Secondary Character. B Rej.	A Accept	∨ 90	
	☐ S_AC100	Acceptance, All Characteristics Accepted	A Accept	∨ 100	

Figure 2.15 Definition of Decision Codes and Code Groups for Embedded EWM

In Customizing follow-up actions, define the follow-up action and take care of each warehouse number and the control parameters of quality control (see Figure 2.16). You then assign the follow-up action to the code groups that you defined in Customizing for decision codes. This can be defined per inspection rule, selection of decision codes, and follow-up actions.

Dialog Structure	Follow-Up Actions for Quality Results							
∨🗀 Follow-Up Actions	War...	FollUpActn	IOT	Int.Action	Ty.	Whse Proc. Type	Reason	Exception Code
⮐ Follow-Up Actions for Quality Results	☐ 1710	PUTA	4	4 Put Away	∨ FF	Y114		
∨🗀 Code Group								
🗀 Assign Follow-Up Actions								

Figure 2.16 Definition of Follow-up Actions

For a decision, you can propose a follow-up action. There is also a BAdI to determine the proposed follow-up action (see Table 2.19 later in this section). A proposed follow-up action is required if you are using external inspections as the external interface does not contain a follow-up action, because this is not a Quality Inspection Engine table but a pure EWM table. Follow-up actions can be defined differently per inspection object type.

Because the decision and therefore the follow-up action on external inspection is communicated only after completion of the inspection document, follow-up processing is called only once. It is implemented as an implementation of Quality Inspection Engine enhancement spot QIE_OBJECTS_INSP_DOCUMENT. The implementation is done in class /SCWM/CL_QFU, with method IF_QIE_INSP_DOC_EVENTS~ON_EVENT_RAISED, calling method DECIDED, which corresponds to a decision on the inspection document header.

Follow-Up Handling

In this section, we describe the different scenarios supported in decentralized EWM for the triggering of a follow-up action that originates from the decision made at the end of quality inspection.

In returns management (SAP CRM or advanced returns management), a follow-up action can already be defined in the order document. All relevant data is passed to decentralized EWM, and no real inspection takes place. A goods receipt is posted according to the previously provided decision information.

Returns management can request follow-up determination in its own system. In this scenario, EWM only inspects the goods and collects the decision. Information is passed back to returns management and a follow-up activity must be triggered from there. In this scenario, field FUPEXT is set in the inspection document. It defines which system is to decide on the follow-up action.

In returns management of SAP CRM and advanced returns management, EWM can also decide that follow-up must be initiated by SAP CRM/advanced returns management.

If this is not a return scenario or a returns system forces a special scenario, the follow-up action is recorded in EWM or determined by the default follow-up action of the decision defined in Customizing.

Any decision can lead to a posting change of the stock to change at least the field's inspection type (field INSPTYP) and optional inspection reference (field INSPID). Depending on the existence of the follow-up decision, these fields are changed when awaiting the follow-up decision or cleared if follow-up is already known. The stock type, product, and batch can be changed as well on follow-up activity.

A decision on the inspection document header is valid for the complete inspection stock. For inspections on the stock level, a decision on the handling unit (complete content of handling unit) or stock level can have its own follow-up action. In a sample inspection, the inspection rule defines if the decision and follow-up are relevant.

Possible outcomes are as follows:

- Follow-up action is relevant to sampling stock only
- Follow-up action is relevant to the sample and the original handling unit; the sample was drawn
- Sample is destructive
- Sample is destructive and follow-up action is relevant to the handling unit where the sample was drawn
- Sample is not relevant for any follow-up (processed with header decision)

If the inspection sample is stock-relevant, the quantity of the sample is marked by value B in field INSPTYP during goods receipt. The value of field INSPID corresponds to the element key (GUID) of the sample.

Follow-up code includes three control parameters and an exception code. The following control parameters are included:

- **Internal action**
  In internal action, the following processes are provided:
  - Creation of a stock transfer order to another warehouse
  - Scrapping
  - Continue putaway to delivery
  - Creation of a warehouse internal inspection for further or more detailed inspection

- **Destination stock category**
  Maintenance of a location-independent stock type in field **Destination Stock Type** will lead to a posting change of the stock type. During decision and follow-up processing, this change will be made on the already called posting change for the inspection document reference.

- **Warehouse process type**
  By definition of a warehouse process type, a warehouse task will be created by the use of this warehouse process type, except for follow-ups with internal action *continue putaway*. For example, on *scrapping*, it is useful to create a warehouse task for a specific storage type used (exclusively) for scrapping purposes.

- **Exception code**
  Exception code handling is called if an exception code is defined.

Customer follow-ups and enhancements to the posting changes are possible upon implementing the BAdIs for follow-up handling. Follow-up processing can be found completely in class /SCWM/CL_QFU for different entering points:

- **Inspdoc_decision**
  Processes complete inspection stock

- **Element_decision**
  Processes the handling unit and or stock referred to in the element according to inspection rule

- **Stock_decision**
  Processes the provided stock information (only possible from work center or RF processing)

All methods do a predetermination of required data to be passed to method stock_action, which includes enhancement spot /SCWM/ES_QFU respective of BAdI /SCWM/EX_QFU.

Objects and Data Model

The inspection object types in Quality Inspection Engine cannot be delivered out of the box. For this reason, inspection object types must be generated in the customer system, relying on the EWM-based configuration. Each inspection object type generation creates a new unique key (GUID) and therefore a new inspection object type version. There can only be one active version of an inspection object type, and defined inspection rules are only valid for the version that was active at the time of their creation.

[»]

Inspection Object Type Version

With the generation or activation of a new inspection object type version, all defined master data for that inspection object type gets lost. The programs work only with the active version of the inspection object. The inspection object type version is independent from the warehouse number and cross-client.

Quality Inspection Engine is programmed in the package named QIE. Its most important subpackages are certainly QIE_COMMON and QIE_OBJECTS_INSP. The latter is responsible for the creation and editing of inspection documents. It also contains the core transparent tables QIE_INSP_DOC for the inspection document and QIE_ELEMENT for the inspection element, which may also be considered inspection document items. EWM-specific data on the respective quality inspection data objects are defined within SAP includes starting with the prefix SI_.

In a similar fashion, the Quality Inspection Engine inspection document and finding tables provide for a customer include with the prefix CI_. These include structures can be created using forward navigation while double-clicking the (initially not fully existing) include itself while displaying the respective database table in Transaction SE11.

Table 2.18 shows the available Quality Inspection Engine tables based on the SAP and customer includes for each data object and table.

Data Object	Database Table	SAP Include	Customer Include
Inspection document	QIE_INSP_DOC	SI_QIE_TS_INSP_DOC_CONS, SI_QIE_TS_IRULE_ARGS_CONS	CI_QIE_TS_INSP_DOC_CONS
Inspection rule arguments	QIE_IRULE_ARGS	SI_QIE_TS_IRULE_ARGS_CONS	
Inspection element	QIE_ELEMENT	SI_QIE_TS_DRWI_ATTR_CONS	
Sample drawing instruction	QIE_SAMP_DRWI	SI_QIE_TS_DRWI_ATTR_CONS	
Finding	QIE_FINDING	SI_QIE_TS_FIND_ATTR	CI_QIE_TS_FIND_ATTR

Table 2.18 Quality Inspection Tables (Structures) Containing Customer Includes

The EWM part of quality inspection is included in package /SCWM/QINSP. An exception is the direct integration with the SAP ERP or SAP S/4HANA system predominantly used for (advanced) returns processing, located in function group /SCWM/ERP_QFU, which can be found in package /SCWM/EWM_INTEGRATION. On the SAP ERP or SAP S/4HANA side, tables /SPE/INSPECRESH (Inspection Outcome: Header), /SPE/INSPECRESP (Inspection Outcome: Item), and /SPE/INSPECRESC (Inspection Outcome: Item Codes), assigned to package /SPE/RET_INSPECTIONS, keep track of returns-based inspection results between systems.

Quality inspection foresees quite a lot of customer enhancement possibilities, in both the Quality Inspection Engine and /SCWM/ domains. Available enhancement spots and included BAdIs for the /SCWM/ component can be found in Table 2.19. You can also find further available BAdIs in Quality Inspection Engine–based enhancement spots via Transaction SE20 or in the IMG.

Enhancement Spot	BAdI	Description
/SCWM/ES_QFU	/SCWM/EX_QFU	Follow-up actions
	/SCWM/EX_QFU_BATCH_DATA	Batch characteristics during inspection decision
	/SCWM/EX_QFU_CLOSE_HU	Close handling unit at header decision
	/SCWM/EX_QFU_SAVE	Save for data created or changed in BAdI /SCWM/EX_QFU
	/SCM/EX_QFU_SET_FUCODE	Determine follow-up code
	/SCWM/EX_QFU_SET_IN_EXTSYST	Maintain and execute follow-up action externally
	/SCWM/EX_QFU_STO	Create purchase order
	/SCWM/EX_QFU_STOCK_ACTION	Influence stock action after decision
	/SCWM/EX_QFU_STOCK_ACTION_WT	Modification of product warehouse tasks after inspection decision
	/SCWM/EX_QFU_STOCK_ITEMS_4_FUP	Follow-up activities before the handling unit(s) lock
/SCWM/ES_QM_CNT	/SCWM/EX_QM_CNT	Overrule counting relevance of inbound delivery items

Table 2.19 Enhancement Spots for Quality Inspection in Decentralized EWM

Enhancement Spot	BAdI	Description
/SCWM/ES_QM_DIV	/SCWM/EX_QGR_CONTROL	Influence the behavior of goods receipt control for inbound delivery items
	/SCWM/EX_QM_SAMPLE_ROUND_QTY	Rounding of sample quantities for external sample size
	/SCWM/EX_QM_STOCK_EXTSMPLE_QTY	Stock selection for sample size
	/SCWM/EX_QM_STOCK_INSP_EXT	Enablement of stock-based quality inspections or defect processing
	/SCWM/EX_QM_STOCK_SAMPLE_SORT	Stock sorting for changed sample size
/SCWM/ES_QM_INSP	/SCWM/EX_QM_INSP_CHANGE	Change inspection (product/batch inspection)
	/SCWM/EX_QM_INSP_CHECK_LOCK	Check lock (product/batch inspection)
	/SCWM/EX_QM_INSP_RELEVANCE	Set inspection relevance (product/batch inspection)
	/SCWM/EX_QM_IOT5_CREA_ALL	Decide whether all stock lines must be processed
/SCWM/ES_QM_PRP	/SCWM/EX_QM_PRP	Write inspection document attribute
/SCWM/ES_QM_SUMMARY	/SCWM/EX_QM_INSPDOC_AUTO_DEC	Control of background decision for inspection document
	/SCWM/EX_QM_INSP_SUMMARY	Custom criteria definition for inspections

Table 2.19 Enhancement Spots for Quality Inspection in Decentralized EWM (Cont.)

Preliminary inspection for handling units is a special case, as here no planning takes place that is completed by a result. The preliminary inspection of handling units is realized in function module /SCWM/QHU_INSPECTION. This function module expects two lists of handling units: the good ones and the bad ones. From this list, a new inspection document is created with one item per handling unit, including the results according to the table where they are passed. Goods receipt is posted for all handling units according to the result.

A standard RF transaction exists to scan those handling units. A custom RF transaction or SAP GUI transaction is conceivable, where this scan could also contain the unloading step.

Integration

In goods receipt processing—especially in product inspection—we have multifunctional requirements. EWM offers a maximum of flexibility regarding inspection of stock and follow-up processing. Enhanced functionality on the inspection is also provided by integrating external inspection systems such as SAP ERP or SAP S/4HANA. Here it is possible to add characteristics-based recording of inspection results, which Quality Inspection Engine itself is not capable of. For returns management, the customer relationship management system (SAP CRM) influences the processing of the stock more than the real quality of the goods, but feedback to the returns system about quality is requested.

In the following section, we present the possibilities of integrating decentralized EWM and SAP ERP or SAP S/4HANA quality management. This will mainly include the creation of an inspection lot in the SAP ERP or SAP S/4HANA system triggered from decentralized EWM and the replication of the usage decision back from SAP ERP or SAP S/4HANA to EWM, potentially initiating logistical follow-up actions.

Inspection in an External System

If required, inspection of incoming goods can be processed in an external system with EWM triggering the creation and replication of inspection documents. Where communication of Quality Inspection Engine with an external system is generally realized by SAP Process Integration (SAP PI), EWM may also directly integrate with the quality management in SAP ERP or SAP S/4HANA (quality management). This integration makes use of inspection type 17 (origin external system) in quality management. This communication path is realized by remote function call (RFC).

To integrate decentralized EWM with an external inspection system, such system must be defined in the Quality Inspection Engine setup (see Figure 2.17) and must also be assigned to the inspection object types on the warehouse level. For the assigned inspection object types, the inspection rule offers additional fields for the external system (e.g., inspection type 17) to activate external inspection for this inspection rule. For inspection documents of this inspection rule, the document is distributed to the external system at document release/creation and expects the results from the external system. For connecting an external quality system, it is important to consider SAP Note 1278425.

[»]

How-To Guide for EWM Quality Management/Quality Inspection Engine Configuration for Decentralized EWM

We recommend going through the how-to guide for EWM configuration for quality inspection with decentralized EWM, named *How-To Configure Quality Management Processes for Decentralized EWM Based on SAP S/4HANA*. You can find it in the SAP Community wiki at *https://wiki.scn.sap.com/wiki/display/SCM/How-To+Guides+for+SAP+EWM*. You might also consider the documentation on quality management for decentralized EWM in the SAP Help Portal (*https://help.sap.com/*) for more details on functionality and configuration options and requirements.

On inspection in an external system, results can be entered only on the sample or document header level. Follow-up processing on the stock level is not possible due to incomplete stock information in the external system. For inspection documents distributed to an external system, result recording is possible in EWM as well, overcoming a potential breakdown of the external system.

The communication between EWM and an external system is completely handled by Quality Inspection Engine. Relevant Customizing can be found via menu path **Cross-Application Components • Quality Inspection Engine • Central Settings • Communication with an External QM System • Define External QM Systems**. Create an external quality management system and assign attributes that need to be maintained in the inspection rule. Figure 2.17 shows an example of integration with quality management in SAP ERP. On the same level, you assign the installation of the system.

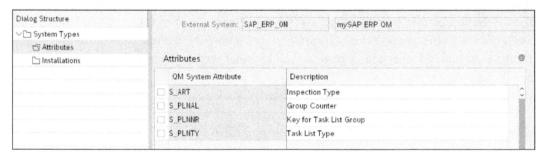

Figure 2.17 Inspection Attributes for External Quality Management System

Result Communication for Returns

For return deliveries, a document flow entry is created for each decision. On quantity classification, the delivery item calculates the completion of the inspection. Completion of the inspection is mandatory for completing the return delivery. After completion, a PPF action is triggered to send the results to SAP ERP or SAP S/4HANA. Depending on the type of the original system or the returns order, the results are then communicated to a corresponding system, such as SAP CRM.

Follow-up Processing from External System

Returns can define that EWM only completes the inspection and records the result, but the decision on follow-up has to be done by the returns system (SAP CRM, advanced returns management, SAP ERP, or SAP S/4HANA). Depending on the decided-upon follow-up, the system creates a delivery with reference to the inspection result or directly calls function module /SCWM/QM_FOLLOW_UP to post the follow-up if no delivery is required (like on *continue putaway*). It is possible to realize other follow-ups by posting changes or outbound deliveries with reference to the inspection result.

2.4.2   Quality Management in Embedded EWM

In this section, we will focus on quality inspection in embedded EWM. Specifically, we will discuss its functions and objects and data model.

Function

As mentioned earlier in the introduction to Section 2.4 for quality management, embedded EWM turns to the classical SAP S/4HANA quality management for triggering and performing quality inspections and their follow-up processing. Core quality inspection–related functionality for embedded EWM is certainly intended to be more or less identical to decentralized EWM. However, moving toward SAP S/4HANA quality management required leaving most Quality Inspection Engine–based objects and functionality behind, which led to some limitations, while simplifications could be achieved in the area of master data redundancy, and new functionality even could be provided, such as defects processing.

In the following sections, we will discuss inspection lot creation, inspection results, follow-up handling, and defect processing.

Inspection Lot Creation

After incoming or already existing stock is found to be relevant for inspection, the creation of an *inspection lot* is triggered from embedded EWM. While Quality Inspection Engine–based objects like inspection documents, inspection elements, and findings in the Quality Inspection Engine–based sample drawing procedure are no longer used, inspection lot creation can still be triggered by an inspection rule requiring an inspection object type to be generated and activated during basic setup. However, as of SAP S/4HANA 1909, configuration allows you to work without inspection rules at all, in which case the system will turn toward the material master's quality management–related data (table QMAT) and the quality inspection info record (table QINF) to determine inspection relevance. IOT3 (Q-Inspection Returns Delivery), IOT4 (Q-Inspection Product/Batch Inbound Delivery), and IOT5 (Q-Inspection Product/Batch Warehouse-Internal), as described in the previous section on quality inspection in decentralized EWM, remain in use within embedded EWM and will still need to be activated, while preliminary inspections (IOT1 and IOT6) and counting (IOT2) have been deprecated. The rather new IOT 7 (Logistical Defect Processing) is available for embedded EWM only in SAP S/4HANA 2022 (and later), which allows you to create quality management–based defects and respective stock postings or scrapping potentially to be turned into quality notifications.

With IOT4, inbound delivery–based inspections, both processes of acceptance sampling and presampling in production, are supported in embedded EWM next to the inspection after goods receipt.

[»]

Quality Management Configuration for Embedded EWM

We recommend going through the documentation on quality management for embedded EWM at the SAP Help Portal (*https://help.sap.com/*) for more details on functionality and configuration options and requirements.

Table 2.20 shows the inspection types that have been made available for embedded EWM processing. They mirror and extend already known SAP S/4HANA quality management–based inspection types, adding the number *17* as a prefix. This relates to the inspection process origin from an *external system*, meaning outside of SAP S/4HANA, being used by both embedded and decentralized deployment options.

Inspection Types Used without Inspection Rules	Description	Inspection Types Used with Inspection Rules	Description
		17	Extended Warehouse Inspection
01	Goods Receipt Insp. for Purchase Order	1701 1702	EWM Inspection External System EWM Acceptance Sampling
04	Goods Receipt Inspection from Production	1704	EWM Goods Receipt Insp. from Production
08	Stock Transfer Inspection	1708	EWM Stock Transfer Inspection
09	Recurring Inspection of Batches	1709	EWM Recurring Inspection of Batches

Table 2.20 Supported Quality Management Inspection Types in Embedded EWM

For IOT4, you can use sampling and activate the sample size calculation available with SAP S/4HANA quality management's sampling procedure. Using split sample quantities, it is possible to separate the sample quantity from the remaining quantity and only move the sample quantity to the quality area. The remaining quantity can then be moved to final putaway. The separation is achieved by posting the sample quantity to a different inspection ID of type 'S'. Both quants of the sample and the remaining quantity carry the same inspection lot ID reference (in case of decentralized EWM inspection document reference). For packed stock, the handling unit will not be split when moved to the quality inspection area, while unpacked stock quantities will be rounded by stock UOM, packaging specification figures, or using BAdI /SCWM/EX_QM_SAMPLE_ROUND_QTY, as it may make sense to round up the quantity to whole units so not to break up containers. The sample split is triggered synchronously after goods receipt. Technically, unpacked stock is processed in class /SCWM/CL_QLOT_S4 using method PROCESS_QINSP_GM_PROD. Packed stock uses method PROCESS_QINSP_GM_HU of the same class.

Inspection Results

In embedded EWM, the usage decision is made based on the SAP S/4HANA quality management–based inspection lot. The inspection lot optionally allows for detailed recording of quality results and characteristics alongside decision-making. Partial decisions are also supported in embedded EWM by reusing the popup UI familiar from the SAP S/4HANA quality management integration with decentralized EWM. This will allow decisions to be made on the handling unit level, for example, where appropriate stock items will need to be selected.

[«]

Partial Decisions with EWM-Triggered Inspection Lots

You can check SAP Note 3298981 for a quick overview of partial decision-making for quality management inspection lots with EWM. The note also contains further information and links to other interesting topics tied to quality management processing.

Decision codes and code groups for usage decision need to be customized via the SAP S/4HANA quality management. See Figure 2.18 for an example of a code group created for quality inspection for EWM inbound delivery processing.

Dialog Structure					
∨ ☐ Code Groups for Usage Decision	Code Group: UD1701	Decision Code Grp Inbound Delivery (EWM)			
☐ Codes for Usage Decision					
	Codes for Usage Decision				
	Code	Short Text for Code		Long Text for Code	Where-Used List ...
	☐ A1	Accepted-unrestricted Stock		☐	☐⁵
	☐ A2	Accepted-unrestricted minor quality Stck		☐	☐⁵
	☐ R1	Rejected-blocked Stock		☐	☐⁵

Figure 2.18 Usage Decision Code Groups for Embedded EWM

Follow-up Handling

Follow-up actions in the context of embedded EWM will again be triggered from usage decisions made in the SAP S/4HANA quality management inspection lot. As SAP S/4HANA quality management is using function modules to flexibly react to decisions, the EWM integration of follow-up handling provides two function modules that can be called behind the EWM-related decision codes to trigger EWM logistical follow-up actions:

- QFOA_EWM_LOG_FOLLOW_UP_S4 for full quantity (inspection lot level) decisions
- QTFA_EWM_LOG_FOLLOW_UP_S4 for usage decisions for partial quantities (partial lots)

For *skip lots*—that is, when quality inspections can be skipped because of the current quality level—embedded EWM immediately receives the information at inspection lot creation and directly initiates the posting to free stock.

Defect Processing

Embedded EWM supports IOT7 for defect processing. Once detected for stock in the warehouse, quality defects can be recorded and followed up on using the Record Warehouse Defect app. The app will allow you to trigger stock-based actions, such as posting stock into blocked or unrestricted status or scrapping to a cost center. Defects can be further processed as quality notifications, based on which further stock-based actions can again be triggered or communications to suppliers or quality experts can be filed. EWM stock will carry reference to the defect or quality notification number with inspection type G.

While creating defects or quality notifications and choosing follow-up actions, methods CHECK_EWM_DATA and CHECK_ERP_DATA of class /SCWM/CL_QUI_DEFECT will be invoked to perform stock checks and selections, called from function module /SCWM/QUI_DEFECT_FUP_S4, which again calls function module /SCWM/QUI_DEFECT_FUP.

When saving the defect, method SAVE_FOLLOW_UP_PROCESSING of class /SCWM/CL_QUI_DEFECT takes care of execution of the follow-up actions using several classes implementing interface /SCWM/IF_QFU, which inherit from class /SCWM/CL_QFU_ACTION. One subclass can be found per follow-up action, e.g., /SCWM/CL_QFU_SCRAP_COMPL for scrapping to a cost center.

Objects and Data Model

Embedded EWM fully integrates into the existing SAP S/4HANA quality management objects and data model. As core data dictionary objects of the quality management module, we would like to mention the following transparent tables:

- QALS stores the SAP S/4HANA quality management quality inspection lot.
- Q_LOT_SERIAL holds serial number related inspection data.
- QALT keeps partial lots.

- QPRS keeps samples.
- QAVE stores the usage decisions that have been made.

Like in decentralized EWM, quality inspection in embedded EWM foresees quite a lot of customer enhancement possibilities, similar to the ones for decentralized EWM. They are fewer in number, however, as some BAdIs were linked to functionality that is not supported in embedded EWM anymore. In general, when dealing with enhancements around quality inspections, we recommend considering the Quality Inspection Engine–based BAdIs in decentralized EWM and qualtiy management–based BAdIs and user exits in embedded EWM. Available enhancement spots and included business add-ins for the components can be found in Table 2.21.

Enhancement Spot	BAdI	Description
/SCWM/ES_QFU	/SCWM/EX_QFU_SAVE	Save Data for Follow-up Action
	/SCWM/EX_QFU_STOCK_ACTION	Influence Stock Action after Decision
	/SCWM/EX_QFU_STOCK_ACTION_WT	Modification of Product Warehouse Tasks after Inspection Decision
/SCWM/ES_QM_DIV	/SCWM/EX_QGR_CONTROL	Influence the Behavior of Goods Receipt Control for Inbound Delivery Items
	/SCWM/EX_QM_SAMPLE_ROUND_QTY	Rounding of Sample Quantities for External Sample Size
	/SCWM/EX_QM_STOCK_EXTSMPLE_QTY	Stock Selection for Sample Size
	/SCWM/EX_QM_STOCK_INSP_EXT	Enablement of Stock-Based Quality Inspections or Defect Processing
	/SCWM/EX_QM_STOCK_SAMPLE_SORT	Stock Sorting for Changed Sample Size
/SCWM/ES_QM_INSP	/SCWM/EX_QM_INSP_CHANGE	Change Inspection (Product/Batch Inspection)
	/SCWM/EX_QM_INSP_RELEVANCE	Set Inspection Relevance (Product/Batch Inspection)
/SCWM/ES_QM_PRP	/SCWM/EX_QM_PRP	Write Inspection Document Attribute

Table 2.21 Enhancements for Quality Inspection in Embedded EWM

2.5   Integration with ERP Systems

As a central part of distribution and production logistics, warehouse management is closely linked with order and stock management, both core components of an ERP system. Transport management, manufacturing execution, and quality management systems can be considered as other potential integration points for warehousing. In this final section of the chapter, however, we explain the nature of the integration of EWM with SAP ERP or SAP S/4HANA, as well as potential integration options for third-party ERP systems. Last but not least, we highlight some differences in the SAP S/4HANA integration when using embedded EWM.

EWM provides a variety of interfaces for integration with SAP and third-party systems using various communication methods and technologies. The list of integration scenarios starts with SAP Business Warehouse (SAP BW) and SAP GTS, leading to various third-party systems for manufacturing execution, material flow control, sampling based inventory, or yard management, just to name a few.

The integration with SAP ERP or SAP S/4HANA, however, offers the most basic and the most comprehensive set of interfaces with EWM. The integration of third-party ERP systems with decentralized EWM is technically possible; however, it should be considered as a customer project in its entirety, as no standard framework or support is given for third-party ERP integration.

In this section, we would like to shed some light on ERP integration. For this purpose, we first introduce the interface blocks that are relevant for integration with SAP ERP or SAP S/4HANA. We highlight inbound and outbound message processing, calling spots, and enhancement options for each interface block's messages. Almost every EWM implementation project uses one or another custom development for the integration with SAP ERP or SAP S/4HANA.

In the second part of this section, you will learn which approaches exist for integration with third-party ERP systems and how you should plan the implementation of such integration. Third, we present further differences using embedded EWM where not already mentioned in the previous sections.

2.5.1   SAP ERP and SAP S/4HANA Systems

The integration of EWM with SAP ERP or SAP S/4HANA has four different aspects that are of the most interest to us, which we will therefore further address:

- Connection of different SAP ERP or SAP S/4HANA releases to EWM (SAP ERP or SAP S/4HANA version control), clearly only applicable for decentralized EWM
- Transactional data interfaces:
  - Delivery interface
  - Goods movement interface

- Shipment interface
- QM interface, only applicable for decentralized EWM as embedded EWM uses the inspection lot of the central system
- Master data interfaces (Application Link Enabling [ALE] or data replication framework-based), only applicable for decentralized EWM as embedded EWM uses the respective data in the central system:
  - Material (IDoc message type MATMAS)
  - Business partner (data replication framework), customer ,and vendor (IDOC message types DEBMAS and CREMAS), through customer-vendor integration (CVI)
  - Batch and batch classification (IDOC message types BATMAS and CLFMAS)
  - Packing instruction to packaging specification (RFC)
- Mapping of stock data models between SAP ERP or SAP S/4HANA and EWM

Most relevant objects for SAP ERP or SAP S/4HANA integration can quickly be found and accessed in the Object Navigator (Transaction SE80) through the package /SCWM/ERP_INTEGRATION.

Shared Customizing in SAP S/4HANA–Based EWM

Before moving to the ERP-EWM interfaces, we would like to talk briefly about shared Customizing tables that have been introduced with SAP S/4HANA–based EWM in order to eliminate data redundancy in SAP S/4HANA and EWM integration. Some previously available SAP ERP–based Customizing data objects, mostly linked to additional material attributes, are being accessed by SAP S/4HANA–based EWM as well. Table 2.22 shows the shared Customizing objects accompanied by the tables used in SAP EWM. Using the CDS redirection views, read accesses to the SAP EWM tables will automatically be redirected to the linked SAP S/4HANA table based on the field mapping contained in the CDS redirect view.

Object	SAP S/4HANA Table	SAP EWM Table	CDS Redirection View
Catch Weight Profile for Catch Weight Quantities	TCWQPROC	/SCWM/TCWPROC	/SCMB/V_TCWPROC
Catch Weight Tolerance Group	TCWQTOLGR	/SCWM/TCWTOLGR	/SCMB/V_TCWTOLGR
Quality Inspection Group	TQGRP	/SCWM/TQGRP	/SCMB/V_TQGRP
Transportation Group	TTGR	/SCMB/V_TTGR	/SAPAPO/TTGR
Warehouse Material Group	TWHMATGR	/SCMB/TWHMATGR	/SCMB/V_TWHMATGR

Table 2.22 Shared Customizing Tables for SAP S/4HANA and EWM

Object	SAP S/4HANA Table	SAP EWM Table	CDS Redirection View
Warehouse Storage Condition	TWHSTC	/SCMB/TWHSTC	/SCMB/V_TWHSTC
Handling Indicator	THNDLCD	/SCMB/THNDLCD	/SCMB/V_THNDLCD
Handling Unit Type	THUTYP	/SCWM/THUTYP	/SCMB/V_THUTYP
Serial Number Profile	TSERIAL	/SCWM/TSERIAL	/SCMB/V_TSERIAL
Packing Group	TVEGR	/SCWM/TPACKGR	/SCMB/V_TVEGR
Delivery Priority	TPRIO	/SCDL/TDLVPRIO	
Incoterms	TINC	/SCMB/TINC	/SCMB/V_TINC
Shipping Conditions	TVSB	/SCDL/TSRVLVL	

Table 2.22 Shared Customizing Tables for SAP S/4HANA and EWM (Cont.)

Keeping an eye on these tables when they are used in custom code will be required when migrating from SAP EWM to EWM based on SAP S/4HANA.

Version Control

For the development of the standalone SAP EWM system, SAP ERP release 6.0 was used. This release offers significantly larger interface functionality for connecting a decentralized warehouse management system than older SAP ERP releases. This is mainly due to several enhancements of the delivery interface, which were already available for the integration to the decentralized logistics execution warehouse management (SAP ERP WM). These mainly include:

- Confirmation of partial goods receipts to SAP ERP
- Inbound delivery split in SAP EWM
- Cancellation of delivery-based goods issue postings in SAP EWM
- Creation of inbound and outbound deliveries in SAP EWM
- Pick denial and changes to outbound delivery in SAP EWM before confirmation to SAP ERP

However, customers also called for the option to connect SAP EWM with SAP ERP release levels lower than 6.0. This is why SAP delivered SAP ERP version control with EWM release 5.1, through which SAP ERP releases from 4.6C onward can be connected to SAP EWM. Integration with such low SAP ERP release levels will come with functional restrictions of SAP EWM though, as it will make use of the limited IDoc-based interface functionality of the older SAP ERP releases. For an overview of the availability of individual interface functions in the various SAP ERP releases, Section 2.5.2. The use of IDoc-based interfaces represents a possible, albeit functionally limited and rarely used, alternative to the integration of SAP EWM with SAP ERP, SAP S/4HANA, and third-party ERP systems.

Business Functions for SAP ERP Integration with EWM

As of SAP ERP EHP 6.03, the `LOG_LE_INTEGRATION` business function is available for advanced SAP ERP integration functionality, especially around the delivery interface. This business function will already be active in an SAP S/4HANA–based ERP system. Check the release notes for EWM and SAP ERP enhancement packages and SAP Support Note 1423321 for exact information about additional features.

Transactional Data Interfaces

The integration of transactional data between SAP ERP or SAP S/4HANA and EWM is mainly based on two interface blocks: the delivery interface and the goods movement interface. While the delivery interface is mostly used to communicate instructions from the SAP ERP or SAP S/4HANA side to the warehouse about planned activities around stock reception or retrieval, as well as posting changes, which will be confirmed from the EWM side with their execution, the goods movement interface is used for any EWM-triggered goods movements, such as stock changes and stock difference postings that are relevant for SAP ERP or SAP S/4HANA inventory adjustments.

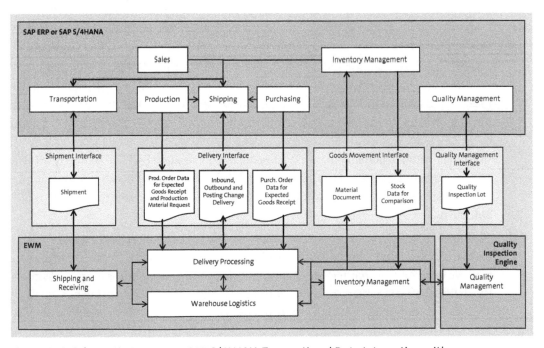

Figure 2.19 Schematic SAP ERP or SAP S/4HANA Transactional Data Integration with Decentralized EWM

In addition, you can activate the usage of two additional interface blocks for transport and quality management integration: while the shipment interface specifically supports the integration with the SAP ERP or SAP S/4HANA transportation management functionality, the quality management interface can be used for connecting any quality management systems. Integration with SAP ERP or SAP S/4HANA quality management is, in this case, only one of several possible system alternatives; however, it is the only one provided by SAP out of the box. Figure 2.19 gives an overview of the individual interfaces for transactional data objects that are described later in the section in more detail.

In the next sections, we take a more detailed look at the four main interfaces that run between EWM and SAP ERP or SAP S/4HANA, going through the individual messages contained in the delivery, goods movement, shipment, and quality management interface blocks.

Editing of SAP ERP or SAP S/4HANA Inbound Queue Content from EWM Messages

Due to ample demand, configurable options have been provided by SAP to allow for changes of the content of hanging queues on the SAP ERP or SAP S/4HANA inbound side of message processing from EWM. We recommend checking out the configuration guide attached to SAP Note 2244179 if you want to make use of the queue content change options.

Delivery Interface

The delivery interface is certainly the most complex and functionally extensive of the four interface blocks between EWM and SAP ERP or SAP S/4HANA. Any planned goods receipts and goods issues initiated from the SAP ERP or SAP S/4HANA side, as well as stock posting changes for the warehouse, are communicated through it. After the distribution of the deliveries from SAP ERP or SAP S/4HANA, the document sovereignty is with EWM. After that event, document changes can only be requested by SAP ERP or SAP S/4HANA and depend on the status of the document in EWM. However, EWM can in turn communicate changes, splits, and confirmations of delivery documents back to SAP ERP or SAP S/4HANA.

Ultimately, the delivery interface will allow for the creation of delivery documents in EWM to be distributed and confirmed to SAP ERP or SAP S/4HANA. In the following section, we describe the architecture of the inbound and outbound message processing of the delivery interface in more detail. You can also find a short description of each message and an explanation of how their usage is differentiated by document category (inbound or outbound delivery, posting change, production material request).

[+]

Debugging SAP ERP or SAP S/4HANA Integration

To debug the SAP ERP or SAP S/4HANA integration and the delivery interface specifically, we recommend using Transaction SAAB to activate the /SCWM/ERPINTEGRATION breakpoint ID. Moreover, we would like to point out the following breakpoint IDs: /SCWM/ERPDETERMINATION for SAP ERP– or SAP S/4HANA–based investigation and /SCWM/ERPVALIDATION for specific checks and validations.

You may also halt the processing of the inbound messages for detailed message content analysis either by deregistering the queue processing within Transaction SMQR on a general level or (for your SAP user individually) by activating the /SPE/IF_DEBUG_QRFC user parameter ID in the SAP ERP or SAP S/4HANA system and the /SCWM/IF_DEBUG_QRFC user parameter ID in EWM.

Within Transaction SMQ2, you can then find the halted message queue entries, as shown in Figure 2.20, and initiate their further processing in debugging mode. Double-click the queue name to display the message contents. Make sure to maintain the correct display applications in the qRFC administration beforehand (Transaction SMQE), as shown in Figure 2.21.

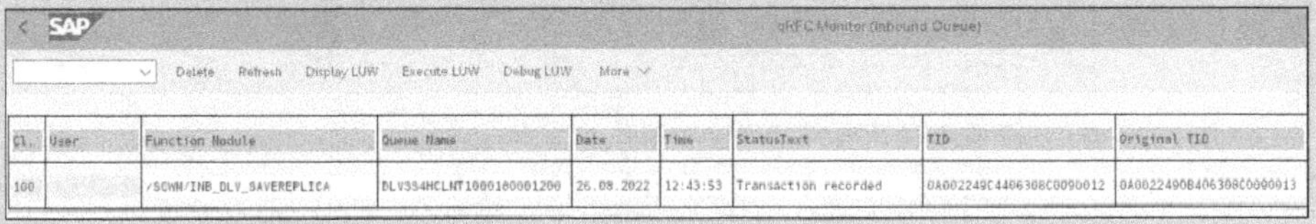

Figure 2.20 Example of Queue Entry in SMQ2

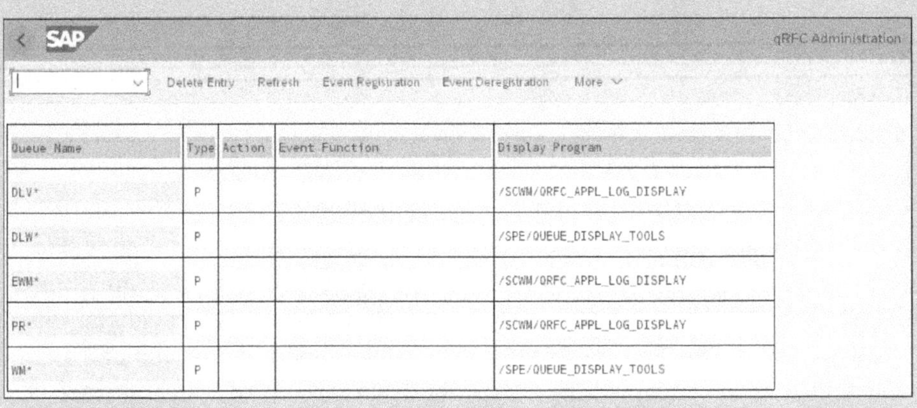

Figure 2.21 qRFC Display Programs in qRFC Administration

EWM Inbound Message Processing

The delivery or warehouse request management in EWM is closely integrated with the SAP ERP or SAP S/4HANA shipping through the delivery interface. Figure 2.22 shows the outbound message processing in SAP ERP or SAP S/4HANA and inbound message processing for delivery documents in EWM.

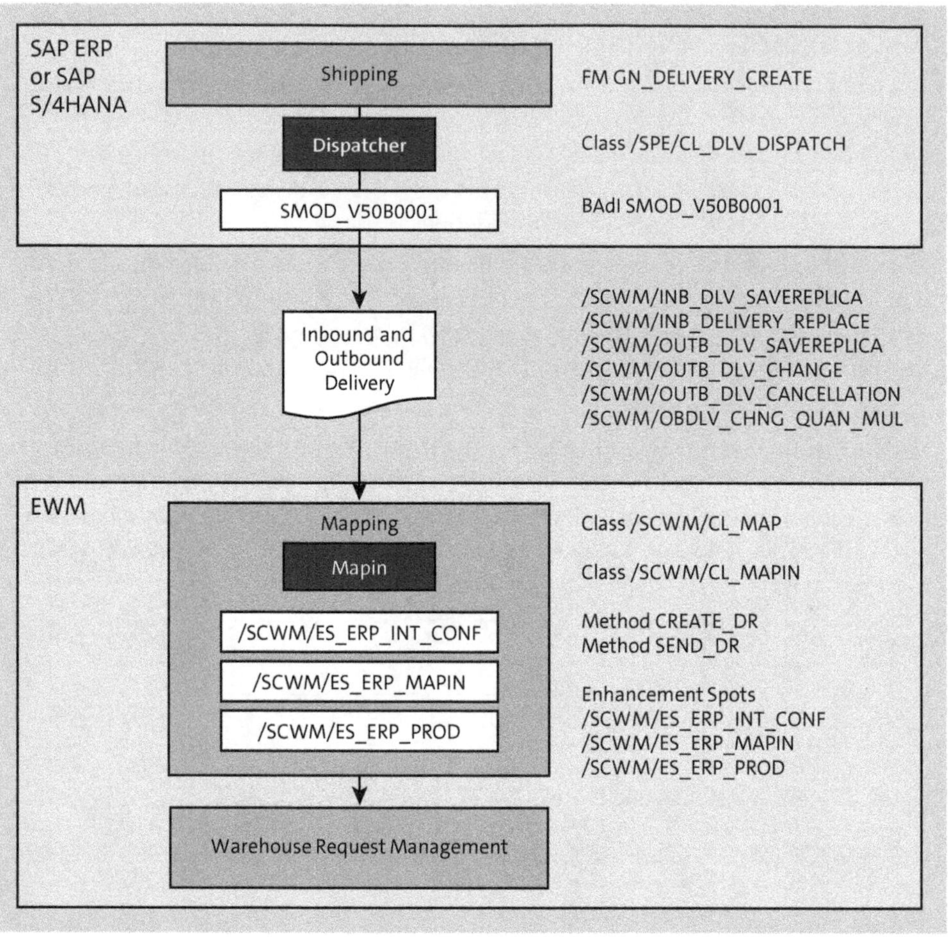

Figure 2.22 Inbound Message Processing of Delivery Interface

The SAP ERP or SAP S/4HANA system's shipping module initiates the message processing. The dispatcher application is responsible for the replication of inbound and outbound deliveries. The various SAP ERP or SAP S/4HANA modules, which are integrated with EWM, can create delivery documents that are routed to EWM through the /SPE/CL_DLV_DISPATCH class. You can control what data will be replicated for inbound and outbound deliveries by implementing the appropriate methods of BAdI SMOD_V50B0001 to pass, for example, additional data to EWM.

[+] **Transmission of Additional Delivery Data**

In SAP Note 351303, you can find detailed information and a sample implementation of BAdI definition SMOD_V50B0001, which can be used to send unstructured custom data with Business Application Programming Interface (BAPI) structure EXTENSION1. Furthermore, it lists the individual methods of the BAdI used within the inbound and outbound message processing.

The inbound message processing in EWM starts with a handover of SAP ERP or SAP S/4HANA delivery object data formats to the data formats of the EWM delivery object. The /SCWM/CL_MAPIN class is responsible for the mapping of the data formats and the data transfer to the EWM delivery management for creating a delivery notification or delivery request. In addition to the mapping of stock and master data, it will perform the determination of document categories, documents, and item types. In the example case of an SAP ERP– or SAP S/4HANA–triggered posting change, the SAP ERP or SAP S/4HANA outbound delivery will be mapped to a EWM posting change document category. Using the BAdIs of enhancement spot /SCWM/ES_ERP_MAPIN, which are called at the end of the mapping process, you can influence the data handover of, for example, custom data according to your own specifications. The delivery management will then conduct further determinations and validations in the follow-on process of transferring the notification or request into a document category that is used for warehouse processing.

[«]

Enhancement Options of EWM Inbound Message Processing

The following enhancement options exist for EWM inbound message processing of the delivery interface:

- BAdI for document and item type determination
- BAdI for changes/enhancements to data mapping
- BAdI for product creation with inbound delivery replication

You can find a more detailed description of the available BAdIs for SAP ERP or SAP S/4HANA integration in Chapter 6, Section 6.1. Table 2.23 through Table 2.44 provide an overview of the individual delivery-related messages. The tables are divided into two groups:

- Inbound messages of inbound warehouse requests (Table 2.23 through Table 2.25)
- Inbound messages of outbound warehouse requests (Table 2.26 through Table 2.30)

Description	Inbound Delivery Replication to EWM
Function	Creates an inbound delivery in EWM after creation and distribution from SAP ERP or SAP S/4HANA
Function module	/SCWM/INB_DLV_SAVEREPLICA
IDoc	SHP_IBDLV_SAVE_REPLICA*

Table 2.23 Inbound Message Processing of the Inbound Warehouse Request: Delivery Replication to EWM

Description	Inbound Delivery Replication to EWM
Called at...	<ul><li>Creation of an SAP ERP or SAP S/4HANA inbound delivery through Transactions VL60 and VL31N.</li><li>Creation of an SAP ERP or SAP S/4HANA inbound delivery through confirmation of a production order</li><li>Transfer of expected goods receipt data on request from the SAP ERP or SAP S/4HANA or EWM side</li><li>Transfer of expected goods receipt data from SAP ERP or SAP S/4HANA at release of manufacturing orders</li></ul>

Table 2.23 Inbound Message Processing of the Inbound Warehouse Request: Delivery Replication to EWM (Cont.)

Description	Change Request for an Inbound Delivery
Function	Requests a change of an inbound delivery after distribution from SAP ERP or SAP S/4HANA
Function module	/SCWM/INB_DELIVERY_REPLACE
Called at...	Change or deletion of an SAP ERP or SAP S/4HANA inbound delivery through Transaction VL60
Note	Will be replied to by calling function module /SPE_INB_DELIVERY_ RESPONSE on the SAP ERP or SAP S/4HANA side

Table 2.24 Inbound Message Processing of the Inbound Warehouse Request: Change Request from SAP ERP or SAP S/4HANA

Description	Change of Priority Points of Inbound Delivery Items
Function	Replicates a change in priority points for inbound delivery items as a result of changes to purchase order items. The change of the EWM delivery does actually not occur through a change of the SAP ERP or SAP S/4HANA delivery; therefore, it is not directly the delivery interface that is being used for the update.
Function module	/SCWM/INB_PO
Called at...	Change of purchase order items priority.

Table 2.25 Inbound Message Processing of the Inbound Warehouse Request: Change of Priority Points

Description	Outbound Delivery Replication to EWM
Function	Creates an outbound delivery in EWM after creation and distribution from SAP ERP or SAP S/4HANA
Function module	/SCWM/OUTB_DLV_SAVEREPLICA
IDoc	SHP_OBDLV_SAVE_REPLICA*
Called at...	<ul><li>Creation of an SAP ERP or SAP S/4HANA outbound delivery through Transactions VL10x, VL01N, and VL01NO</li><li>Creation of an SAP ERP or SAP S/4HANA customer returns delivery, turned into an EWM inbound delivery</li><li>Creation of an SAP ERP or SAP S/4HANA vendor returns delivery</li><li>Creation of an SAP ERP or SAP S/4HANA outbound delivery for component staging of a production order</li><li>Creation of an SAP ERP or SAP S/4HANA outbound delivery for component consumption with a production order confirmation</li><li>Creation of an SAP ERP or SAP S/4HANA outbound delivery with a consumption posting through Transaction MB1A</li><li>Creation of a posting change in SAP ERP or SAP S/4HANA through Transactions MIGO or MB1B</li></ul>

Table 2.26 Inbound Message Processing of the Outbound Warehouse Request: Delivery Replication to EWM

Description	Status Transfer of an Unchecked Delivery to EWM
Function	Replicates the deletion of unchecked deliveries from SAP ERP or SAP S/4HANA, which will trigger the deletion of unchecked deliveries in EWM
Function module	/SCWM/OUTB_DLV_CHANGE
Called at...	Transfer of unchecked to checked deliveries in SAP ERP or SAP S/4HANA initiated from SAP CRM

Table 2.27 Inbound Message Processing of the Outbound Warehouse Request: Status Change of Unchecked Deliveries

Description	Cancellation of Outbound Delivery
Function	Communicates the cancellation of an SAP ERP or SAP S/4HANA outbound delivery when canceling a production confirmation
Function module	/SCWM/OUTB_DLV_CANCELLATION
Called at...	Cancellation of production confirmation in SAP ERP or SAP S/4HANA through Transaction CO13

Table 2.28 Inbound Message Processing of the Outbound Warehouse Request: Cancellation

Description	Quantity Change of Outbound Delivery
Function	Requests a delivery item quantity change in EWM
Function module	/SCWM/OBDLV_CHNG_QUAN_MUL
Called at...	Changes to sales order in SAP ERP or SAP S/4HANA through Transaction VA02 or SAP CRM
Availability	SAP ERP 6.04 (business function LOG_LE_INTEGRATION) for Sales and Distribution sales order

Table 2.29 Inbound Message Processing of the Outbound Warehouse Request: Quantity Change Request

Description	Creation and Status Updates of Production Material Request in EWM
Function	Creates a production material request in EWM on the basis of an SAP ERP or SAP S/4HANA manufacturing order and updates relevant changes from the SAP ERP or SAP S/4HANA side
Function module	/SCWM/PRODUCTION_WHR_MAINTAIN
Called at...	Request warehouse management staging, completion, and closing of SAP ERP or SAP S/4HANA manufacturing order
Availability	SAP ERP 6.06/SAP EWM 9.2 (advanced production integration)

Table 2.30 Extended Warehouse Management Outbound Message Processing

The outbound message processing of changes, splits, or confirmations of deliveries in EWM is scheduled and triggered by corresponding actions of the PPF. These search the message log, which is updated by the stock or delivery management, for relevant change entries of the respective document. If an entry is found, the output processing is initiated by calling the respective function module in the SAP ERP or SAP S/4HANA system in method SEND_BAPI of class /SCWM/CL_MAPOUT after completion of mapping the EWM delivery object to the required SAP ERP or SAP S/4HANA format. The inbound processing of the SAP ERP or SAP S/4HANA system performs the appropriate function for the delivery document. As in SAP ERP or SAP S/4HANA outbound processing, the SMOD_V50B0001 BAdI definition is also available in inbound processing, providing different methods for processing and validation of the incoming document data. Figure 2.23 shows a schematic overview of the EWM outbound message processing.

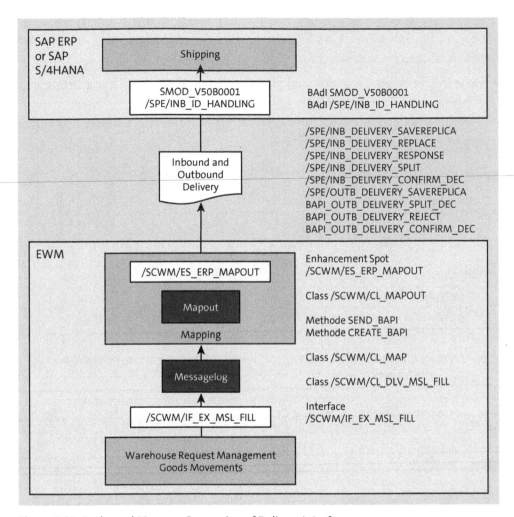

Figure 2.23 Outbound Message Processing of Delivery Interface

[«]

Enhancement Options of EWM Outbound Message Processing

The following enhancement options exist for EWM outbound message processing of the delivery interface:

- BAdI for changes of document data mapping
- BAdI for adding entries to the message log

You can find more detailed descriptions of the available BAdIs for SAP ERP or SAP S/4HANA integration in Chapter 6, Section 6.1.

In the following tables, we list the function modules that are called by EWM for sending document data to the SAP ERP or SAP S/4HANA system. In cases where an IDoc-based interface message is available and SAP ERP or SAP S/4HANA integration setup works via IDocs, this interface will alternatively be called from the SEND_BAPI method. The tables are divided into two groups:

- Function modules for outbound message processing of inbound warehouse requests (Table 2.31 through Table 2.38)
- Function modules for outbound message processing of outbound warehouse requests (Table 2.39 through Table 2.44)

Description	Inbound Delivery Replication to SAP ERP or SAP S/4HANA
Outbound message processing	/SCWM/CL_MAPOUT_ID_REPLICA
Function	Replicates an EWM-created inbound delivery to SAP ERP or SAP S/4HANA
Called at...	Creation of inbound delivery in EWM
Calls SAP ERP or SAP S/4HANA function module	/SPE/INB_DELIVERY_SAVEREPLICA

Table 2.31 Outbound Message Processing for Inbound Warehouse Request: Replication to SAP ERP or SAP S/4HANA

Description	Inbound Delivery Change to SAP ERP or SAP S/4HANA
Outbound message processing	/SCWM/CL_MAPOUT_ID_REPLACE
Function	Communicates changes of EWM inbound deliveries to SAP ERP or SAP S/4HANA
Called at...	■ Creation of batch split items ■ Changes to batch characteristics ■ Creation of new inbound delivery item ■ Deletion of inbound delivery
Calls SAP ERP or SAP S/4HANA function module	/SPE/INB_DELIVERY_REPLACE

Table 2.32 Outbound Message Processing for Inbound Warehouse Request: Changes to SAP ERP or SAP S/4HANA

Description	Response to a Change Request for an Inbound Delivery
Outbound message processing	/SCWM/CL_MAPOUT_ID_RESPONSE
Function	Answers to the change request initiated by message /SPE/INB_DELIVERY_REPLACE
Called at...	Change request triggered through Transaction VL60
Calls SAP ERP or SAP S/4HANA function module	/SPE/INB_DELIVERY_RESPONSE

Table 2.33 Outbound Message Processing for Inbound Warehouse Request: Response to Change Request

Description	Inbound Delivery Split in EWM
Outbound message processing	/SCWM/CL_MAPOUT_ID_SPLIT_DEC
Function	Communicates an inbound delivery split from EWM to SAP ERP or SAP S/4HANA
Called at...	▪ Partial confirmation of an inbound delivery with exception code ▪ Partial confirmation of an inbound delivery in the kit-to-stock scenario (SAP ERP– or SAP S/4HANA–triggered) ▪ Deletion of an inbound delivery item through Transaction /SCWM/PRDI
Calls SAP ERP or SAP S/4HANA function module	/SPE/INB_DELIVERY_SPLIT

Table 2.34 Outbound Message Processing for Inbound Warehouse Request: Inbound Delivery Split

Description	Inbound Delivery Confirmation to SAP ERP or SAP S/4HANA
Outbound message processing	/SCWM/CL_MAPOUT_ID_REJECT /SCWM/CL_MAPOUT_ID_CONF_DEC /SCWM/IDOC_OUTPUT_IBDLV_CONFDC
Function	Confirms the goods receipt and completion of inbound deliveries to SAP ERP or SAP S/4HANA

Table 2.35 Outbound Message Processing for Inbound Warehouse Request: Confirmation to SAP ERP or SAP S/4HANA

Description	Inbound Delivery Confirmation to SAP ERP or SAP S/4HANA
Called at...	■ Goods receipt confirmation (header or handling unit level), full and partial quantity goods receipt ■ Cancellation of goods receipt ■ Completion of inbound delivery item ■ Rejection of inbound delivery
Calls SAP ERP or SAP S/4HANA function module	/SPE/INB_DELIVERY_CONFIRM_DEC
Sends IDoc	SHP_IBDLV_CONFIRM_DECENTRAL*

Table 2.35 Outbound Message Processing for Inbound Warehouse Request: Confirmation to SAP ERP or SAP S/4HANA (Cont.)

Description	Request Expected Goods Receipt Data from EWM, SAP ERP, or SAP S/4HANA
Function	Creation or deletion of expected goods receipt data in EWM
Called at...	Request of expected goods receipt data for manufacturing orders through Transaction /SCWM/ERP_EGR_DELETE (EWM) or /SPE/EGR (SAP ERP or SAP S/4HANA)
Calls SAP ERP or SAP S/4HANA function module	/SPE/INB_EGR_CREATE_PROD
Note	Data is replicated to EWM through message /SCWM/INB_DLV_SAVEREPLICA

Table 2.36 Outbound Message Processing for Inbound Warehouse Request: Request of Expected Goods Receipt for Manufacturing Orders

Description	Request Expected Goods Receipt Data from EWM or SAP ERP or SAP S/4HANA
Function	Creation or deletion of expected goods receipt data in EWM
Called at...	Request of expected goods receipt data for purchase orders and scheduling agreements through Transaction /SCWM/ERP_EGR_DELETE (EWM) or /SPE/EGR (SAP ERP or SAP S/4HANA)
Calls SAP ERP or SAP S/4HANA function module	/SPE/INB_EGR_CREATE_POSA

Table 2.37 Outbound Message Processing for Inbound Warehouse Request: Request of Expected Goods Receipt for Purchase Orders or Scheduling Agreements

Description	Request Expected Goods Receipt Data from EWM or SAP ERP or SAP S/4HANA
Note	Data is replicated to EWM through message `/SCWM/INB_DLV_SAVEREPLICA`

Table 2.37 Outbound Message Processing for Inbound Warehouse Request: Request of Expected Goods Receipt for Purchase Orders or Scheduling Agreements (Cont.)

Description	Call of Transaction VL60
Function	Allows for calling SAP ERP or SAP S/4HANA Transaction VL60 from EWM inbound delivery handling
Called at...	Creation of an inbound delivery through Transaction /SCWM/PRDI; call to Transaction VL60 needs to be implemented via BAdI
Calls SAP ERP or SAP S/4HANA function module	`/SPE/INB_CALL_TRX_VL60`

Table 2.38 Outbound Message Processing for Inbound Warehouse Request: Call of Transaction VL60

Description	Outbound Delivery Replication to SAP ERP or SAP S/4HANA
Outbound message processing	`/SCWM/CL_MAPOUT_OD_SAVEREPLICA`
Function	Replicates an EWM-created outbound delivery to SAP ERP or SAP S/4HANA
Called at...	Creation of an outbound delivery in EWM (direct outbound delivery order)
Calls SAP ERP or SAP S/4HANA function module	`/SPE/OUTB_DELIVERY_SAVEREPLICA`
Available from	SAP ERP 6.03 (business function `LOG_LE_INTEGRATION`)

Table 2.39 Outbound Message Processing for Outbound Warehouse Request: Replication

Description	Outbound Delivery Split
Outbound message processing	`/SCWM/CL_MAPOUT_OD_SPLIT_DEC` `/SCWM/IDOC_OUTPUT_OBDLV_SPLTDC`

Table 2.40 Outbound Message Processing for Outbound Warehouse Request: Outbound Delivery Split

Description	Outbound Delivery Split
Function	Communicates an outbound delivery split
Called at...	■ Goods issue posting for an outbound delivery with partial pick confirmation ■ Creation of an outbound delivery with different routes at item level (route determined in EWM) ■ Partial confirmation of a posting change
Calls SAP ERP or SAP S/4HANA function module	BAPI_OUTB_DELIVERY_SPLIT_DEC
Sends IDoc	SHP_OBDLV_SPLIT_DECENTRAL01

Table 2.40 Outbound Message Processing for Outbound Warehouse Request: Outbound Delivery Split (Cont.)

Description	Response to a Change Request
Outbound message processing	/SCWM/CL_MAPOUT_OD_REJECT_CRM
Function	Answers to the change request initiated through message /SCWM/OBDLV_CHNG_QUAN_MUL
Called at...	Answering change request posted from SAP ERP or SAP S/4HANA Transaction VA02
Calls SAP ERP or SAP S/4HANA function module	BAPI_OUTB_DELIVERY_REJECT
Available from	SAP ERP 6.04 (business function LOG_LE_INTEGRATION)

Table 2.41 Outbound Message Processing for Outbound Warehouse Request: Response to Change Request

Description	Outbound Delivery Confirmation
Outbound message processing	/SCWM/CL_MAPOUT_OD_CONF_DEC /SCWM/IDOC_OUTPUT_OBDLV_CONFDC
Function	Confirms goods movements to outbound deliveries, posting changes, and return deliveries to SAP ERP or SAP S/4HANA

Table 2.42 Outbound Message Processing for Outbound Warehouse Request: Confirmation

Description	Outbound Delivery Confirmation
Called at...	■ Creation of a final delivery (outbound delivery in an invoice before goods issue scenario ■ Goods issue posting ■ Confirmation of a posting change
Calls SAP ERP or SAP S/4HANA function module	BAPI_OUTB_DELIVERY_CONFIRM_DEC
Sends IDoc	SHP_OBDLV_CONFIRM_DECENTRAL*

Table 2.42 Outbound Message Processing for Outbound Warehouse Request: Confirmation (Cont.)

Description	SAP ERP or SAP S/4HANA Availability Check
Outbound message processing	/SCWM/CL_AVAIL_CHECK_ERP
Function	Checks availability of stock in SAP ERP or SAP S/4HANA
Called at...	Checking availability at creation of EWM-triggered outbound deliveries
Calls SAP ERP or SAP S/4HANA function module	BAPI_MATERIAL_AVAILABILITY
Available from	SAP ERP 6.03 (business function LOG_LE_INTEGRATION)

Table 2.43 Outbound Message Processing for Outbound Warehouse Request: Availability Check-In SAP ERP or SAP S/4HANA

Description	Invoice Request from EWM
Outbound message processing	/SCWM/SR_INVOICE_CREATE
Function	Requests creation of invoice in SAP ERP or SAP S/4HANA
Called at...	Request of invoice creation from EWM outbound delivery via Transaction /SCWM/FDO or from transportation unit via Transaction /SCWM/TU
Calls SAP ERP or SAP S/4HANA function module	/SPE/CREATE_NEW_BILLING_CALL

Table 2.44 Outbound Message Processing for Outbound Warehouse Request: Invoice Request

Description	Invoice Request from EWM
Available from	SAP ERP 6.00

Table 2.44 Outbound Message Processing for Outbound Warehouse Request: Invoice Request (Cont.)

Goods Movement Interface

The goods movement interface consists of a single message with the name /SPE/GOODS-MVT_CREATE, which reports to SAP ERP or SAP S/4HANA stock adjustments triggered in EWM without delivery reference. You can find all the relevant dictionary objects in package /SCWM/ERP_INTEGRATION. In the SAP ERP or SAP S/4HANA system, corresponding material documents are created via the interface message. The stock management of EWM recognizes from the respective goods movement whether it must be reported to SAP ERP or SAP S/4HANA. This, for example, is the case with stock transfers containing EWM stock types, which differ in terms of availability group or location-independent stock type (SAP ERP or SAP S/4HANA stock type). Figure 2.24 shows the architecture of the goods movement interface in graphical representation. A BAdI for changing the material document data is available to allow for a custom enhancement for the goods movement interface.

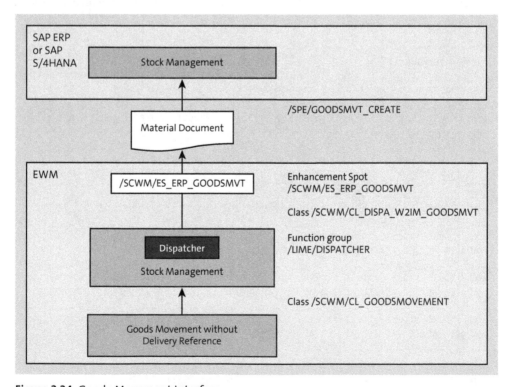

Figure 2.24 Goods Movement Interface

Table 2.45 contains some further technical and functional background information for the goods movement interface. You also can find descriptions of the function modules that read the stock data for the stock comparison between SAP ERP or SAP S/4HANA and EWM in Table 2.46.

Description	Replication of Goods Movement to SAP ERP or SAP S/4HANA
Outbound message processing	/SCWM/CL_DISPA_W2IM_GOODSMVT /SCWM/IDOC_OUTPUT_GOODSMVT_CR
Function	Replicates goods movements without delivery reference to SAP ERP or SAP S/4HANA
Called at...	▪ Posting of stock differences via Transactions /SCWM/DIFF_ANALYZER, /SCWM/WM_ADJUST, and /SCWM/ERP_STOCKCHECK ▪ Unplanned goods issue via Transaction /SCWM/ADGI ▪ Posting changes (e.g., **Received on Dock** to **Available for Sales** stock types) via Transaction /SCWM/POST
Calls SAP ERP or SAP S/4HANA function module	/SPE/GOODSMVT_CREATE
Sends IDoc	MBGMCR*
Available from	SAP ERP 4.6C (IDoc) SAP ERP 6.00 (function module)

Table 2.45 Outbound Message Processing for EWM-Triggered Goods Movements: Replication to SAP ERP or SAP S/4HANA

Description	SAP ERP or SAP S/4HANA Stock for Stock Comparison
Function	Reads SAP ERP or SAP S/4HANA stock
Called at...	Stock comparison via Transaction /SCWM/ERP_STOCKCHECK
Calls SAP ERP or SAP S/4HANA function module	/SPE/MATERIAL_STOCK_READ; alternatively, the older version, L_MM_MATERIALS_READ_QUANTITY
Available from	SAP ERP 6.00

Table 2.46 Selection of SAP ERP or SAP S/4HANA Stock for EWM Stock Comparison

Shipment Interface

You can use the shipment interface with SAP ERP or SAP S/4HANA as of EWM release 7.01. The /SCWM/ERP_TM_INTEGRATION package contains the interface's associated development objects. Incoming and outgoing transports that you plan in SAP ERP or SAP S/4HANA can be replicated to EWM as transportation units or vehicles through the SHPMNT05 IDoc. In this integration scenario, SAP ERP or SAP S/4HANA will therefore play the role of transportation planning system. In the event that you are planning transportation in EWM itself or in a third-party external transportation planning system that you have integrated with EWM, you can also replicate the EWM transportation units or vehicles to SAP ERP or SAP S/4HANA at the time of shipment confirmation. This way, processing of shipping, document printing, or freight cost accounting can still be done in the SAP ERP or SAP S/4HANA system as a follow-up activity of shipment confirmation. Figure 2.25 shows the integration of the shipment execution in EWM for replication and confirmation of or changes to shipments in SAP ERP or SAP S/4HANA.

[»]

Availability of LE-TRA in SAP S/4HANA

Per the compatibility scope matrix described in SAP Note 2269324, LE-TRA is not the strategic solution for freight management. It will be available for usage until end of 2030, however, so we still mention the interface here.

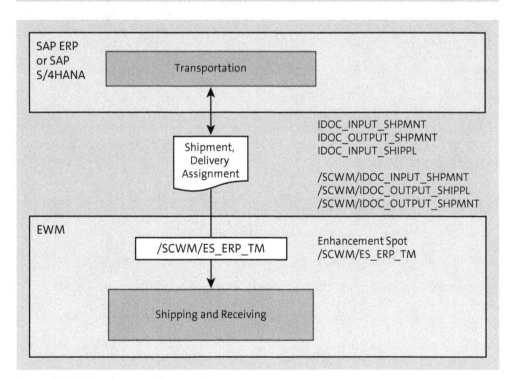

Figure 2.25 Shipment Interface

Several BAdIs are available for enhancing the shipment interface and changing the shipment data. For replication of a shipment from SAP ERP or SAP S/4HANA to EWM, there is an IDoc available, as described in Table 2.47.

Description	Replication of a Shipment
Inbound message processing	/SCWM/IDOC_INPUT_SHPMNT
Receives IDoc	SHPMNT05
Function	Replicates an SAP ERP or SAP S/4HANA shipment as an EWM transportation unit or vehicle
Called at...	Activation of a planned shipment in SAP ERP or SAP S/4HANA
Available from	SAP EWM 7.01

Table 2.47 Inbound Message Processing for Replication of SAP ERP or SAP S/4HANA Shipments to EWM

Two IDocs are available for communication of shipments from EWM to SAP ERP or SAP S/4HANA. One will replicate and confirm the EWM transportation unit or vehicle to SAP ERP or SAP S/4HANA as a shipment, while the other is used to cancel the assignment of deliveries to a shipment. More detailed descriptions can be found in Table 2.48 and Table 2.49.

Description	Replication/Confirmation of a Shipment
Outbound message processing	/SCWM/IDOC_OUTPUT_SHPMNT
Sends IDoc	SHPMNT05
Function	Replicates and confirms a EWM transportation unit or vehicle as shipment to SAP ERP or SAP S/4HANA
Called at...	Check out of a transportation unit or vehicle
Available from	SAP EWM 7.01

Table 2.48 Outbound Message Processing for Replication of Transportation Units or Vehicles to EWM

Description	Deletion of Delivery Assignment
Outbound message processing	/SCWM/IDOC_OUTPUT_SHIPPL
Receives IDoc	TPSSHT01
Function	Communication of delivery assignments to an EWM transportation unit

Table 2.49 Outbound Message Processing for Deletion of Delivery Assignments to Shipments

Description	Deletion of Delivery Assignment
Called at...	Changing of delivery assignments in EWM or deletion of an EWM transportation unit
Available from	SAP EWM 7.01

Table 2.49 Outbound Message Processing for Deletion of Delivery Assignments to Shipments (Cont.)

Quality Management Interface

To replicate and update inspection documents as part of quality control in the warehouse, the SAP ERP or SAP S/4HANA system and decentralized EWM do not communicate with each other directly, but instead do so through Quality Inspection Engine. Quality Inspection Engine is closely connected to EWM, being a consumer application. The data dictionary package QIE_COMMUNICATION includes the relevant development objects for the integration of consumer applications with Quality Inspection Engine.

Quality Inspection Engine takes on the task of preparing and saving the inspection documents, while EWM initiates the creation of inspection documents and follow-up actions based on inspection results. The quality inspection can now be performed either in EWM or in SAP ERP or SAP S/4HANA, where inspection lots can be created alongside the creation of Quality Inspection Engine inspection documents. SAP ERP or SAP S/4HANA provides a full-fledged quality management system for the processing of inspection lots, making available extensive functionality and offering the opportunity to manage all relevant quality management actions of your business on a single system. Figure 2.26 shows the architecture of quality management. Quality Inspection Engine can also communicate with an SAP ERP or SAP S/4HANA system or other quality systems through SAP PI based on IDocs. However, using queued remote function calls (qRFCs) might be more suitable, as this integration technology is also used for the majority of other interfaces between EWM and SAP ERP or SAP S/4HANA.

[+]
Activation of qRFC Technology for the Quality Management Interface

SAP Note 1278425 provides information on activities necessary for the use of quality management and includes a sample implementation for the QPLEXT_COMM_TEC BAdI that determines the integration technology to be used for the SAP ERP or SAP S/4HANA integration.

A BAdI for changing the Quality Inspection Engine communication is available and can serve as an enhancement option for quality management communication. This BAdI offers the necessary flexibility for running the interface via custom means.

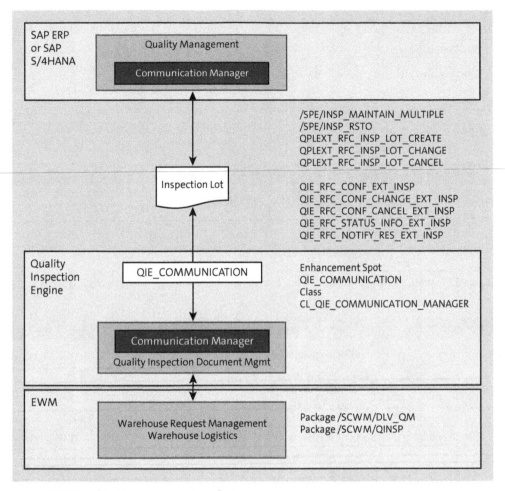

Figure 2.26 Quality Management Interface

The following tables describe messages used by the qRFC technology. The tables are divided into two groups:

- Function modules for the inbound message processing of the inspection lot (see Table 2.50 through Table 2.54)
- Function modules for the outbound message processing of the inspection lot (see Table 2.55 through Table 2.58)

Description	Inspection Lot Creation
Function	Confirms inspection lot creation
Function module	QIE_RFC_CONF_EXT_INSP
Called at...	Creation of inspection lot

Table 2.50 Inbound Message Processing of the Inspection Lot: Confirmation of Creation

Description	Inspection Lot Change
Function	Confirms inspection lot change
Function module	QIE_RFC_CONF_CHANGE_EXT_INSP
Called at...	Change of inspection lot

Table 2.51 Inbound Message Processing of the Inspection Lot: Confirmation of Change

Description	Inspection Lot Cancellation
Function	Confirms inspection lot cancellation
Function module	QIE_RFC_CONF_CANCEL_EXT_INSP
Called at...	Cancellation of inspection lot

Table 2.52 Inbound Message Processing of the Inspection Lot: Confirmation of Cancellation

Description	Inspection Lot Status Update
Function	Confirms inspection lot status update
Function module	QIE_RFC_STATUS_INFO_EXT_INSP
Called at...	Status update of inspection lot

Table 2.53 Inbound Message Processing of the Inspection Lot: Confirmation of Status Update

Description	Inspection Lot Result
Function	Confirms inspection lot result
Function module	QIE_RFC_NOTIFY_RES_EXT_INSP
Called at...	Confirmation of inspection lot result

Table 2.54 Inbound Message Processing of the Inspection Lot: Confirmation of Inspection Result

Description	Inspection Lot Creation in SAP ERP or SAP S/4HANA
Function	Requests inspection lot creation in SAP ERP or SAP S/4HANA
Called at...	Inspection document creation in EWM

Table 2.55 Outbound Message Processing of the Inspection Lot: Request for Inspection Lot Creation

Description	Inspection Lot Creation in SAP ERP or SAP S/4HANA
Calls function module	QPLEXT_RFC_INSP_LOT_CREATE

Table 2.55 Outbound Message Processing of the Inspection Lot: Request for Inspection Lot Creation (Cont.)

Description	Inspection Lot Change in SAP ERP or SAP S/4HANA
Function	Requests inspection lot change in SAP ERP or SAP S/4HANA
Called at...	Inspection document change in EWM
Calls function module	QPLEXT_RFC_INSP_LOT_CHANGE

Table 2.56 Outbound Message Processing of the Inspection Lot: Request for Inspection Lot Change

Description	Inspection Lot Cancellation in SAP ERP or SAP S/4HANA
Function	Requests inspection lot cancellation in SAP ERP or SAP S/4HANA
Called at...	Inspection document cancellation in EWM
Calls function module	QPLEXT_RFC_INSP_LOT_CANCEL

Table 2.57 Outbound Message Processing of the Inspection Lot: Request for Inspection Lot Cancellation

Description	Inspection Lot Result of a Return
Function	Communicates inspection lot results for return items to SAP ERP or SAP S/4HANA for further distribution to SAP CRM
Called at...	Confirming inspection result of return items
Calls function module	/SPE/INSP_MAINTAIN_MULTIPLE

Table 2.58 Outbound Message Processing of the Inspection Lot: Confirmation of Inspection Results for Return Items

[»]

Checks for Issues with Quality Management Interfaces Not Triggered from SAP ERP or SAP S/4HANA

If you encounter issues with the confirmations of SAP ERP or SAP S/4HANA quality management in EWM, we recommend performing the activities listed in SAP Note 2787311 for issue resolution.

Master Data Interfaces

For the distribution of master data between SAP ERP or SAP S/4HANA and EWM, ALE and data replication framework technologies are used, the earlier of which has been in place for long time while the latter is rather new. The EWM integration, however, only makes use of a fraction of the data objects that would normally be communicated. The following master data objects are communicated from SAP ERP or SAP S/4HANA to EWM via these technologies:

- Business partner (supplier/carrier and customer), using ALE or data replication framework
- Material, using ALE
- Quality inspection rules via quality data for material, using ALE
- Quality inspection rules via quality info record, using RFC (can be triggered via business transaction event)
- Batch (including classification), using ALE
- Packing instruction to packaging specification, using RFC (core interface)

Figure 2.27 gives an overview of the individual interfaces for master data objects that are described later in more detail.

[»]

Enhanced Settings for ALE Data Transfer

SAP Note 2881061 contains information on the configuration options for enhanced settings for ALE data transfer, such as additional filtering options for IDoc communication. You may check the attached *Decentralized EWM Enhanced Settings for ALE Data Transfer* document for more example use cases and details, including configuration.

For the replication of business partners from SAP ERP or SAP S/4HANA to EWM, ALE is used. Material master records, batches, and batch classification are also replicated via ALE. For a description of the called function modules in EWM, see Table 2.59 through Table 2.69.

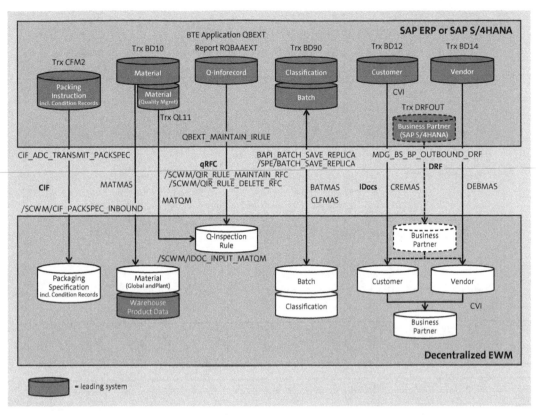

Figure 2.27 Overview of SAP ERP or SAP S/4HANA Integration for Master Data Objects in Decentralized EWM

Description	Replication of SAP ERP or SAP S/4HANA Customers
Function	Creates customers in EWM alongside business partners via CVI
IDoc message type	DEBMAS
Called at...	Transaction BD12 (Send Customers)

Table 2.59 Replication of Customers to EWM

Description	Replication of SAP ERP or SAP S/4HANA Vendors
Function	Creates vendors in EWM alongside business partners via CVI
IDoc message type	CREMAS
Called at...	Transaction BD14 (Send Vendor)

Table 2.60 Replication of Vendors to EWM

[+] **Conflicting Number Ranges for Business Partners**

If number ranges for your SAP ERP vendors and customers overlap, you might run into numbering conflicts with the business partners created in EWM. We recommend checking SAP Note 3194346 for potential solutions to this problem.

Description	Replication of SAP S/4HANA Business Partners via Data Replication Framework
Function	Creates business partners in EWM. Will also create underlying customers or vendors via CVI. Can be set up in SAP S/4HANA only and will not require CREMAS and DEBMAS IDocs to be activated.
Function module	MDG_BS_BP_OUTBOUND_DRF
Called at...	Transaction DRFOUT (Execute Data Replication)

Table 2.61 Replication of Business Partners to EWM via Data Replication Framework

Description	Replication of SAP ERP or SAP S/4HANA Materials/Articles
Function	Creates materials (products) in EWM
IDoc message type	MATMAS
Called at...	Transaction BD10 (Send Material)

Table 2.62 Replication of Materials to EWM

Description	Replication of SAP ERP or SAP S/4HANA Material Quality Data
Function	Creates quality inspection rules in EWM when using IDoc inbound function module /SCWM/IDOC_INPUT_MATQM (instead of IDOC_INPUT_MATQM, which would replicate the quality master data of the material)
IDoc message type	MATQM
Called at...	Transaction QL11 (Send Inspection Setup)

Table 2.63 Replication of Materials to EWM

Description	Replication of SAP ERP or SAP S/4HANA Batches
Function	Creates batches

Table 2.64 Replication of Batches to EWM

Description	Replication of SAP ERP or SAP S/4HANA Batches
IDoc message type	BATMAS
Called at...	Transaction BD90 (Batch Master Record Initial Transfer)

Table 2.64 Replication of Batches to EWM (Cont.)

Description	Replication of SAP ERP or SAP S/4HANA Classification Data
Function	Creates (Batch) Classification data in EWM
IDoc message type	CLFMAS
Called at...	Transaction BD90 (Batch Master Record Initial Transfer)

Table 2.65 Replication of Classification Data to EWM

Description	Creation/Changes of Batches in EWM
Function	Creates/Changes Batches in SAP ERP or SAP S/4HANA
Called at...	Creation of a batch in EWM with reference to inbound delivery and production request or via Transaction MSC1N (Create Batch) and MSC2N (Change Batch)
Calls function module	BAPI_BATCH_SAVE_REPLICA or /SPE/BATCH_SAVE_REPLICA depending on batch update mode from SAP ERP or SAP S/4HANA version control.

Table 2.66 Creation of Batches in SAP ERP or SAP S/4HANA from EWM

Description	Replication of Valuation Prices to EWM
Function	Reading and updating of valuation prices from SAP ERP or SAP S/4HANA to EWM
Called at...	Downloading of valuation prices via EWM Transaction /SCWM/VALUATION_SET
Calls function module	/SPE/MBEW_GEN_ARRAY_READ
Available from	SAP ERP 6.00

Table 2.67 Replication of Valuation Prices

Description	Replication of Account Assignment Data to EWM
Function	Reading and updating of account assignment data from SAP ERP or SAP S/4HANA to EWM
Called at...	Downloading of account assignment data via EWM Transaction /SCWM/ ACC_IMP_ERP
Calls function module	/SPE/AAC_DETERMINATION
Available from	SAP ERP 6.03

Table 2.68 Replication of Account Assignment Data

Description	Replication of Production Supply Areas to EWM
Function	Reading and updating of production supply areas from SAP ERP or SAP S/4HANA to EWM
Called at...	Downloading of production supply areas via EWM Transaction /SCWM/ PSA_REPLICATE
Calls function module	L_WM_GET_DATA
Available from	SAP ERP 6.00

Table 2.69 Replication of Production Supply Areas

Additional master data objects that you will need in order to operate your warehouse with EWM (e.g., warehouse product data, storage bins, or packaging specifications) can be uploaded to EWM via upload reports from file locations. Migration tools from SAP ERP or SAP S/4HANA warehouse management, which provide options for file downloads from warehouse management data to import into SAP EWM, are available. Further options to load SAP EWM master data to SAP S/4HANA–based EWM exist when migrating from SAP EWM. Such features are provided with the migration cockpit. You can find further information on migrating SAP EWM to EWM based on SAP S/4HANA in Appendix B.

Mapping of SAP ERP or SAP S/4HANA and EWM Stock Models

Another core aspect of the integration between SAP ERP or SAP S/4HANA and EWM is the difference in stock data models used by the two systems. Many interfaces need to apply a mapping of stock data in their input and output message processing. Figure 2.28 shows the stock key fields for the mapping between SAP ERP or SAP S/4HANA and EWM.

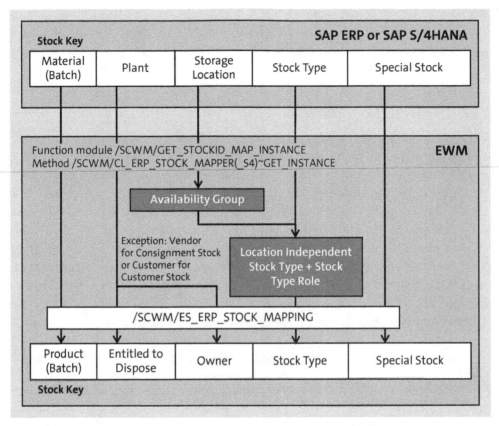

Figure 2.28 Mapping of Stock Models between SAP ERP or SAP S/4HANA and EWM

The /SCWM/CL_MAP class for SAP ERP or SAP S/4HANA integration represents a good example of the mapping of stock data. In the constructor of this central class, the /SCWM/ GET_STOCKID_MAP_INSTANCE function module is called to generate instances for the mapping of stock data between SAP ERP or SAP S/4HANA and EWM. This function module forms part of the /SCWM/ERP_STOCKID_MAPPING function group, which controls the stock data mapping on local classes. The function module calls a BAdI for custom enhancements of the stock data mapping shortly after the execution of the standard mapping procedure. Should you consider implementing this BAdI, we recommend doing so with extreme caution, as incorrect implementation could lead to severe damage of your stock data in EWM. EWM with SAP S/4HANA also allows for the service adapter framework to be used for instantiation of stock key mappings between SAP ERP or SAP S/4HANA and EWM stock models. Classes /SCWM/CL_ERP_STOCK_MAPPER and /SCWM/CL_ERP_STOCK_MAPPER_S4 implement the underlying /SCWM/IF_STOCKID_MAPPING interface and contain all required business logic.

The EWM stock model can, for example, be enhanced by creating additional stock types. But you must always consider the situation of the storage locations in the SAP ERP or SAP S/4HANA system. Additional stock types will in most cases need additional storage locations in the SAP ERP or SAP S/4HANA system because the default mapping of SAP ERP or SAP S/4HANA to EWM will determine the SAP ERP or SAP S/4HANA stock type and the storage location based on a unique EWM stock type. You could, however, implement the aforementioned BAdI to define a custom mapping rule.

2.5.2   Third-Party ERP Systems (Non-SAP)

Integration of EWM with a third-party ERP system is technically possible. It will, however, require a feasibility analysis for your unique situation and should be structured as a subproject of its own within the EWM implementation project. You should not underestimate the required effort. In this section, we will discuss some aspects that you should consider as part of the integration of a third-party ERP system with EWM. First, you will need to decide on an integration approach. There are two main approaches that appear feasible, the first of which represents the usual way, with the connection of the third-party ERP system with EWM via a middleware solution that takes care of mapping and routing the various messages. Figure 2.29 shows a potential system landscape for this approach. The second approach is a direct connection of the third-party ERP system with EWM (without middleware); however, this is not a sensible option in our view.

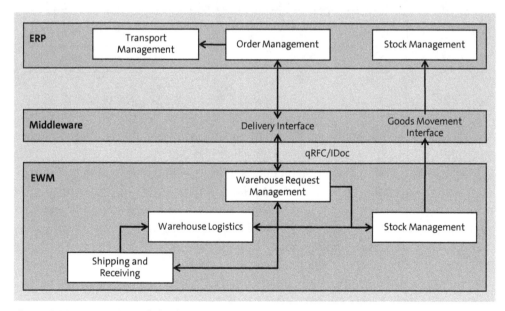

Figure 2.29 Integration of Third-Party ERP System via Middleware

[»]

Integration with a Third-Party ERP System via Middleware

When integrating EWM with a third-party ERP system via a middleware solution, you must be aware that the middleware solution will probably require access to the metadata of all the interfaces used. Because EWM calls function modules from ERP in the outbound message processing, you must find a way to make the metadata of the respective ERP function modules available. One possible approach to this would be to retrieve the metadata from another ERP system, if available in your system landscape. Otherwise, you could define the ERP function modules at least in their structure in EWM or another repository system to make the necessary metadata available.

In addition, there is the possibility of putting an ERP system between the middleware and EWM. This approach is especially useful if you are already planning to introduce ERP sometime in the future. One possible advantage of this solution is that you can use the full functionality of the delivery interface and may have less customization and mapping effort with the interfaces between order management and inventory management in your ERP system. The additional integration of an SAP ERP or SAP S/4HANA system appears less disadvantageous if you plan to use it more extensively in the future anyway. In this setup, you would need to plan for additional configuration, testing, and migration effort.

See Figure 2.30 for a schematic diagram of this integration approach. You should accurately identify and weigh the advantages and disadvantages against your own situation, especially in the light of available integration possibilities and interfaces of the ERP system.

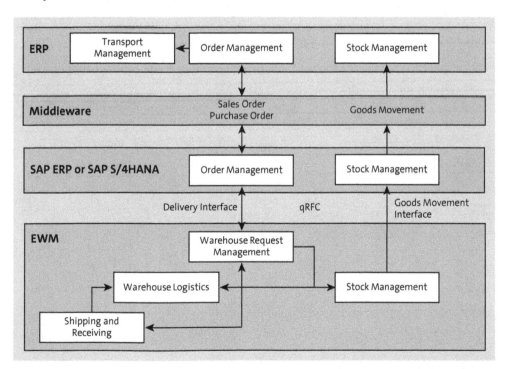

Figure 2.30 Integration of Third-Party ERP System via Middleware and SAP ERP or SAP S/4HANA

The next decision you have to make will concern the integration technology you will use: qRFC or IDoc. Integration with IDocs is intended to be a technically simpler solution, but it will also bring limited functionality of the delivery interface. The functional restrictions on IDocs are shown in Table 2.70, Table 2.71, and Table 2.72. If you will require functionality that is not possible to implement with IDocs, you may prefer the usage of the qRFC technology.

[»]

How-To Guide for IDoc-Based Non-SAP ERP Integration

SAP Note 3140478 provides information about connecting decentralized EWM to non-SAP ERP systems via IDoc-based interfaces as of SAP S/4HANA 2021 FPS 1. A how-to guide is available that shows how a basic scenario using inbound and/or outbound deliveries can be set up using ALE IDocs. You can find the guide named *How to Integrate a Non-SAP ERP System with a Decentralized EWM on SAP S/4HANA via ALE IDoc* in the SAP Community wiki at *https://wiki.scn.sap.com/wiki/display/SCM/How-To+Guides+for+SAP+EWM*.

The SAP ERP or SAP S/4HANA version control settings, mentioned at the beginning of this section, will enable you to configure the integration independently of the chosen integration technology (IDoc/qRFC) so that it will meet your functional requirements. The settings certainly do not support all of your integration requirements out of the box, though. You might, for example, want to prevent the possibility of cancelling goods receipt postings because your legacy ERP system will not support this. You can make such settings via the SAP ERP or SAP S/4HANA version control.

[»]

Preventing the Use of Outbound Delivery Splits

SAP Note 1600871 provides information about how to prevent the creation of split deliveries in EWM. Because your non-SAP ERP system will likely not support this SAP ERP/SAP S/4HANA feature, you should consider the information contained in this SAP Note.

Functionality of Goods Receipt Processes	Supported by IDoc?
Full confirmation of goods receipt	Yes
Partial goods receipt confirmation (multiple)	No
Goods receipt with quantity changes	Yes, at goods receipt
Batch creation/change in inbound delivery	No
Rejection of inbound delivery	Yes, at goods receipt
Inbound delivery split	No

Table 2.70 Supported Interface Functionality for Goods Receipts with IDocs

Functionality of Goods Receipt Processes	Supported by IDoc?
Reversal of inbound delivery	No
Creation of inbound delivery from EWM	No
In Yard status	Yes, only EWM
Expected goods receipt	No

Table 2.70 Supported Interface Functionality for Goods Receipts with IDocs (Cont.)

Functionality of Goods Issue Processes	Supported by IDoc?
Full confirmation of goods issue	Yes
Outbound delivery split	Yes
Goods issue for scrapping	Yes
Deletion of batch split item	Yes
Zero confirmation of outbound delivery	Yes
Batch splits	Yes, at goods issue
Batch changes	Yes, at goods issue
Reversal of goods issue	No
Pick denial	No
Reversal of delivery split	No
Invoice before goods issue	No
Deletion of outbound delivery	No
Creation of outbound delivery in EWM	No
Additional item from EWM (e.g., packaging)	No

Table 2.71 Supported Interface Functionality for Goods Issues with IDocs

Functionality of Internal Processes	Supported by IDoc?
Posting change from any ERP system	Yes
Posting change from EWM	Yes
Stock comparison EWM to any ERP system	Yes

Table 2.72 Supported Interface Functionality for Internal Processes with IDocs

Functionality of Internal Processes	Supported by IDoc?
Posting of differences to any ERP system	Yes
Valuation price upload from any ERP system (physical inventory tolerance)	No

Table 2.72 Supported Interface Functionality for Internal Processes with IDocs (Cont.)

In addition to these rather technical issues, you should not forget some key points of the functional system integration. Analyze the application architectures of your ERP system and of EWM in order to understand whether the systems' logistical execution processing logics fit each other at all. The decisive factor here is the question of whether the necessary interfaces in the ERP system are already present, or at least conceptually feasible. We described the availability and functionality of interfaces provided by EWM in Section 2.5.1.

Furthermore, it is important to decide which of the two systems has to adapt to the prevailing conditions and the interface situation of the other. This question is not easily answered. It is good to argue that the EWM standard should not be changed, specifically to allow for a future connection to SAP ERP or SAP S/4HANA. On the other hand, changes to the existing ERP system might be difficult because it may be technically obsolete, poorly supported, or inadequately documented.

After clarification of the integration architecture, you should analyze the nature of the required interfaces and address the mapping of fields for each message. Stopping message processing by queue deregistration, as described earlier, will be essential to an understanding of which data is expected to be received and sent out by EWM. For this purpose, it is useful to have an SAP S/4HANA installation available that is integrated with EWM in order to understand how ERP communicates with EWM in various process scenarios with regard to messages and data.

Integration with a Third-Party ERP System via the Delivery Interface

SAP Note 1465477 provides five possible solutions for creating custom outbound messages or interfaces based on EWM deliveries. Should you plan for custom interfaces within your EWM implementation project, consider the information contained in the SAP Note for the technical solution design.

The final aspect that you need to consider when integrating with the third-party ERP system is the mapping of the stock models. As already described in the previous section, EWM provides its own stock mapping in the inbound and outbound message processing in its integration with ERP. Particular importance is attached to the EWM stock type that is ultimately mapped to the ERP storage location and stock type via the availability group and the location-independent stock type and the stock type role. When integrating with a third-party ERP system, you will have to map the stock model of the third-party ERP system, not only to the EWM stock model, but also to the ERP stock model.

The interfaces only know the fields of the ERP stock model, which can prove to be a bottleneck in your integration project. Therefore, you either have to enhance the relevant interfaces with custom fields for stock data or map the stock model of the third-party ERP system to a "virtual" ERP stock model before it is again mapped to the EWM stock model in the EWM system itself. In the latter case, you would communicate stock data to EWM as if EWM was connected to ERP, which makes this aspect of the integration, at least from the EWM side, appear easy to handle. This approach is especially useful if you are planning to introduce ERP in the near future and might have already defined the setup of the ERP stock.

2.5.3 SAP S/4HANA Integration in Embedded EWM

Apart from the earlier described differences between decentralized and embedded EWM in respect to quality inspection and master data, there are some partly configurable differences to further reduce process complexity and data redundancy in embedded EWM. These shall be outlined in the following paragraphs. Figure 2.31 gives an overview of the further and optional interfaces between the ERP part of SAP S/4HANA and EWM components. Dotted arrows mark optional interfaces that will likely not be used in integration of embedded EWM in customer implementations as per activation of their concurrent options for leaner and more direct integration, depicted as solid arrows.

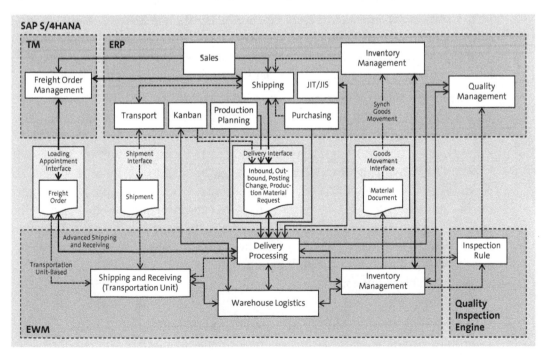

Figure 2.31 Schematic SAP S/4HANA Transactional Data Integration with Embedded EWM

However, you could still opt for the less lean integration option, in order to be able to use further EWM functionality that is available with this option only. Good examples might be choosing not to eliminate delivery processing from Kanban so as to be able to use wave management alongside the deliveries for Kanban supply or not eliminating the transportation unit for freight order management integration so as to still be able to use EWM-based yard management for status tracking and movements of transportation units and vehicles. On the other hand, options for eliminating inspection rules for inspection lot creation or activating synchronous goods movements (at least from EWM to SAP S/4HANA) seem more likely to occur as positive aspects of data redundancy reduction and tighter integration prevail.

Elimination of Expected Goods Receipts

To simplify processes and eliminate the need for data redundancy replicating and updating transactional data objects between SAP S/4HANA and EWM, the use of persistent expected goods receipt documents was eliminated in embedded EWM. Instead, wherever SAP S/4HANA document data is required in EWM for the creation of inbound deliveries, direct access to purchase orders and manufacturing orders from EWM delivery processing has been made available. Once again, the service adapter framework is used to differentiate between embedded and decentralized EWM contexts.

For expected goods receipt, the service adapter framework will return an instance of class /SCWM/CL_EGR_MANAGER_S4 in context of embedded EWM for service interface /SCWM/IF_EGR_MANAGER. Furthermore, class /SCWM/CL_DLV_EGR2PDI_S4 reuses class /SCWM/CL_DLV_EGR2PDI for inbound delivery creation using the purchase or manufacturing order data calling class, /SCWM/CL_EGR_READER_S4. It is in this class that reading and mapping of given transactional data from SAP S/4HANA to EWM objects takes places emulating transient expected goods receipt data.

In this process, enhancement spot /SCWM/ES_EGR_S4 (Enhancements to Expected Goods Receipt in SAP S/4HANA) has been made available to allow for custom determinations and data mapping toward the emulated expected goods receipt data. It contains BAdIs /SCWM/EX_MAP_EGR_DOCTYPE_S4 (Mapping Document and Item Type for EGR) and /SCWM/EX_MAP_EGR_S4 (Mapping of EGR Data), which can be used to influence the expected goods receipt document and item type determination and the mapping of transactional data from SAP S/4HANA to transient EWM expected goods receipt objects. This expected goods receipt data is then finally used for copying into inbound deliveries, mainly reusing existing copying functionality. BAdIs of enhancement spot /SCWM/ES_DLV_EGR2PDI (Enhancement Create Inbound Delivery from Expected Goods Receipt) remain available in this context.

Elimination of Notification Documents in Delivery Processing

The use of any notification documents in the delivery interface was eliminated for embedded EWM, also referred to as *skip (delivery) request* functionality. The ability to create notification documents in a decentralized environment in case of, for example, missing master data is not required in an embedded environment anymore. Therefore, only processing documents remain for the delivery objects in embedded EWM. We will not go into much technical detail about how the skip is achieved; basically, the logic of the transfer or transition service between the notification and the processing document (see Section 2.1.1) was moved to the message processing layer of the respective document category during mapping into EWM. BAdIs for custom determination of EWM delivery aspects remain fully available.

Optional Elimination of Quality Inspection Engine Inspection Rules

Embedded EWM optionally supports the usage of quality management without using Quality Inspection Engine–based inspection rules. For checking relevancy of quality inspection, the system can be configured to access the quality management material master directly, thereby eliminating redundancy in objects controlling the quality management planning. Transparent table /SCWM/QIOTWM_NIR holds EWM process–relevant data when no inspection rule is used. The location-dependent stock type and the external process step hence can be derived from the warehouse number, inspection object type, inspection process, and quality inspection group.

Again, the service adapter framework has been leveraged to detect the right inspection settings for service /SCWM/IF_AF_QINSP_INT per the given context. For embedded EWM, class /SCWM/CL_QLOT_S4 will be instantiated, retrieving Customizing settings via class /SCWM/CL_QCUST_SEL_INT_S4. The quality management material master data, as stored in table QMAT, will then be enriched by the EWM-relevant data to create the inspection lot (table QALS).

Optional Synchronous Integration for Kanban and Stock Postings

For embedded EWM, there was an initiative early on to bring EWM-triggered goods movements closer to the SAP S/4HANA-based inventory management component, thereby eliminating potentially stuck queues in the until then asynchronous goods movement interface by changing the posting method to synchronous. In synchronous mode, which can optionally be activated on the warehouse number level, any issues or errors arising from either EWM or the materials management's stock management will be shown to the user when trying to execute the posting from EWM transactions, like /SCWM/POST, /SCWM/DIFF_ANLALYZER, /SCWM/ADGI, and /SCWM/ISU.

At the same time, further attempts have been made to simplify SAP S/4HANA materials management–triggered stock postings and production planning-triggered Kanban events to EWM, optionally eliminating the delivery interface, and have EWM creating (goods movement) warehouse tasks alongside the initiation of materials management–based material documents or production planning-based Kanban status updates. In addition, the synchronous setup for stock postings would also allow for combined EWM and materials management storage locations in one material document, triggered from the respective materials management transactions—specifically, MIGO. In the following sections, we will take a closer look at the rather newly available functionality of synchronous postings.

SAP S/4HANA to EWM

SAP S/4HANA inventory management uses the central MB_CREATE_GOODS_MOVEMENT function module for its stock postings. This function module can import a parameter on the goods movement header level (IMKPF-EWM_SYNC_POST_REQ) in order to synchronously post a goods movement from SAP S/4HANA to EWM. The function module will still check if the intended movement is really EWM-relevant, basically checking for an embedded EWM warehouse number (IMSEG-EWM_LGNUM) and an EWM-relevant movement type.

Also, the EWM storage bin must be provided (IMSEG-EWM_LGPLA). Should these prerequisites not be fulfilled, the function module might fall back into delivery creation, such as if the warehouse number was managed decentrally. Otherwise, the EWM class for synchronous goods movements, /SCWM/CL_EWM_GOODSMVT_SYNC, is called via its interface, /SCWM/IF_EWM_GOODSMVT_SYNC. Finally, either EWM function module /SCWM/GM_CREATE will be used for triggering an EWM goods movements or function module /SCWM/GM_CANCEL will be called in case of goods movement cancellations.

Enhancement spot /SCWM/ES_CORE_GM contains BAdIs /SCWM/EX_CORE_GM_GMDOC_PACK (Packaging Proposal upon Goods Receipt) and /SCWM/EX_CORE_GM_GMDOC_WT (Automatic Warehouse Task Creation upon Goods Receipt). These can be implemented with custom logic to determine if and how automated packing and warehouse task creation should be performed for goods receipt postings triggered in synchronous goods movements from SAP S/4HANA to EWM.

Transaction MIGO

Over the different SAP S/4HANA versions, more and more goods movement postings, initiated not just by Transaction MIGO but most manufacturing-related transactions for goods movements, have been enabled for synchronization between SAP S/4HANA and EWM. Transaction MIGO offers most extended features for EWM integration however, up to the point of dialog enhancements. Figure 2.32 shows an example of a goods issue to cost center processing with movement type 201. Once the movement type has been activated for synchronous goods movements in the respective warehouse number, Transaction MIGO offers the **Warehouse Management** tab for input of further EWM-related data, like the aforementioned storage bin. It also allows for direct access to the stock overview of the respective warehouse and pulls the stock situation once the material to be posted has been defined.

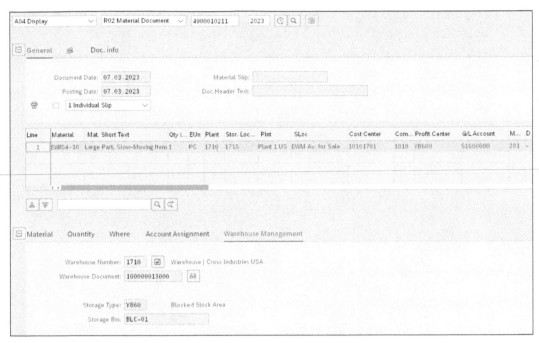

Figure 2.32 Transaction MIGO: Warehouse Management Tab for Synchronous Goods Movement Postings

The **Warehouse Management** tab for input of EWM-related data has been available through implementation /SCWM/CL_EI_MIGO_WHSE_TAB_S4 of the BAdI definition MB_MIGO_BADI_INT, internally used and owned by SAP. The BAdI implementation basically dispatches any further calls to class /SCWM/CL_MIGO_S4, which contains the main business logic. Several further classes exist, which are needed for the various processes and reference documents to support the Transaction MIGO–triggered processing of synchronous goods movements to EWM, named /SCWM/CL_MIGO_*_S4—for example, /SCWM/CL_MIGO_WHSE_S4, responsible for the mapping of SAP S/4HANA and EWM warehouse numbers and several additional checks. Other classes manage the handling of reference documents alongside packaging or bin proposals that are available within the different processes. We recommend walking through such classes for a more detailed overview of the technical implementation.

Kanban

Simplified Kanban is less about synchronization of goods movements, even though goods issue for Kanban supports synchronous stock postings. It focuses instead on the elimination of the delivery object in the SAP S/4HANA to EWM communication for replenishment of stocks, kept, for example, in Kanban containers, from external suppliers or warehouses to the production line. In this case, a replenishment warehouse task is created directly for production supply at container event **Empty** and may also be confirmed directly at container event **Full**, both triggered from the Kanban control board. It also supports warehouse task display, cancellation, and reversal.

The demand and supply relationship is maintained by so-called control cycles. Such control cycles have been enhanced to allow for additional EWM-related data maintenance—predominantly, the destination storage bin and the activation of simplified Kanban via the stock transfer replenishment strategy (see Figure 2.33).

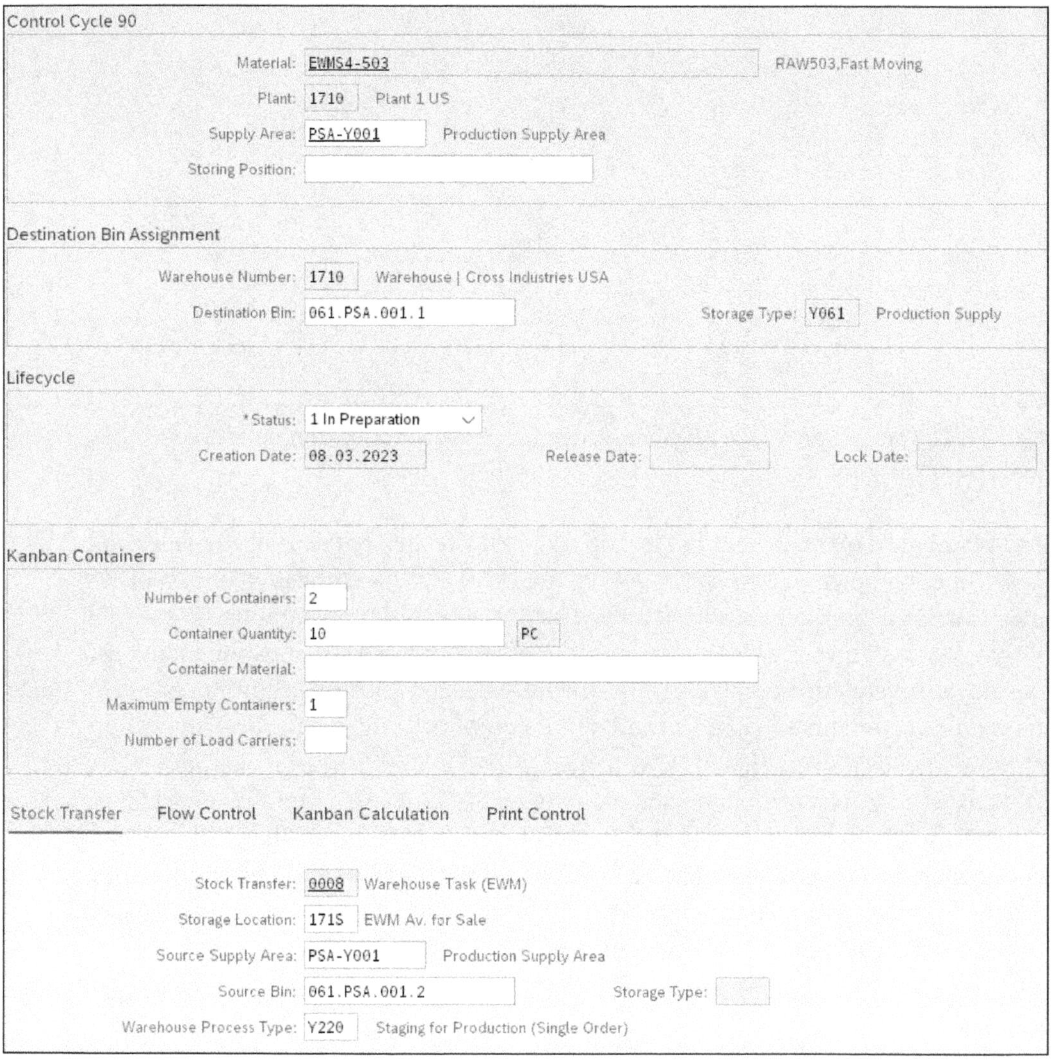

```
Control Cycle 90

                    Material: EWMS4-503                          RAW503,Fast Moving

                      Plant: 1710      Plant 1 US

                Supply Area: PSA-Y001       Production Supply Area

            Storing Position:

Destination Bin Assignment

           Warehouse Number: 1710       Warehouse | Cross Industries USA

             Destination Bin: 061.PSA.001.1              Storage Type: Y061   Production Supply

Lifecycle

                    * Status: 1 In Preparation      v

              Creation Date: 08.03.2023          Release Date:              Lock Date:

Kanban Containers

        Number of Containers: 2

          Container Quantity: 10                      PC

          Container Material:

    Maximum Empty Containers: 1

      Number of Load Carriers:

Stock Transfer    Flow Control    Kanban Calculation    Print Control

              Stock Transfer: 0008    Warehouse Task (EWM)

            Storage Location: 171S    EWM Av. for Sale

          Source Supply Area: PSA-Y001       Production Supply Area

                  Source Bin: 061.PSA.001.2              Storage Type:

      Warehouse Process Type: Y220    Staging for Production (Single Order)
```

Figure 2.33 Extended Control Cycle Settings for EWM-Related Data

The EWM-related Kanban events are mostly triggered from subroutines of function group MPKB (Container Maintenance for Kanban), belonging to package MD05. All integration between Kanban in production planning in SAP S/4HANA and EWM is done via direct method calls going through interface /SCWM/IF_KANBAN_WT_CONTROL, implementing class /SCWM/CL_KANBAN_WT_CONTROL. On the other hand, in the direction of EWM to Kanban in production planning in SAP S/4HANA, all calls go through interface /SCWM/IF_KANBAN_WT_POST_PRC_S4 and implement class /SCWM/CL_KANBAN_WT_POST_PRC_S4. Here the service adapter framework has been used for class determination and instantiation, following service /SCWM/IF_KANBAN_WT_POST_PRC.

EWM to SAP S/4HANA

The service adapter framework provides service and interface /SCWM/IF_ERP_GOODSMVT_SYNC to instantiate class /SCWM/CL_ERP_GOODSMVT_SYNC_S4 in the context of embedded EWM (S4_OP_INT). From here, class /SCWM/CL_ERP_GM_MAPOUT is called for a lean simulation of the SAP S/4HANA goods movement posting. The service class itself is called in the central function module of EWM-based goods movements, /SCWM/GM_CREATE. If the current stock posting is relevant for synchronous ERP posting, and there are no errors coming back from the SAP S/4HANA posting simulation, the EWM goods movement will be committed using function module /SCWM/GM_POST.

Thereafter, the SAP S/4HANA goods movement posting will be performed using function module /SCWM/ERP_GM_SYNC_UPD_S4 with a synchronous call of function module /SPE/GOODSMVT_CREATE, meaning in the same logical unit of work. BAdI /SCWM/EX_ERP_GOODSMVT_EXT is available for custom changes to the goods movement posting (e.g., for custom movement type determination logic) beforehand. However, if the stock has a delivery or production material request document reference, or is in any way not relevant for synchronous posting, the SAP S/4HANA goods movement posting will again be performed with an asynchronous call of function module /SPE/GOODSMVT_CREATE, triggered via a respective logistics inventory management engine collection in a separate logical unit of work, using function module /LIME/DOCUMENT_POST.

Optional Elimination of EWM Shipping and Receiving Transportation Unit

While the formerly available transportation unit–based EWM integration with SAP TM works with the EWM transportation unit, the advanced shipping and receiving integration of SAP TM and EWM has a different, simplified design. The transportation unit is basically skipped, and the EWM deliveries and handling units are directly integrated with the TM freight order on the single freight unit level. In addition, a new document type called the consignment order has been introduced with SAP S/4HANA 2020 and is supported by the advanced shipping and receiving integration only. This document type can group transportation requirements based on certain criteria, such as the same source and destination location or the same delivery date and time. On top of that, more statuses are introduced, which allow for a higher frequency of data synchronization between the SAP S/4HANA or EWM delivery and the SAP TM freight order. Last but not least, advanced shipping and receiving allows for a combination of EWM- and materials management–managed storage locations in one freight order.

The service adapter framework has again been used to differentiate between different transportation planning types stored on the EWM delivery header level. Service and interface /SCWM/IF_AF_SR_TRANSPORT instantiate class /SCWM/CL_AF_SR_TRANSPORT, which implements common methods for either shipping and receiving or advanced shipping and receiving environments.

The entire EWM and SAP TM integration with its different integration options is too large a topic to be handled here. We therefore recommend checking out additional information sources, like the SAP Help information for both EWM and SAP TM.

Integration of Just-in-Time Processing with EWM

Just-in-time (JIT) processing is a common and frequently used concept in repetitive and discrete manufacturing, such as in the automotive industry, dealing with supply-to-line processes for large quantities of products and allowing for accurate forecasting of replenishment. It is based on tight alignment between suppliers and production warehouses. Embedded EWM can create (and update) stock transfer deliveries from JIT calls, which represent replenishment requests generated from the JIT processing application. We recommend checking out the SAP Help on EWM for a good overview of JIT processing in regard to integration with embedded EWM.

Enhancement spot /SCWM/ES_JIT includes BAdIs for custom fields in JIT deliveries (/SCWM/EX_JIT_CUSTOM_FIELDS, Use of Custom Fields in Warehouse Requests for JIT Processing) and monitor selections (/SCWM/EX_JIT_CUSTOM_SELECT_MON, Custom Selection Fields in Warehouse Monitor Nodes for JIT), as well as delivery document and item type mappings (/SCWM/EX_JIT_MAP_DOCTYPE, Definition of Document & Item Type at Warehouse Request Creation for JIT Call).

Extensibility Guide for JIT and EWM Integration

We strongly recommend reading the *Extensibility Guide for JIT-EWM-Integration* for further information on the JIT and EWM integration architecture and enhancement options in supply-to-line processing, considering not just JIT-based processes, but also further EWM components' BAdIs that might be of interest in extending the overall process with custom logic. The guide is available from the SAP Community wiki at *https://wiki.scn.sap.com/wiki/display/SCM/How-To+Guides+for+SAP+EWM*.

2.6 Summary

In this chapter, we introduced the basic architecture elements of the EWM solution, including delivery and warehouse request processing, shipping and receiving, warehouse orders, warehouse tasks, and the functionality and data model of quality management. We also provided an overview of the technical coherency between the different objects of stock management. This should give a good understanding of how stocks are managed with EWM, especially regarding the segregation and differentiation.

Finally, we described the communication interfaces and methods between SAP ERP or SAP S/4HANA and EWM, including master data and transactional data for both decentralized and embedded EWM. You should now have a good basis for understanding how the communication flow works back and forth between the two systems and what to keep in mind even when connecting EWM to a third-party ERP system.

In the next chapter, we will describe the most important frameworks used by EWM, such as the warehouse monitor, the RF framework, and the PPF, and how to use them most efficiently in your enhancements.

Chapter 3

Frameworks and Development Tools in Extended Warehouse Management

Custom developments can be stable and easy with the proper use of frameworks and their developer tools. In this chapter, you will learn which frameworks can be found in EWM and their uses. With the help of examples, you will learn to handle the frameworks and tools.

In this chapter, we would like to give you an understanding of the flexibility of EWM regarding custom developments based on existing frameworks and development tools. For this purpose, we will use vivid descriptions and numerous examples of which frameworks and development tools are available in EWM to realize custom developments. We will elaborate on two types of frameworks. One the one hand, we will discuss the EWM-specific frameworks, including the warehouse management monitor, Easy Graphics Framework (EGF), radio frequency framework (RF framework), and the work center. On the other hand, we will look at the SAP-wide Post Processing Framework (PPF) component, and the SAP S/4HANA–based key user extensibility for custom fields.

SAP product development teams have intensively used all of these frameworks during the development of EWM. Thus, there are numerous templates available, and the frameworks are well suited to implement project-based requirements for warehouse management with EWM.

3.1 Warehouse Management Monitor

Always be well informed about the situation in your warehouse by using the *warehouse management monitor* (the warehouse monitor for short). In this section, we show you how the warehouse management monitor, which is designed with its own framework, can be enhanced quickly and easily. A basic requirement for each warehouse management software application is to provide tools for monitoring the current day-to-day situation in the warehouse. EWM provides one central tool for this purpose: the warehouse management monitor. The warehouse management monitor application is modeled as a framework (package /SCWM/MONITOR_FRAMEWORK) that allows you to configure one or more monitors, or views, within the monitor, according to your organization's requirements based on the warehouse number. With this tool, you can select and monitor all warehouse-related documents and stock, providing node-specific methods to trigger actions on the respective objects. It is also capable of providing functionality for maintenance of storage bin and warehouse product master data. In addition, the *alert monitor* allows you to detect specific time-critical warehouse processes and to trigger necessary actions.

Start the warehouse management monitor via menu path **Extended Warehouse Management • Monitoring • Warehouse Management Monitor** (or Transaction /SCWM/ MON).

In the following sections, we describe how the warehouse management monitor is constructed. In addition, we show you what options there are—other than Customizing— to integrate individual requirements.

3.1.1 Basics and Technical Structure

An essential benefit of this framework is that you can enhance the warehouse management monitor with your own nodes or functions very easily. In the warehouse management monitor, there are more than 300 monitor nodes, divided into the following categories:

- Outbound
- Inbound
- Physical inventory
- Documents
- Stock and bin
- Resource management
- Product master data
- Alert
- Labor management
- Billing
- Material flow system
- Tools

The graphical UI of the warehouse management monitor is based on the ALV grid control and is divided into three view areas, which can be aligned flexibly and user-specifically with regard to their respective size (see Figure 3.1). On the left, you find the node hierarchy tree, with the upper and lower view areas to the right. The hierarchy tree is only for navigation purposes.

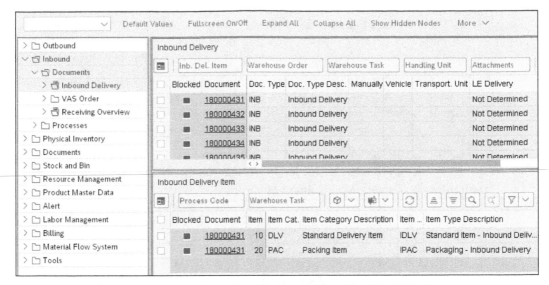

Figure 3.1 Warehouse Management Monitor: Structure of Graphical User Interface

The node hierarchy tree consists of two types of nodes: category nodes and profile nodes. The difference is in their tasks:

- *Category nodes* are just collection folders where other category nodes and/or profile nodes will be grouped. They do not have a node profile assigned. The arrangement of the hierarchy tree is sorted logically. Related information is typically grouped into nodes.

- The *profile nodes* contain information—according to their assigned node profile— that can be shown in the right view area after double-clicking the corresponding node. A profile node represents a specific object class. The subnodes (child nodes) of the main profile nodes are also profile nodes and have a logically, hierarchically subordinate relation to their parent nodes. They can, for example, represent a subset of their parent nodes (e.g., parent node **Warehouse Order**, child node **Warehouse Task**). This is done via drill down: for a selection result, more data of a dependent object will be selected without having to enter selection criteria again. The selection criteria and the display of the child data depend logically on those of the parent node.

[Ex]

Dependencies in the Node Hierarchy

Select the **Documents • Warehouse Order** node (parent node) to select warehouse orders. Within the upper view area on the right side of the screen, you can then use the **WT** button for the selected warehouse orders to view the associated warehouse tasks in the lower view area (drill down). These very same warehouse tasks are also displayed when you open/unfold the node **Warehouse Order** and select these warehouse tasks on the corresponding **WT** child node directly with the same selection conditions. Technically, function module /SCWM/WO_TO_MON is called in both cases.

However, there are warehouse tasks that have no corresponding warehouse order (e.g., inactive warehouse tasks or goods movement warehouse tasks). These objects cannot be selected in the **WT** child node because they obviously do not have a reference to the parent node.

Such warehouse tasks have to be selected via the specific **Warehouse Task** parent node (**Documents • Warehouse Task**).

The technical structure and the relations of the node hierarchy are displayed again in Figure 3.2. You can find the corresponding Customizing settings in the IMG at **EWM • Monitoring • Warehouse Management Monitor**.

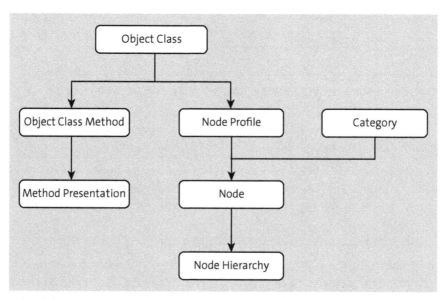

Figure 3.2 Technical Structure of Warehouse Management Monitor

In addition to structure and node hierarchy, the framework of the warehouse management monitor provides two other important features, which are monitor methods and hotspots:

- The *monitor methods* can be assigned to each object in Customizing at **EWM • Monitoring • Warehouse Management Monitor • Define Object Class Methods**. With these methods, which contain their own ABAP logic, you can execute specific functions with the help of buttons within the respective context—for example, to confirm or cancel selected warehouse tasks. Whether a method is presented as a function key with or without text, you have to define it in the *methods presentation*. You do not need a special screen or ABAP List Viewer knowledge. The framework manages the entire integration and UI control for you.

- There is also the possibility for specific objects to integrate navigation jumps into the object-specific transactions. These objects then become *hotspots*. An overview of the objects or the available services is provided in Table 3.1. You will recognize hotspots because they are underlined in the ALV grid (see, for example, **Storage Bins** in Figure 3.1). Via the hotspot, you can reach, from the appropriate service method, a detailed display of the corresponding object—for the storage bin, for example, Transaction /SCWM/LS03. Besides the already preconfigured hotspots, you can also implement your own hotspots if needed. You can make the necessary settings in the IMG at **EWM • Monitoring • Warehouse Management Monitor • Define Navigation**.

Service	Description
ATTACH	Attachment
BATCH	Batch
BIN	Storage bin
CUSTOM	Custom
DLV	Delivery
DOCKEY	Document key
GENERIC	Generic
HU	Handling unit
ILT	Indirect labor
MMDOC	Material document (embedded)
MMDOCITM	Material document item
MSGTXT	Long text
PI	Physical inventory
PROD	Product
PSHU	Planned shipping handling unit
PSPEC	Packaging specification
QINSPDOC	Quality inspection document
SLG1	Application log
TO	Warehouse task
TU	Transportation unit
URL	URL
VAS	Value-added services (VAS) order

Table 3.1 Available Services for Hotspots in Warehouse Monitor

Service	Description
VEH	Vehicle
WAVE	Wave
WO	Warehouse order
WORKC	Work center
YARDMOVE	Yard move

Table 3.1 Available Services for Hotspots in Warehouse Monitor (Cont.)

To be able to adjust the monitor in the customer-specific processes and special features in the warehouse, EWM offers two options that can be combined:

- **Create a new monitor via Customizing**
  Using Customizing, you can implement completely new monitors or even monitor variants of the standard monitor with your own nodes and hierarchies and new features within a flexible framework without modifications.

- **Variant maintenance via the context menu**
  The end user can also directly use the context menu for each hierarchy node to create his own *variant node*, assign layout variants, or hide nodes completely. Another beautiful feature of variant maintenance is that you can assign individual selection variants to your own variant node. For this, you just create a personal selection variant in a selection screen and then assign it using the **Assign Selection Variant** function of the context menu (see Figure 3.3).

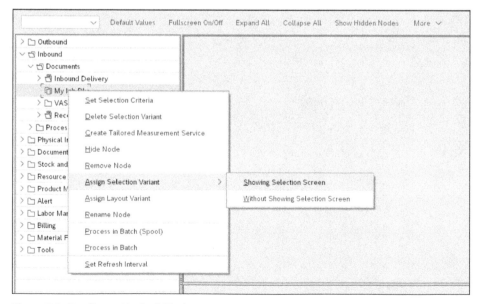

Figure 3.3 Configure Variant Node

Without Showing Selection Screen has the effect that double-clicking this variant node skips the selection screen and starts the selection with the maintained variant and values directly. **With Showing Selection Screen** shows your customized selection screen instead of the standard selection screen. In addition, you can also maintain cross-user selection variants and ALV layouts for a monitor node in Customizing. You find the corresponding settings in the IMG under **EWM • Monitoring • Warehouse Management Monitor • Define Nodes** (**Define Nodes** folder). Thus, you will have made these settings available to all users, and they can also be provided via the transport management system in all systems.

Context Menu of Nodes

For several nodes, SAP also provides a feature that allows you to create tailored measurement services directly via the context menu. More information about the EWM measurement services is provided in Section 3.2.

We assume that you want to create in your project a new customer-tailored monitor. For this purpose, you have the option to realize this procedure either dependent directly on the warehouse number or independent of it per wildcard logic. Even with the wildcard logic, if your new monitor is later started with a specific warehouse number, it will then be warehouse number–dependent. However, the monitor, once configured, can be reused in the same way for several warehouse numbers without a warehouse number–specific customizing.

Customize Monitor Tree IMG Activity

Use the **Customize Monitor Tree** IMG activity to configure the warehouse management monitor. With the easy to use graphical interface, changes and enhancements can be done much more simply (see Figure 3.4).

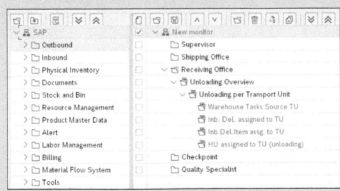

Figure 3.4 Customize Monitor Tree IMG Activity

When customizing the warehouse management monitor, we recommend that you always copy the standard monitor first. You can accomplish this activity in the IMG at **EWM • Monitoring • Warehouse Management Monitor • Define Monitors**. Enter "****" in the **Warehouse No.** field and "SAP" in the **Monitor** field and choose the **Copy As...** button. Assign a new monitor name and save the data. The important benefit of this approach is that you always have the possibility to switch to the standard monitor, especially in production.

You should apply all node hierarchies at this copy step. If you do not need specific nodes for your project (e.g., the node for labor management), we recommend that you just hide these nodes. It is much easier to show the hidden nodes again if they are needed later than to reconstruct a complete hierarchy. You perform this activity in the same Customizing activity. Set the **Hide Node** checkbox for the corresponding node combination, as shown in Figure 3.5.

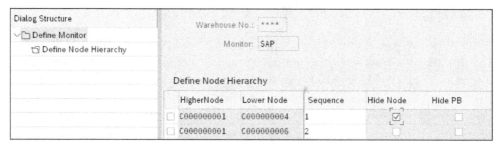

Figure 3.5 Node Hierarchy Maintenance

If you don't have a desired node right away, you can choose the /SCWM/MON_TECH user parameter for your user profile and set the value to "X". Start the warehouse management monitor in a new mode after that. Now the system displays the technical node names instead of the usual descriptions (see Figure 3.6).

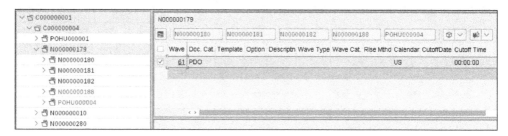

Figure 3.6 Node Hierarchy: Technical Terms

You can find the required information while switching between these two modes. Consider that the displayed main nodes in the hierarchy tree are all subnodes of the virtual superordinate ROOT node. All other node descriptions can be derived.

According to the various fields of activities in a warehouse and the resulting different requirements of the monitor nodes and functions, you can now adjust one or more own monitors in this way.

[«]

Authorizations in the Monitor

You can restrict access to single nodes of a specific monitor and their integrated functions (e.g., monitor methods) with the authorization control on the user level. Use the /SCWM/MO authorization object for this purpose.

3.1.2 Enhancement Options

In addition to the option of configuring your own monitors with easy Customizing activities, there is often a requirement for individual queries. For example, maybe you need warehouse orders to be selectable on the basis of specific warehouse task attributes, or you have enhanced standard business objects with custom fields using the available extension includes and now you may want to select these business objects based on such custom fields. For that, you can define your own nodes in the corresponding hierarchy context. We describe how to work with extension includes in Section 3.5.

To implement your own monitor node, you need a function module that will be assigned to the new node in Customizing. In Chapter 4, Section 4.3.4, we will show a specific example of what such an implementation may look like and which Customizing steps it will require.

You should use the following standard parameters for the declaration of the function module. Table 3.2 shows the standard parameters that are available. This allows you to apply all options that the framework provides in the area of the node hierarchy tree.

Parameter	Associated Type	Function
Importing		
IV_LGNUM	/SCWM/LGNUM	Warehouse number
IV_VARIANT (optional)	VARIANT	Selection variant the function module should be called with (optional)
IV_MODE	/SCWM/DE_MON_FM_MODE	Execution mode: ■ 1 = normal ■ 2 = no selection screen ■ 3 = only choose selection variant ■ 4 = refresh

Table 3.2 Standard Parameters for Definition of Function Interface

Parameter	Associated Type	Function
IT_DATA_PARENT (optional)	For example, /SCWM/TT_WO_DET_MON_OUT	Data from parent node
Changing		
CT_TAB_RANGE	RSDS_TRANGE	Selection options of previous nodes
CT_FIELDCAT	LVC_T_FCAT	Field catalog for list viewer control
Exporting		
EV_RETURNCODE	XFELD	User-canceled selection
EV_VARIANT	VARIANT	Selected ABAP report variant
ET_DATA	For example, /SCWM/TT_TO_DET_MON_OUT	Selection result

Table 3.2 Standard Parameters for Definition of Function Interface (Cont.)

When implementing the new function, you should perform the following steps:

1. Check if the selection variant is used.
2. Clear Dynpro elements.
3. Map selection options and parameters to database tables and fields.
4. Fill selection criteria on the basis of the selection variant used, if available.
5. Apply selection criteria from the parent node in case of drilling down.
6. Check if the selection screen will be displayed.
7. Export selection criteria.
8. Convert and enrich selection results (e.g., with descriptions), if required.

Pay special attention to the performance of your own monitor nodes. Most of the nodes of the warehouse management monitor are designed for operational use. That means that the user must be able to reach the respective information fast and at any time. That's why the monitor provides different nodes, each with its own selection focus. The project often comes down to the question: Why can't individual information from multiple nodes (e.g., warehouse tasks and handling unit information) be grouped together in one single node?

The explanation lies in the fact that specific search strategies and database accesses are adapted for the respective node context in an optimized way. A combination may lead to the undermining of these optimizations, which might make the runtime behavior for the user no longer acceptable. In addition, you should consider a further aspect that can negatively affect the runtime behavior: if the user chooses too few selection conditions or none at all, you should add a warning so that the user has the option to cancel the selection before it has completed the tedious load of a database table. As an orientation, you can check the use of the /SCWM/CHK_PARENT_FIELD_SEL function module.

During the conception and implementation phase of a monitor node, you should always consider that data volumes will be much bigger in a production environment than in development and test systems.

[«]

Further Information about the Extension of the Warehouse Monitor

For more information on enhancing the warehouse management monitor, see SAP Note 1824039 at the SAP Support Portal (*http://support.sap.com*). Attached to this support note, you will find a how-to guide on warehouse monitor enhancements, which contains detailed technical descriptions and also a lot of valuable sample coding. You can also find the guide in the SAP Community wiki at *https://wiki.scn.sap.com/wiki/display/SCM/How-To+Guides+for+SAP+EWM*.

3.2   Easy Graphics Framework and Measurement Services

You can monitor and supervise processes in your warehouse by displaying key figures graphically within the *warehouse cockpit* (Transaction /SCWM/EGF). With the help of big flat screens—mounted, for example, in the receiving and goods issue areas of the warehouse—the latest graphs are displayed to the warehouse operators, telling them, for example, in which warehouse areas work is waiting or overdue. An example of how such a screen could look is shown later in Figure 3.8.

SAP delivers EGF and measurement services for the warehouse cockpit, two kits you can use and enhance in every EWM project. With more than 50 measurement services delivered and 18 different chart types (from vertical bars to a speedometer), many customer requirements can be met without any additional development. To display more than one key figure within the same graphic or to add, for example, a target line, an additional development is required. In the following sections, we will first introduce the foundation of EGF and then show an additional development using this framework.

[«]

Warehouse KPIs

EWM in SAP S/4HANA offers an interesting alternative for graphical data representation: warehouse KPIs, which can be accessed by the identically named SAP Fiori app. EWM provides many KPIs and CDS views delivered standard. We recommend checking the available KPI and CDS view scope in the latest available version of SAP S/4HANA in the SAP Help Portal for EWM. You will find them under **Analytics**.

The Manage KPIs and Reports app will allow you to use standard and custom-built CDS views to come up with individual KPIs. For a short example of KPI creation, you might consider checking out the guide called *Outbound Delivery Order CDS Query for SAP Smart Business in S/4HANA Cloud*, available in the SAP Community wiki at *https://*

wiki.scn.sap.com/wiki/display/SCM/How-To+Guides+for+SAP+EWM. Figure 3.7 shows an example for warehouse KPIs.

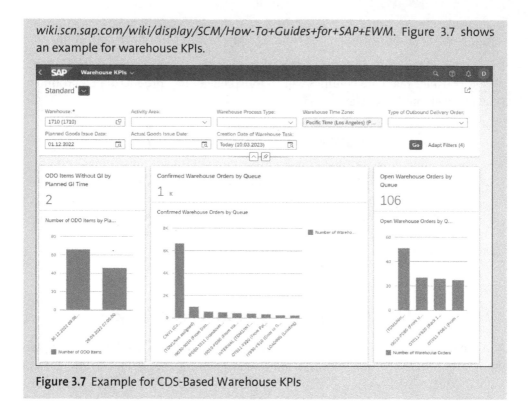

Figure 3.7 Example for CDS-Based Warehouse KPIs

3.2.1   Foundations

We will start by introducing some important terms and components of EGF and the measurement services framework. In short, you use a *measurement service* to determine the value of a key figure (part 1), and you use EGF to display the key figure graphically (part 2).

Part 1: Determine a Key Figure with the Measurement Service Framework

In the IMG, via path **Monitoring • Measurement Services • Define Basic Measurement Service (BMS)**, you will find the SAP-delivered basic measurement services. Popular examples include the number of outbound delivery items and the number of warehouse tasks, among others. In addition to a name, a basic measurement service consists of a description and two function modules that are entered in the basic measurement service framework:

- **Selection screen**
  The first function module defines the selection screen. A user will use this screen to enter selection parameters and to define selection variants (as you'll see later in Figure 3.11). The selection variant is the result of using this function module.

- **Query**

  The second function module will execute the database selection based on the selection variant and returns the resulting key figure. A user can tailor a basic measurement service from the basic measurement service framework using a wizard. The steps in the wizard will support the user to enter, in addition to a name, a selection variant (mandatory) and thresholds (optional). The result of the wizard is then a new *tailored measurement service*. If you run a tailored measurement service, the system will return a key figure without a unit—for example, "Number of urgent outbound delivery items today" = 2930. With the help of a second wizard, a user can define a formula, combining several tailored measurement services and operators, hence creating a *calculated measurement service*—for example, "Average number of delivery items by user" = 2930 ÷ 30 = 97.3.

Part 2: Visualization of a Key Figure

A graphic or a chart in the warehouse cockpit is called an *EGF object*. A warehouse cockpit consists of one or several EGF objects. Figure 3.8 shows the **EGF Demo Cockpit** in the warehouse cockpit, showing four different EGF objects. Any key figure determined by a tailored measurement service or calculated measurement service can be displayed in the warehouse cockpit using one of the following chart types: traffic light, speedometer, bars, or timeline.

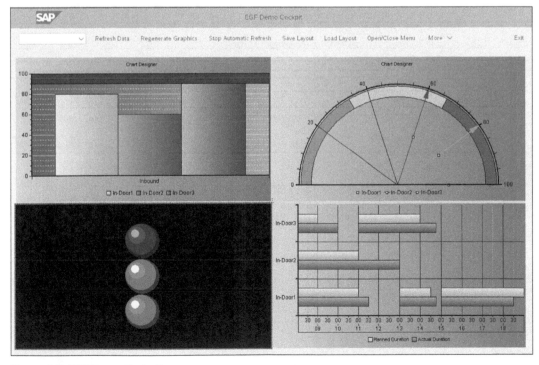

Figure 3.8 EGF Demo Cockpit

There are predelivered EGF objects that are not based on a tailored measurement service. For example, for monitoring a material flow system, the *MFS Resource Status* EGF object displaying a traffic light is available. The figures for this EGF object are determined by an individual database selection.

In the warehouse cockpit (WHS_COCKPIT), you can find predefined EGF objects. If a user starts this cockpit, the framework will call the service methods of a service provider class to determine and display the key figures. For an EGF object based on a tailored or calculated measurement service, the GET_DATA method of class /SCWM/CL_EG_SP_MS is called to determine the value and to create a chart-independent object using class /SCWM/CL_EGF_CHART_DATA. This chart object will be converted by the framework into one of the 18 available chart types of the Internet Graphics Service.

With the GET_DATA method, the framework will query for categories and series of a chart object. If you were using a table (see Table 3.3), the categories would reflect the columns and the series would correspond with lines.

	Category A	Category B	Category C
Series 1	Value 1.1	Value 1.2	Value 1.3
Series 2	Value 2.1	Value 2.2	Value 2.3

Table 3.3 Categories and Series for Chart Object

Further Information on EGF Implementation

In the *EGF Implementation* guide, you can find further basics and examples of how to use and extend the framework. The document is available via the SAP Community wiki (*https://wiki.scn.sap.com/wiki/display/SCM*). The best way to find the latest version of the guide is to use the document search within the wiki, entering "EGF implement" as a search term.

3.2.2 Custom Development: Basic Measurement Service

A new basic measurement service should be developed in a project if one of the following requirements exists:

- The service will be reusable for several applications.
- A user will have the option to influence the key figure with predefined selection parameters.

If neither of these requirements exist, the project can use an individual database selection by implementing the GET_DATA method of the EGF (Section 3.2.4).

A developer can create with little effort a basic measurement service for many of the key figures that are found in the warehouse management monitor. In our example, we will develop a basic measurement service for the number of wave items. This basic measurement service can then be used for several key figures, such as the number of employees required for picking within the labor management application or for a wave picking overview chart in the warehouse cockpit.

The number of wave items key figure can be found in the warehouse management monitor by a user if he summarizes the values of the **No.Itm** (number of items) column in the **Outbound • Documents • Wave** monitor node (see Figure 3.9).

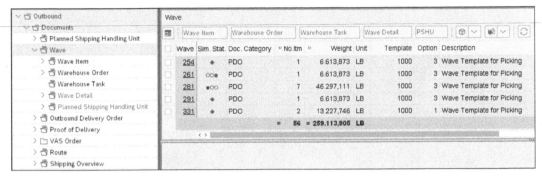

Figure 3.9 Key Figures KPI 1: Number of Wave Items

If you can find the key figure in the monitor, you can reuse the existing selection function for the basic measurement service. If, however, the monitor selection does not meet the project's performance requirements, a new database selection needs to be developed. One advantage of reusing the monitor selection is that you do not need to know the details of the database model.

To develop a basic measurement service, the following steps are necessary:

1. Create a new function group in Transaction SE80 (ABAP Workbench), such as ZBKS_ WAVE_KPI.

2. Create a function module for the selection screen within the new function group, such as Z_BKS_WAVE_SELSCREEN (see Listing 3.1).

3. Create a function module for the value determination within the new function group, such as Z_WAVE_KPI_1 (see Listing 3.2).

4. Define the new basic measurement service in the IMG for the basic measurement service framework.

5. Create a tailored measurement service based on the basic measurement service.

The function module for the selection screen in step 2 (e.g., Z_BSK_WAVE_SELSCREEN) must have exactly the given interface; otherwise, the framework and the wizard will not be able to call it dynamically. You can either specify a new selection screen within the function module or just call the selection screen, which is used in the warehouse management monitor. If you choose the latter approach, you have the advantage of testing the selection and the result within the monitor.

```
FUNCTION z_bks_wave_selscreen.
*"----------------------------------------------------------------------
*"*"Local Interface:
*"  IMPORTING
*"     REFERENCE(IV_DYNNR) TYPE  DYNNR
*"  CHANGING
*"     REFERENCE(CV_VARIANT) TYPE  VARIANT
*"----------------------------------------------------------------------
  DATA: lv_lgnum TYPE /scwm/lgnum.
  "Provide the hidden WH field for the WH MON screens
  GET PARAMETER ID '/SCWM/LGN' FIELD lv_lgnum.
  CALL FUNCTION '/SCWM/WAVEHDR_MON'
    EXPORTING
      iv_lgnum   = lv_lgnum
      iv_variant = cv_variant
    IMPORTING
      ev_variant = cv_variant.
  "Return current variant
  cv_variant = sy-slset.

ENDFUNCTION.
```

Listing 3.1 Function Module for Selection Screen of New Basic Measurement Service

Also, the function module for the value determination in step 3 (e.g., Z_WAVE_KPI_1; see Listing 3.2) requires a predefined interface to ensure that the framework and wizard can call it dynamically. In our example, the monitor query is reused. To do so, we looked up the /SCWM/WAVEHDR_O_MON function module of the corresponding node profile P0000179 in IMG activity **Monitoring • Warehouse Management Monitor • Define Nodes**.

```
FUNCTION z_wave_kpi_1.
*"----------------------------------------------------------------------
*"*"Local Interface:
*"  IMPORTING
*"     REFERENCE(IV_LGNUM) TYPE  /SCWM/LGNUM
*"     REFERENCE(IV_VARIANT) TYPE  VARIANT
*"     REFERENCE(IV_REPID) TYPE  /SCWM/DE_MS_REPID
*"  EXPORTING
*"     REFERENCE(EV_RESULT) TYPE  /SCWM/DE_MS_RESULT
*"     REFERENCE(EV_UNIT) TYPE  /SCWM/DE_UNIT
*"  EXCEPTIONS
*"     ERROR
*"----------------------------------------------------------------------

  DATA: lt_data TYPE /scwm/tt_wavehdr_det_mon_out,
```

```
      lv_rc    TYPE sysubrc.

"1.Check the existence of the variant
CALL FUNCTION 'RS_VARIANT_EXISTS'
  EXPORTING
    report  = iv_repid
    variant = iv_variant
  IMPORTING
    r_c     = lv_rc
  EXCEPTIONS
    OTHERS  = 99.
IF lv_rc NE 0 OR sy-subrc NE 0.
  RAISE error.
ENDIF.
"2.Call the monitor selection with selscreen IV_Variant
CALL FUNCTION '/SCWM/WAVEHDR_O_MON'
  EXPORTING
    iv_lgnum      = iv_lgnum
    iv_variant    = iv_variant
    iv_mode       = '2'
  IMPORTING
    et_data       = lt_data
  EXCEPTIONS
    error_message = 99.
IF sy-subrc NE 0.
  RAISE error.
ENDIF.
"3.Summarize the number of items in the wave
LOOP AT lt_data ASSIGNING FIELD-SYMBOL(<ls_data>).
  ev_result = ev_result + <ls_data>-noitm.
ENDLOOP.


ENDFUNCTION.
```

Listing 3.2 Function Module for the Value Determination of New Basic Measurement Service

To perform step 4, choose IMG activity **Monitoring • Measurement Services • Define Basics Measurement Service (BMS)**. Create a new entry (e.g., ZWV1), and enter the names of the function modules from steps 2 and 3 (see Figure 3.10). In the **Report ID** and **Selection screen** fields, you have to enter the program name and number where the selection screen coding is located. As we are reusing the one from the monitor here, we enter that one, /SCWM/SAPLWIP_WAVE, screen 100. For **BMS Group**, you can choose either an existing one (e.g., "08" for the Miscellaneous group) or define a new group in the previous IMG activity.

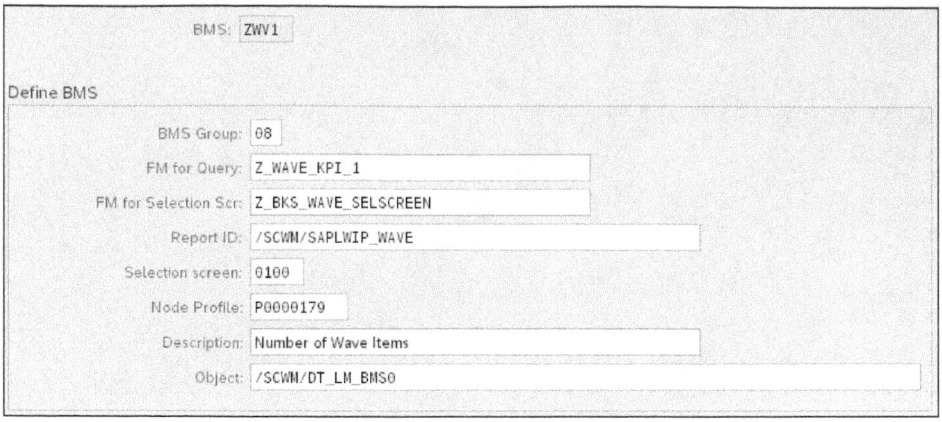

Figure 3.10 Define New Basic Measurement Service in IMG

To complete the steps, you tailor the new basic measurement service with the wizard. You have two options:

- Create a local tailored measurement service using Transaction /SCWM/TLR_WIZ-ARD (Tailored Measurement Service with Wizard) in the SAP menu.
- Create a tailored measurement service that can be transported to follow-up systems using IMG activity **EWM • Monitoring • Measurement Services • Tailored Measurement Service with Wizard**.

In both cases, the wizard will help you to create a new tailored measurement service within seven steps. First you enter a name (e.g., WV01) and the warehouse number. Then you select your new basic measurement service (e.g., ZWV1), which you can find in group 08 (Miscellaneous). In the **Select Variant** wizard step, you can create or edit selection variants and hence test the Z_BKS_WAVE_SELSCREEN function module from step 2. In our example, we enter the current date and select wave items in the time slot from 8:00 to 10:00 a.m., as shown in Figure 3.11.

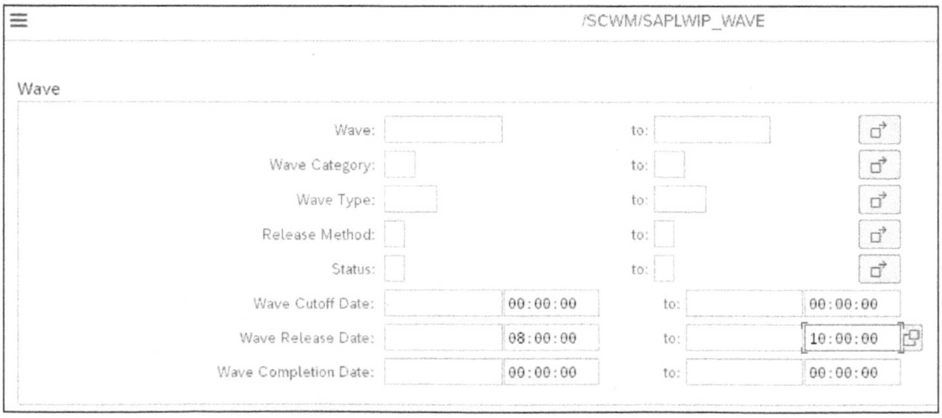

Figure 3.11 Selection Variant with Wave Release Date and Time

The wizard will create all necessary settings for the EGF object (e.g., _<Whse>WV01T) of the tailored measurement service, as with the settings in Figure 3.12. Now you can now display a chart for the tailored measurement service in the warehouse cockpit (see Figure 3.13).

Warehouse No.:	1710
Measmnt Service:	WV01

Maintain/Define TMS

BMS:	ZWV1
Variant:	Z_WV01
MS Description:	Wave Items

Details

Check Uppr Threshold:	✓
Upper Threshold:	300
Upper Exception:	
Check Low Threshold:	✓
Lower Threshold:	100
Exception Low:	
Min. Rep. Intvl:	

Figure 3.12 Definition of Tailored Measurement Service WV01

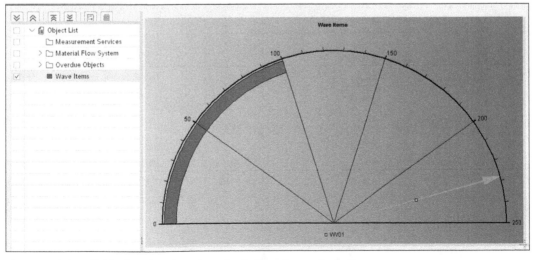

Figure 3.13 Result Displayed as Speedometer in Warehouse Cockpit

If you do not want to use the wizard, you have to manually create the settings in the following IMG activities/transactions:

- **Define TMS** (Transaction /SCWM/MS_TLR_A)
- **Define EGF-Object** (Transaction /SCWM/EG_OBJECT)
- **Define Warehouse Cockpit** (Transaction /SCWM/EGF_COCKPIT)

Key Figure Series

Repeat the last step and create also tailored measurement services WV02, WV03, and WV04 by changing the time interval in the selection screen to 10 a.m. to 12 p.m., 12–2 p.m., and 2–6 p.m. (reflecting the important time slots in your warehouse). With the four tailored measurement services/key figures, you will be able to do the exercise in Section 3.2.4 in which several key figures are displayed in the same chart.

Now start the warehouse cockpit (Transaction /SCWM/EGF) with the delivered EGF implementation WHS_COCKPIT and your warehouse number. Use the **Show Hidden Objects** button to add the EGF object <Whse>WV01T to the object list. Double-click the new object and the system will display the chart for the key figure. The system chooses the chart type **Time**, but with the context menu you can change the chart type to, for example, **Speedometer** (see Figure 3.14).

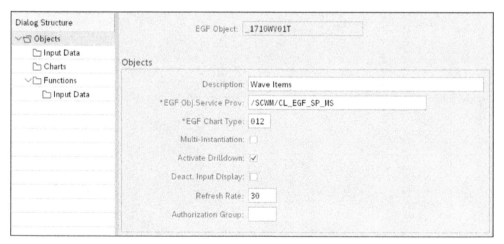

Figure 3.14 Changing EGF Chart Type to Speedometer

You can use the **Save Layout** button to avoid the steps to unhide and start the key figure every time you start the transaction. The popup window shown in Figure 3.15 will appear, and you can set it as the default layout, storing the current layout, including the input data.

Figure 3.15 Save Layout for Warehouse Cockpit

The wizard will automatically set the chart type for a measurement service to time (value 011). To change this afterward, run Transaction /SCWM/EGF_OBJECT and enter "012" (speedometer).

3.2.3 Adjust Chart Template

Without coding, you can improve the look and feel of the chart template for an EGF object. The optics of the warehouse cockpit can be made more attractive for the user just by changing colors, fonts, and the like.

To do so, start Transaction /SCWM/EGF_CHART (Process Chart Template). In the **Chart Template • Load From Database** menu, you can, for example, load chart type 012 (speedometer). As a first step, you save your own template specifically for your EGF object from Section 3.2.2. Use the **Value** menu button, as shown in Figure 3.16, to load the actual result value of your EGF object. Switch to change mode by using the **Change Template** menu button. Now you can change the background color or the width and color of the speedometer needle in the global settings. You also can change the descriptions or add some labels.

When you are done, you save the chart template again; with the **Cross-User** option, you can make your changes visible to all users.

In the EGF implementation guide mentioned in Section 3.2.1, you'll find an alternative to this EWM transaction: the Chart Designer.

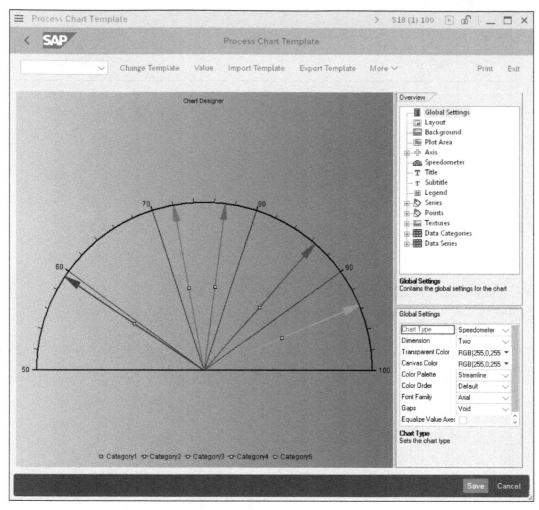

Figure 3.16 Adjusting Your Chart Template for Your EGF Object

3.2.4   Custom Development: Easy Graphics Framework Object Service Provider

With the EWM standard solution, you get several *EGF object service providers*, which contain the coding that is used to display, for example, material flow system key figures, tailored measurement services, and overdue warehouse objects. In Transaction SE24 (Class Builder), you can find the complete list of standard service provider classes. You can look up the classes that implement the /SCWM/IF_EGF_SP EGF object service provider interface.

As the warehouse cockpit is a framework, you are invited to develop your own EGF object service providers and your own EGF objects.

To develop a new EGF object, including a new service provider, the following steps are necessary:

1. **Specification**
   Based on the customer requirement, you specify which key figure will be displayed in which way.

2. **Design**
   What user input is required to evaluate the key figure? Either no input is required, or you make the user enter options (e.g., warehouse number and dates). You also have to decide if you want to develop a generic service provider class, using it for several EGF objects.

3. **Realization**
   Create a new class (e.g., ZEGF_SP_TMS) in Transaction SE24, which has to implement the /SCWM/IF_EGF_SP interface. In our example, we will implement the GET_DATA method.

4. **Configuration**
   Create a new EGF object in the SAP menu or in the IMG. Assign the chart type, input parameters, and the EGF service provider. Last but not least, you add the new EGF object to the warehouse cockpit.

5. **Fine-tuning**
   Adjust colors, lines, and headings for your new EGF object (see Section 3.2.3).

In the next section, you will find the details on how to perform all of these steps.

Specification

Together with the business team, you specify the new key figure and how it will be displayed. In our example, for wave items daily monitoring, we want to display the actual number of wave items for several points of time in one chart (**Actual**). Furthermore, we want to also show the expected number of wave items (**Target**) within the same chart. You can use, for example, a Microsoft Excel chart for a mock-up of the display (see Figure 3.17).

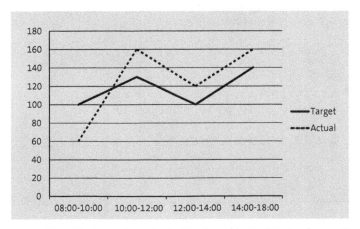

Figure 3.17 Chart Mock-up to Be Displayed in EWM Warehouse Cockpit

Design

In our example, we will use two user inputs: the warehouse number, and the wave item tailored measurement services (e.g., WV01, WV02, WV03, and WV04) from Section 3.2.2.

In a new database table ZEGF_MS_TARGET, you enter the target values for tailored measurement services WV01–WV04. To do so, start Transaction SE11 (ABAP Dictionary) and create the fields as specified in Table 3.4. Do not forget to activate the table.

Field	Data Element	Key	Check Table or Search Help
CLIENT	MANDT	Yes	None
LGNUM	/SCWM/LGNUM	Yes	/SCWM/T300
MEAS_SERV	/SCWM/DE_MS	Yes	/SCWM/SH_MS_TLR
VALUE	/SCWM/DE_EGF_VALUE	No	None

Table 3.4 Fields of ZEGF_MS_TARGET

You then generate a maintenance view using Transaction SE55 (Table Maintenance Generator).

In Transaction SM30 (Maintain Table Views), you start your maintenance view and enter the target values for keys WV01 to WV04, such as 70, 150, 90, or 12.

Realization

When you create the new EGF object service provider ZEGF_SP_TMS, you assign the /SCWM/IF_EGF_SP interface in Transaction SE24 (Class Builder) and implement the GET_DATA method (see Listing 3.3).

```
METHOD /scwm/if_egf_sp~get_data.
  DATA: lv_label      TYPE /scwm/de_egf_label,
        ls_title      TYPE /scwm/s_egf_chart_title,
        ls_subtitle   TYPE /scwm/s_egf_chart_title.

  BREAK-POINT ID zewmdevbook_324.

  "1. Get uservinput: get warehouse number
  ASSIGN it_object_input[ tablename = '/SCWM/S_MS_RESULT_SEL_UI' ]
    TO FIELD-SYMBOL(<ls_selection>).
  IF sy-subrc IS NOT INITIAL.
    RETURN.
  ENDIF.
  ASSIGN <ls_selection>-frange_t[ fieldname = /scwm/if_ui_pl_c=>sc_field_lgnum ]
    TO FIELD-SYMBOL(<ls_frange_t_read>).
  IF sy-subrc IS NOT INITIAL
```

```
OR <ls_frange_t_read> IS INITIAL.
  RETURN.
ENDIF.
DATA(ls_selopt) = VALUE rsdsselopt( <ls_frange_t_read>-selopt_t[ 1 ] ).
DATA(ls_tms)    = VALUE /scwm/s_ex_ms_result( lgnum = ls_selopt-low ).
IF ls_tms-lgnum IS INITIAL.
  RETURN.
ENDIF.
"2. Get uservinput: table of measurement services
ASSIGN <ls_selection>-frange_t[ fieldname = 'TMS' ]
  TO <ls_frange_t_read>.
IF sy-subrc IS NOT INITIAL.
  RETURN.
ENDIF.
"3. Set the labels for the two series: Actual and Target
DATA(ls_data_result) = VALUE /scwm/s_egf_point_general(
             label = 'Actual Values'
             id    = 'ACTUAL' ).
DATA(ls_data_target) = VALUE /scwm/s_egf_point_general(
             label = 'Target Values'
             id    = 'TARGET' ).
eo_chart_data = NEW /scwm/cl_egf_chart_data( ).
"4. For each meas. serv., create values in the 2 series
LOOP AT <ls_frange_t_read>-selopt_t INTO ls_selopt.
  CLEAR: ls_tms-meas_serv, ls_tms-ms_result.
  ls_tms-meas_serv = ls_selopt-low.
  "5. Get description of measurement service for category
  SELECT SINGLE meas_serv_txt
    FROM  /scwm/tms_text
    INTO  lv_label
    WHERE langu = sy-langu
    AND   lgnum = ls_tms-lgnum
    AND   meas_serv = ls_tms-meas_serv
    AND   ms_type = 'T'. "tailored ms
  eo_chart_data->add_category(
    EXPORTING
      iv_category = lv_label ).
  "6. Get result of the meas. service (=ACTUAL series)
  CALL FUNCTION '/SCWM/MS_EVALUATE'
    EXPORTING
      iv_lgnum     = ls_tms-lgnum
      iv_meas_serv = ls_tms-meas_serv
      iv_ms_type   = 'T'
      iv_update_db = abap_false
```

```
          iv_alert    = abap_true
      IMPORTING
          ev_result   = ls_tms-ms_result.
    ls_data_result-value = ls_tms-ms_result.
    eo_chart_data->add_series_general(
      EXPORTING
        iv_label = ls_data_result-label
        is_point = ls_data_result
        iv_id    = ls_data_result-id ).
    "7. Get target value from a Z database (= target series)
    SELECT SINGLE value
      FROM  zegf_ms_target
      INTO  ls_data_target-value
      WHERE lgnum     = ls_tms-lgnum
      AND   meas_serv = ls_tms-meas_serv.
    IF sy-subrc IS INITIAL.
      eo_chart_data->add_series_general(
        EXPORTING
          iv_label = ls_data_target-label
          is_point = ls_data_target
          iv_id    = ls_data_target-id ).
    ENDIF.
  ENDLOOP.
ENDMETHOD.
```

Listing 3.3 GET_DATA Method of New Service Provider Class

The GET_DATA method will do the following:

- In coding areas "1 and "2, the user input (warehouse number and tailored measurement service) is taken over from the import parameter. This generic setup will allow you to use this class for several tailored measurement services, not only the wave items key figures.

- In coding area "3, we define two sets of data values (Actual and Target).

- In coding areas "4 and "5, we loop over all tailored measurement services and hand over each one as a category to the chart.

- In coding areas "6 and "7, we determine for each category two values: the value of the tailored measurement service key figure and the target value from the Z table.

Configuration

For the configuration of the new wave items daily monitoring EGF object, you do the following:

1. In Transaction /SCWM/EGF_OBJECT (Define Measurement Service in the Warehouse Cockpit), create a new entry with the following attributes:
   - **Name**: "_ZWAVE02"
   - **Description**: "Wave-Items Daily Monitoring"
   - **EGF Object Service Provider**: "ZEGF_SP_TMS" (from the previous step)
   - **EGF Chart Type**: "004" (Vertical Bars)
   - **Multi-Instantiation**: yes
   - **Refresh Rate**: 30 minutes

2. After you save the new entry, choose the **Input Data** folder and create two new entries (see Figure 3.18):
   - Entry for the warehouse number:
     - **Table Name**: "/SCWM/S_MS_RESULT_SEL_UI"
     - **Field Name**: "LGNUM"
     - **Sequence**: "1"
     - **Multiple Values**: no
     - **From-Value Required Entry**: yes
     - **Title**: yes
     - **Parameter ID**: "/SCWM/LGN"
   - Entry for one or several TMS:
     - **Table Name**: "/SCWM/S_MS_RESULT_SEL_UI"
     - **Field Name**: "TMS"
     - **Sequence**: "2"
     - **Multiple Values**: yes
     - **From-Value Required Entry**: yes
     - **Title**: no

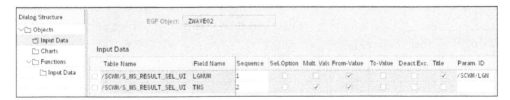

Figure 3.18 Configuration of Input Data

With those two new entries, you give the user the option to enter input selection criteria when starting the key figure chart (which you'll see later in Figure 3.20). EGF generates the selection popup based on this definition maintained in the two new entries.

3. Now choose the **Charts** folder and list all allowed chart types: 001 (Stacked Lines), 002 (Profiles), 003 (Horizontal Bars), 004 (Vertical Bars), 008 (Ring), and 009 (Split Circle).

Thereafter, the user will have the option to change the display of the key figure. Note that you should only list chart types that are supported by the service provider class.

4. As a last step, assign your new _ZWAVE02 EGF object to a cockpit (e.g., ZWAVE_COCKPIT) in Transaction /SCWM/EGF_COCKPIT (Configure Measurement Services in the Warehouse Cockpit). For fine-tuning, you can add the title "Wave Items" in your EGF object or display the target values as a line instead of bars.

Now you can test the new chart in the warehouse cockpit. Figure 3.19 shows the EGF object.

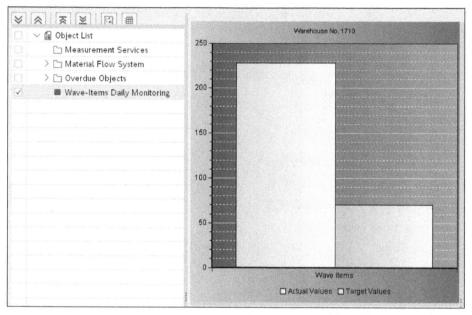

Figure 3.19 New EGF Object Results for Tailored Measurement Service WV01

The layout will save the EGF object display (e.g., chart type) and the user input, so only the very first user needs to type in the warehouse and tailored measurement service names. If required at a later point, a user can change the input for the selection criteria using the context menu (see Figure 3.20).

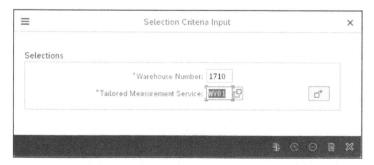

Figure 3.20 Selection Criteria for EGF Object (Generated Popup)

3.3   Radio Frequency Framework

In many EWM projects, a new or enhanced RF transaction is required to meet customer requirements. In this section, you will find out how you can use the RF framework to develop a new RF transaction.

RF transactions are simple, highly specialized UIs. While performing a physical task in the warehouse (e.g., moving a pallet from a high rack to the goods issue zone), the warehouse operator is at the same time using a mobile device to confirm the task in the system. Besides a mobile device usually consisting of a screen with a small keyboard, a headset with microphone can also be used (pick-by-voice). The RF UI will give small amounts of precise information to the user to ensure that he can execute the physical task step by step.

SAP delivers a collection of more than 80 RF transactions, which can be used as is or used as templates. An RF transaction is developed and maintained in the RF framework and cannot run on its own like a classical SAP transaction. Therefore, the full description is *logical RF transaction*. RF transactions run in the *RF environment* (Transaction /SCWM/RFUI).

By developing function modules and maintaining Customizing entries, you can add customer-specific RF transactions in the RF framework. The RF framework will support the developer to strictly separate the UI from the business logic. In a typical EWM project, at least two kinds of RF devices are used: a handheld device with a small screen and a mounted forklift device with a big screen. The same RF transaction can run on both devices using the same business logic (captured in function modules) but different displays (small screen and big screen).

Besides the option to use it for developing your own RF transactions, the RF framework also offers the following features:

- A generation report, to adjust all standard screens to your new screen size
- A wizard to copy and adjust single screens
- The possibility to define RF menus for different user groups

An RF transaction can run in the SAP GUI or in a web browser using ITSmobile.

Technical Documentation on the RF Framework and SAP Screen Personas

We invite you to check out the how-to guide *Radio Frequency* (formerly known as the *RF Cookbook*) for further technical information and *SAP Screen Personas for Mobile RF Devices in Extended Warehouse Management in SAP S/4HANA* for achieving an SAP Fiori–like easily adoptable design without the need to use ITSmobile. You can find both guides in the list of available EWM how-to guides in the SAP Community wiki at *https://wiki.scn.sap.com/wiki/display/SCM/How-To+Guides+for+SAP+EWM*.

In the following sections, all referenced IMG activities are found in the path **EWM • Mobile Data Entry • Radio Frequency (RF) Framework**. We will now walk through each of the required Customizing activities provided by the RF framework in more detail, explaining its parameters and control options.

3.3.1 Basics

In this section, we will introduce the most important terms and definitions for the RF framework. We will also illustrate how these terms/definitions could apply in a project:

- **Display profile**
  The display profile defines the screen size (usually in number of rows and columns) and the number of buttons. The display profile ** is delivered by SAP and can be used for RF devices with a size of eight lines and forty columns. It shows four buttons.

  Typical use in a project: In a project, you typically have two sets of screens: mounted screens on forklifts (e.g., eight lines and 40 columns) and handhelds with small screens (e.g., 30 lines and 12 columns).

- **Application**
  The application is the organizational unit of the RF framework. Initially the framework was built to host applications other than EWM. EWM RF transactions use application 01.

  Typical use in a project: Always use the value 01 for your new RF transactions.

- **Presentation profile**
  With the presentation profile, you can specify warehouse-specific logic in an RF transaction. You link each warehouse to exactly one presentation profile, but you can use the same presentation profile in several warehouses. The presentation profile is a key in many Customizing tables of the framework. During runtime, the framework will first try to find presentation profile specific entries. If no entries are found, it will use entries with ****, which is the standard presentation profile.

  Typical use in a project: A rule of thumb is to have one presentation profile for each warehouse.

- **Personalization profile**
  A personalization profile defines, for one group of users, which set of RF transactions is available and in which menu structure those transactions are listed. For one presentation profile, you can define one or several personalization profiles. In the IMG, under **RF Menu Manager**, you maintain the personalization profiles. In the SAP menu, under **Master Data • Resource Management • Maintain Users** (Transaction /SCWM/USER), you assign the personalization profile to a user. With the personalization profile, you can also influence the number of fields to be validated on a screen; for example, a beginner has to validate the bin and quantity during picking process, whereas an advanced user only needs to verify the bin.

Typical use in a project: Instead of the standard personalization profile ** (with more than 80 RF transactions in a three-level menu hierarchy), you should create a master menu containing only those RF transactions that are used in your warehouse. Further personalization profiles (e.g., O1 for goods issue and R1 for goods receipt) can be set up to make sure that special user groups are restricted only to the RF transactions they need, and they can quickly access them in a lean menu.

- **RF environment**
  With Transaction /SCWM/RFUI, you start the RF environment in SAP GUI (see Figure 3.21). The first screen is the logon screen ❶, where you specify the warehouse, resource, and presentation device. The second screen is the main menu ❷, where you can drill down into further submenus or RF transactions ❸. Each RF transaction can consist of one or several screens.

  Typical use in a project: In the early phases of the project, you use this SAP GUI Transaction /SCWM/RFUI to develop and test the RF transactions. Later on, you change to ITSmobile.

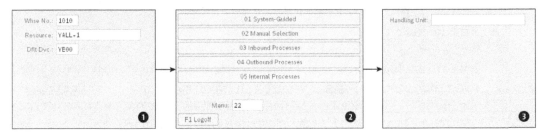

Figure 3.21 Flow Logic in RF Environment: Screen Size 8 x 40

- **(Logical) RF transaction**
  An RF transaction is a user dialog running in the RF environment. Each RF transaction is started from the RF menu and usually consists of one or several screens.

  Typical use in a project: In a project, the new logical RF transactions are created in the Z* namespace. An easy-to-understand RF transaction usually has one or two screens, up to four max.

- **Step**
  One RF transaction combines one or several steps. Usually, one step consists of one screen, several function codes, and several function modules (as you'll see later in Figure 3.24).

  Typical use in a project: You first specify the steps and screens of your new RF transaction, then link the screens using function codes. It is also quite typical to enhance standard RF transactions such that certain steps are skipped or processed automatically.

- **Validation profile**
  The validation profile is part of an RF transaction. You list all fields for a step/screen where validation is useful. An example is the **Bin** field, which is usually displayed

first to the user. To make sure the user did go to the right bin to perform the warehouse task, you set up a validation field, and the system will ask the user to scan the bin barcode before confirming the step. *Note:* In the **Verification Control** IMG activity, you can control which validation fields are mandatory in which context.

Typical use in a project: For any field on your screen where the user can scan a barcode (e.g., product, bin, handling unit), you typically set up a validation field.

- **Application parameter**
  An application parameter can be an ABAP table or structure. The application parameters are handed over from the framework to the function modules within one RF transaction. The framework will update the application parameter with the values the user entered on the screen and will display the values of the application parameters after they were changed in the function module.

  Typical use in a project: Group all display fields required in your RF transaction in one structure (e.g., ZZS_RF1) in the ABAP data dictionary. Then define an application parameter ZSRF1 for this structure; afterward, you can use this parameter in the interface of your function modules.

- **Function code**
  A function code can be up to six characters. Each button on the RF screen can be linked to one function code (see Figure 3.22); for example, the **F1 End** button is linked to function code COMPLT and to the F1 function key. If the user is using this button or the F1 function key, the framework will translate this into function code REVERS and hand this code to the application function modules.

  Not every function code is presented to the user with a button, as this would consume too much space on small screens. Thus, the most common function codes (and function keys) for all RF transactions are not displayed as buttons in the standard RF transactions:

  - F7 (BACKF): With this function key, you can go back one step.
  - F6 (CLEAR): With this function key, you delete the value of the actual input field.
  - F6 and F6 (CLEAR ALL): This will clear all input fields of the current screen.
  - F5 (More): The user can look at the second set of buttons.
  - F9 (FULLMS): The user can display the full message text in case the system issues an error or success message.
  - F8 (LIST): If a value help is provided for a field, this will show all allowed values.

  Typical use in a project: Reuse the aforementioned function codes in your new RF transaction to make sure that the user experiences the same system behavior across all RF transactions.

- **Function code group**
  As you can have only a limited number of buttons (e.g., four) on one screen, the framework allows you to use two groups. So, the F1, F2, F3, and F4 function

keys define group O1 (Figure 3.22 ❶), which is the group displayed to the user by default. If the user enters function key [F5] (more), then the framework displays the buttons/function keys of group O2 ❷. The [F5] function key is displayed by a small button, showing [>] (shown in Figure 3.22).

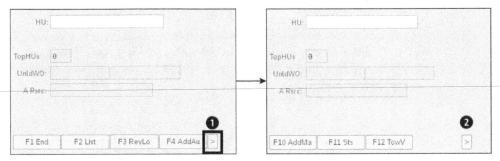

Figure 3.22 Screen with Two Function Code Groups

Typical use in a project: As too many functions on one screen usually adds complexity, try to use only one function code group. In many standard RF transactions, you can use the **Hide** flag to eliminate buttons and to keep the number of functions small.

- **Data entry type**
  This new field was introduced for the pick-by-voice application. The RF framework can also be used for voice applications. In a voice application, the user does not have an RF device with a display. The user is working with a headset and microphone only. All information on a very simple RF screen is read to the user and the user input is done by voice only.
  Typical use in customer project: Use the default value space (General Data Entry Type) if you set up a handheld device. For voice devices, use value 1 (Voice Recognition).

To understand the RF framework fully, we can recommend making use of two checkpoint groups:

- /SCWM/RF_FRAME_STEP (Step Flow)
- /SCWM/RF_FRAME_VERIF (Verification Profile)

The technical values of a screen in an RF transaction during testing can be found by pressing [Ctrl]+[Shift]+[F1] or by setting the /SCWM/RF_TECH_TITLE user parameter.

Now that you are familiar with the basic definitions, we will create a new RF transaction in the following sections. This will give you the chance to discover the features of the RF framework while applying them in a simple example.

[»]

New BAdIs to Eliminate Extensive RF Customizing

In SAP S/4HANA 2021, the new /SCWM/ES_RF_CUST enhancement spot was introduced, containing a couple of BAdIs that aim to eliminate potentially extensive RF customizing. Should you want to integrate your own customizing into the RF framework, controlling the step flow, function code profile, or RF subscreen determination, or you would like to use same the RF transaction with different default values or field controls without needing to add or copy customizing, we recommend checking out the BAdIs contained in the enhancement spot. For further details, look at the BAdI and the interface documentation of the included BAdI definitions.

3.3.2   Radio Frequency Framework and the Web Dynpro ABAP Transaction

When using the RF framework, the developer does not add programming logic in the process before output (PBO) or process after input (PAI) Web Dynpro ABAP events. The framework will set up the SAP GUI status with the function codes that are defined in the IMG for the RF transaction. It will look up which screen is to be shown and which function module is to be called for which function code or verification field in the IMG tables (see Figure 3.23).

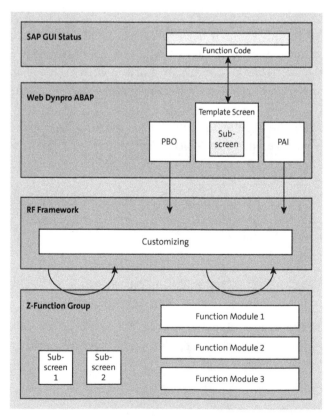

Figure 3.23 Web Dynpro ABAP Interacting with RF Framework

In a new custom function group, you develop the subscreens and the function modules. For each step, you develop the following:

- One subscreen
- One or several function modules (usually one for PBO and several for PAI)
- The customizing for the step flow in the RF framework

Before manually creating the customizing entries in the RF framework, it is helpful to draw a flow chart with the screens, function codes, and function modules. The flow chart in Figure 3.24 shows that for function code INIT, the framework will call the ZPBO_1 function module before displaying the ZB1 screen. In the ZPBO_1 function module, we will add logic to clear and prefill values of screen ZB1. On the ZB1 screen, the user has two application-specific function codes available: ENTER and ZF1. With the ENTER user input, the framework will call the ZPAI_E1 function module to, for example, apply context validation of the user input. If the user wants to finish the transaction, he will use function code ZF1. Function module ZPAI_ZF1 is called and will implement logic to store the application data entered by the users.

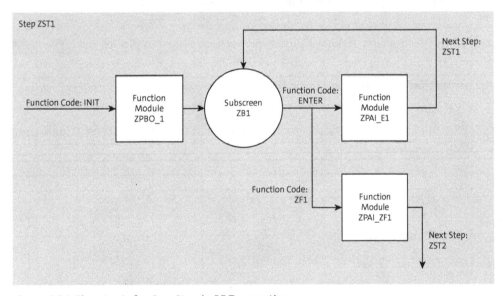

Figure 3.24 Flow Logic for One Step in RF Transaction

You can use the predefined INIT and ENTER function codes. If you have the requirement for more function codes, you can define new ones in the framework, such as ZF1, and link them to function keys. As not every RF device offers all function keys (F1 to F12), you should first check against the hardware that will be used before setting up a function key.

Figure 3.25 shows the necessary step flow Customizing entries required for the flow of the example RF transaction we will build up in Section 3.3.6.

	Define Logical Transaction step flow						
Dialog Structure	Pres. Prof	Log Trans.	Step	Func. Code	Valid.Prof	Function Module	Next Step
🗀 Define Application Parameters	****	ZSORT	ZST1	ENTER	☐	Z_SORT_ZST1_PAI	ZST2
∨🗀 Define Presentation Profiles	****	ZSORT	ZST1	INIT	☐	Z_SORT_ZST1_PBO	
🗀 Define Personalization Profiles	****	ZSORT·	ZST2	ENTER	☑	Z_SORT_ZST2_PAI	
∨🗀 Define Steps	****	ZSORT	ZST2	EXCEPT	☐	Z_SORT_ZST2_EXCEPTIONS	ZST2
🗀 Define States	****	ZSORT	ZST2	HULIST	☐		ZST3
∨🗀 Define Function codes	****	ZSORT	ZST2	INIT	☐	Z_SORT_ZST2_PBO	
🗀 Define Function code text	****	ZSORT	ZST3	ENTER	☐	Z_SORT_ZST3_PAI	ZST2
🗀 Define Validation Objects	****	ZSORT	ZST3	INIT	☐	Z_SORT_ZST3_PBO	
∨🗀 Define Logical Transactions							
🗀 Define Presentation texts							
🗐 Define Logical Transaction step flow							

Figure 3.25 Customizing Entries Required for Step ZST1 from Flow Chart

Furthermore, in the **Map Logical Transaction Step to Subscreen** folder, you have to maintain the ZB1 subscreen for the ZST1 step. For each RF transaction (e.g., ZBOOK1), you have to define one initial step, which is, in this case, ZST1.

3.3.3   Create a New Display Profile

As soon as you know what RF hardware will be used in your project, you can start adjusting the screens to the hardware display size. In our example, we will convert the screens to a display size with 12 lines and 20 columns.

Adjusting the screens requires three steps:

1. Generate a new display profile in the IMG.
2. Adjust the layout of the new Dynpros manually in the screen painter (Transaction SE51), if required.
3. Create a new entry for the presentation device and assign the display profile to it.

Next, we will detail how to run these three steps.

Generate New Display Profile

To generate a new display profile in the IMG, you have to do the following:

1. Start the **RF Screen Manager** IMG activity. On the **Display Profile** tab, you enter the value "**"** in the display profile field (**SrcDispProfile**) and then use the **Copy Profile** button. In the popup, you enter the name of the new display profile (e.g., "H1") and the screen size: "12" for **Screen Height** and "20" for **Screen Width** in this example; see Figure 3.26. Also, the menu item length (**Menu Item Lngth**) must be shortened to, for example, "20".

2. Continue to enter the function group for the template screens (e.g., "ZRF_H1_ TMPL"). The system will generate this function group and will copy the two standard RF template screens into it. The newly created template screens will have the new size but will usually require some manual adjustment.

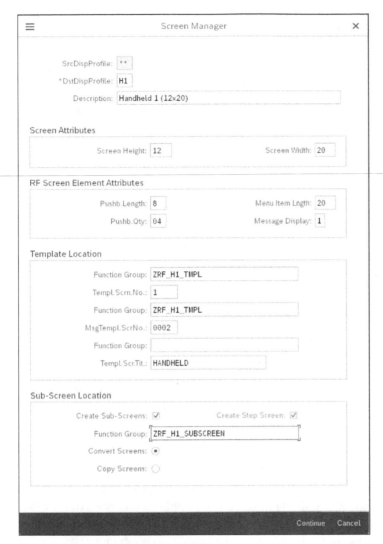

Figure 3.26 Create Display Profile H1

3. In the **Sub-Screen Location** area, you set the **Create Sub-Screens** checkbox and enter a second function group (e.g., "ZRF_H1_SUBSCREEN"). The system will then copy all subscreens found in the RF framework for display profile ** and also convert them to the new size. If the system encounters size conflicts, you will get a success message protocol after you press ⎡Enter⎤.

[«]

Create Sub-Screens Checkbox

If you choose not to set the **Create Sub-Screens** checkbox, you will miss not only the application-specific RF transaction screens but also the general screens for log on, log off, and menu.

4. When the creation is finished, change to the **Screens** tab and enter the new display profile H1. You'll see the newly created Customizing entries for all RF transactions, as shown in Figure 3.27. The traffic light icon for each subscreen will indicate if the conversion worked without any technical conflict. A technical conflict means that the system was not able to copy a field as there was, for example, not enough space on the screen. The system will shorten fields as much as required if the new display profile has less screen space than the template one.

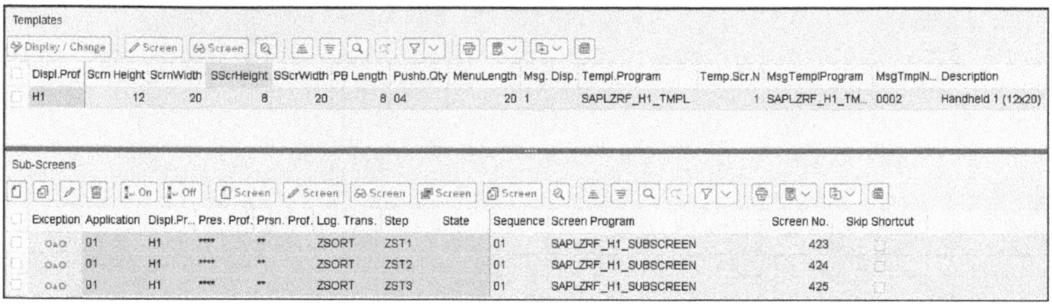

Figure 3.27 RF Framework Entries for New Subscreens

Adjust Layout of the Dynpros

If the space on the screens with the new size is smaller than on the standard screen, it will take some effort to adjust the automatically created screens manually. Many fields (e.g., bin, handling unit) are shortened and hence important information is not displayed to the user. In Figure 3.28 and Figure 3.29, you see the screens before and after manual adjustments.

Start Transaction SE80 and verify the layout of the Dynpros in the screen painter. First start with the template screens 1 and 2 in function group ZRF_H1_TMPL and make sure the generated space for the subscreens is maximized. You might want to move the buttons so that you can increase the number of lines in the subscreen from eight to ten. The subscreens are the screens for the central RF transactions log on ❶ (RFLOGN), log off (RFLOGF), menu ❷ (RFMENU), and list ❸ (RFLIST), which you should verify in the screen painter as well.

The RFMENU subscreen (e.g., screen number ❷ in Figure 3.28) shows six menu entries, as it was on the template screen of display profile **. As you have more lines available now, you can add more menu lines in the screen painter by using the fields of structure /SCWM/S_RF_SCRELM and create more buttons (see Figure 3.29). Make sure you add the value "001" in screen group 003 so that the RF framework can deactivate unused menu lines.

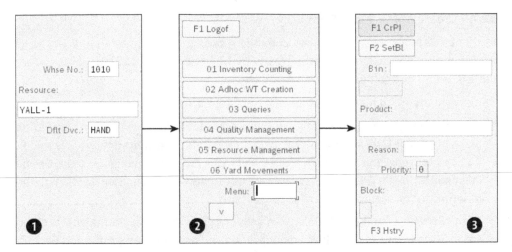

Figure 3.28 RF Screens before Manual Adjustments

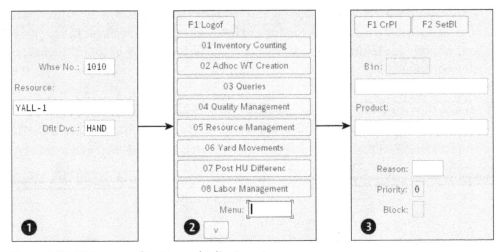

Figure 3.29 RF Screens after Manual Adjustments

Create and Assign New Entry

To use the new display profile H1, go to the SAP menu and start Transaction /SCWM/ PRDVC (Maintain Presentation Devices). Create a new entry, such as "HAND", and assign the display profile H1 to it. If you set the **Default** checkbox, then the logon screen of this display profile will be shown to the users when logging on to RF environment. You can now compare the standard screen size (refer back to Figure 3.21) with the new handheld screen size (see Figure 3.29).

3.3.4   Create a New Radio Frequency Menu

In this section, we show you how to copy the standard RF menu to a project-specific master menu. You should do this step early in the project to avoid adjusting the standard RF menu by adding or deleting menu entries.

To copy the standard menu, the following four steps are required:

1. Create a new presentation and personalization profile. This is done in the **Define Steps in Logical Transactions** IMG activity. In the **Define Presentation Profiles** folder, you create a new entry, such as "P001." Mark this entry and navigate to the **Define Personalization Profiles** folder. There you create a new entry, such as, "MM", with the description "master menu."

2. In the **RF Menu Manager** IMG activity, keep the default values on the entry screen and use the **Copy** function. In the popup, enter the presentation profile and personalization profile from step 1 (e.g., P001 and MM) and continue with ⌜Enter⌟. The system will now display the new RF menu in a tree control on the right side of the screen. On the left side of the screen, you see a list with all possible RF transactions and menu/submenu items. As soon as a new RF transaction is available in your project, you can add it into the master menu. If you already know of some RF transactions or submenus that are not used in the project, you can remove them with the **Delete** button.

3. Assign the new presentation profile (e.g., P001) to the warehouse number used in your project. This is done in IMG activity **Assign Presentation Profile to Warehouse**.

4. In Transaction /SCWM/USER (Maintain Users), assign the new MM menu to users.

Now log onto the RF environment (Transaction /SCWM/RFUI) and verify the new menu structure.

3.3.5   Specification and Design of a New Radio Frequency Transaction

In this section, we will show you how to specify and design a new RF transaction. We will start with a fictitious specification, for a *sort pick handling unit*. A specification should contain the business context and describe the gap in the standard software. Make sure you mention the straightforward case first and list the exceptions separately. This will ensure that the design of the RF transaction can focus on the main use case with regard to usability.

RF transactions support highly specialized work steps in the warehouse, which means each RF transaction usually fits one specific task. If you develop an RF transaction with too many options and screens, keep in mind that it might become difficult for end users to use, or it may require special training.

Specification: Sort Pick Handling Unit

This fictitious specification for a sort pick handling unit might have the following description in the blueprint:

- **Process**

  Goods issue for small parts.

- **Context**

  A forklift moves the pick handling units to the *mixed handling unit* staging bin after finishing the multiorder picking tour. A user at this staging bin scans each item of the pick handling unit and repacks and sorts the items into the ship handling unit of the corresponding customer. The user repeats this step until all items of the pick handling unit are repacked into the corresponding ship handling units.

- **Custom development**

  For this repack step, a new RF transaction is required. The straightforward case (~80%) will run in the system as follows:

  - On the entry screen (subscreen 1), the user scans the picking label barcode, and the system will identify the item that needs to be repacked.

  - On the second screen (subscreen 2), the system will display the product name, product description, consolidation group, and quantity, which were identified by the barcode. This way, the user can check if the system identified the right stock and if the item in his hand matches the system data.

  - The user scans the ship handling unit on the second screen, and the system will check if the item is allowed into this ship handling unit (by checking the consolidation group). If it is allowed, the system will repack the item into the ship handling unit and navigate to screen 1 such that the user can scan the next item.

The following exceptions can occur and must be handled by the system:

- The forklift driver forgot to confirm the pick handling unit and the user at packing got the **Open Warehouse Task Exists** error message after scanning the first barcode of this pick handling unit. As this will happen rarely (estimation is < 1%), the user will be trained to use standard RF Transaction WKMNHU (Manual Selection by Handling Unit) to confirm the open task.

- The user scans a wrong ship handling unit. The system issues the **Consolidation group not matching** error message and clears the handling unit field.

- If the user decides that the pick handling unit is full, the user will use standard RF Transaction PAHUCH (Maintain Handling Unit) to close the handling unit. The final ship handling unit label with the ship-to address and weight is printed by the system.

- The user will use the standard RF Transaction PAHUCS (Create Shipping Handling Unit) to create new ship handling units. At this point, the system prints a preliminary handling unit label, which contains just the barcode of the handling unit and the consolidation group.

Design

For the design, we recommend creating the screens first as a mock-up, such as in Word or Excel (see Figure 3.30). Due to the small screen size, there are many restrictions that may impact the process or usability. Include the business key user in the design and simulate the workflow with the mock-ups as much as possible.

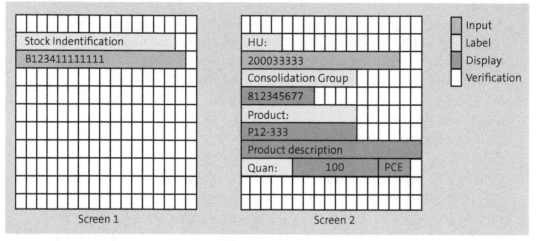

Figure 3.30 Mock-Up of New RF Screens

To define the flow logic of the required function codes and function modules, first create a flow chart (see Figure 3.31). The user starts in the RF menu, with the new RF Transaction ZSORT. This consists of two steps, ZST1 and ZST2, each assigned to one subscreen.

For the starting step, ZST1, the function code INIT is used to handle the event PBO with function module Z_SORT_ZST1_PBO. This function module will initialize the values on screen 1. When the user confirms the input on screen 1 by pressing [Enter], the Z_SORT_ZST1_PAI function module will be called by the framework. It will verify the input and if, for example, the barcode can't be decoded by the system, an error message will occur on screen 1.

If no error occurs, the framework will continue with step ZST2 and call the Z_SORT_ZST2_PBO function module for function code INIT of screen 2. The user scans the handling unit barcode and, after the user presses [Enter], the PAI event is triggered. The framework will call function module Z_SORT_ZST2_PAI and verify the input. If the handling unit is accepted, the system will update the database, and with function code CMPTRS (complete transaction), the RF transaction is finished and will automatically restart. On both screens, the user can navigate back with function key [F7] (function code BACK). With the flow chart, it will be easier to do the required Customizing entries in the RF framework.

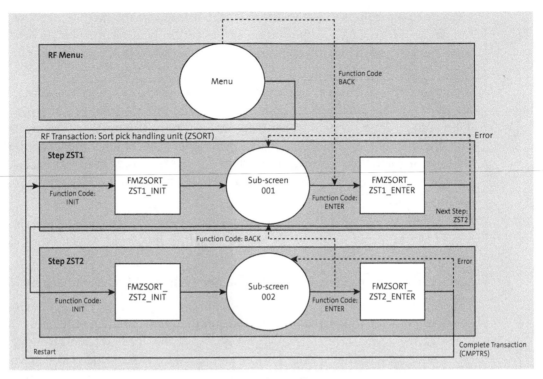

Figure 3.31 Flow Chart for RF Transaction Sort Pick Handling Unit

3.3.6 Realization of the New Radio Frequency Transaction in the System

The realization of the new RF transaction can be done in two phases:

- In phase A, you create the RF transaction with all its RF framework Customizing and empty function modules/screens.
- In phase B, you add the business logic in the function modules.

If your project requires several new RF transactions, you can split the work so that one developer is focusing on the RF framework and does the tasks described in phase A. The application developer can then focus on the business logic in phase B and will not necessarily have to have detailed knowledge of the RF framework.

In the following step-by-step description of the realization, we refer to the display profile H1 of Section 3.3.3 and the specified Sort Pick Handling Unit RF transaction of Section 3.3.5.

Phase A: Realization of the Empty Transaction in the Radio Frequency Framework

There are five steps to complete in this phase:

1. Create a new function group, such as ZRF_SORT, in Transaction SE80. Create four function modules: Z_SORT_ZST1_PBO, Z_SORT_ZST1_PAI, Z_SORT_ZST2_PBO, and Z_SORT_ZST2_PAI.

Navigate to the main SAPLZRF_SORT program and insert the /SCWM/IRF_SSCR RF framework include. No coding is required within the function modules at this point in time; however, if you add a breakpoint into the empty function modules, you can test the navigation easily later.

2. Within the ZRF_SORT function group, you create two screens, 0001 and 0002. Change the screen type to **Subscreen** for both screens. In the **Other Attributes • Lines/Columns** section, enter "10" in the **Lines** field and "20" in the **Column** field if you work with display profile H1. Navigate to the layout (screen painter) and for now just put one label on each of the screens, such as "Screen 1" and "Screen 2." On the **Flow Logic** tab, add one line to call the status_sscr module in the PBO and one line in the PAI to call the user_command_sscr module.

3. In the Customizing of the RF framework, create the entries for the new RF Transaction ZSORT. This step is quite tricky, and you will find all necessary details for this step in the following section.

4. Add the new RF transaction to the RF menu. See Section 3.3.4, step 2 for details on how to do that.

5. Log onto the RF environment and start the new RF transaction. Navigate between the two screens with the ⌈Enter⌋ and ⌈F7⌋ keys. Verify that the flow logic is working, as shown in Figure 3.32. When starting the transaction from the RF menu ❶, you will first see a screen with the text **Screen 1** ❷. With ⌈Enter⌋, you will move to a screen with the text **Screen 2** ❸. Pressing ⌈Enter⌋ again will make the system restart the transaction and you will see a screen with the text **Screen 1**. With the ⌈F7⌋ function key, you can go back to the menu.

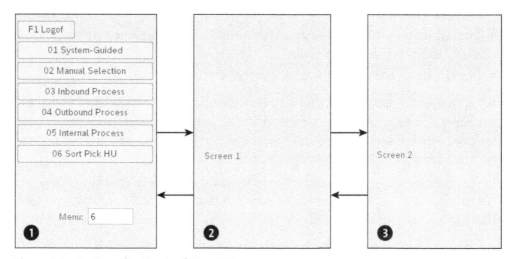

Figure 3.32 Testing Flow Logic of New RF Transaction

With the successful test of all function codes in the RF environment, phase A is completed.

Create Customizing Entries

To create the necessary Customizing entries for the new RF transaction, complete the following steps:

1. Start the **Define Steps in Logical Transactions** IMG activity. Create two new entries in the **Define Steps** folder: ZST1 and ZST2.

2. In the **Define Logical Transactions** folder, create one new entry: ZSORT. Enter a description, and in the **Initial Step** field, enter "ZST1". Save and mark the new entry before further setup.

3. In the **Define Presentation Texts** folder, define the description in all project-relevant languages (see Table 3.5). If you work with more than one display profile, which differ in the length of their menus, then you have to maintain the description by length and language. Keep in mind that even if the screen has twenty columns, the framework will require two columns to generate the menu number into the displayed text.

Language	Presentation Profile	Personalization Profile	Size	Presentation Text
EN	****	**	20	Sort Pick Handling Unit
EN	****	**	40	Sort Picking Handling Unit
DE	****	**	20	Pick-HU sortieren

Table 3.5 Entries in Define Presentation Texts Folder

4. In the **Define Inter-Transaction Flow** folder, create a new entry for logical Transaction ZSORT (see Table 3.6), and in the **Default Navigation** field, choose option **3— Same Transaction**. This option is recommended if the user will work in the same transaction more or less all day.

Presentation Profile	Personalization Profile	Logical Transaction	Default Navigation
****	**	ZSORT	3—Same Transaction

Table 3.6 Entry in Define Inter-Transaction Flow Folder

5. In the **Map Logical Transaction Step to Sub-Screen** folder, create two new entries in Customizing for the two new screens (see Table 3.7), as follows:
   - **Application**: Always enter "01" for EWM.
   - **Presentation and personalization profile**: Define your new transaction for template profiles **** and **.
   - **Display profile**: Enter the display profile H1.
   - **State**: Always enter the template value ******.
   - **Screen sequence**: Always put the value "01".

Application, Presen-tation, and Personal-ization Profile	Display Profile	Logical Transaction	Step, State, Sequence	Program and Screen Number
01,****,**	H1	ZSORT	ZST1, ******,01	SAPLZRF_SORT, 1
01,****,**	H1	ZSORT	ZST2, ******,01	SAPLZRF_SORT, 2

Table 3.7 Assign Subscreens to Steps

6. In the **Define Function Code Profile** folder, create four new entries with the values of Table 3.8. The key fields that are not displayed in the table are fixed:
   - **Presentation profile:** ****
   - **Personalization profile:** **
   - **Push button quantity:** **
   - **Number of function keys:** **
   - **Logical transaction:** "ZSORT"
   - **State:** *******
   - **Screen sequence:** "01"

Step	Function Code Group	Function Code	Function Key
******	01	ENTER	[ENT]
******	01	BACK	[F7]
******	01	FULLMS	[F9]
******	01	CLEAR	[F6]

Table 3.8 Entries in Define Function Code Profile Folder

7. As you maintain value ****** in the **STEP** field, the function codes apply to all steps of this logical transaction.

[+]

Use Standard Function Codes

As all other RF transactions use function key [F7] for function code BACK, you should do the same in a new RF transaction. The same applies for function codes FULLMS and CLEAR. Add them to your new RF transaction, as the user will need these sooner or later:

- [F9] **(FULLMS)**
  A user can look up the full text of an error message.
- [F6] **(CLEAR)**
  A user can clear the current input field or, if using it twice, it will clear all input fields on this particular screen.

8. In the **Define Logical Transaction Step Flow** folder, create four new entries for presentation profile **** and logical RF Transaction ZSORT; see Table 3.9. All entries must match to the flow chart (see Figure 3.31).

For step ZST2 and function code ENTER, we will set the **Processing Mode** to 0 (defined during execution), as we want the developer to decide if the transaction can be completed or not.

Step	Function Code	Function Module	Next Step	Processing Mode and Background Function Code
ZST1	INIT	Z_SORT_ZST1_PBO		2—Foreground
ZST1	ENTER	Z_SORT_ZST1_PAI	ZST2	1—Background, INIT
ZST2	INIT	Z_SORT_ZST2_PBO		2—Foreground
ZST2	ENTER	Z_SORT_ZST2_PAI		0—Defined during execution, CMPTRS

Table 3.9 Entries in Define Logical Transaction Step Flow Folder

Phase B: Develop the Business Logic

Phase B is structured into five steps:

1. Create a new application parameter in ABAP Dictionary and in the RF framework.
2. Design the layout of the two new subscreens by using the fields of the new application parameter.
3. Create a new checkpoint group, ZEWMDEVBOOK_336, in Transaction SAAB and switch the **Break** option on.
4. Add the application parameter in the interface of the four new function modules and add the business logic:
   - TOP include of function group ZRF_SORT (see Listing 3.4)
   - Function module Z_SORT_ZST1_PBO (see Listing 3.5)
   - Function module Z_SORT_ZST1_PAI (see Listing 3.6)
   - Function module Z_SORT_ZST2_PBO (see Listing 3.7)
   - Function module Z_SORT_ZST2_PAI (see Listing 3.8)

   The coding examples you find at the end of each step give details.
5. Test your new RF transaction in the RF environment with some test data.

The details of these five steps are discussed in the following sections.

Create New ABAP Structure

Create a new ABAP structure, ZRF_SORT, in ABAP Dictionary (Transaction SE11) with the fields listed in Table 3.10. Some of the fields (e.g., IDPLATE, RFHU) will be used to display info on the screens; other fields (e.g., SOURCE_HU, GUID_STOCK) are used internally for processing the data.

Component	Component Type	Use
IDPLATE	/SCWM/DE_RF_IDPLATE	Subscreen 1, input field
RFHU	/SCWM/DE_RF_RFHU_LONG	Subscreen 2, input field
DSTGRP	/SCWM/DE_RF_DSTGRP	Subscreen 2, output field
MATNR	/SCWM/DE_RF_MATNR	Subscreen 2, output field
MAKTX	/SCWM/DE_RF_MAKTX	Subscreen 2, output field
VSOLA	/SCWM/DE_RF_VSOLA	Subscreen 2, output field
ALTME	/SCWM/DE_RF_ALTME	Subscreen 2, output field
LGNUM	/SCWM/LGNUM	Internal
SOURCE_HU	/SCWM/GUID_HU	Internal
GUID_STOCK	/LIME/GUID_STOCK	Internal

Table 3.10 Fields of ABAP Structure ZRF_SORT

In the IMG activity **EWM • Mobile Data Entry • Radio Frequency (RF) Framework • Define Steps in Logical Transactions**, go to the **Define Application Parameters** folder and create a new entry for parameter ZSORT. In the **Parameter Type** field, enter the structure name, "ZRF_SORT".

Barcode Fields in Radio Frequency

If you want to use an input field for scanning a barcode (e.g., handling unit), try to reuse the existing standard fields. The RFHU field is used in many RF transactions for scanning the handling unit barcode. It is longer (50 characters) than the handling unit identification (20 characters), and furthermore, the RFHUL conversion exit is linked to this field. Hence the RF framework will automatically decode the barcode using, for example, the EAN128 specification maintained in Customizing, so a prefix specified in EAN128 will be removed from the user input and the handling unit identification will be handed over to the application.

Add New Fields to Subscreens

Add the new fields to the subscreens by using the graphical screen painter in ABAP Object Navigator (Transaction SE80). Start with subscreen 1 and use the **Dictionary/Program Fields Window** F6 button to import fields of structure ZRF_SORT. Place field IDPLATE onto screen 1.

For screen 2, place fields RFHU, DSTGRP, and so on onto the screen. See Figure 3.9, where the **Use** column shows subscreen 2, and see Figure 3.30 for layout details.

Save and activate both screens.

If you want to test your application in ITSmobile later on, not in SAP GUI, you also have to create the HTML templates for the new screens.

Call Packing Logic

In the example coding, we are using the /SCWM/CL_WM_PACKING service class for repacking the item from the pick handling unit into the ship handling unit. These service class methods provided by the standard take care of the locking (check this in Transaction SM12). We want to make sure that several users can work on the same pick handling unit at the same time (but on different items only) and that only one user can pack something into the ship handling unit. You can verify the locking logic in Transaction SM12.

Test New Transaction

To test the RF transaction, you need to prepare a pick handling unit for one or several outbound deliveries and apply multiorder picking. Each item in the pick handling unit must have a stock identification, which usually consists of the concatenation of warehouse number and warehouse task. This item label was printed during picking and can now be scanned by the user. Next, you prepare empty ship handling units (one for each customer) at the packing station, and then you are ready to test the RF transaction.

Log onto the RF environment and choose the **Sort Pick HU** transaction from the menu. If you are testing in SAP GUI and without the hardware device, try to simulate the handling by not using the mouse. The warehouse worker later on will not have a mouse either. Check that the system automatically focuses on the right input field, type in the barcode, and press [Enter] after each input (see Figure 3.33). Select RF transaction **06** and press [Enter] ❶. If you type in a feasible stock identification, you will make it to the second screen ❷. The display fields for the product, consolidation group, and quantity are prefilled for display.

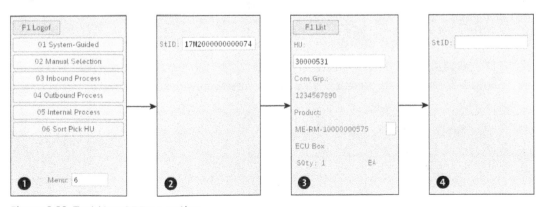

Figure 3.33 Test New RF Transaction

The user can verify the product and quantity and choose the right destination handling unit by comparing the consolidation group ❸. With the next press of ⌷Enter⌷ after the handling unit barcode, the system will repack the stock and the transaction restarts ❹. For monitoring the repacking, you might use the work center (Transaction /SCWM/ PACK) and refresh the display after each scan in RF. You can also look up the stock identification of an item at the work center.

Do not forget to test the exceptions; for example, try typing in a wrong stock identification or a wrong handling unit. The system should respond with an error message.

[»]

Success, Warning, and Error Messages in Radio Frequency

After a successful repack, the system does not give a success message. This is quite different from the usual desktop transactions. Not giving success messages is part of the EWM RF philosophy, as this might be annoying for the user. If a user in our example does 200 repacks per hour, a success message would be quite superfluous. However, an error message, which is only displayed, might get overlooked by the user. Most mobile devices are able to give a sound or vibration signal. You can set up EWM to send success or error sound values (e.g., 1 = error, 2 = success) to the mobile device in Transaction /SCWM/PRDVC (Maintain Presentation Devices). However, this error sound value must be translated by the CSS in the web browser so that a sound file on the hardware is played.

In some applications where fast scanning is done (e.g., loading), you might add a success message (with a small sound) so that the user is aware when the system is ready for the next scan.

In the following listings, you will find the coding for the four function modules. Start with the coding required in the TOP include of the function group (see Listing 3.4).

```
FUNCTION-POOL zrf_sort.
TYPE-POOLS: wmegc.
DATA: go_pack TYPE REF TO /scwm/cl_wm_packing,
      go_stock TYPE REF TO /scwm/cl_ui_stock_fields.
```

Listing 3.4 Global Parameters in Function Group

Then enter the coding for function module Z_SORT_ZST1_PBO (see Listing 3.5), which will run before displaying screen 1. It will initialize the required objects and clear the screen field.

```
FUNCTION z_sort_zst1_pbo.
*"----------------------------------------------------------------------
*"*"Local Interface:
*"  CHANGING
*"     REFERENCE(ZSORT) TYPE  ZRF_SORT
```

```
*"------------------------------------------------------------------
  DATA: ls_rsrc TYPE /scwm/rsrc.

  BREAK-POINT ID zewmdevbook_336.

  "1. Init the work area
  CLEAR zsort.
  "Get warehouse number of this resource
  CALL FUNCTION '/SCWM/RSRC_RESOURCE_MEMORY'
    EXPORTING
      iv_uname = sy-uname
    CHANGING
      cs_rsrc  = ls_rsrc.
  zsort-lgnum = ls_rsrc-lgnum.

  "2. Init packing & transaction manager
  /scwm/cl_tm=>set_lgnum( iv_lgnum = zsort-lgnum ).
  IF go_pack IS NOT BOUND.
    go_pack = NEW /scwm/cl_wm_packing( ).
  ENDIF.
  DATA(ls_pack_controle) = VALUE /scwm/s_pack_controle(
    cdstgrp_mat    = abap_true "take over cons.group
    chkpack_dstgrp = '2' "check while repack products
    processor_det  = abap_true ).
  go_pack->init(
    EXPORTING
      iv_lgnum         = zsort-lgnum
      is_pack_controle = ls_pack_controle
    EXCEPTIONS
      error            = 1
      OTHERS           = 2 ).
  IF sy-subrc <> 0.
    /scwm/cl_pack_view=>msg_error( ).
  ENDIF.

  "3. Init stock-ui
  IF go_stock IS INITIAL.
    CREATE OBJECT go_stock.
  ENDIF.

ENDFUNCTION.
```

Listing 3.5 Interface and Coding for Function Module Z_SORT_ZST1_PBO

Now implement the Z_SORT_ZST1_PAI function module, which is called after the user scans a barcode into the input field of screen 1; see Listing 3.6. The system will validate if the user input is feasible (see comments "1 and "2) and checks if there are open warehouse tasks for the source handling unit (see comment "3). Then the system will hand over the values into structure ZSORT for further processing on the next screen (see comment "4).

```
FUNCTION z_sort_zst1_pai.
*"----------------------------------------------------------------------
*"*"Local Interface:
*"  CHANGING
*"     REFERENCE(ZSORT) TYPE  ZRF_SORT
*"----------------------------------------------------------------------
  DATA: lt_rng_idplate TYPE rseloption,
        lt_huitm       TYPE /scwm/tt_huitm_int,
        lv_lines       TYPE sy-tabix,
        lv_open_to     TYPE xfeld.

  BREAK-POINT ID zewmdevbook_336.

  "1. Validation of user input
  CLEAR: zsort-source_hu, zsort-guid_stock.
  IF zsort-idplate IS INITIAL.
    MESSAGE 'Enter a stock identification' TYPE wmegc_severity_err.
  ENDIF.
  "2. Check if ID is a valid stock identification
  DATA(ls_rng_idplate) = VALUE rsdsselopt(
    low    = zsort-idplate
    sign   = wmegc_sign_inclusive
    option = wmegc_option_eq ).
  APPEND ls_rng_idplate TO lt_rng_idplate.

  CALL FUNCTION '/SCWM/HU_SELECT_QUAN'
    EXPORTING
      iv_lgnum   = zsort-lgnum
      ir_idplate = lt_rng_idplate
    IMPORTING
      et_huitm   = lt_huitm
    EXCEPTIONS
      OTHERS     = 99.
  DELETE lt_huitm WHERE vsi <> wmegc_physical_stock.
  TRY.
      DATA(ls_huitm) = VALUE #( lt_huitm[ idplate = zsort-idplate ] ).
    CATCH cx_sy_itab_line_not_found.
```

```
      CLEAR zsort-idplate.
      MESSAGE 'Stock Identification not found' TYPE wmegc_severity_err.
      RETURN.
  ENDTRY.
  "3. Validations
  CALL FUNCTION '/SCWM/CHECK_OPEN_TO'
    EXPORTING
      iv_hu    = ls_huitm-guid_parent
      iv_lgnum = zsort-lgnum
    IMPORTING
      ev_exist = lv_open_to
    EXCEPTIONS
      OTHERS   = 99.
  IF sy-subrc <> 0.
    MESSAGE ID sy-msgid TYPE sy-msgty NUMBER sy-msgno
    WITH sy-msgv1 sy-msgv2 sy-msgv3 sy-msgv4.
  ENDIF.
  IF lv_open_to IS NOT INITIAL.
    MESSAGE 'Open Task exists for pick-HU' TYPE wmegc_severity_err.
  ENDIF.
  "4. Set technical fields in RF application
  zsort-source_hu  = ls_huitm-guid_parent.
  zsort-guid_stock = ls_huitm-guid_stock.

ENDFUNCTION.
```

Listing 3.6 Interface and Coding for Function Module Z_SORT_ZST1_PAI

Before displaying screen 2, the RF framework will call function module Z_SORT_ZST2_PBO and run the coding (see Listing 3.7). The system will read the values that are displayed on the screen (see comment "1) and set them to the ZSORT handover structure (see comment "2).

```
FUNCTION z_sort_zst2_pbo.
*"----------------------------------------------------------------------
*"*"Local Interface:
*"  CHANGING
*"     REFERENCE(ZSORT) TYPE  ZRF_SORT
*"----------------------------------------------------------------------

  BREAK-POINT ID zewmdevbook_336.

  "1. Get item details
  go_pack->get_hu_item(
    EXPORTING
```

```
      iv_guid_hu    = zsort-source_hu
      iv_guid_stock = zsort-guid_stock
    IMPORTING
      es_huitm = DATA(ls_huitm)
    EXCEPTIONS
      OTHERS = 99 ).
  IF sy-subrc <> 0. "technical error
    MESSAGE ID sy-msgid TYPE sy-msgty NUMBER sy-msgno
    WITH sy-msgv1 sy-msgv2 sy-msgv3 sy-msgv4.
  ENDIF.
  "2. Set application screen fields
  zsort-dstgrp = ls_huitm-dstgrp.
  zsort-vsola  = ls_huitm-quana.
  zsort-altme  = ls_huitm-altme.
  CALL METHOD go_stock->get_matkey_by_id
    EXPORTING
      iv_matid = ls_huitm-matid
    IMPORTING
      ev_matnr = zsort-matnr
      ev_maktx = zsort-maktx.

ENDFUNCTION.
```

Listing 3.7 Interface and Coding for Function Module Z_SORT_ZST2_PBO

Last but not least, enter the coding for the Z_SORT_ZST2_PAI function module (see List-ing 3.8). The function module will check if the user scanned a feasible ship handling unit (see comments "1 and "2) and if so, it will repack the item from the pick handling unit into the ship handling unit (see comment "3). Then a save will commit everything to the database (see comment "4).

```
FUNCTION z_sort_zst2_pai.
*"----------------------------------------------------------------------
*"*"Local Interface:
*"  CHANGING
*"     REFERENCE(ZSORT) TYPE  ZRF_SORT
*"----------------------------------------------------------------------

  BREAK-POINT ID zewmdevbook_336.

  "0. Stay on this screen (default)
  /scwm/cl_rf_bll_srvc=>set_prmod(
  /scwm/cl_rf_bll_srvc=>c_prmod_foreground ).
  "1. Validation of user input
  IF zsort-rfhu IS INITIAL.
```

```abap
    MESSAGE 'Enter Handling Unit' TYPE wmegc_severity_err.
ENDIF.
"2. Get destination handling unit
go_pack->get_hu(
  EXPORTING
    iv_huident = CONV #( zsort-rfhu )
  IMPORTING
    es_huhdr   = DATA(ls_dest_hu)
  EXCEPTIONS
    OTHERS = 99 ).
IF sy-subrc <> 0.
  CLEAR zsort-rfhu. "Scanning Error
  MESSAGE ID sy-msgid TYPE sy-msgty NUMBER sy-msgno
  WITH sy-msgv1 sy-msgv2 sy-msgv3 sy-msgv4.
ENDIF.
IF ls_dest_hu-copst IS NOT INITIAL.
  MESSAGE 'HU is closed' TYPE wmegc_severity_err.
ENDIF.
"3. Repack item into  dest. handling unit
DATA(ls_quan) = VALUE /scwm/s_quan( quan = zsort-vsola
                                    unit = zsort-altme ).

go_pack->repack_stock(
  EXPORTING
    iv_dest_hu    = ls_dest_hu-guid_hu
    iv_source_hu  = zsort-source_hu
    iv_stock_guid = zsort-guid_stock
    is_quantity   = ls_quan
  EXCEPTIONS
    OTHERS = 99 ).
IF sy-subrc <> 0.
  MESSAGE ID sy-msgid TYPE sy-msgty NUMBER sy-msgno
  WITH sy-msgv1 sy-msgv2 sy-msgv3 sy-msgv4.
ENDIF.
"4. Save
go_pack->/scwm/if_pack_bas~save(
  EXPORTING
    iv_commit = abap_true
    iv_wait   = abap_true
  EXCEPTIONS
    OTHERS = 99 ).
IF sy-subrc <> 0.
  ROLLBACK WORK.
  /scwm/cl_tm=>cleanup( ).
  MESSAGE ID sy-msgid TYPE sy-msgty NUMBER sy-msgno
```

```
  WITH sy-msgv1 sy-msgv2 sy-msgv3 sy-msgv4.
 ENDIF.
 "5. Navigate to the transaction end
 /scwm/cl_rf_bll_srvc=>set_prmod(
    /scwm/cl_rf_bll_srvc=>c_prmod_background ).
```

ENDFUNCTION.

Listing 3.8 Interface and Coding for Function Module Z_SORT_ZST2_PAI

3.3.7   Realization of a Verification Profile

In this section, we want to introduce validation objects and validation profiles. We will also enhance RF Transaction ZSORT with a validation profile.

Validation Object

A *validation object* in the RF framework usually consists of a display field and a (single-character) input field. In Figure 3.34, you see a screen where the user gets the information concerning which bin is the next destination (display field with value 021.01.06.02). Besides this display field, the single-character field is open for input. It is the verification field where the user scans the barcode from the rack. Due to space restrictions, the verification field only uses one character. However, it is scrollable, and the scanned barcode (e.g., 021010602) will fit into it. The system will validate the input with the corresponding display field, and if it is not an exact match, a validation function module is called to, for example, allow a barcode without the hyphen to match the bin with a hyphen.

In our example, this is the /SCWM/RF_PICK_BIN_CHECK function module. If the input is accepted by the system, the field is set to display and the focus will move to the next input field, such as the quantity. Here the quantity verification field (**AQty**) is several characters long as we expect the user to type in a value with the help of the keyboard rather than scanning a barcode.

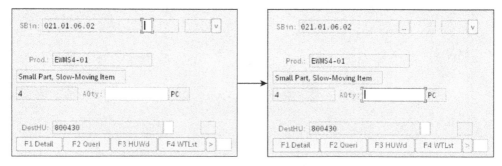

Figure 3.34 Validation Objects for Bin and Quantity

The goal of validation objects is to increase quality in the warehouse concerning the stock situation and to check that the user is taking or bringing stock to the correct bin. However, the more the user has to validate, the more time is required to perform the task in the system. So, for example, instead of having the user verify the source handling unit and the product with two scans, only make him verify the product with one scan. If 3,000 picks are performed each day in a warehouse, then this means there are only 3,000 scans instead of 6,000 scans.

If the user scans a wrong barcode, the RF framework will give an error and automatically clear the field. If the scanned barcode contains an application identifier of a GS1 barcode, the RF framework will decode it in the most common cases. So if, for example, an SSCC barcode contains the string [FNC1]00123456780000000001, the RF framework will translate it into 123456780000000001, for which EWM can find a handling unit using function module /SCWM/RF_EAN128_SPLIT_VALID.

Validation Profile

For each RF transaction, you can set up a validation profile with a list of validation objects per step. For each validation object, the framework will call the specified function modules. The RF framework starts searching for an entry in the validation profile with the full key (display profile, personalization profile, logical transaction, and step). If an entry for the full key is not found, the RF framework will use special wildcard logic to determine an entry: presentation profile is set to **, personalization profile is set to ****, and for the logical transactions, wildcards XX****, XXXX**, and ****** are used. If you want to check out the details, look up the /SCWM/CL_RF_BLL_DB=>VALID_PRF_GET method.

Enhance Radio Frequency Transaction ZSORT with a Validation Object

In RF Transaction ZRF_SORT, we now want to add verification for the field product. We are assuming here that each product in our project warehouse has a barcode attached to it. Usually, the manufacturing department does this labeling as a part of the production step. To increase the quality, we want the user to scan the product barcode and the picking label stock identification.

The goal of this exercise is to illustrate how you set up validation objects in the RF framework. The following five steps are required for this exercise:

1. Enhance the ZRF_SORT structure in ABAP Dictionary (Transaction SE11) with the MATNR_VERIF field using data element /SCWM/DE_RF_MATNR_VERIF.

2. Start the screen painter for screen 2 in the ZRF_SORT function group. Add the new MATNR_VERIF field right beside the MATNR field. Add the attributes of the MATNR_VERIF field as displayed in Figure 3.35:
   - **Scrollable** = yes
   - Third **Group** field = 002
   - **Vis.Length** (visible length) = 1

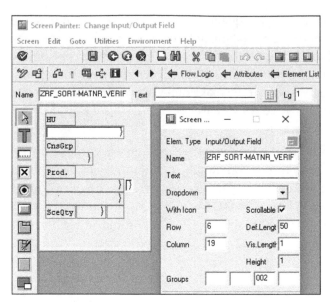

Figure 3.35 Screen Painter Attributes for Verification Field MATNR_VERIF

The value 002 in the third group field will make the RF framework recognize that this is a validation field. The RF framework will make sure that the field is open for input before and closed for input after validation.

3. Start the **Define Steps in Logical Transactions** IMG activity. In the **Define Validation Objects** folder, you will find an existing MATNR entry for the product field. In a custom project, you might add a new object here if none of the standard objects fit.

4. Select the new RF Transaction ZSORT and move to folder **Define Validation Profile**. Here you create one entry with the following values:

   - **Presentation profile**: ****
   - **Personalization profile**: **
   - **Logical transaction**: ZSORT
   - **Step**: ZST2
   - **State**: ******
   - **Validation object**: MATNR
   - **Application parameter**: ZSORT
   - **Validation input field**: MATNR_VERIF
   - **Validation value field**: MATNR
   - **Checkbox verification field**: yes

5. In the **Define Logical Transaction Step Flow** folder, you have to set the **Validation Profile** checkbox for step ZST2 and function code ENTER. With this checkbox, the RF framework will first focus on the validation fields and then interrupt the user with an error message if verification fails.

Now test RF Transaction ZSORT again (see Figure 3.36) and check out the verification field. The difference in the solution without the verification field is that the system will not let you confirm the repacking unless you scanned the product.

Figure 3.36 Verification of Product

If you want the system to allow the scan of EAN/UPC barcodes, you have to enter a function module for verification in the verification profile. Examples include function module /SCWM/RF_MATNR_VALID or /SCWM/RF_PICK_MATID_CHECK.

3.3.8 Value Helps in Radio Frequency with Function Key F8

Value helps in the RF framework are different than those in an SAP GUI desktop transaction or web browser. In a desktop transaction, a field can have a value help with a function key [F4], or it can have a dropdown list. A web browser typically works with dropdown lists. In the early years of RF devices, screens were not touchscreens and hence the RF framework solution is linked to a function key [F8] for value help (see Figure 3.37). If the user presses [F8] ❶, the RF framework will check if a value help is defined for the field that is in focus (see, for example, the **Resource** field on the logon screen in Figure 3.37). The framework will display all defined values for this field in a list screen, and the user can choose an entry by typing in a sequence number (e.g., the value "1" if the second entry in the list is to be chosen, as shown in Figure 3.37 ❷). Pressing [Enter] will show the next screen ❸.

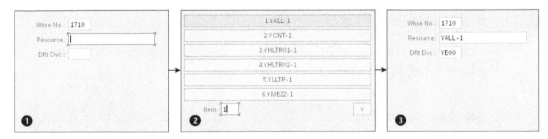

Figure 3.37 Value Help for Resource Field

To add a value help to your own RF screens, you just have to call two framework methods in the PBO function module. Then the RF framework will display the values on the framework screen and also return the chosen value to the input field.

First you call method /SCWM/CL_RF_BLL_SRVC=>INIT_LISTBOX, where you pass the name of the field. In a loop and with method /SCWM/CL_RF_BLL_SRVC=>INSERT_LISTBOX, you hand over all allowed values to the framework.

Examples can be found in the RF transaction for log on (RFMAIN, step RFLOGN, function code INIT). The /SCWM/RSRC_USER_DEF_SET_GET PBO function module will create the value help for the resource (see form resource_listbox_fill in Listing 3.9).

```
FORM resource_listbox_fill
  USING    value(iv_lgnum)  TYPE /scwm/lgnum.

 CONSTANTS cc_fieldname TYPE fieldname
             VALUE '/SCWM/S_RSRC-RSRC'.
 FIELD-SYMBOLS <ls_rsrc> TYPE /scwm/rsrc.
 DATA         lv_char40_val TYPE /scwm/de_rf_text.
 DATA         lt_rsrc TYPE  TABLE OF /scwm/rsrc.


 /scwm/cl_rf_bll_srvc=>init_listbox( cc_fieldname ).
 SELECT * FROM /scwm/rsrc INTO TABLE lt_rsrc
       WHERE lgnum = iv_lgnum.
       CHECK sy-dbcnt IS NOT INITIAL.

* Pass the listbox values to the framework
  LOOP AT lt_rsrc ASSIGNING <ls_rsrc>.
     lv_char40_val = <ls_rsrc>-rsrc.
     /scwm/cl_rf_bll_srvc=>insert_listbox(
              iv_fieldname = cc_fieldname
              iv_value = lv_char40_val ).
  ENDLOOP.
**----

ENDFORM.                    " resource_listbox_fill
```

Listing 3.9 Prepare Value Help for Resource

As a last step, you have to add the function code LIST [F8] in your function code profile in the RF framework Customizing settings.

3.3.9   Realization of Lists

Lists in the RF framework differ from the value help, as they show more columns and hence provide more information. Depending on the screen size, lists usually show two or three columns.

In this section, we will continue with the ZSORT exercise and add a list of possible ship handling units. This way, the user can use the list to look up all open ship handling units in his work area for this customer. Besides the handling unit number, the list will also show the handling unit type (carton, pallet, etc.).

This enhancement consists of three steps:

1. Create a new subscreen for the handling unit list.
2. Create two new function modules for the processing before and after the list.
3. Add some Customizing entries for the new ZST3 step such that the framework can call the new screen and function modules.

The details of these three steps are given in the following sections.

Create a New Subscreen

We want to have the **Handling Unit Identification** and **HU Type** columns on the new screen. Furthermore, the first column will show a line sequence number such that the user later can easily choose a line by typing in the sequence number.

To make this step easier, we will copy an existing list screen 0201 from function group /SCWM/RF_INQUIRY to our function group zrf_sort and also reuse the inquiry structure. This can be done in the ABAP Object Navigator (Transaction SE80). With this copy approach, we just need to adjust the columns, as shown in Figure 3.38.

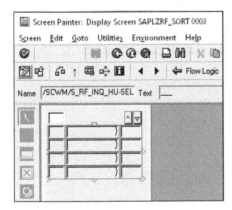

Figure 3.38 Subscreen 3 with Step Loop

To adjust the columns, change the name of column field 2 to /SCWM/S_RF_INQ_HU_LOOP-HUIDENT with display length 12 and set the checkbox to scrollable. In field 3, change the name to /SCWM/S_RF_INQ_HU_LOOP-LETYP with length 4. All columns are display fields only as we do not expect the user to do any input in the list.

Remove all other fields on the screen except the selection field (/SCWM/S_RF_INQ_HU-SELNO, input field) and the buttons for page up and page down (/SCWM/S_RF_SCRELM-PGUP and /SCWM/S_RF_SCRELM-PGDN). The buttons will help the user to scroll through the list in case the lines on the screen are not enough.

Verify the flow logic of the screen; it differs from our screens 1 and 2 as here the framework has to handle the list in a loop, as shown in Listing 3.10.

```
PROCESS BEFORE OUTPUT.

 MODULE status_sscr_loop.
 LOOP.
    MODULE loop_output.
 ENDLOOP.
 MODULE loop_scrolling_set.


PROCESS AFTER INPUT.

 LOOP.
    MODULE loop_input.
  ENDLOOP.
 MODULE user_command_sscr.
```

Listing 3.10 Flow Logic of Subscreen 3: List Screen

Create Two New Function Modules

Create the new Z_SORT_ZST3_PBO function module with the coding as shown in Listing 3.11. The function module will query the database to find all handling units that matching the bin and the customer (see comments "1 and "2). This list will be handed over to the RF framework by filling the CT_INQ_HU_LOOP application parameter (see comment "3) and introducing it to the framework with method /SCWM/CL_RF_BLL_SRVC=>SET_SCR_TABNAME (see comment "4).

```
FUNCTION z_sort_zst3_pbo.
*"----------------------------------------------------------------------
*"*"Local Interface:
*"  CHANGING
*"     REFERENCE(ZSORT) TYPE  ZRF_SORT
*"     REFERENCE(CT_INQ_HU_LOOP) TYPE  /SCWM/TT_RF_INQ_HU_LOOP
*"----------------------------------------------------------------------
  DATA: lt_huhdr   TYPE /scwm/tt_huhdr_int,
        ls_hu_loop TYPE /scwm/s_rf_inq_hu_loop,
        lt_dstgrp  TYPE rseloption,
        lt_lgpla   TYPE rseloption.

  BREAK-POINT ID zewmdevbook_336.

  "1. Get bin of the pick handling unit
  go_pack->get_hu(
```

```
  EXPORTING
    iv_guid_hu = zsort-source_hu
  IMPORTING
    es_huhdr    = DATA(ls_huhdr)
  EXCEPTIONS
    OTHERS      = 99 ).
IF sy-subrc <> 0. "technical error
  MESSAGE ID sy-msgid TYPE sy-msgty NUMBER sy-msgno
  WITH sy-msgv1 sy-msgv2 sy-msgv3 sy-msgv4.
ENDIF.
DATA(ls_selopt) = VALUE rsdsselopt(
  low    = ls_huhdr-lgpla
  sign   = wmegc_sign_inclusive
  option = wmegc_option_eq ).
APPEND ls_selopt TO lt_lgpla.
ls_selopt-low = zsort-dstgrp.
APPEND ls_selopt TO lt_dstgrp.
"2. Get all handling units on this bin with same consol. group
CALL FUNCTION '/SCWM/HU_SELECT_GEN'
  EXPORTING
    iv_lgnum  = zsort-lgnum
    ir_lgpla  = lt_lgpla
    ir_dstgrp = lt_dstgrp
  IMPORTING
    et_huhdr  = lt_huhdr
  EXCEPTIONS
    OTHERS    = 99.
IF sy-subrc <> 0.
  MESSAGE ID sy-msgid TYPE sy-msgty NUMBER sy-msgno
  WITH sy-msgv1 sy-msgv2 sy-msgv3 sy-msgv4.
ENDIF.
"3. Prepare list of handling units
CLEAR ct_inq_hu_loop.
DELETE lt_huhdr WHERE copst IS NOT INITIAL.
LOOP AT lt_huhdr ASSIGNING FIELD-SYMBOL(<huhdr>).
  CLEAR ls_hu_loop.
  ls_hu_loop-seqno = sy-tabix.
  MOVE-CORRESPONDING <huhdr> TO ls_hu_loop.
  APPEND ls_hu_loop TO ct_inq_hu_loop.
ENDLOOP.

"4. Set screen elements for RF framework
/scwm/cl_rf_bll_srvc=>init_screen_param( ).
/scwm/cl_rf_bll_srvc=>set_screen_param('CS_INQ_HU').
```

```
/scwm/cl_rf_bll_srvc=>set_screen_param('CT_INQ_HU_LOOP').
CALL METHOD /scwm/cl_rf_bll_srvc=>set_scr_tabname
  EXPORTING
    iv_scr_tabname = '/SCWM/TT_RF_INQ_HU_LOOP'.
CALL METHOD /scwm/cl_rf_bll_srvc=>set_line
  EXPORTING
    iv_line = 1.


ENDFUNCTION.
```

Listing 3.11 Interface and Coding of Function Module Z_SORT_ZST3_PBO

The second new function module, Z_SORT_ZST3_PAI (see Listing 3.12), will check if the user selected a handling unit from the list by typing in a sequence number (see comment "1). If the user did so, the selected line will be returned by filling application parameter ZSORT-RFHU (see comment "2).

```
FUNCTION z_sort_zst3_pai.
*"----------------------------------------------------------------------
*"*"Local Interface:
*"  CHANGING
*"     REFERENCE(ZSORT) TYPE  ZRF_SORT
*"     REFERENCE(CT_INQ_HU_LOOP) TYPE  /SCWM/TT_RF_INQ_HU_LOOP
*"     REFERENCE(CS_INQ_HU) TYPE  /SCWM/S_RF_INQ_HU
*"----------------------------------------------------------------------

  BREAK-POINT ID zewmdevbook_336.

  "1. Validation of user input
  DATA(ls_inq_hu) = VALUE /scwm/s_rf_inq_hu_loop(
    ct_inq_hu_loop[ cs_inq_hu-selno ] ).
  IF sy-subrc IS NOT INITIAL.
    MESSAGE e108(/scwm/rf_en) WITH cs_inq_hu-selno.
  ENDIF.
  "2. Forward user selection to screen 2
  zsort-rfhu = ls_inq_hu-huident.
  /scwm/cl_rf_bll_srvc=>set_screen_param('ZSORT').


ENDFUNCTION.
```

Listing 3.12 Interface and Coding for Function Module Z_SORT_ZST3_PAI

Add Customizing Entries

Now we will add the required Customizing entries in the RF framework.

We start in IMG activity **Define Steps in Logical Transactions**, where we will first create a new step, ZST3, in the **Define Steps** folder. In the **Define Logical Transactions** folder, we select RF Transaction ZSORT and navigate to the **Map Logical Transaction Step to Sub-Screen** subfolder. Here you should copy an existing line (e.g., for step ZST2) and change the step to ZST3 and the screen number to 3.

In subfolder **Define Function Code Profile**, copy an existing entry and change the step to ZST2. Change the function code to HULIST and assign it to press button 1 with function key F1. The impact of this Customizing entry is that screen 2 will show the **F1 List** push button.

In subfolder **Define Logical Transaction Step Flow**, create three new entries as shown in Table 3.11. With function code HULIST, the framework will navigate to the new step ZST3 and process the function code INIT automatically in the background. With function code ENTER, the framework will navigate back to step ZST2.

Step	Function Code	Function Module	Next Step	Processing Mode and Background Function Code
ZST2	HULIST		ZST3	1—Background, INIT
ZST3	INIT	Z_SORT_ZST3_PBO		2—Foreground
ZST3	ENTER	Z_SORT_ZST3_PAI	ZST2	1—Background, INIT

Table 3.11 Step Flow Entries for Integration Step ZST3

Now, as shown in Figure 3.39, when you test RF Transaction ZSORT ❶, you will notice the new **F1 List** push button on the second screen in the top area ❷. When you use function key F1, the framework will bring you to the new screen ❸ showing a list of possible handling units. Here type in the number of the line you want to choose, such as "3". This will bring you back to screen 2 and the value for the **HU** field is prefilled with the chosen, third handling unit ❹.

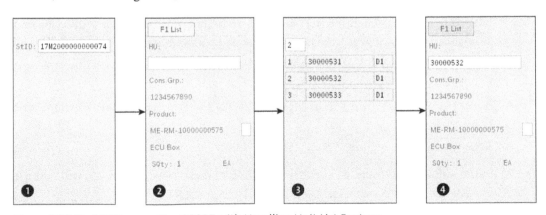

Figure 3.39 Test RF Transaction ZSORT with Handling Unit List Feature

Adding a list screen to your RF transaction will not take too much effort as the RF framework supports you a lot for this step. The tricky part is to choose the right columns within the limited available space on the screen so that a user can make the right decision for his selection.

3.3.10   Exception Handling in Radio Frequency

The RF framework supports the user in many RF transactions and in anticipated exceptional situations. For example, in RF picking, the *not enough stock on source bin* exception is predefined: the user enters an exception code, types in the quantity difference, and can continue with his work. Without this predefined exception, the user would have to interrupt his picking tour and go to a supervisor or clearing office for help. The more often an exception can occur, the more often the software should be capable of handling it without much user effort.

In RF transactions, we have the exception code field on all screens where exceptions are supported by the system. The field is usually located in the lower-right corner of the screen. For some exceptions, such as *pick handling unit is full* (exception code NEXT), no further user input is required. For other exception codes, such as *stock missing* (exception code DIFF), a separate screen for user input of the difference quantity is needed.

All exceptions require user training, and if an exception requires too much input (e.g., stock found on bin during physical inventory), the RF transaction might not be the right choice to handle the exception immediately.

You will learn in this section how to enhance RF Transaction ZSORT with two exception codes, LIST and SKFD:

- Enter the SKFD (skip validation field) exception if the user cannot verify the product barcode.
- Enter the LIST exception code to see all allowed exceptions for a particular transaction.

Both exceptions can be found in standard RF transactions, so we will just describe how to enable them in a new RF transaction. This requires three steps:

1. Create a new business context 9PA in the IMG and assign exception codes SKFD and LIST within your warehouse number.
2. Extend the step flow for RF Transaction ZSORT to allow the framework to react on exceptions.
3. Create function module Z_SORT_ZST2_EXCEPTIONS.

In the following sections, we present the details of these steps, which you will perform in ABAP Object Navigator (Transaction SE80) and in the IMG.

Create a New Business Context

We start with the IMG for exception handling, at **EWM • Cross-Process Settings • Exception Handling • Maintain Business Context for Exception Codes**. Here you create a new business context. Enter "9PA" for the **Context Name** and enter "Repack pick items" for the **Description**. Navigate to the **Assign Operation to Business Context** subfolder for your new entry and assign step **18 RF Packing HU Items** to it. Again, select this entry and navigate to the **Assign Internal Process Codes** subfolder, where you create two new entries with the LIST and SKFD internal process codes; see Figure 3.40.

In the **Define Exception Codes** IMG activity, you will now define the user-specific exception codes with the internal exception codes in the warehouse (e.g., 1710).

Figure 3.40 IMG for Creating New Business Context 9PA

First choose the **Create Exception Code** folder and create two new entries:

- 111: Enter your warehouse, enter exception code 111, and enter a description, "Skip Product Verification".
- 999: Enter your warehouse, enter exception code 999, and enter a description, "List all exception codes".

Select one entry after the other and navigate to the **Define Exception Code** subfolder, where you create one entry with business context 9PA and step 18. Continue with the **Maintain Process Parameters** subfolder and assign internal process code SKFD to exception code 111. For exception code 999, add an entry with internal process code LIST.

Numeric Exception Codes

So long as the RF device consists of a screen with a small keyboard, it is better to choose numeric exception codes rather than character-based codes. On most devices, it is easier for the user to type in "111" rather than "SKFD", as often the characters are not on the primary set of keys on the keyboard.

Extend the Step Flow

Go to the **Define Steps in Logical Transactions** IMG activity and teach the RF framework to allow and handle exceptions.

Select RF Transaction ZSORT in folder **Define Logical Transactions** and navigate to the **Define Function Code Profile** subfolder. Here, copy an existing entry and replace the step (new value ZST2) and the function code (new value EXCEPT). Set the **Exception** checkbox, and in the **Shortcut** field enter "****". With this setting, you enable the display of the exception code field on screen 2 of RF Transaction ZSORT.

Navigate to subfolder **Define Logical Transaction Step Flow** and copy an existing entry. Change the **Step** to ZST2 and **Function Code** to EXCEPT. In the **Function Module** field, type in "Z_SORT_ZST2_EXCEPTIONS". The value of the **Next Step** field is ZST2, and in the **Processing Mode** field, choose option "O" (defined during execution).

Create Function Module

In the last step, create the Z_SORT_ZST2_EXCEPTIONS function module, where the exceptions of screen 2 are handled (see Listing 3.13).

The coding will check first that a user entered a valid exception code (see comment "2) by using a standard verify_exception_code method of class /SCWM/CL_EXCEPTION_APPL. Here the system will check the Customizing entries completed in step 1.

The coding is linked to the internal process codes LIST and SKFD (see comments "3 to "5), so the coding is independent of the external process codes 111 or 999.

Now when you test the enhanced RF Transaction ZSORT, you will find the exception code field in the lower-right part of the screen (see Figure 3.41). You can use ⎡Tab⎤ to navigate to the field, rather than using the mouse. If you type in "111" and press ⎡Enter⎤, the verification field for the product changes from the input field to a verified output field ❸ and ❹. If you type "999" in the first screen ❶, the system shows a list screen with all allowed exceptions ❶ and ❷. On the list screen ❷, you can enter the sequence number of the line and the system will automatically take this exception code into the exception code field.

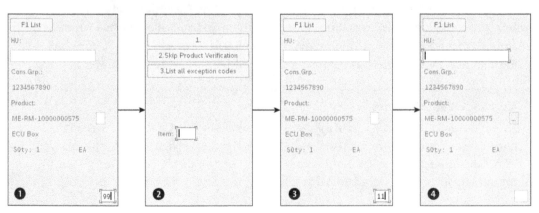

Figure 3.41 Test Exception Codes in RF Transaction ZSORT

Many standard RF transactions handle exceptions, so before you develop your own exceptions, it is worth checking the standard. You can find the function modules in Function Builder (Transaction SE37) by searching for "/SCWM/RF_*_EXCEPTION".

```
FUNCTION z_sort_zst2_exceptions.
*"----------------------------------------------------------------
*"*"Local Interface:
*"  CHANGING
*"     REFERENCE(ZSORT) TYPE  ZRF_SORT
*"----------------------------------------------------------------

  CONSTANTS: lc_buscon(3)   VALUE '9PA',
             lc_execstep(2) VALUE '18'.

  DATA: ls_exccode TYPE /scwm/s_iexccode,
        lv_fcode   type /scwm/de_fcode.

  BREAK-POINT ID zewmdevbook_336.

  "1. Checks & initializations
  IF zsort-source_hu IS INITIAL.
    RETURN.
  ENDIF.
  "Get shortcut
  DATA(lv_shortcut) = /scwm/cl_rf_bll_srvc=>get_shortcut( ).
  "Create instance of Exception object
  DATA(lo_excep) = /scwm/cl_exception_appl=>create_exception_object( ).
  "2. Verify exception code entered by the user
  ls_exccode-exccode = lv_shortcut.
  /scwm/cl_exception_appl=>verify_exception_code(
    EXPORTING
      is_appl_item_data = zsort
      iv_lgnum          = zsort-lgnum
      iv_buscon         = lc_buscon
      iv_execstep       = lc_execstep
      ip_excep          = lo_excep
    CHANGING
      cs_exccode        = ls_exccode ).
  "Exception code is not maintained in Customizing
  IF ls_exccode-valid <> abap_true.
    "Exception code is not allowed
    MESSAGE e003(/scwm/exception)
    WITH ls_exccode-exccode.
    RETURN.
  ENDIF.
  "3. Handle exceptions
  CASE ls_exccode-iprcode.
    WHEN wmegc_iprcode_list.
```

```
      "4. Handle exception code "list"
      CALL FUNCTION '/SCWM/RSRC_EXCEPTION_LIST_FILL'
        EXPORTING
          iv_lgnum     = zsort-lgnum
          iv_buscon    = lc_buscon
          iv_exec_step = lc_execstep.
      lv_fcode = wmegc_iprcode_list.
      /scwm/cl_rf_bll_srvc=>set_fcode( lv_fcode ).
      /scwm/cl_rf_bll_srvc=>set_prmod(
        /scwm/cl_rf_bll_srvc=>c_prmod_background ).
      CALL METHOD /scwm/cl_rf_bll_srvc=>set_field
        EXPORTING
          iv_field = '/SCWM/S_RF_SCRELM-SHORTCUT'.
    WHEN wmegc_iprcode_skfd.
      "5. Handle exception code "Skip verification field"
      zsort-matnr_verif = zsort-matnr. "verify the product
      /scwm/cl_rf_bll_srvc=>set_prmod(
        /scwm/cl_rf_bll_srvc=>c_prmod_foreground ).
    WHEN OTHERS.
      "Exception code is not allowed
      MESSAGE e003(/scwm/exception) WITH lv_shortcut.
  ENDCASE.
  /scwm/cl_rf_bll_srvc=>clear_shortcut( ).

ENDFUNCTION.
```

Listing 3.13 Interface and Coding for Function Module Z_SORT_ZST2_EXCEPTIONS

3.3.11   Process Functions in Background Mode in Radio Frequency Transactions

In the Customizing of the RF framework, you can choose for each combination a step and a function code if another function code and step will be processed automatically in the background. By changing the setting from **Foreground** to **Background**, you can, for example, optimize some standard RF transactions where too many steps (screens) are shown to the user. For example, in RF receiving, with this kind of customizing, you can skip the screen that displays the vendor's information.

In some RF transactions, the decision whether to continue in the background to the next screen or to stay on the current screen can only be made at runtime, depending on the user input. In this case, set the third option, **Defined during execution**.

Examples include RF picking and RF packing. In RF picking, the extra screen for the low stock check will only be displayed for the user when the current bin becomes empty. In RF packing, the system will only show the logon screen to the work center once per user session.

If you choose the **Defined during execution** option, you can use the /SCWM/CL_RF_BLL_SRVC=>SET_PRMOD method to change to foreground (use constant /SCWM/CL_RF_BLL_SRVC=>C_PRMOD_FOREGROUND) or to background (use constant /SCWM/CL_RF_BLL_SRVC=>C_PRMOD_BACKGROUND).

3.3.12   Enhance Standard Radio Frequency Transactions, and the Use of Radio Frequency BAdIs

There are three approaches for enhancing a standard RF transaction. Each can have advantages and disadvantages depending on the project:

1. **Wrap standard function modules**

   If you, for example, require an additional check or new information on the screen, you can often add this program logic at the beginning or end of the standard function (e.g., function module SF) that is called for a certain screen in RF. Therefore, you create a new function module (e.g., NF), which calls the standard SF function. Before or after the call of SF, you enter your own program logic. In the RF Customizing, you copy the standard Customizing entry for SF to your presentation profile and link it to the NF function module. The benefit of this approach is that you keep to the standard as much as possible, so any coding fixes provided by SAP standard will also apply in your project. Furthermore, you limit the new coding to run only for a certain presentation profile/warehouse. If you encounter a software error, you can switch presentation profiles back to standard and hand over the example to SAP support. As with presentation profile ****, only standard function modules are called.

2. **Copy the standard function module**

   If you need an enhancement that cannot be added at the beginning or end in a function module, you will have to copy the standard function module and change the coding lines somewhere in the middle. Similar to approach 1, you copy the Customizing entry to your warehouse/presentation profile and enter the copied function module. The disadvantage of this approach is that you take over maintenance for all of the coding copied into your project. Very often, you end up copying the complete function group. The fixes provided by SAP will have no impact as you detour from the standard processing.

3. **Use the RF BAdIs**

   You can use the two RF framework BAdIs and call your own function modules and hence replace the standard program logic. One advantage of this approach is that you do not need to understand or use the RF framework Customizing. The disadvantage is that no Customizing is used and thus everything is solved by coding. This results in less transparency for other developers or projects. In the worst case, the developers using these BAdIs start developing new Customizing tables, which is just another RF framework. If you take this approach, try to keep a switch so that you can easily change to plain standard processing in case of an error that needs to be investigated by SAP support.

The two RF framework BAdIs are /SCWM/EX_RF_FLOW_PRE and /SCWM/EX_RF_FLOW_POST. One is called before each step is processed by the RF framework, and the other one is called after each step.

Besides the option to enhance a standard RF transaction, you can also reuse some core RF transactions. A *core RF transaction* usually cannot run in the RF environment, and you recognize it by the wildcards in its name; for example, RF picking uses core transaction PI**** and RF putaway uses PT**** and PTHU**. The standard developments of RF picking were clustered and reused entries in the RF framework. The Customizing entries in logical transaction PI**** will apply to the whole family of RF picking transactions. So, picking by handling unit (logical Transaction PIBHU), picking system guided (logical Transaction PISYSG), and so on all use the same Customizing entries that you can find for PI****.

One choice you have is also to reuse the core RF transactions. To do so, you would, for example, create the logical Transaction PIZZO1, which would reuse settings of PI****. The namespace rule here is changed so that the Z is not necessarily in the beginning of the name.

For the step flow, the RF framework always selects entries for the logical transaction (e.g., PIZZO1) and also for the two possible core RF Transactions PI**** and PIZZ**. With the concept of the core RF transactions, the number of Customizing entries is minimized if you have a group of transactions that are similar.

3.4   Post Processing Framework

For various business processes, it may be useful or even necessary to trigger defined follow-up actions that are event-driven. If these actions do not influence the current process, they may be decoupled from the initiating process and run parallel or afterward. The processing is asynchronous from that point.

In contrast is synchronous processing. In this case, all actions within one *logical unit of work* are processed sequentially and posted together at the end. Compared to asynchronous processing, this increases the total runtime, but it also ensures that all routines are executed without errors.

Printing Forms

A typical use case is the printing of forms. If a user posts the goods issue for a delivery within a dialog transaction, the relevant shipping documents should be printed directly afterward. Usually, it's not necessary to process these steps in a synchronous manner. In fact, the user would only need to post the goods issue in his dialog transaction and then receive a success message. He should not have to wait for another message that the printing was also successful, because he will notice this from the documents that are being printed. Here you can simply assign the actual printing of shipping documents as a follow-up action to the *successful goods issue posting* status.

In Basis, there are different methods to trigger event-driven actions. The most important features and enhancement options of PPF are shown and explained in the following section.

3.4.1   What Is Post Processing Framework?

PPF is a software component that is deployed cross applications to trigger actions based on events. With the help of standardized interfaces (class interfaces), the framework allows the various SAP applications to trigger actions (e.g., printing of forms, generating follow-on documents, starting workflows, sending emails or alerts). The decision of whether an action is triggered or not can be made via configurable conditions or by just using ABAP logic.

PPF was developed as an object-oriented successor to message control. With easy access to different SAP applications and simple expandability, PPF offers high flexibility and is frequently used for custom extensions in EWM implementation projects. In the following sections, we'll look at the structure of PPF and then discuss its flow logic.

Structure and Functions

Within PPF, there are several sets of action definitions—grouped under action profiles and applications—that contain certain ABAP logic. These action definitions are the defined frame for an action that is to be executed during a business process. They contain all the information about processing type, processing time, and the conditions that must be fulfilled to process the action.

The Customizing settings for action definitions are stored in table PPFTTTCU.

At runtime, the PPF generates triggers (instances of an action definition) for all relevant action definitions. The relevance depends on the calling application. These triggers will release the actual action processing (ABAP logic).

The triggers are stored in table PPFTTRIGG.

Logic Flow

In Figure 3.42, the logical sequence of the framework is illustrated in simplified form to help you understand the relationship between the application and the main functions of PPF schematically, as follows:

1. The application program calls the PPF manager (CL_CONTEXT_MANAGER_PPF) and passes the distinct application and the action profile.

2. The PPF manager pushes the determination of the trigger for a PPF action definition (CL_TRIGGER_PPF). All action definitions, which are grouped under the specific action profile of the application, will be checked.

3. For all activated action definitions, the corresponding schedule conditions will be analyzed.

4. If the schedule condition is met, the set merging logic will be examined to see if the action is to be carried out again.

5. When all previous checks are positive, the start condition—if any—will be finally evaluated.

6. Execution starts for all permissible triggers (unless the **Processing using selection report** option is set as a processing time).

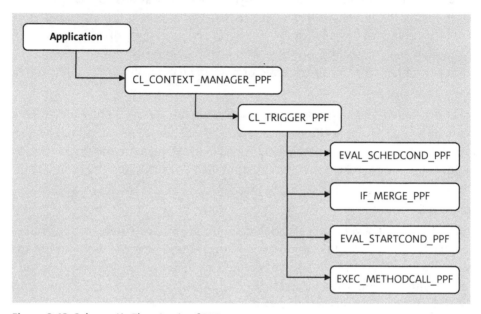

Figure 3.42 Schematic Flow Logic of PPF

The execution of a PPF action is, among other things, dependent on the processing time of the action definition. The configuration options for the processing times of PPF actions are described in Section 3.4.2.

> **Further Information about Post Processing Framework**
>
> For more information on PPF, check the SAP Community wiki at *https://wiki.scn.sap.com/wiki/display/SCM/How-To+Guides+for+SAP+EWM*. In the *How to Use PPF in SAP EWM* how-to-guide, you can find detailed technical descriptions for the available class interfaces and service classes of PPF.

3.4.2   Extended Warehouse Management and Post Processing Framework

In EWM, several PPF actions are already delivered within the standard shipment and are either strongly required for correct processing logic of individual processes, particularly within integration into SAP S/4HANA modules, or to be used optionally as the sample templates for rapid process implementation.

The following PPF applications are available for EWM in SAP S/4HANA:

- /SCDL/DELIVERY—New delivery
- /SCWM/SHP_RCV—Shipping and receiving
- /SCWM/WME—Warehouse management engine
- QIE—Quality Inspection Engine (decentralized EWM)

Transaction SPPFCADM takes you to the central Customizing menu. Here you can manage specific settings for existing action definitions as well as assign start and schedule conditions. In this context, you also have the option to create your own action definitions as well as start and schedule conditions.

You can reach the Customizing of an action definition as follows:

1. Mark the application and press the **Define Action Profile and Actions** button.

2. Mark the action profile and choose it in the dialog structure by double-clicking **Action Definition**.

3. Mark the action definition and press the **Detail** button. Then you will be on the screen shown in Figure 3.43.

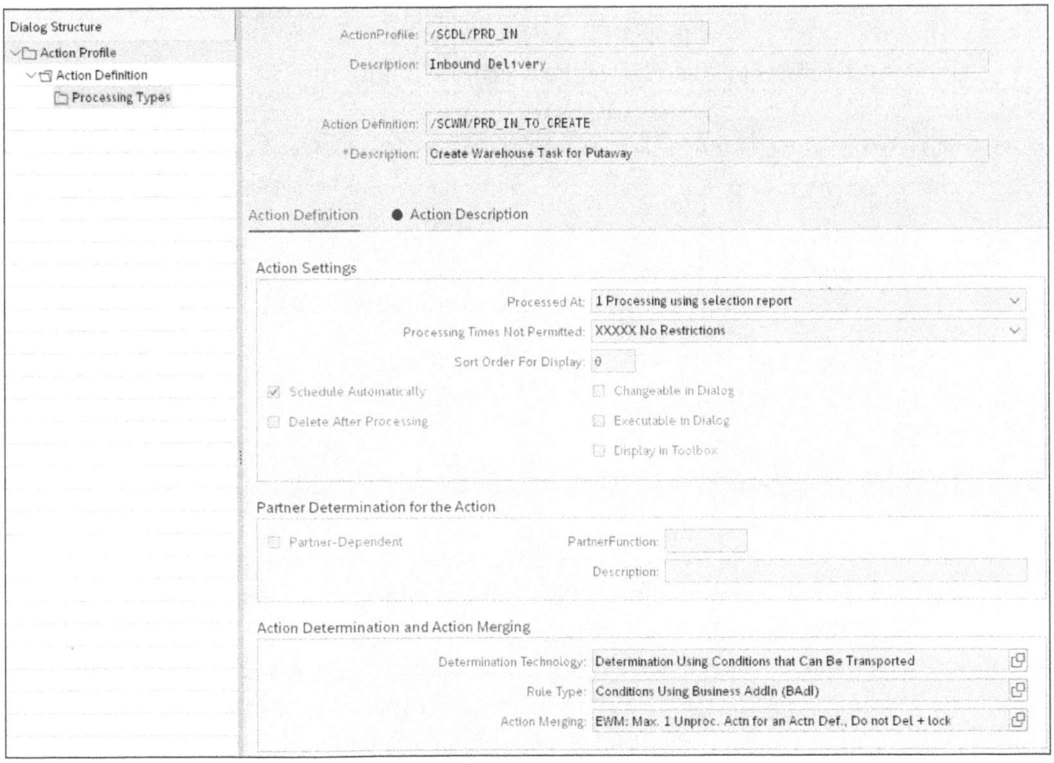

Figure 3.43 Customizing of Action Definitions

You can find the ABAP logic behind each action definition by choosing **Processing types** by double-clicking in the dialog structure and then pressing the **Show implementation** button. In Chapter 4, Section 4.5.2, we will elaborate on these settings.

4. On the **Action Definition** tab, you will find a range of Customizing options.

As described before in Section 3.4.1, PPF is not an EWM-specific application. Therefore, we will only explain the settings that are essential for standard processing in EWM in the following sections: processing time, action merging, further options, and conditions.

Processing Time

The following options are available for the processing time using the **Process At** field:

- Immediate processing
- Processing when saving the document
- Processing using selection report

The **Processing when saving the document** and **Processing using selection report** settings trigger an asynchronous execution of the PPF action. This means that the action is being processed decoupled from the main logical unit of work.

Table 3.12 contains an overview of the execution methods.

Option	Execution Methods
Immediate processing	Within the current logical unit of work before COM-MIT WORK (synchronously)
Processing when saving the document	Immediately after finishing the current logical unit of work with COMMIT WORK (asynchronous)
Processing using selection report	After finishing the current logical unit of work using COMMIT WORK via report RSPPFPROCESS at any time—for example, as a periodic job (asynchronous)

Table 3.12 Overview Processing Times

In general, you should avoid (if possible) the **Immediate processing** setting. For the standard PPF actions in the /SCDL/DELIVERY application, this processing time is explicitly not allowed. This is because there is a risk of infinite loops or other side effects if the PPF action changes the current delivery itself. Also note that the **Immediate processing** setting has a direct impact on the runtime behavior of the main process because it has to wait until the execution of the action definition is completed. Therefore, you should always check carefully if you really need immediate processing. It can be used when printing labels if the user expects the labels to be printed before he saves the document, and the labels can be printed repeatedly without restrictions.

Action Merging

With the help of the merging options, you can control whether a PPF action for a specific application key may be re-executed. More specifically, the PPF trigger is checked. Depending on the setting, the merging logic also checks already existing triggers for an application key and deletes them (if necessary).

Usually, you want to run a PPF action only once (e.g., the printing of a handling unit label). But this setting can be too general sometimes. For example, if the action was processed with errors, it has been executed once and therefore must not run a second time, even if the result for the end user has not been sufficient.

The following options for **Action Merging** are currently available in EWM:

- EWM: Max. 1 Action for Each Action Definition
- EWM: Max. 1 Action for Each Action Definition, Do not Delete
- EWM: Max. 1 Unproc. Actn for an Actn Def., Do not Del + lock
- EWM: Max. 1 Unprocessed Action for Each Action Definition
- EWM: No Aggreg. of Actions for Each Actn Def., Do not Delete
- Max. 1 Action for Each Action Definition
- Max. 1 Unprocessed Action for Each Action Definition
- Max. 1 Unprocessed Action for Each Actn Def., Do not Delete
- Max. 1 Unprocessed Action for Each Processing Type
- Set Highest Number of Processed Actions

Some of these merge logics have been introduced specifically in EWM for delivery processing. They contain a specific locking logic. Further details are described in Section 3.4.3. All merge logics are implementations for the IF_MERGE_PPF interface. You can also implement your own action merging options by creating an implementation to this interface.

Further Options

In the view of the transaction in which you make the Customizing settings for the action definitions (refer back to Figure 3.43), there are further Customizing options for the previously explained points. In the following section, we will briefly describe the options that are undocumented or not self-explanatory.

The **Schedule Automatically** flag should always be set in EWM. Otherwise, a PPF trigger must be triggered manually from a UI add-on, as it is known from the ENJOY transactions in SAP S/4HANA. These add-ons are not used within the UI pattern of EWM.

The ability to execute and make changes in the dialog refers exclusively to specific application transactions (e.g., /SCWM/PRDI) that have integrated the PPF view (refer back to Figure 3.5). EWM provides this capability because end users in productive systems usually have no authority for administration Transaction SPPFP. With this transaction, you can always edit the corresponding PPF actions independent of these settings.

Partner determination logics are not used in EWM. For the determination technology, only use the **Using Transportable Conditions** setting. All other options are not supported.

For the rule type, you can choose between BAdI and workflow conditions. This setting refers to which logic is used in the determination of schedule and start conditions. In EWM, the conditions for all standard PPF action definitions are determined using BAdI filters and not workflow configurations.

Notes on Performance

Because most PPF action definitions for EWM are shipped by SAP in the activated state, you should look closely before a productive start at what PPF actions you actually need for your business processes. All other actions should be deactivated; otherwise, all activated action definitions' schedule conditions are executed unnecessarily. The appropriate settings can be found in Customizing for action definitions before you jump to the detail screen.

In addition, we recommend that you regularly delete the persistent PPF objects from the database tables using the corresponding standard features.

Conditions

Triggering a PPF action does not necessarily mean that it will be processed. *Triggering* it just means that there will be an executable PPF action object created for later usage by a given application object. The execution time of this object depends on the processing time, which has been set in the corresponding PPF action definition.

The PPF provides two types of conditions:

- Schedule condition
- Start condition

Through the schedule condition, the PPF action is triggered, but its progress can be stopped by a start condition. The PPF action then gets the **Not processed** status and is quasi-buffered. Using report RSPPFPROCESS, which you schedule as a periodic job, you can trigger these PPF actions again. The corresponding start condition will be checked each time, whereas the schedule conditions are no longer relevant at this point.

From a technical point of view, there is a big difference between the schedule and the start conditions. With the schedule conditions, data is used from memory, which is evaluated before the main process updates the database by memory. The evaluation of start conditions, however, takes place only after the database has already been updated. Therefore, the starting conditions use the data from this updated database.

Therefore, checking the starting conditions means checking the persistent object states. For the schedule conditions, there are transient object states used. You should be aware of this fact. To assign an action definition with a schedule, and possibly a starting condition, select the application in Transaction SPPFCADM and press the **Condition Configuration (Transportable Conditions)** button. You should see the screen shown in Figure 3.44.

Double-click **Action Profile** in the upper-left area of the screen and then **Action Definition** in the upper-right area of the screen.

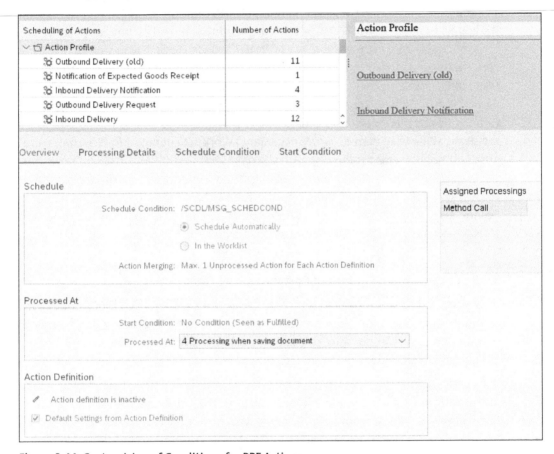

Figure 3.44 Customizing of Conditions for PPF Actions

Technical Names

If you click the **Technical Names** button, you will see the familiar technical names of the action profiles and definitions in the upper-left and upper-right parts of the transaction.

The **Overview** and **Processing Details** tabs each include administration information and general Customizing settings.

In the **Schedule Condition** and **Start Condition** tab, you can set each one of the available conditions. You can reach the corresponding BAdI implementation by selecting the **Edit Condition** button.

When evaluating conditions, besides the static—that is, hardcoded—ABAP logic, EWM also offers dynamic findings, which you can configure. The basis for this is the SAP CRM condition technique. Because this technique is not part of PPF, we will not go into detail on it here. However, you should remember that there is an alternative to user-coded conditions.

The condition technique is, for example, used in PPF application /SCWM/WME. Also, in the application /SCDL/DELIVERY, you can use condition records, if you have set the corresponding schedule condition (e.g., /SCWM/DLV_CONF_SC). If you want to evaluate conditions on the basis of condition records, you have to perform the corresponding setup in Customizing for EWM first (e.g., under **Cross-Process Settings • Handling Units • Basics • Print**). Then you create condition records, which include corresponding conditions. For example, you can set condition records to print handling units by choosing menu path **Extended Warehouse Management • Work Scheduling • Print • Settings • Create Condition Records for Printing (HUs)** (or Transaction /SCWM/PRHU6). At runtime, the system finds the current values of an object and compares them with the condition records you defined. If a matching record is found, the condition is true. In Chapter 4, Section 4.5.3, you will find a custom development that shows you how the condition technique plays along with PPF for warehouse orders.

3.4.3   Enhancement Options of Post Processing Framework

In projects, it is normally not necessary to create your own applications or your own action profiles. The more common case is that, in certain processes, due to special requirements, you do not want to use the standard SAP PPF modules. For such cases, the framework provides several enhancement options.

Before you start with your own implementation, you should first check exactly which of the options described in the following section makes the most sense in your case. For example, it could already be sufficient to assign your own schedule condition to an SAP standard action definition instead of developing the entire set.

If you want to use your own schedule and start conditions, keep in mind that you should avoid using logics that are too complex at these points and especially should not use potentially expensive database calls. This would have a negative impact on the total runtime of the individual processes. Note that schedule conditions will always be executed when the respective action definition must be checked. This happens with every call of the related action profile.

Performance in the Schedule Condition

Whenever an inbound delivery is changed, all action definitions are checked, which are grouped under the action profiles /SCDL/PRD_IN and /SCDL/PRD_CMMN. Thus, all assigned schedule conditions will be executed.

Say you confirm 10 warehouse tasks that have reference to an inbound delivery, one after another, via Transaction /SCWM/RFUI. With each confirmation, the delivery is updated and therefore changed. This means that with each confirmation, all relevant schedule conditions will be executed again.

It does not matter if the change of the delivery is initiated by background processing or a dialog transaction.

Therefore, you should make sure that your own schedule condition for the delivery only reads the to-be-processed delivery item and that you do not inadvertently cause a read of the complete delivery with all of the items.

We will now go into more details around the procedure of creating custom schedule and start conditions, action execution, and further enhancement options of PPF.

Your Own Schedule Condition

If you would like to use your own schedule condition, you have to create an implementation for the classic EVAL_SCHEDCOND_PPF BAdI. Make sure you create a filter value or set an existing one.

In the method of your implementing class, you can place the logic that you need. In your implementation, you have to be aware that you have to inform the framework if scheduling should be executed or not. This information is controlled by the return code of your method. If the schedule condition is true, set the value of the EP_RC variable to 0. Then you need to assign your new schedule condition to an action definition in Customizing, as described in Section 3.4.2.

If you want to implement your own schedule condition for PPF actions of the application /SCDL/DELIVERY, you should take note of some particular features. Within the delivery processing, a special locking mechanism is used within PPF, which affects both schedule condition and merging logic.

For performance reasons, many EWM processes within the delivery processing, which work at the item level, do not load all items of the respective delivery in the memory. For this reason, the main process treats this single position in memory as the only one associated with the delivery. At the same time, these processes often run in parallel tasks. Because the evaluation of conditions for PPF actions works at the delivery header level and the parallel processing of tasks at the delivery item level, the corresponding PPF actions will be evaluated for each and every affected parallel task. To prevent this behavior and thus the resulting side effects, logical unit of work overarching locking mechanisms are used.

At the end of your scheduling method (see Listing 3.14), you should therefore implement the ABAP code.

```
METHOD if_ex_eval_schedcond_ppf~evaluate_schedule_condition.

  CASE flt_val.
    WHEN 'ZEWMDEVBOOK_343_FILTER'.
      ep_rc = 0.
    WHEN OTHERS.
      MESSAGE e001(zewmdevbook_343) WITH flt_val ip_ttype INTO DATA(msg).
      cl_log_ppf=>add_message(
        ip_problemclass = sppf_pclass_1
        ip_handle       = ip_protocol ).
      ep_rc = 99.
  ENDCASE.

  IF ep_rc = 0.
    "Check for already scheduled PPF actions
    ep_rc = /scdl/cl_common_ppf=>set_sched_cond_lock(
      io_context = io_context
      ip_ttype   = ip_ttype ).

  ENDIF.
ENDMETHOD.
```

Listing 3.14 Call Locking Logic in Delivery Environment

[»]

/SCDL/ Delivery and Schedule Conditions

If you implement your own action definition at application /SCDL/DELIVERY and you do not want to use explicit schedule conditions, you have to use the default schedule condition /SCWM/EMPTY_SCHED as filter. This way the described locking logic will be used (compare class /SCWM/CL_IM_PARPPF_BASIC_SCOND).

Your Own Start Condition

A start condition can be made project-specific by creating an implementation of BAdI EVAL_STARTCOND_PPF. Assign the new start condition to the action definition in the Customizing for PPF. As a template, you can refer to the /SCWM/CL_IM_DLV_CONF_ST class.

Your Own Action Execution

If you want to implement your own ABAP logic for your action definition, create an implementation for BAdI EXEC_METHODCALL_PPF. Then assign the filter of the new implementation to your action definition.

In Chapter 4, Section 4.5.2, we will explain the individual steps with an example.

Note that for the ABAP logic, it is your responsibility to notify the framework if the processing was successful or not. This message is similar to schedule and start conditions and uses the same return codes. If all relevant processing steps of your method have been executed without any errors, set the value of the variable RP_STATUS to sppf_status_processed; otherwise, set it to sppf_status_error. You can include the PPF constants in your coding with the SPPF type group.

Don't Get Confused

Some PPF actions (e.g., /SCWM/PDI_01_WT_CREATE, Creation of Warehouse Tasks for Warehouse Request) only trigger background processing, which means that the actual function for the warehouse task creation will be executed decoupled from the PPF action. This may lead to the **Successfully processed** status of the action, but the respective warehouse tasks might not actually have been created. You may refer to the application log in such a situation or try to create such warehouse tasks manually, checking the creation log.

Other Enhancement Options

PPF actions that are meant to run in background processing (with processing time **Processing when saving the document**) are processed by the SPPF_PROCESS function module. This processing takes place by default as a *transactional RFC* (tRFC). In some situations, it may make sense to serialize this action processing. For example, if you carry out an update to an object, you have to assume that this object can be updated simultaneously by parallel processing. To ensure serialization, you have to implement the COMPLETE_PROC_PPF BAdI, and then assign a queue via the COMPLETE_METHOD method. In this case, the SPPF_PROCESS function module will be called as a *queued RFC* (qRFC).

When a particular PPF action has been determined to run, you want to trigger a further specific action in parallel (e.g., an email notification or an alert).

This option is also offered by the COMPLETE_PROC_PPF BAdI. It is called if it is ensured that the determined trigger will be executed for an action definition.

In addition, you can also create your own application and your own action profiles for action definitions in PPF, if needed.

3.5   Key User Extensibility for Custom Fields

Custom field extensions of business object—interfaces and UIs—are one of the most common requirements in standardized software based implementation projects. Forming part of the *in-app extensibility* options available in SAP S/4HANA, *key user extensibility* provides SAP Fiori application–based tools that support you in this activity, among others.

In this section, we will roughly show how the Custom Fields and Logic app can be used to create EWM- related field enhancements. Furthermore, we present manual custom field enhancement options for EWM business objects that are not (yet) available for key user extensibility.

3.5.1   Introduction to Key User Extensibility

Key user extensibility enables you to implement various kinds of enhancements to existing standard business objects as well as create more simplistic business objects anew. The main purpose of this extensibility concept is to empower key users to configure field and UI enhancements rather easily for their user group while having developers and designers take care of more complex development activities. Among other features, key user extensibility allows for the creation of field extensions of business objects, interfaces, and UIs alongside custom logic for, say, field control, value validation, or prepopulating default values.

However, the business object to be extended by custom fields must provide for such extensibility. The SAP software architect will lay the basic groundwork for the extensibility of a business object in the development process of an SAP software product. Data structures and programs need to be flexibly and coherently designed and configured so that an extension of the respective business object by automatic generation will be possible while providing for the required software stability. Such extension often refers not only to the adding of fields to structures or tables but also to UIs and any type of interfaces.

The underlying mechanism for such key user–provided custom field extensions is technically based on include structures following a special naming convention, making use of the `INCL_EEW` string, and being defined for a specific business context in the business context repository. We will refer to such include structures as *extension includes*.

In contrast to the generally available extension option of appends, extension includes are already actively present in standard structures and tables. When publishing custom fields within a key user extensibility application, such fields will be added to the respective extension structures of the enhanced objects, also referred to as the *business context*, using automatically generated append structures.

Two procedures are generally available for this purpose:

- **Manual creation of ABAP-managed fields**
  Manual processing includes the assignment of custom fields to an extension include via Transaction SE11 (ABAP Dictionary) using an append structure. To do so, you need to know that an extension include is actually available in the corresponding ABAP Dictionary structure or table that you wish to enhance. This way, you will not need to make use of key user extensibility, which will allow you to name the

custom fields to your liking, regardless of the SAP naming convention, using persistence suffixes added to the field names defined in key user extensibility. Use suffixes to avoid field naming conflicts. However, there is a way to make these ABAP-managed fields available within the key user extensibility tools at a later stage using Transaction SCFD_EUI.

[+]

Naming Proposal for New ABAP-Managed Fields

To avoid name clashes of your manually created extension fields (e.g., during activation or system upgrade), SAP strongly recommends creating them with an appropriate field suffix, which belongs to the business context of the relevant extension include (see Transaction SCFD_REGISTRY). Ideally, you should follow the naming that the system would otherwise generate itself. This is not a prerequisite, but it can minimize the risk of name clashes in future.

- **Automatic generation of custom fields leveraging key user extensibility applications**

  In this case, you define the custom field of the selected business context by using the Custom Fields app. Changes to the respective extension include for the enhanced business context will be automatically generated and dependent dictionary objects activated. The application will thereby allow you to extend data dictionary objects without specific ABAP knowledge and speed up development and maintenance of field enhancements. Custom fields generated as such can be made available in defined contexts.

[+]

Activation of Key User Extensibility

Before using key user extensibility, ensure that it has been activated in your system. SAP Note 2283716 can be referenced for this purpose. In particular, the adaptation transport organizer will need to be set up before any custom extension will be possible. As transportable ABAP DDIC objects will be generated, the adaptation transport organizer will take care of creating the respective transport requests in the background.

3.5.2   Extended Warehouse Management and Key User Extensibility

As mentioned earlier, key user extensibility is a newer enhancement framework based on SAP S/4HANA. Table 3.13 shows business objects that might be interesting for custom field enhancements in EWM leveraging key user extensibility.

For these business objects, referred to as business contexts, you can create and publish custom fields using the Custom Fields and Logic application. Check database table CFD_W_BUS_CTXT (Custom Fields: Business Context Registry) for further business object references.

Business Object	Business Context	Suffix	Extension Include
Business partner	BP_CUSTVEND1	BUS	INCL_EEW_BUT000
General product data	PRODUCT	PRD	PRD_INCL_EEW_PS
Plant-related product data	PRODUCT_PLANT	PLT	PLNT_INCL_EEW_PS
Warehouse product data	/SCWM/PRODUCT_WAREHOUSE_DATA	WHD	/SCWM/S_PRD_WH_INCL_EEW_PS
Storage type–related product data	/SCWM/PRODUCT_STORAGETYPE_DATA	SST	/SCWM/S_PRD_WHST_INCL_EEW_PS
EWM delivery item	/SCWM/DLV_ITEM_STR	CDI	/SCDL/INCL_EEW_DLV_ITEM_STR

Table 3.13 EWM-Related Key User Extensibility Business Contexts

To create enhancements with the Custom Fields app, follow these steps:

1. **Check adaptation transport organizer setup**
   Call Transaction S_ATO_SETUP and define the adaptation transport organizer parameters. Figure 3.45 shows an example adaptation transport organizer setup. In addition to the namespace or prefix setup, it will be important to provide the package under which the changes are to be stored.

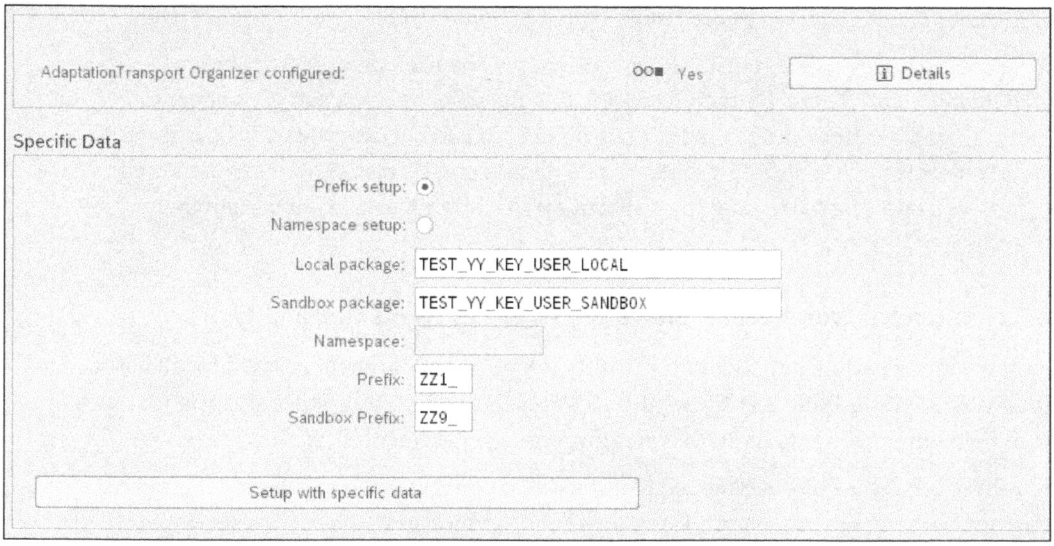

Figure 3.45 Adaptation Transport Organizer Setup

2. **Create and publish a custom field**

Start the Custom Fields and Logic app, then click the **Create** button in the upper-right corner. In the popup screen, select the business context (data object) to be extended. Figure 3.46 shows available contexts for the /SCWM/ EWM namespace.

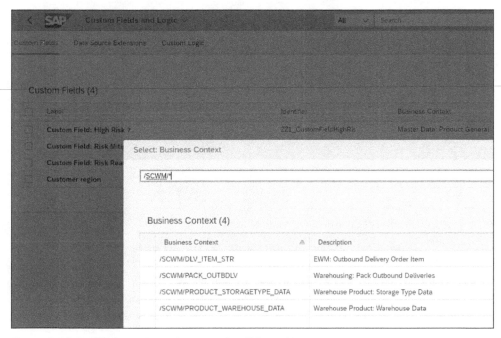

Figure 3.46 Available Business Contexts for /SCWM/ Namespace

3. Choose a context from the list (e.g., **/SCWM/PRODUCT_WAREHOUSE_DATA** to extend the warehouse product), and go on to define the field parameters, as shown in Figure 3.47.

Figure 3.47 Define Parameters of New Custom Field

233

4. **Define custom field availability**

Go to the **UIs and Reports** tab to define availability for the custom field. Figure 3.48 shows the availability of the custom field. Choose the **Enable Usage** action for the field in the respective function and then **Publish** the field.

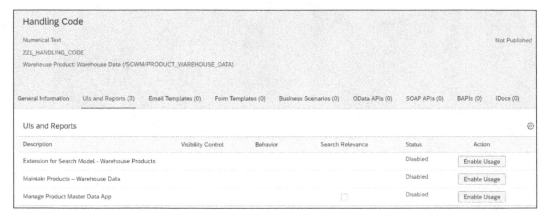

Figure 3.48 Definition of Custom Field Availability

5. **Checking the results**

You can immediately check the results of the field generation after publication by calling Transaction /SCWM/MAT1 (Warehouse Product Data Maintenance). In our example case, the additional field can be found on the **Warehouse Data** tab, where it is ready for input (see Figure 3.49).

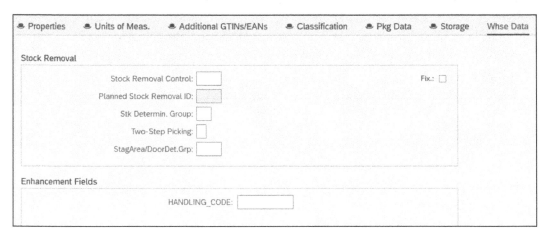

Figure 3.49 Result of Custom Field Publication in Enhancement Fields Subscreen

3.5.3 Extended Warehouse Management Extension Includes

In contrast to the business objects or business contexts of key user extensibility mentioned earlier, you can further enhance EWM-specific business objects, which were not foreseen for key user extensibility, in a manual way. Such extension includes, which we will call *EWM extension includes*, can be manually extended by adding an append structure, which is possible without registered modifications to standard DDIC objects. EWM extension includes can be found for the following applications and business objects:

- Delivery (including expected goods receipt, production material request, and JIT call)
- Warehouse task
- Warehouse order
- Handling unit
- Transportation unit
- Vehicle
- Door
- Available and physical stock
- Packaging specification
- VAS order
- Quality inspection document
- Indirect labor task
- Measurement services framework telegram
- Preallocated stock
- Stock consolidation
- Warehouse product data
- Warehouse product storage type data
- Warehouse billing
- ABC analysis result
- Historical workload
- Initial stock upload

These EWM extension includes were built in by SAP to associated structures, or database tables directly, belonging to a DDIC object. For example, adding a field in the extension include for the handling unit header will make the field appear in the handling unit header database table, as well as in the internal handling unit header structures and in the structures for handling unit header data display—for example, in warehouse monitor lists for the handling unit header. The where-used references of such extension includes give you information about where the new field will potentially appear. Again, adding custom fields for these business objects should follow the regular procedure of using append structures with the respective EWM extension includes.

Automatically generated or customizable screen enhancements are not supported by manual enhancements of EWM extension includes. However, many UIs of individual business objects in EWM use the SAP List Viewer (ALV) and the EWM extension includes are mostly present in the respective ALV lists underlying the structures used for data display. This is why custom fields are often found in the list view of EWM business objects but not in the form view. If available for the object, you can implement BAdIs so as to have the fields appear in the form view as well. A list of available BAdIs for business objects of delivery processing and warehouse logistics can be found in Table 3.14. Further implementation advice for the respective BAdIs can be found in the Customizing documentation under the listed paths.

Business Object	Enhancement Spot for UI Extension
Delivery	/SCWM/ES_DLV_UI_SCREEN

IMG path: **Business Add-Ins (BAdIs) For Extended Warehouse Management • Cross-Process Settings • Delivery - Warehouse Request • Screen Enhancements for Customer Enhancement Structures**

Applicable in the following transactions:

- /SCWM/EGR
- /SCWM/FD
- /SCWM/GRN
- /SCWM/IDN
- /SCWM/IM_DR
- /SCWM/IM_PC
- /SCWM/IM_ST
- /SCWM/ODR
- /SCWM/PRDI
- /SCWM/PRDO

Expected goods receipt	/SCWM/ES_GR

IMG path: **Business Add-Ins (BAdIs) For Extended Warehouse Management • Goods Receipt Process • Enhancements for Goods Receipt Process • Define Enhancements for Goods Receipt Processes**

Applicable in the following transactions:

- /SCWM/GRPE
- /SCWM/GRPI
- /SCWM/GR

VAS order	/SCWM/ES_VAS_UI

IMG path: **Business Add-Ins (BAdIs) For Extended Warehouse Management • Cross-Process Settings • Value-Added Services (VAS) • BAdI: Screen-Exit for a VAS Header**

Table 3.14 Enhancement Spots for UI Extensions

Business Object	Enhancement Spot for UI Extension
Applicable in the following transactions: ■ /SCWM/VAS ■ /SCWM/VASEXEC ■ /SCWM/VAS_I ■ /SCWM/VAS_INT ■ /SCWM/VAS_KTR ■ /SCWM/VAS_KTS ■ /SCWM/VAS_KTO	
Packaging specification	**/SCWM/ES_PS_UI**
IMG path: **Business Add-Ins (BAdIs) For Extended Warehouse Management • Master Data • Packaging Specification • Packaging Specification User Interface** Applicable in the following transaction: ■ /SCWM/PACKSPEC	

Table 3.14 Enhancement Spots for UI Extensions (Cont.)

Finding EWM-Related Include Structures for Field Enhancements

The ABAP Data Dictionary object search (Transaction SE11) can be used to find Include structures easily for custom field enhancements. For the warehouse logistics EWM component, use the wildcard search input "/SCWM/INCL_EEW*". Try search string "/SCDL/ INCL_EEW*" to widen your search for component delivery processing.

We will use the delivery object to provide an example of a manual custom field extension in EWM. You can find the corresponding include structures in Table 3.15. You should particularly note that several delivery document types (e.g., inbound delivery notification and outbound delivery request) use the same structures. This leads to an enhancement being simultaneously available in several document types.

Extension Include for Document Header	Extension Include for Document Item
Request and Notification	
/SCDL/INCL_EEW_DR_HEAD_STR	/SCDL/INCL_EEW_DR_ITEM_STR
Delivery Order (Processing Document)	
/SCDL/INCL_EEW_DLV_HEAD_STR	SCDL/INCL_EEW_DLV_ITEM_STR

Table 3.15 Extension Includes for EWM Delivery Documents

The outbound delivery (final delivery) thereby uses the same structures as the outbound delivery order (processing document). There are a range of BAdIs available from which the new fields can be supplied with data. It should be noted for the delivery processing that the fields are often supplied from SAP ERP or SAP S/4HANA, and then passed into the different delivery document types and potentially into the succeeding warehouse tasks as well. Such custom enhancement requires the use of various BAdIs, in which the following activities will be performed:

1. Transfer of the field values from the SAP ERP or SAP S/4HANA system into the message for delivery replication

2. Handover of field values to EWM within inbound message processing for the delivery within EWM

3. Transfer of field values from the delivery notification to processing delivery document type (only applicable for decentralized EWM while not skipping the notification document)

4. Transfer of the field values from the delivery to the warehouse task

You can find a detailed version of this procedure in the enhancement example for the simple outbound process in Chapter 4, Section 4.4.

Screen Enhancements for Web Dynpro UIs in Extended Warehouse Management

Several newer EWM applications, such as the shipping cockpit, have been built on Web Dynpro UI technology. SAP provides further frameworks, such as the floorplan manager, to enable you to enhance such applications. For a detailed description of how to go about doing so, refer to SAP Note 1902754.

3.6 Work Center

In this section, we will explain the UI EWM work center and its role as a framework. First let's have a look at the architecture, the different use cases in standard, and the enhancement possibilities. Then we will experience the framework with some specific custom development exercises.

SAP Fiori Apps for Packing in Extended Warehouse Management

EWM in SAP S/4HANA provides some newer SAP Fiori apps for certain functionalities, such as delivery creation, cart picking, and packing. You can find a list of available SAP Fiori apps for EWM in the SAP Fiori apps reference library at *https://fioriapps-library.hana.ondemand.com/*. Filter by component SCM-EWM. While the SAP Fiori apps allow for some configuration, they do not offer the enhancement options provided with the classical work center. We encourage you to evaluate the different app options in your project to make an optimal choice of which app to use.

3.6.1   Basics and Architecture

The UI work center is made for warehouse employees working in packing. Their main work is to pack, label, and consolidate stock into, for example, cartons or pallets, either for shipping or for storing within the warehouse. Besides the physical work, they have to document the results in the system on desktop computers. We will now go into detail about the use of the work center transaction and its screen areas, finally looking at its architectural structure and available BAdIs.

Usage of the Work Center Transaction in the Warehouse

After the user has finished his physical work (e.g., packing 10 cartons on a pallet), he documents the packing steps in the system. Ideally, the desktop computer located in the warehouse is equipped with a keyboard scanner and a printer. A mouse is often not available, as users do the physical work with gloves and the environment is dusty. There are usually a limited number of different workflows that the user has to enter in EWM: repacking of stock, repacking of pallets, closing a pallet, and so on.

The EWM work center (see Figure 3.50) might fit into the required workflows in your warehouse, as it offers several tabs, with each designed for one specific packing workflow. If the tabs do not exactly fit, you can add your own tabs via screen BAdIs in which you optimize the input fields for the workflows in your warehouse.

The tabs in the UI can be switched on or off using IMG activity **EWM • Master Data • Work Center • Specify Work Center Layout**. Ideally, you would reduce the layout to three to eight tabs out of the 40 available so that, for example, the user in packing outbound has only those tabs required for his tasks. The BAdI tabs can also be switched on or off in this IMG activity.

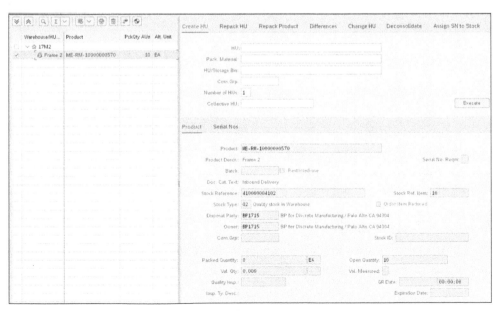

Figure 3.50 Work Center Packing Outbound User Interface

Screen Areas

The UI (shown in Figure 3.51) has four screen areas: tree control ❶, scanner tabs ❷, detail tabs ❸, and status ❹.

For the different areas, you have the following enhancement options (there are no enhancement options for the status area):

- In the tree control, you can use the Change of Display in Tree Control BAdI to, for example, change the icons.

- In the scanner area, you can add up to three of your own tabs by using the Individual Screens on User Interface of the Workcenter BAdI. A tab has space for simple packing workflows as it offers approximately six lines.

- Use the Separate Detail Screens on Workstation Desktop UI BAdI to add up to five tabs in the details area. A new tab has space for approximately fifteen lines, so it can be used to show tables or support more complex workflows.

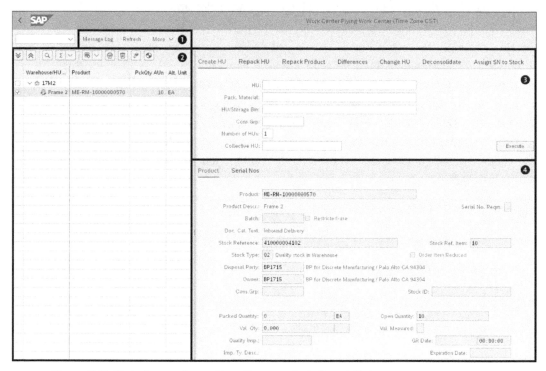

Figure 3.51 Main Screen Areas: Tree, Scanner, Detail, and Status

Architecture and BAdI Usage

The UI work center is used in several standard transactions. Table 3.16 lists the transaction names as well as the report names.

Name	Transaction	Report
Packing General	/SCWM/PACK	/SCWM/RPACKENTRY
Deconsolidation in Goods Receipt	/SCWM/DCONS	/SCWM/RSPREADENTRY
Create Confirmation for VAS	/SCWM/VASEXEC	/SCWM/RVASENTRY
Quality Inspection and Count	/SCWM/QINSP (decentralized EWM)	/SCWM/RQINSPENTRY
Maintain Planned Shipping HUs	/SCWM/CAP	/SCWM/RPOPACKENTRY
Packing for Inbound or OD	/SCWM/PRDI and /SCWM/PRDO, then navigate to **Follow-on Functions • Pack**	/SCWM/RCALL_PACK_IBDL /SCWM/RCALL_PACK_OBDL
HU Display	/SCWM/MON, then select the monitor method **HU Display**	/SCWM/RHU_PACKING

Table 3.16 Usage of UI Work Center

All transactions have the display and/or processing of handling units in common. In the transactions for VAS (/SCWM/VASEXEC) and quality inspection (/SCWM/QINSP), in addition to handling units, you can also process VAS or quality inspection documents.

All transactions in Table 3.16 consist of two parts:

- An entry screen, which is usually a program with select options
- A main screen (refer back to Figure 3.50)

You will find the different reports for the work center transactions in package /SCWM/PACKING.

Figure 3.52 shows the architecture of the work center with regards to the model-view-controller levels:

- The view/controller level consists of several entry screens ❶ and the main screen ❷. With the central function module /SCWM/PACKING_UI in function group /SCWM/UI_PACKING, the main screen is started.
- The /SCWM/UI_PACKING function group ❷ takes care of all the SAP GUI elements (the tree control, grid controls, etc.) and will ensure that all relevant controls are updated after each user interaction (e.g., deleting a handling unit). It translates the user input into technical keys and forwards iti via the global GIF_MODEL model instance to the model level.
- The model level ❸ consists of several service classes all inheriting from class /SCWM/CL_PACK, which implements the /SCWM/IF_PACK interface. The service class offers simple

methods such as create_hu, delete_hu, pack_stock, and so on. If a method was successful, it triggers an event that can be handled by the view/controller level to update the screen.

- If packing takes place for a planned handling unit, the /SCWM/CL_DLVPACK_IBDL service class is used. For a planned handling unit, the stock items are not posted to goods receipt in the warehouse yet. After stock is posted to goods receipt, the /SCWM/CL_WM_PACKING service class is used to document repacking of handling units. Stock that has left the warehouse via a goods issue posting cannot be repacked as no service class exists.

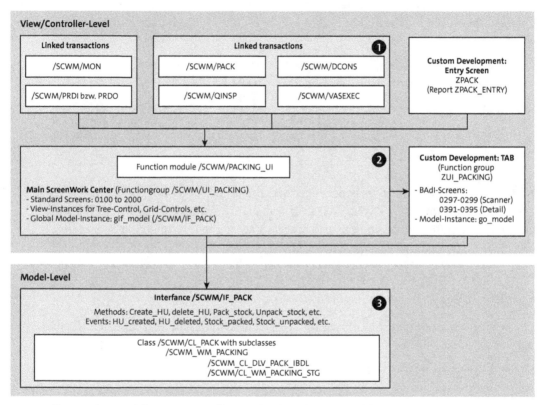

Figure 3.52 Model-View-Controller Levels of Application Work Center

The model level with its /SCWM/CL_WM_PACKING service class is used also in many RF transactions. If you plan to develop a new UI for packing, such as in Web Dynpro, and would rather not use the work center, you certainly should reuse the methods of service class /SCWM/CL_WM_PACKING.

All enhancement options via BAdIs for the work center can be found in IMG folder **Business Add-Ins (BAdIs) for Extended Warehouse Management • Master Data • Work Center • Adjust User Interface for Work Center**. They are all grouped into the /SCWM/ES_WRKC_UI enhancement spot.

Table 3.17 is intended to support you in finding the right BAdI for your requirement. Besides the IMG name and the technical name in the first two columns, you will find the information about which model/view/controller level the BAdI is located in in the Level column (Figure 3.52 ❷ and ❸). The Screen Area/Tab column references the location of the BAdI call on the screen; see Figure 3.51. So, for example, BAdI /SCWM/EX_WRKC_UI_DEST_BIN is called in the scanner area ❷ on the **Create HU** tab. In the last column, you will find the information about which service method of interface /SCWM/IF_PACK the BAdI is called in. If the column is empty, then the call of this BAdI does not take place in a service method.

BAdI Name In IMG	Technical Name	Level	Screen Area/Tab	Method Context
Additional Activities before and after Packing	/SCWM/EX_WRKC_PACK	❸	❶ and ❷	Repack_stock, Pack_HU, Pack_by_to
Target Storage Bin Proposal for Putaway HU	/SCWM/EX_WRKC_UI_DEST_BIN	❷	❷, Create HU	
Determination of Warehouse Task for Deconsolidation	/SCWM/EX_WRKC_UI_WHTA_DCONS	❷	❷, Deconsolidate	
Reaction to Changes to HU	/SCWM/EX_WRKC_UI_HU_CHANGED	❷	❸, Capacity	
Repack HU or HU Contents	/SCWM/EX_WRKC_UI_FLAG_REPACK	❷	❷, Repack HU	
Selection of HU from Possible Destination HUs	/SCWM/EX_WRKC_UI_DETERMINE_HU	❷	❷, Repack HU, Repack Product	
Determination of HU Weight Using Scale	/SCWM/EX_WRKC_UI_GET_WEIGHT	❷	❷, Change HU	
Determine a Packaging Material for an HU Identification	/SCWM/EX_WRKC_UI_PAMT_FR_IDENT	❷	❷, Create HU	

Table 3.17 Work Center BAdIs

BAdI Name In IMG	Technical Name	Level	Screen Area/Tab	Method Context
Change of Display in Tree Control	/SCWM/EX_WRKC_UI_TREE_CONTROL	❷	❶	
Change of Active Tab Page in Desktop Detail Area	/SCWM/EX_WRKC_UI_DETAIL_TABS	❷	❸	
Setting the GUI-Status	/SCWM/EX_WRKC_UI_GUI_STATUS	❷	❹	
Push Button for Navigating in the Product Master	/SCWM/EX_WRKC_UI_PRO-DUCTMASTER	❷	❸, Product	
Individual Screens on UI of the Work Center	/SCWM/EX_WRKC_UI_SCAN_SCREENS	❷	❷	
Separate Detail Screens on Workstation Desktop UI	/SCWM/EX_WRKC_UI_DETA_SCREENS	❷	❸	
Method Called after Save	/SCWM/EX_WRKC_UI_AFTER_SAVE	❸	❹	Save
Destination HUs and Packaging Materials from PSHUs	/SCWM/EX_WRKC_UI_PO_PROP	❷	❷, Repack HU, Repack Product	
Set Proposal for Quantity and Unit for HU Item Repacking	/SCWM/EX_WRKC_PACK_QTY_PROPOSE	❷	❷, Repack Product	

Table 3.17 Work Center BAdIs (Cont.)

[»]

Impact of Business Add-In Implementations

Keep in mind that the BAdIs listed earlier are called in several work center transactions. You might want to limit your implementation to certain use cases. The functional BAdIs, especially the ones that are listed with level 3, are called in many standard functions, such as ad hoc warehouse task creation and RF transactions.

Besides the aforementioned BAdIs, there are also object-specific BAdIs available for handling units, warehouse tasks, and the like.

3.6.2   Enhancing the Entry Screen

If you need to enhance the entry screen (see Figure 3.53) with, for example, further or different selection parameters or application checks, you can do this with little effort.

All the listed reports in Table 3.16 show the same flow logic. First a screen with some selection parameters is displayed, and then some checks are done. As a last step, the /SCWM/CALL_PACKUI function module is called with a list of handling units in order to navigate to the work center main screen.

After you copy the short report /SCWM/RPACKENTRY in the ABAP Editor (Transaction SE38) to report ZPACK, you can add your own selection criteria or remove the unused selection parameters. You could also add some further checks before you let the user continue on the main screen.

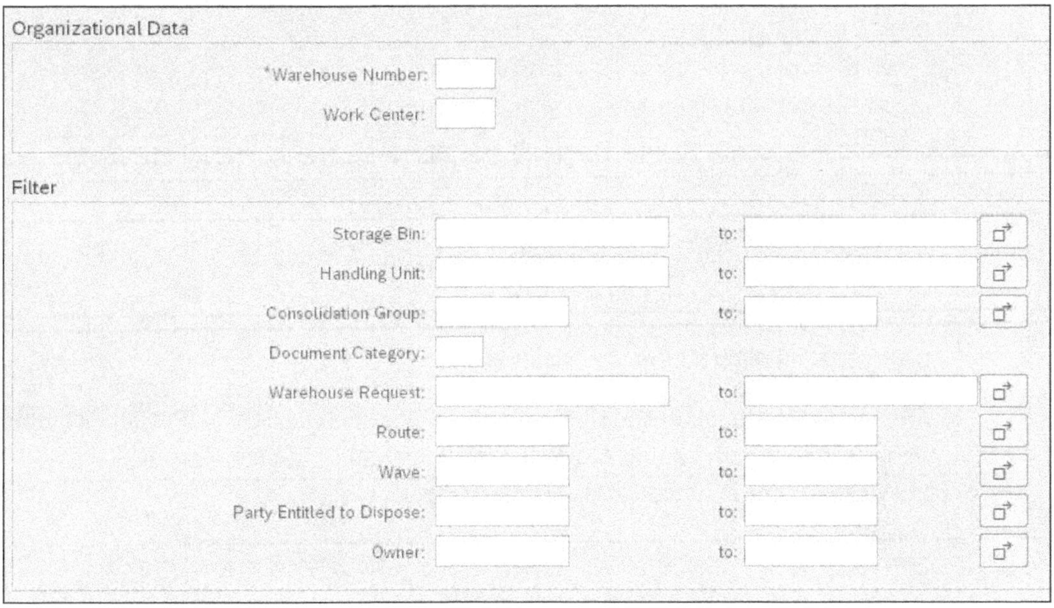

Organizational Data		
*Warehouse Number:		
Work Center:		

Filter		
Storage Bin:	to:	
Handling Unit:	to:	
Consolidation Group:	to:	
Document Category:		
Warehouse Request:	to:	
Route:	to:	
Wave:	to:	
Party Entitled to Dispose:	to:	
Owner:	to:	

Figure 3.53 Entry Screen for Transaction /SCWM/PACK: Packing—General

Start Packing Only for Fully Picked Deliveries

If you need to require that a packer at the work center will only start packing outbound deliveries for which the picking is completed, you can copy the report as described earlier and add a check on the delivery status.

245

3.6.3 Custom Development: Change Icons in the Tree Control

On the work center main screen, the tree control on the left side (see Figure 3.50) presents the objects' handling units, stock, and bins with different icons. To make the work for the user easier, you can set your own icons for the stock in special situations. In our example, we will use the yellow traffic light icon to indicate to the user that this stock line is still in quality inspection and in his work list. Also, we will change the icon for handling units that are closed to one that shows a carton with a dotted border line.

To create an enhancement implementation of this type, take the following steps:

1. Begin by starting with the IMG activity **BAdI: Change of Display in Tree Control** (Transaction SE19), for BAdI Z_EI_WRKC_UI. Implement the CHANGE_TREE_LINE method of BAdI /SCWM/EX_WRKC_UI_TREE_CONTROL. Do not forget to add the ICON type group on the **Properties** tab of your new BAdI class—for example, ZCL_IM_WRKC_UI.

2. The sample coding for the yellow traffic light is shown in Listing 3.15.

```
METHOD /scwm/if_ex_wrkc_ui_tree_cntrl~change_tree_line.
  BREAK-POINT ID zewmdevbook_363.
  IF  cs_line-guid_type = '07' "product line
  AND cs_line-cat(1)     = 'Q'. "stock type
    cs_line-icon_node = icon_yellow_light.
  ENDIF.
  IF  cs_line-guid_type = '06' "hu line
  AND cs_line-copst IS NOT INITIAL. "hu completed
    cs_line-icon_node = icon_wf_replace_workitem.
  ENDIF.
ENDMETHOD.
```

Listing 3.15 Set Different Icon for Quality Stock

3. After activating the BAdI and the coding, start Transaction /SCWM/PACK (Packing—General) to test your coding. Stock that is under quality inspection is displayed with the yellow traffic light icon as displayed in Figure 3.54.

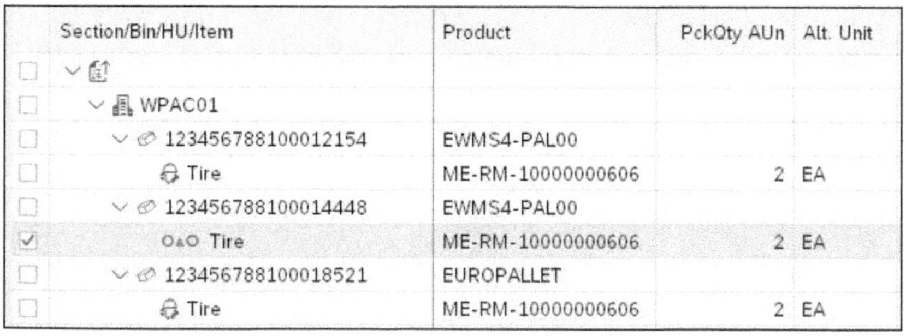

	Section/Bin/HU/Item	Product	PckQty	AUn	Alt. Unit
☐	∨ 🗂				
☐	∨ 🗐 WPAC01				
☐	∨ ⊘ 123456788100012154	EWMS4-PAL00			
☐	🔀 Tire	ME-RM-10000000606	2	EA	
☐	∨ ⊘ 123456788100014448	EWMS4-PAL00			
☑	O▲O Tire	ME-RM-10000000606	2	EA	
☐	∨ ⊘ 123456788100018521	EUROPALLET			
☐	🔀 Tire	ME-RM-10000000606	2	EA	

Figure 3.54 Work Center with New Icons in Tree Control

Remember that your coding will run with every refresh the user executes, so you have to avoid database-intensive logic for determining the right icon.

3.6.4   Custom Development: New Tab in Scanner Area

In the next example, we will show you how to use the screen BAdI to handle a project-specific requirement for repacking stock. Let's assume the standard **HU Repacking** tab is too complex for use in your project.

Specification

A user will first scan a destination handling unit (e.g., pallet). In the next input field, the user will scan one or several pick handling units (e.g., cartons; see Figure 3.55). Then, the system will create a nested handling unit (e.g., several cartons on one pallet). The pallet can be used in the next warehouse processing steps for scanning, such as loading.

The value of the destination handling unit will stay the same in this UI as long as the user does not actively change it. The **F8 New Dest-HU** button is offered to allow the user to change to an empty new pallet. The goal of this specification is to minimize the number of scans.

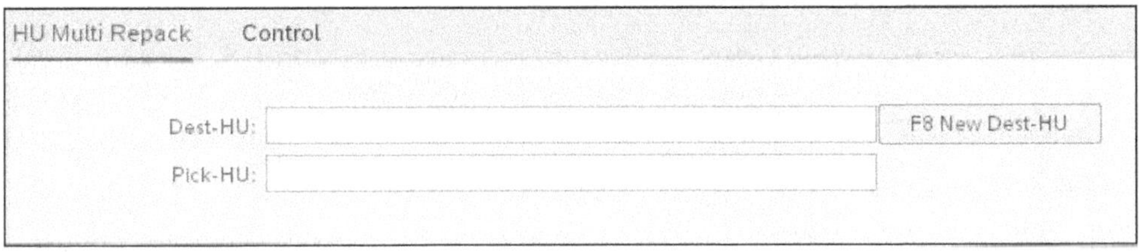

Figure 3.55 New HU Multi Repack Tab in Scanner Area

Realization

To create a new tab in the work center UI, follow these steps:

1. Create a function group, such as ZUI_PACKING, in ABAP Object Navigator (Transaction SE80).

2. In the new TOP include, such as LZUI_PACKINGTOP, of the ZUI_PACKING function group, create the global parameters for the source and destination handling unit (see Listing 3.16).

```
FUNCTION-POOL ZUI_PACKING.
TABLES: /scwm/s_pack_view_scanner.
DATA: gs_dest_hu    TYPE /scwm/s_huhdr_int,
      gs_source_hu  TYPE /scwm/s_huhdr_int,
      go_model      TYPE REF TO /scwm/cl_wm_packing.
```

Listing 3.16 Coding of TOP Include

3. Copy screen 0205 of function group /SCWM/UI_PACKING to your new function group from step 1. Name the new screen–for example, 999.

4. Change the flow logic of screen 999 as described in Listing 3.17.

```
PROCESS BEFORE OUTPUT.
  MODULE status_999.

PROCESS AFTER INPUT.

  FIELD /scwm/s_pack_view_scanner-dest_hu_prop_ui
  MODULE scan_dest_hu_999 ON REQUEST.
  FIELD /scwm/s_pack_view_scanner-source_hu_ui
  MODULE scan_source_999 ON REQUEST.
  MODULE user_command_999.
```

Listing 3.17 Flow Logic for Screen 999

5. Start the screen painter for the screen 999. Change the layout so that only two input fields are showing (destination handling unit and pick handling unit). One button with the description **F8 New Dest-HU** will be placed next to the destination handling unit field. See details for the layout in Figure 3.55. Use the field names SOURCE_HU_UI and DEST_HU_PROP_UI of structure /SCWM/S_PACK_VIEW_SCANNER.

6. Create the status_999 PBO module in a new include (see Listing 3.18). With this module, you make sure that the system focuses automatically on the next input field so that the user can just scan barcodes and does not have to interrupt his work by using the keyboard.

```
MODULE status_999 OUTPUT.
  "Get the model instance for packing
  IF go_model IS INITIAL.
    /scwm/cl_wm_packing=>get_instance( IMPORTING eo_instance = go_model ).
  ENDIF.
  "Focus on the next field for input
  IF /scwm/s_pack_view_scanner-dest_hu_prop_ui IS INITIAL.
    SET CURSOR FIELD '/SCWM/S_PACK_VIEW_SCANNER-DEST_HU_PROP_UI'.
    EXIT.
  ENDIF.
  IF /scwm/s_pack_view_scanner-source_hu_ui IS INITIAL.
    SET CURSOR FIELD '/SCWM/S_PACK_VIEW_SCANNER-SOURCE_HU_UI'.
    EXIT.
  ENDIF.
ENDMODULE.
```

Listing 3.18 Status_999 PBO Module

7. Create the scan_dest_hu_999, scan_source_999, and user_command_999 PAI modules in a new include (see Listing 3.19). In those modules, the system will check and process

the input of the screen fields and will react to the use of the [F8] button. Activate the function group.

```
MODULE scan_dest_hu_999 INPUT.
  "User scanned a destination handling unit -> read handling unit
  CLEAR gs_dest_hu.
  IF NOT /scwm/s_pack_view_scanner-dest_hu_prop_ui
  IS INITIAL.
    /scwm/s_pack_view_scanner-dest_hu =
    /scwm/s_pack_view_scanner-dest_hu_prop_ui.
    go_model->get_hu(
      EXPORTING
        iv_huident = /scwm/s_pack_view_scanner-dest_hu
      IMPORTING
        es_huhdr   = gs_dest_hu
      EXCEPTIONS
        OTHERS     = 99 ).
    IF sy-subrc <> 0.
      CLEAR /scwm/s_pack_view_scanner-dest_hu_prop_ui.
      MESSAGE ID sy-msgid TYPE sy-msgty NUMBER sy-msgno
      WITH sy-msgv1 sy-msgv2 sy-msgv3 sy-msgv4.
    ENDIF.
  ENDIF.
ENDMODULE.

MODULE scan_source_999 INPUT.
  "User scanned a source handling unit -> read handling unit
  CLEAR gs_source_hu.
  IF NOT /scwm/s_pack_view_scanner-source_hu_ui IS INITIAL.
    /scwm/s_pack_view_scanner-source_hu =
    /scwm/s_pack_view_scanner-source_hu_ui.
    go_model->get_hu(
      EXPORTING
        iv_huident = /scwm/s_pack_view_scanner-source_hu
      IMPORTING
        es_huhdr   = gs_source_hu
      EXCEPTIONS
        OTHERS     = 99 ).
    IF sy-subrc <> 0.
      "Scan error -> user must repeat the scan
      CLEAR /scwm/s_pack_view_scanner-source_hu_ui.
      MESSAGE ID sy-msgid TYPE sy-msgty NUMBER sy-msgno
      WITH sy-msgv1 sy-msgv2 sy-msgv3 sy-msgv4.
    ENDIF.
```

```
    ENDIF.
* 2-98: Additional Checks...
* to be implemented
   "99 Repack the source-hu into the target-handling unit
   IF gs_source_hu IS NOT INITIAL AND
   gs_dest_hu IS NOT INITIAL.
     go_model->pack_hu(
       EXPORTING
         iv_source_hu = gs_source_hu-guid_hu
         iv_dest_hu   = gs_dest_hu-guid_hu
       EXCEPTIONS
         error        = 1
         OTHERS       = 2 ).
     IF sy-subrc <> 0.
       MESSAGE ID sy-msgid TYPE sy-msgty NUMBER sy-msgno
       WITH sy-msgv1 sy-msgv2 sy-msgv3 sy-msgv4.
     ENDIF.
     /scwm/cl_pack=>go_log->init( ).
     "Clear input field for the next source handling unit
     CLEAR: gs_source_hu,
     /scwm/s_pack_view_scanner-source_hu_ui.
   ENDIF.
ENDMODULE.


MODULE user_command_999 INPUT.
   "User wants to scan a new target handling unit, clear the field
   IF sy-ucomm = 'F8'.
     CLEAR /scwm/s_pack_view_scanner-dest_hu_prop_ui.
     "Set function code to default
     CALL FUNCTION 'SAPGUI_SET_FUNCTIONCODE'
       EXCEPTIONS
         OTHERS = 99.
     IF sy-subrc <> 0.
       MESSAGE ID sy-msgid TYPE sy-msgty NUMBER sy-msgno
       WITH sy-msgv1 sy-msgv2 sy-msgv3 sy-msgv4.
     ENDIF.
   ENDIF.
ENDMODULE.
```

Listing 3.19 Include for PAI Modules

To make the new tab visible in the work center, you have to follow the next few steps:

1. Use the IMG and create an enhancement implementation for the **BAdI: Individual Screens on User Interface of the Workcenter** activity—for example, Z_EI_WRKC_UI_ SCAN. Enter a name for the BAdI implementation, such as ZEX_WRKC_UI_SCAN, and

select the /SCWM/EX_WRKC_UI_SCAN_SCREENS BAdI. Enter a class name (e.g., ZCL_IM_WRKC_UI_SCAN) and continue. As shown in Figure 3.56, link to the new SAPLZUI_PACKING program and subscreen 999 on the **Enh. Implementation Elements** tab for screen 297 (BADI_SCANNER_TAB3).

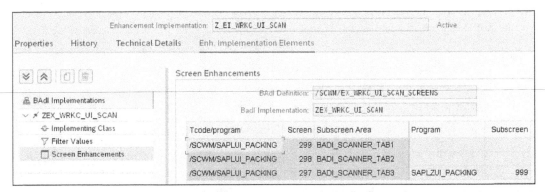

Figure 3.56 Assign Subscreen and Program to Enhancement Implementation

2. In Listing 3.20, you will find sample coding for method set_tab_name that you will implement in class ZCL_IM_WRKC_UI_SCAN. Here you set the name of the new tab, such as, "HU Multi Repack," which you maintain via text element TEXT-001. Do not forget to activate the class and the BAdI implementation.

```
METHOD /scwm/if_ex_wrkc_ui_scan_scr~set_tab_name.
  BREAK-POINT ID zewmdevbook_364.
  ev_text_scanner_badi_3 = TEXT-001. "HU Multi Repack
ENDMETHOD.
```

Listing 3.20 Set_tab_name Method

You have now finished all of the development steps. To make the new tab visible, the following IMG steps are required.

1. Start activity **EWM • Master Data • Work Center • Specify Work Center Layout** in the IMG, and create a new layout, such as ZBD1. Choose **1—Packing General** for **Transaction Type**, and in the **Tab Pages in Scanner Area** frame, select the checkboxes for **Display Scanner Area** and **BAdI 3**. Save and exit this IMG activity.

2. Start the following **Define Work Center** IMG activity, select an existing entry, and copy it to, for example, work center ZBD1. In the **Work Center Layout** field, enter "ZBD1", from the previous step. For the **Check Stop on Route** field, choose **2—Check while repacking handling units and products**. Afterward, the system will make sure you consolidate only cartons of the same route on one pallet handling unit.

3. In the SAP menu, start Transaction /SCWM/TWORKST (Define Master Data Attributes) and assign a storage bin to work center ZBD1—for example, bin PACK-O01.

To test the new work center, run Transaction /SCWM/PACK (Packing—General). On the entry screen, select warehouse 1710 and work center ZBD1.

You'll find the new **Multi HU Repack** tab, as shown in Figure 3.55. Scan an existing pallet handling unit barcode into the first field, **Dest-HU**. The system will navigate automatically to the next field, **Pick-HU**. Here, scan one or several carton handling units. Verify the result in the tree control area of the work center: a nested handling unit should show up, showing a pallet handling unit containing one or several carton handling units.

[+]

Use Central Model Class for Packing

To use the work center packing model class in your implementations, make sure you call the static GET_INSTANCE method:

/scwm/cl_wm_packing=>get_instance(IMPORTING eo_instance = go_model)

This will ensure that the work center framework will handle any repacking events—for example, display updates of the tree control after each repack scan. Furthermore, the automatic save and refresh is triggered by the framework. This way, you do not have to take care of saving, refreshing, or locking in your custom BAdI implementation; in most cases, the model class and the framework will complete these tasks for you. Try to use the methods of the /SCWM/CL_WM_PACKING model class as much as possible, like method PACK_HU (to repack a handling unit) or method HU_PROCESS_COMPLETED (to close a handling unit).

3.6.5   Custom Development: Close Handling Unit

In this section, you will become familiar with BAdI /SCWM/EX_WRKC_UI_AFTER_SAVE, which is called after each save in the work center. Here you will have the chance to add your own follow-up activities or to change existing follow-up activities.

We recommend that you switch on the **Save after Each Action** setting in the **Define Work Center** IMG activity so that after each user action, the system writes the changes to the database. If the user closes a handling unit, such as with the **Complete Process Step for HU** button, the system issues a saving command and a default follow-up activity: it creates a warehouse task as a follow-up for this handling unit in its next destination. This is done in the /SCWM/CL_EI_WRKC_UI_AFTER_SAVE fallback class of the /SCWM/EX_WRKC_UI_AFTER_SAVE BAdI. If you create your own implementation of this BAdI, you will automatically switch off the fallback class. If that is not intended, you can call the fallback class within your implementation by, for example, adding it before or after some checks.

Specification

In our project, a user in the goods receipt area will use the work center for building the handling units for putaway. For the finished handling units, the system will determine a putaway bin and also will confirm the task automatically. The user will do the putaway without system interaction as the putaway bins are close by. The user might select one or several handling units and use the **Complete Process Step for HU** button. The system will determine the putaway bins for those handling units one after the other, as the storage concept allows several handling units on the same bin.

Realization

Start the BAdI builder (Transaction SE19) and create a new enhancement implementation (e.g., Z_EI_WRKC_UI_AFTER_SAVE) for enhancement spot /SCWM/ES_WRKC_UI. Select BAdI /SCWM/EX_WRKC_UI_AFTER_SAVE and enter a name (e.g., "ZEX_WRKC_UI_AFTER_SAVE") and a class (e.g., "ZCL_IM_WRKC_UI_AFTER_SAVE"). Navigate to the AFTER_SAVE method and enter the coding shown in Listing 3.21.

Within the BAdI, the IT_MOVEHU import parameter lists all handling units for which a follow-up warehouse task is required. In coding paragraph "1, we change the follow-up warehouse tasks to immediate confirmation (field squit). And in paragraph "3, we make sure the tasks run in the same background queue, one after the other. Here we have set the queue name to be the bin of the work center. The standard sets the queue name to the handling unit identification, which results in parallel processing rather than in sequenced processing. In paragraph "2, we make sure that for all other work centers, the standard default coding is called.

```
METHOD /scwm/if_ex_wrkc_ui_after_save~after_save.
  BREAK-POINT ID zewmdevbook_365.
  "Note, with this implementation the standard implementation is switched off
  DATA: lv_qname  TYPE trfcqnam.

  "1. Your own logic for follow-up warehouse tasks
  DATA(lt_movehu) = it_movehu.
  LOOP AT lt_movehu ASSIGNING FIELD-SYMBOL(<ls_movehu>).
    "Immediate conf. WT when Work Center = "1234"
    IF is_workstation-workstation = 'ZBD1'.
      <ls_movehu>-squit = abap_true.
    ENDIF.
  ENDLOOP.
  "2. Call standard impl. to switch on follow-up warehouse task creation
  IF is_workstation-lgpla <> 'Y831.001.01'.
    DATA(lo_std) = NEW /scwm/cl_ei_wrkc_ui_after_save( ).
    lo_std->/scwm/if_ex_wrkc_ui_after_save~after_save(
      EXPORTING
        it_movehu      = lt_movehu
        it_closedhu    = it_closedhu
        is_workstation = is_workstation
      IMPORTING
        ev_save        = ev_save ).
```

```
      ELSE.
        "3. Change queue name to BIN (instead of HU)
      IF it_movehu IS NOT INITIAL.
        LOOP AT it_movehu INTO DATA(ls_movehu).
          CLEAR: lt_movehu, lv_qname.
          "Prepare rfc queue
          MOVE: wmegc_qrfc_hu_prcs   TO lv_qname,
                is_workstation-lgpla TO lv_qname+4.

          DATA(ls_rfc_queue) = VALUE /scwm/s_rfc_queue(
            mandt = sy-mandt
            queue = lv_qname ).
          CALL FUNCTION 'GUID_CREATE'
            IMPORTING
              ev_guid_16 = ls_rfc_queue-guid.

          CALL FUNCTION 'TRFC_SET_QIN_PROPERTIES'
            EXPORTING
              qin_name = lv_qname.
          APPEND ls_movehu TO lt_movehu.
          "Call process-oriented storage control for each handling unit
          CALL FUNCTION '/SCWM/TO_CREATE_MOVE_HU'
            IN BACKGROUND TASK
            AS SEPARATE UNIT
            EXPORTING
              iv_lgnum       = is_workstation-lgnum
              iv_commit_work = abap_false
              iv_bname       = sy-uname
              is_rfc_queue   = ls_rfc_queue
              iv_wtcode      = wmegc_wtcode_procs
              it_create_hu   = lt_movehu.
        ENDLOOP.
        ev_save = abap_true.
        CLEAR: ls_rfc_queue.
      ENDIF.
    ENDIF.
ENDMETHOD.
```

Listing 3.21 Sample Coding for Close Handling Unit

You can test the development with an inbound delivery, which is the posted goods receipt, for which no putaway step has been completed yet. Start Transaction /SCWM/ PACK (Packing—General) for your warehouse (e.g., 1710) and work center (e.g., Y831). Enter the inbound delivery in the **Warehouse Request** field. Pack the items into one or several handling units, then select the handling units and use the **Complete Process Step for HU** button.

As a result, the handling units should be confirmed to their final bins, where one or several handling units had the same destination bin. If you stop the queue with the bin name in Transaction SMQ2 (qRFC Monitor), you can see several queue entries for warehouse task creation.

3.6.6 Custom Development: Packing of Inbound Deliveries

To pack items of an inbound delivery before goods receipt, you can use Transaction /SCWM/GR (Physical Goods Receipt). Select the inbound delivery; by pressing the **Pack** button, you'll end up in the packing work center. Transaction /SCWM/GR is designed for an office user. For warehouse operators on the shop floor, several other RF transactions, such as Receiving of Handling Units, are available.

Specification

A warehouse operator will have a desktop transaction where he scans one inbound delivery and then can pack the items.

Realization

The following steps are required to implement the solution for the new desktop transaction:

1. In the **EWM • Master Data • Work Center • Specify Work Center Layout** IMG activity, create a new entry (e.g., IB1) with **Transaction Type** set to **1—Packing General**. In the **Tab Pages in Scanner Area** frame, select the checkboxes for **Display scanner Area**, **Create HU**, **Repack Product**, and **Change HU**. Also select the **Display Tree Control** checkbox in the **Tree** frame.

2. Navigate to the next IMG activity in the same folder, **Define Work Center**, and create a work center, such as ZWP1, with **Description** set to **Packing Inbound Delivery**. In the **Work Center Layout** field, enter layout IB1 from the previous step. Do not select the **Save Action** checkbox.

3. Create a new report ZRCALL_PACK_IBDL in ABAP Editor (Transaction SE38). Copy the coding of Listing 3.22 and create the selection texts with reference to ABAP Dictionary. You can also create a transaction code (e.g., ZPACKIBD) to call the new selection report. Within the report, first define the selection parameters that the user will have (see coding paragraph "1). In paragraph "2, the work center Customizing settings are read and adjusted. Within a while loop, the main screen of the work center is called (see "3).

```
REPORT zrcall_pack_ibdl.

BREAK-POINT ID zewmdevbook_366.

TYPE-POOLS: wmegc.
TABLES: /scwm/s_wrk_pack.
DATA: ls_worksttyp    TYPE /scwm/twrktyp,
      lt_docid        TYPE /scwm/tt_docid,
      ls_docid        TYPE /scwm/s_docid,
      ls_workstation  TYPE /scwm/tworkst,
      lo_pack_ibdl    TYPE REF TO /scwm/cl_dlv_pack_ibdl,
      lv_ucomm        TYPE sy-ucomm VALUE 'SAVE'.

"1. Selection screen
PARAMETERS: pa_lgnum TYPE /scwm/s_wrk_pack-lgnum OBLIGATORY,
            pa_wrkst TYPE /scwm/s_wrk_pack-workstation,
            paprd    TYPE /scwm/s_wrk_pack-docno.

AT SELECTION-SCREEN.
  "2. Validate workcenter and delivery document number
  CALL FUNCTION '/SCWM/TWORKST_READ_SINGLE'
    EXPORTING
      iv_lgnum       = pa_lgnum
      iv_workstation = pa_wrkst
    IMPORTING
      es_workst      = ls_workstation
      es_wrktyp      = ls_worksttyp
    EXCEPTIONS
      OTHERS         = 3.
  IF sy-subrc <> 0.
    MESSAGE ID sy-msgid TYPE sy-msgty NUMBER sy-msgno
    WITH sy-msgv1 sy-msgv2 sy-msgv3 sy-msgv4.
  ENDIF.
  ls_workstation-save_act = space. "not recommended
  ls_worksttyp-tr_004 = abap_true. "Auto-Pack
  "validate that this workcenter is feasible
  "for inbound packing
  CALL FUNCTION '/SCWM/RF_DOCNO_TO_DOCID'
    EXPORTING
      iv_docno     = paprd
      iv_whr_doccat = wmegc_doccat_pdi
    IMPORTING
      ev_rdocid    = ls_docid-docid
    EXCEPTIONS
```

```
      OTHERS          = 99.
    IF sy-subrc <> 0.
      MESSAGE e000(/scwm/rf_en) WITH paprd.
    ENDIF.
    "3. Call workcenter UI
    CREATE OBJECT lo_pack_ibdl.
    APPEND ls_docid TO lt_docid.
    WHILE lv_ucomm = 'SAVE' OR lv_ucomm = 'REFRESH' .
      /scwm/cl_tm=>set_lgnum( ls_workstation-lgnum ).
      "Calculate the open quantity, but no refresh
      lo_pack_ibdl->init(
        EXPORTING
          iv_lgnum        = ls_workstation-lgnum
          it_docid        = lt_docid
          iv_doccat       = wmegc_doccat_pdi
          iv_no_refresh   = abap_true
          iv_lock_dlv     = abap_true
        IMPORTING
          ev_foreign_lock = DATA(lv_foreign_lock) ).
      IF NOT lv_foreign_lock IS INITIAL.
        MESSAGE i097(/scwm/ui_packing).
      ENDIF.
      /scwm/cl_dlv_pack_ibdl=>gv_online = abap_true.
      ls_worksttyp-lgnum = pa_lgnum.
      ls_worksttyp-trtyp = '6'. "Packing Inbound
      CALL FUNCTION '/SCWM/PACKING_UI'
        EXPORTING
          iv_display    = space
          iv_plan       = abap_true
          iv_model      = lo_pack_ibdl
        IMPORTING
          ev_fcode      = lv_ucomm
        CHANGING
          cs_workstation = ls_workstation
          cs_worksttyp   = ls_worksttyp.
      /scwm/cl_tm=>cleanup( ).
    ENDWHILE.
```

Listing 3.22 Sample Coding for Inbound Packing

When testing the new report/transaction, the entry screen will look as shown in Figure 3.57. You will need to enter values in **Warehouse Number** and **Work Center** and an inbound delivery in **Warehouse Request** before starting the selection.

Figure 3.57 New Entry Screen for Packing of Inbound Deliveries

On the main screen (see Figure 3.58), you will see the tabs as configured in the IMG, and you can create handling units, pack delivery items into them, and save. The system will create planned handling units at this point in time as the inbound delivery has not posted the goods receipt yet.

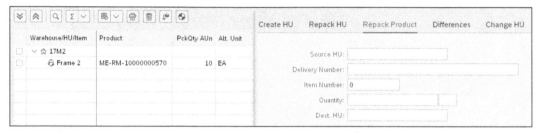

Figure 3.58 New Main Screen for Packing of Inbound Deliveries

We hope that with all those small examples of how to enhance the work center, you now have good ideas about how to do custom developments in your own project.

3.7   Summary

In this chapter, we described the important existing frameworks and development tools used by EWM. You should have a good idea now about how to enhance the warehouse management monitor, EGF, the RF framework, and the work center. In addition, you should be able to implement your own custom developments using PPF and key user extensibility.

In Chapter 4, more practical examples will be presented that will help you to understand the development tools even better and to learn what you can leverage from them.

Chapter 4

Enhancing SAP Best Practices for Embedded EWM

In this chapter, we provide a number of custom developments that you can adopt and use for your own projects. The foundation for these example enhancements is SAP Best Practices for embedded EWM with SAP S/4HANA.

In the previous chapters, you learned about the architecture of EWM and the enhancement frameworks that it offers. Now we would like to give you the opportunity to put into practice what you have learned.

Skilled project personnel that are both functionally and technically oriented, and who dare to look beyond their own expertise, provide the foundation of a successful EWM implementation project. Robust custom developments are most likely to come about when all parties of the development process bring to the table a clear understanding of software requirements and a solid solution approach for optimal implementation. It is from this perspective that we have written this chapter.

As both solution architects and developers alike, you will get an overview of the processes in the warehouse and an understanding of core processes in EWM. In addition, you will get to know the use of features, frameworks, and best practices that should be considered for the realization of custom developments in EWM. This chapter therefore applies to more functionally oriented consultants and to technically oriented developers who want to broaden their horizons for custom development options in EWM.

We have decided to use the available SAP Best Practices for embedded EWM scenarios and processes as the foundation on which to present custom development examples for EWM. SAP Best Practices for embedded EWM contain the core functionalities used in warehouses and can be quite rapidly installed on any SAP S/4HANA system landscape. We will enlarge the functionality within some of these processes by custom developments.

In the first section of this chapter, you will learn about the functionality used within the SAP Best Practices processes, technically referred to as *scope items*, and how to install them. Then you will learn how to locate and test custom developments within the selected processes. Further sections deal with single, specific process scenarios for warehouse management. We'll cover two processes for goods receiving, two for goods issue, and one for warehouse internal activities:

- Basic warehouse inbound processing from a supplier (Section 4.2)
- Warehouse inbound processing from a supplier with batch management (Section 4.3)
- Basic warehouse outbound processing to a customer (Section 4.4)
- Advanced warehouse outbound processing to a customer (Section 4.5)
- Physical inventory in the warehouse (Section 4.6)

For each process, we will pay special attention to the custom developments for you to reenact.

Adopting and Testing the Custom Developments in a Project

Consider the example custom developments as templates. If you plan to use one or another custom development presented in this chapter within your project, you should thoroughly check its fit and correctness within your project's context. In particular, you should pay attention to how the performance of your custom developments fit with the data volumes processed and the overall system load.

4.1 Introduction to SAP Best Practices for Embedded EWM

SAP Best Practices for SAP S/4HANA have been made available to allow for quick implementation of core standard based organizational structures and process flows. They contain preconfiguration and optional demo data content that can easily be activated in a system using the respective solution implementation tools. SAP Best Practices align to SAP S/4HANA versions and span several countries and languages.

In the area of supply chain management, and warehouse management specifically, the SAP Best Practices content is provided for both embedded and decentralized EWM. Embedded EWM-based processes will be used and described within this chapter.

A subset of the preconfigured processes for embedded EWM forms the basis for a variety of custom developments that we will explain in the following sections. You can certainly try out and use the examples within your self-configured processes, but they might have to be adapted first to the individual situation. However, if you have the opportunity to install SAP Best Practices for EWM in your system before you start programming, we recommend doing so, because it forms the basis upon which our custom developments were built and tested.

We will now look at the functional scope of the SAP Best Practices for embedded EWM and present an overview of the enhancements within the scope items, which will be described in much detail in the following sections. Last but not least, we will provide some information on how to get your system prepared to reenact the processes and enhancements.

4.1.1   Functional Scope of SAP Best Practices for Embedded EWM

As mentioned earlier, SAP Best Practices for SAP S/4HANA represent a library of scope items. The contained scope items for embedded EWM include typical warehouse management scenarios of inbound, outbound, and internal operation within one warehouse number. Fundamental settings have been included for organizational structure, master data, and resource management, as well as for integration with the SAP S/4HANA system, which is critical in ensuring the operation of all processes. The 11 scenarios and processes shown in Table 4.1 are available in SAP Best Practices for embedded EWM in SAP S/4HANA 2022. During activation of the SAP Best Practices solution, items from this set of processes can be chosen for custom installation.

Scenario	ID	Process
Inbound	1FS	Basic warehouse inbound processing from supplier
	1V5	Warehouse inbound processing from supplier with batch management
	1V9	Basic warehouse inbound processing from supplier with quality management
Outbound	1G2	Basic warehouse outbound processing to customer
	1V7	Warehouse outbound processing to customer with batch management
	1VD	Advanced warehouse outbound processing to customer
	1G0	Scrapping in warehouse
Internal	1FY	Replenishment in warehouse
	1FW	Physical inventory in warehouse
Cross	1FU	Initial stock upload for warehouse
	1VB	Production integration—component consumption and receipt in warehouse

Table 4.1 Scope Items of SAP Best Practices for Embedded EWM

In the following paragraphs, we will provide you with an overview of SAP Best Practices for embedded EWM in terms of organizational structures and integration with other SAP S/4HANA functionality—predominantly materials management and logistics execution.

Figure 4.1 provides an overview of the organizational structures used for the integration with SAP S/4HANA. The SAP S/4HANA warehouse number is directly linked to the EWM warehouse number, whereas the SAP S/4HANA storage locations are mapped to EWM stock types via availability groups. You can find further details on the mapping of SAP S/4HANA and EWM stock models in Chapter 2, Section 2.5. When setting up the SAP

S/4HANA integration, you will be able to choose the organizational structures of the SAP S/4HANA modules that you would like to integrate with the EWM warehouse number.

[»]

How-to Guide for Basic Settings for SAP EWM in SAP S/4HANA (Embedded EWM)

We recommend reading the *How-To Guide for Basic Settings for SAP EWM in SAP S/4HANA* when setting up the SAP S/4HANA to EWM integration configuration for using embedded EWM in SAP S/4HANA. It contains valuable information on configuration of qRFC communication, warehouse creation, and integration into the enterprise organizational structure. Alternatively, search for "Pre-Activation Settings for Embedded EWM Scope Items" in the SAP Help Portal (*https://help.sap.com/*).

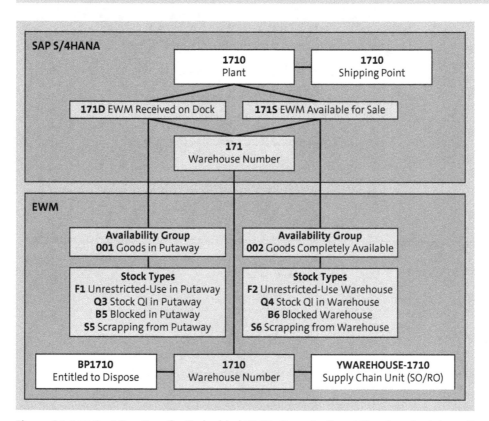

Figure 4.1 SAP Best Practices for Embedded EWM: Organizational Structure for Integration with SAP S/4HANA

Figure 4.2 shows the organizational structure of warehouse number 1710 as used in the individual processes. Warehouse number 1710 is assigned a variety of storage types that are used for the different material movements within the processes. These primarily differ by product size. Inside the storage types you can find storage sections, which again are broken down by product demand—namely, fast, medium, and slow movers. Doors, staging areas, and work centers can be found for inbound and outbound operations.

Warehouse number 1710 also includes storage types for clarification and scrapping. The use of storage types is documented in detail in the process descriptions of the various processes, which are included with the documentation of the respective SAP Best Practices scope items.

You can find additional information for the use of master data and settings for resource management in the test cases of SAP Best Practices scope items as well as individual step-by-step process descriptions. They contain detailed information on the procedures and transactions used for each of the 11 available scope items. You can find them in the Process Navigator by SAP on the SAP for Me platform at *https:// me.sap.com/processnavigator*. You need registration with SAP (S-User) to be able to access this content.

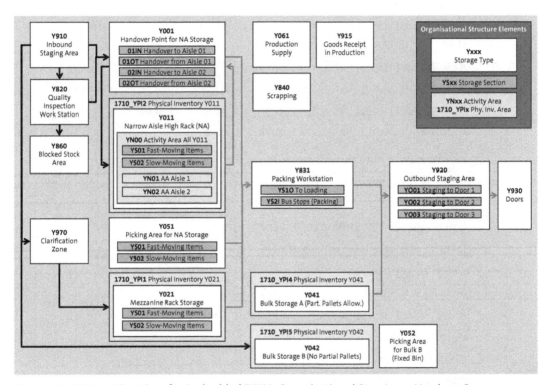

Figure 4.2 SAP Best Practices for Embedded EWM: Organizational Structures Used per Scope Item

Let's get an overview of the inbound functionality of the EWM system used in the scope items for embedded EWM:

- **Delivery processing**
  - Creation of inbound delivery in SAP S/4HANA with purchase order reference
  - Creation of inbound delivery in EWM with purchase order reference
  - RF-based receiving of handling units
  - (Partial) goods receipt posting on handling unit level

- **Warehouse logistics**
  - Automatic warehouse task creation for inbound delivery via PPF action
  - Process-oriented storage control
  - Layout-oriented storage control
  - Usage of quality inspection work center
  - Printing of warehouse order
  - Warehouse task confirmation with difference correction (supplier/warehouse)
  - Warehouse task confirmation with put-away physical inventory
  - Warehouse task/warehouse order confirmation with RF
- **Quality inspection**
  - Warehouse task creation as follow-up activity of quality inspection usage decision
- **Stock management**
  - Automatic posting change from received on dock to available for sales stock
  - Automatic posting change from quality to un-restricted use stock
  - Automatic posting change from quality to scrap stock

Let's also look at the functionality of outbound scope items, as follows:

- **Delivery processing**
  - Creation of outbound deliveries in SAP S/4HANA with sales order reference
  - Batch selection in outbound delivery item
  - Printing of outbound delivery note
- **Warehouse logistics**
  - Manual warehouse task creation via PPF action
  - Automatic wave assignment via PPF action (advanced)
  - Process-oriented storage control
  - Layout-oriented storage control
  - Warehouse order creation with packing profile
  - Picking partial handling unit quantities
  - Packing and confirmation of pick handling units as ship handling units via RF
  - Printing of shipping labels
  - Warehouse task confirmation via RF
  - Warehouse task confirmation with exception handling for differences in picking and packing
  - Movement of handling units to staging area
  - Controlled loading of handling units to transportation unit

- **Shipping**
  - Manual creation of transportation units (advanced)
  - Manual assignment of doors
  - Manual assignment of deliveries to transportation units
  - Printing of loading lists
- **Stock management**
  - Manual goods issue posting for outbound delivery
  - Manual goods issue posting for transportation unit (advanced)

The internal warehouse processes use the standard functionality as provided for inventory procedures (periodic and cycle counting), scrapping, and automatic replenishment.

4.1.2   Overview of Enhancements within the Scope Items

The basic inbound and outbound scope items of the SAP Best Practices for embedded EWM already contain much of the core warehouse management functionality, focusing on delivery processing, SAP S/4HANA integration, and a variation of different putaway and picking procedures. Further scope items then broaden the scope of warehouse management to include the advanced functionality of batch management, shipping and receiving, and more complex warehouse logistics supported by the use of wave management and quality management. We have tried to position the example enhancements within the scope items accordingly. Table 4.2 gives an overview of the enhancements that we present in this chapter, indicating the framework or enhancement technique used for each development.

ID	Custom Development	Realized By
1FS	1FSa: Automatic handling unit creation without packaging specifications	BAdI
	1FSb: Simplify the screen flow for RF putaway	RF framework
1V5	1V5a: Permit activation of the transportation unit only after entering the license plate and pager	BAdI
	1V5b: Putaway depending on quarantine period	BAdI
	1V5c: Enhancing the warehouse monitor	Warehouse monitor
	1V5d: Delay inbound delivery with missing batch	BAdI

Table 4.2 Overview of Enhancements

ID	Custom Development	Realized By
1G2	1G2a: Enhancing the delivery interface by custom data	EEW, BAdI
	1G2b: Transfer of custom data from outbound delivery order to warehouse task	EEW, BAdI
	1G2c: Showing custom data in the form view of the outbound delivery order item	BAdI
	1G2d: Determination and transfer of handling unit type from packaging specification to pick warehouse task	BAdI
	1G2e: Determination of the operative UOM by packaging specification of goods receipt	BAdI
	1G2f: Prohibit goods issue for incomplete packing	BAdI
1V7	1V7a: Take over transportation unit after unloading	PPF, BAdI
	1V7b: Print picking labels on a mobile printer	Condition technique, PPF
1FW	1FWa: Enhancing the goods movement interface by additional data	BAdI

Table 4.2 Overview of Enhancements (Cont.)

4.1.3   Installation of SAP Best Practices for Embedded EWM

For setting up the SAP Best Practices scope items in an on-premise EWM system, you will need to use the *solution builder* (Transaction /N/SMB/BBI). We recommend following the *Administration Guide to Implementation of SAP S/4HANA 2022 with SAP Best Practices*, which you can find in the help portal for SAP S/4HANA at *https://help.sap.com/*. The guide will take you through prerequisite settings, implementation, and upgrade procedures for loading, scoping, and activation of SAP Best Practices in your on-premise system. There is also a dedicated section on SAP S/4HANA–based scope items that you will need to activate on top of the EWM scope items so as to enable end-to-end processes.

4.1.4   Activating an SAP Cloud Appliance Library Instance

The fastest and easiest way to run SAP Best Practices processes and reenact the provided development examples would be for you to activate an SAP Cloud Appliance Library instance. This will specifically be easy if you already have an account at one of the following available cloud service providers:

- Amazon Web Services
- Microsoft Azure
- Google Cloud Platform

If you do not have an account with one of these providers yet, you might consider getting a trial account for a limited time, which often comes with a free budget allowing you to run the appliance actively for a decent number of hours.

With your cloud provider's account available, it should be fairly easy to create a trial instance of the latest SAP S/4HANA version. Go to *http://cal.sap.com* and explore the available fully activated appliance templates for SAP S/4HANA. To create an SAP Cloud Appliance Library instance, you will need a valid SAP ID before selecting your cloud provider, and then will need to specify your account credentials for the provider accordingly. Thereafter, you should be ready for the instance activation. If you run into activation issues, check the provided error log. You might likely need to request a parameter change at your cloud provider to fit the requirements of the SAP recommended virtual machine (VM) sizes. Once this is settled, it will only take a few hours before you have an SAP Cloud Appliance Library instance available for activation and connection. Make sure to suspend the instance when not actively using it to save some budget. Check out the SAP Cloud Appliance Library support page for further information and for how-to videos about instance activation.

Let's now continue with the process enhancements per SAP Best Practice scope item.

4.2   Basic Warehouse Inbound Processing from Supplier: 1FS

In this section, we will first introduce the complex goods receipt process of the SAP Best Practices, in which the functions of the transport control and the RF-based processing of handling units in the processing of incoming goods are in the foreground. Second, we will explore the following variants through custom developments and enhancements:

- **1FSa: Automatic handling unit creation without packaging specifications**
  You will get familiar with the BAdI for automatic handling unit creation.

- **1FSb: Simplify the screen flow for RF putaway**
  We will adjust the RF framework Customizing to skip the entry screen of the RF putaway transaction.

With most enhancements that we introduce in this section, you will find the BREAK-POINT ID ABAP statement in the coding. For each enhancement, we use a corresponding checkpoint group. You can create and activate the checkpoint groups using Transaction SAAB (Checkpoints that Can Be Activated).

4.2.1   Process Description of Scope Item 1FS

In Table 4.3, you will find in an overview of the steps for scope item 1FS (Basic Warehouse Inbound Processing from Supplier). We list the physical activities and the system activities in separate columns. The process steps in SAP S/4HANA modules are skipped, and we start with the description of the EWM steps. A purchase order was created in materials management in SAP S/4HANA as preparation.

Steps 3, 5, and 8 are completed by a goods receipt office clerk with system access via a desktop or a tablet PC using either SAP GUI or SAP Fiori–based apps. The warehouse operators who are physically moving the pallets from the truck (step 2), packing at the packing station (step 4) and moving to the final bin (step 7) work with mobile RF guns so that they post the movements in the system as they occur using RF based apps.

During the putaway operation, there are a couple of variants to be found in the scope item. These variants are based on different products requiring different packaging, storage concepts, and final destination storage types. They include piece- or carton-based small part rack storage in a mezzanine, pallet-based narrow aisle high rack storage (including handover locations for the narrow aisle truck) for medium size parts, and ground floor–based bulk storage (mainly full pallets stacked in front and on top of each other) for large parts, allowing for either full pallet or partial pallet putaway. Another process variant includes clarification and repacking of small parts that arrived in the wrong packaging.

Step	Physical Activity	System Activity
1: A truck arrives at the checkpoint and drives to the door.	A truck arrives. The warehouse clerk receives the delivery paper and communicates the door. The truck drives to the door.	
2: Unload the truck and check the goods.	A warehouse worker unloads the truck. A warehouse clerk checks the goods against the delivery note.	
3: Create EWM inbound delivery via the Create Inbound Delivery app (SAP Fiori app F1705).		The warehouse clerk creates the inbound delivery based on the delivery paperwork.
4: Pack the goods, creating handling units and posting goods receipt (EWM).		A warehouse worker creates and labels the handling units, posts the good receipt per handling unit.

Table 4.3 Steps in Inbound Scope Item 1FS

Step	Physical Activity	System Activity
5: Create warehouse orders (EWM).		The warehouse clerk creates putaway warehouse tasks and warehouse orders per the good receipts posted for the handling unit.
6: The truck leaves.	The truck leaves.	
7.1: Putaway the handling units to the mezzanine (EWM).		A warehouse worker logs on as a resource. The warehouse worker scans the handling units. The system determines the open warehouse orders for the handling units.
	The warehouse worker moves the handling units to the final bin in the mezzanine.	The warehouse worker confirms the warehouse orders.
7.2: Putaway the handling units to narrow aisle high bay racks (EWM).		A warehouse worker logs on as a resource. The warehouse worker scans the handling units. The system determines the open warehouse orders for the handling units.
	The warehouse worker moves the handling units to the handover zone for the narrow aisle high bay.	The warehouse worker confirms the warehouse orders. The system activates the next warehouse task for final putaway in the background.
		A narrow aisle forklift driver scans the handling units. The system determines the open warehouse orders for the handling units.
		The forklift driver confirms the warehouse orders.

Table 4.3 Steps in Inbound Scope Item 1FS (Cont.)

Step	Physical Activity	System Activity
7.3: Putaway the handling units to bulk ground floor area (EWM).		
7.4: Putaway the handling units to the clarification zone and repacking.		
	The packer identifies the goods and creates putaway handling units.	
		The packer closes the putaway handling units. The system prints handling unit labels and creates warehouse orders.
	The packer labels the putaway handling units.	
		A warehouse worker logs on as a resource. The warehouse worker scans a putaway handling unit. The system determines the open warehouse order for the putaway handling unit.
The warehouse worker moves the putaway handling unit to the final bin.		
	The warehouse worker confirms the warehouse order.	
8: Check the inbound delivery (EWM).		

Table 4.3 Steps in Inbound Scope Item 1FS (Cont.)

The process description of scope item 1FS can also be found in the flow chart and test script of the scope item.

4.2.2   Enhancement 1FSa: Automatic Handling Unit Creation without Packaging Specifications

In custom development 1FSa, we will enhance the inbound steps with a function called Automatic Handling Unit Creation without Packaging Specifications. Step 3 of standard scope item 1FS will change with this custom development, making step 4 obsolete (see Table 4.4). All other process steps stay the same as described in Table 4.3.

> **Consider Unified Package Builder Functionality**
>
> EWM offers a rather new feature that allows you to activate data sources other than the packaging specification for packaging requirements or proposals. These include SAP S/4HANA–based packing instructions and SAP Supply Chain Management–based package builder rules (e.g., alternative units of measure from the global material data).

Step	Physical Activity	System Activity
3: Create EWM inbound delivery (EWM) via GUI Transaction /SCWM/PRDI and create handling units.	N/A	The warehouse clerk checks the quantities, creates handling units in the system, and prints the new handling unit labels. She then posts the goods receipt.

Table 4.4 Process Steps with Deviation for Enhancement 1FSa

The main difference between scope item 1FS and enhancement 1FSa is that the pallets arriving from the office clerk create the handling unit labels instead of the warehouse operator, while the latter will apply them on the shop floor. The handling unit label will stay with the pallet as long as possible and can, for example, be used for an internal move, replenishment, or stock removal.

In standard EWM, you could let the system automatically create handling units in the inbound process based on packaging specifications or unified package builder profiles. So for each product (or reference product), you have to maintain a packaging specification that defines the pallet quantity, the handling unit type, and the packaging material for the pallet. If you do not have packaging specifications for each product, and the unified package builder might not be an option, the solution shown in this chapter might be a suitable alternative in your project.

To realize enhancement 1FSa, the following steps are necessary:

1. Create a new master data table ZHU_PMAT to determine the packaging material for the handling units.
2. Implement the HU_PROPOSAL method of BAdI /SCWM/EX_HU_BASICS_AUTOPACK.
3. Switch on automatic packing for the inbound delivery.
4. Create a condition record to print handling unit labels. Deactivate the printing for warehouse order labels.

We describe the details for these four steps in the following sections. First, however, let's look at the pallet building process in 1FS and discuss the prerequisites for this enhancement. We'll also close the section by discussing how to test process 1FSa.

Pallet Building in Process 1FS

Process 1FS uses the *quantity classification* based on alternative UOM to determine the warehouse task quantity when putting away product from the clarification area. The alternative UOMs are defined in the product (see Figure 4.3), so, for example, 192 EA is one pallet, and 8 EA is one carton.

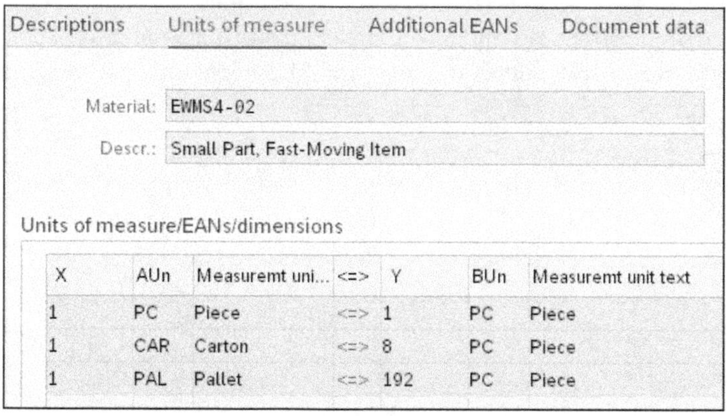

Descriptions	Units of measure	Additional EANs	Document data

Material: EWMS4-02

Descr.: Small Part, Fast-Moving Item

Units of measure/EANs/dimensions

X	AUn	Measuremt uni...	<=>	Y	BUn	Measuremt unit text
1	PC	Piece	<=>	1	PC	Piece
1	CAR	Carton	<=>	8	PC	Piece
1	PAL	Pallet	<=>	192	PC	Piece

Figure 4.3 Material Master with UOM: Additional Data

In the **EWM • Master Data • Product • Define Unit of Measure Attributes** IMG activity, the UOMs are assigned to quantity classifications (see Figure 4.4). So, for example, **Quantity Classification P** (Pallets) is assigned to **Unit PAL**. Based on this setting, the system will split the warehouse task quantities during warehouse task task creation in put-away and could also determine different storage types for putaway.

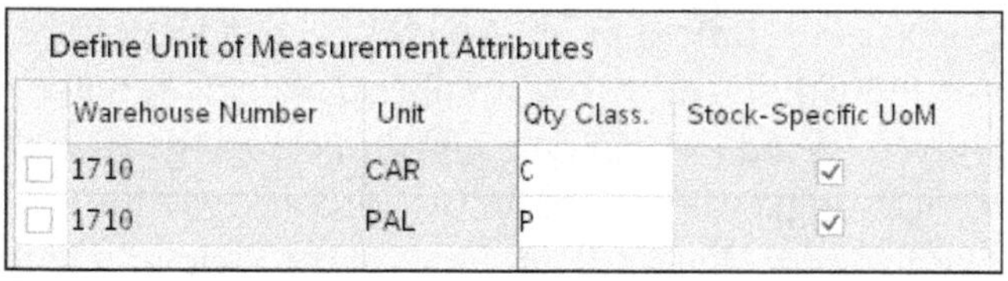

Define Unit of Measurement Attributes			
Warehouse Number	Unit	Qty Class.	Stock-Specific UoM
☐ 1710	CAR	C	☑
☐ 1710	PAL	P	☑

Figure 4.4 IMG Activity to Assign Quantity Classification to Units

So if, for example, an inbound delivery with a quantity of 400 EA is received in the warehouse, the system would create four product warehouse tasks (see Figure 4.5, where we simulate inbound delivery packing in Transaction /SCWM/PRDI):

- Two warehouse tasks with 192 EA = 1 PAL
- Two warehouse tasks with 8 EA = 1 CAR

Warehouse/HU/Item	Product	PckQty AUn	Alt. Unit
☐ ∨ ⌂ 1710			
☑ 🗟 Small Part, Fast-Moving Item	EWMS4-02	400	PC
☐ ∨ 🗃 800367	EWMS4-WBTRO00		
☐ 🗟 Small Part, Fast-Moving Item	EWMS4-02	192	PC
☐ > 🗃 800368	EWMS4-WBTRO00		
☐ ∨ 🗃 800369	EWMS4-STOCON00		
☐ 🗟 Small Part, Fast-Moving Item	EWMS4-02	8	PC
☐ > 🗃 800370	EWMS4-STOCON00		

Figure 4.5 Automatic Handling Unit Creation in Inbound Delivery Packing

Prerequisites for Enhancement 1FSa

Enhancement 1FSa is useful in a warehouse if these prerequisites are met:

- No packaging specifications by product exist.
- The unified package builder is not a valid option.
- The pallet and/or carton quantity is available as an alternative UOM by product.

Create New Master Data Table

To create a handling unit in the system, a packaging material is mandatory. The system takes over the tare weight, volume, and handling unit type from the packing material master and also the kind of numbering (e.g., number range, Serial Shipping Container Code [SSCC]) specified via the packaging material. Hence, we will use a new, simple master data table to determine the packaging material based on the quantity classification. We will also determine a handling unit type that could be used to influence the putaway strategy and to find the optimal bin type.

Create a new database in ABAP Dictionary (Transaction SE11). Enter the name, such as ZHU_PMAT, and a description. In **Delivery Class**, choose option **A (master and transactional data)**, and in the **Data Browser/Table View Maintenance** field, make sure you choose option **X—Display/Maintenance Allowed**. On the **Fields** tab, maintain the fields as they are listed in Table 4.5.

Field	Data Element	Key	Check Table/Search Help
CLIENT	MANDT	Yes	
LGNUM	/SCWM/LGNUM	Yes	/SCWM/SH_LGNUM
QUANCLA	/SCWM/DE_QUANCLA	Yes	/SCWM/TQUANCLA
HUTYP	/SCWM/DE_HUTYP	No	/SCWM/THUTYP
PACKMAT	/SCWM/DE_PMAT	No	/SCWM/SH_PMAT_ONLY

Table 4.5 Fields of Custom Table ZHU_PMAT

For the technical settings of the new table, choose "APPLO" for **Data Class**, "O" for **Size Category**, and switch on the buffering (fully buffered).

After you have saved and activated the table, navigate to the table maintenance generator (Transaction SE55) and generate a maintenance view (e.g., with authorization group SCEA and function group ZHU_PMAT).

Last but not least, maintain a few entries in the new table using Transaction SM31 (Maintain Table Views; see Figure 4.6).

Packaging Material			
Warehouse Number	Qty Class.	HU Type	Packaging Material
☐ 1710	C	YN02	EWMS4-STOCON00
☐ 1710	P	YN03	EWMS4-WBTR000

Figure 4.6 Maintain Packaging Material and Handling Unit Type in Table ZHU_PMAT

Implement the HU_PROPOSAL Method

To implement method HU_PROPOSAL, you have to start the BAdI Builder (Transaction SE19) and create an implementation for enhancement spot /SCWM/ES_HU_BASICS. First enter the name of the enhancement implementation (e.g., ZEI_HU_BASICS) and then choose BAdI definition /SCWM/EX_HU_BASICS_AUTOPACK. As a name for the BAdI implementation, you can enter, for example, ZEX_HU_BASICS_AUTOPACK, and as a class name, choose ZCL_IM_HU_BASICS_AUTOPACK. Navigate to the HU_PROPOSAL method and enter the coding as shown in Listing 4.1. Define one static, private attribute, ST_TUOM_QCLA, of type /SCWM/TT_UOM_QCLA for the class.

Activate the coding and also the BAdI implementation:

- In coding paragraph "1, we first fetch the quantity classification table (/SCWM/TUOM_QCLA) from the IMG.

- We loop over all delivery items, and for each product we determine the list of alternative UOMs (see paragraph "2).

- By using standard function module /SCWM/QUANCLA_DET_UOM, we determine the quantity classification depending on the unpacked, open quantity (see "3).

- Based on the quantity classification, we determine in our new table ZHU_PMAT the packaging material and handling unit type (see "4).

- To determine the handling unit target quantity, we look up the first alternative unit that matches the required quantity classification. The numerator of this unit becomes the target quantity (see paragraph "5).

- In the last two paragraphs, "6 and "7, we finally create a handling unit and pack the delivery item into it.

- Note that we do not use the save method or the commit statement. As this is a BAdI implementation, we expect the calling environment to take care of saving and database commits.

```abap
METHOD /scwm/if_ex_hu_basics_autopack~hu_proposal.

  DATA: lt_mat_uom TYPE /scwm/tt_material_uom,
        lv_quancla TYPE /scwm/de_quancla.

  BREAK-POINT ID zewmdevbook_1fsa.
  DATA(lo_pack)  = CAST /scwm/cl_hu_packing( io_pack_ref ).
  DATA(lo_stock) = NEW /scwm/cl_ui_stock_fields( ).
  "1 Get quantity classification (prefetch)
  IF st_tuom_qcla IS INITIAL.
    SELECT * FROM /scwm/tuom_qcla
             INTO TABLE st_tuom_qcla
             WHERE lgnum = lo_pack->gv_lgnum.
    IF st_tuom_qcla IS INITIAL.
      RETURN.
    ENDIF.
  ENDIF.

  LOOP AT ct_pack ASSIGNING FIELD-SYMBOL(<pack>).
    CLEAR: lt_mat_uom.
    "2 Get product master for each delivery item
    TRY.
        CALL FUNCTION '/SCWM/MATERIAL_READ_SINGLE'
          EXPORTING
            iv_matid   = <pack>-matid
          IMPORTING
            et_mat_uom = lt_mat_uom.
      CATCH /scwm/cx_md.
        io_pack_ref->go_log->add_message( ).
        cv_severity = sy-msgty.
        CONTINUE.
    ENDTRY.
    WHILE <pack>-quan > 0.
      "3 Get quantity classification based on open quantity
      TRY.
          CALL FUNCTION '/SCWM/QUANCLA_DET_UOM'
            EXPORTING
              iv_lgnum   = lo_pack->gv_lgnum
              iv_matid   = <pack>-matid
              iv_batchid = <pack>-batchid
              iv_quan    = <pack>-quan
              iv_unit    = <pack>-unit
              it_mat_uom = lt_mat_uom
```

```abap
        IMPORTING
          ev_quancla = lv_quancla.
    CATCH /scwm/cx_core.
      io_pack_ref->go_log->add_message( ).
      cv_severity = sy-msgty.
      CONTINUE.
ENDTRY.
"4 Determine packmat and hu_typ for the quantity classification
SELECT SINGLE * FROM zhu_pmat
  INTO @DATA(ls_zhu_pmat)
  WHERE lgnum = @lo_pack->gv_lgnum
  AND quancla = @lv_quancla.
IF ls_zhu_pmat-packmat IS INITIAL.
  "Error: No Packaging Material maintained for Quan.Class. &1.
  MESSAGE e001(zewmdevbook_1fsa) WITH lv_quancla.
  io_pack_ref->go_log->add_message( ).
  EXIT.
ENDIF.
DATA(lv_packmatid) = lo_stock->get_matid_by_no(
                       iv_matnr = ls_zhu_pmat-packmat ).
"5 Determine target quantity and UoM
LOOP AT st_tuom_qcla INTO DATA(ls_quancla) WHERE quancla = lv_quancla.
  DATA(ls_mat_uom) = VALUE #( lt_mat_uom[ matid = <pack>-matid
                                          meinh = ls_quancla-unit ] ).
  IF sy-subrc IS NOT INITIAL.
    EXIT.
  ENDIF.
ENDLOOP.
"6 Create new handling unit
DATA(ls_hu_crea) = VALUE /scwm/s_huhdr_create_ext(
  hutyp = ls_zhu_pmat-hutyp ).
DATA(ls_huhdr) = io_pack_ref->create_hu(
  EXPORTING
    iv_pmat      = lv_packmatid
    is_hu_create = ls_hu_crea ).
IF sy-subrc <> 0.
  io_pack_ref->go_log->add_message( ).
  EXIT.
ENDIF.
"7 Pack item
DATA(ls_quan) = CORRESPONDING /scwm/s_quan( <pack> ).
IF <pack>-quan >= ls_mat_uom-umrez.
  ls_quan-quan = 1.
```

```
        ls_quan-unit = ls_mat_uom-meinh.
        <pack>-quan  = <pack>-quan - ls_mat_uom-umrez.
      ELSE.
        ls_quan-quan = <pack>-quan.
        <pack>-quan = 0.
      ENDIF.
      DATA(ls_mat) = CORRESPONDING /scwm/s_pack_stock( <pack> ).
      io_pack_ref->pack_stock(
        EXPORTING
          iv_dest_hu  = ls_huhdr-guid_hu
          is_material = ls_mat
          is_quantity = ls_quan ).
      IF sy-subrc <> 0.
        io_pack_ref->go_log->add_message( ).
        EXIT.
      ENDIF.
      CLEAR: ls_mat, ls_quan, ls_hu_crea, lv_quancla,
             ls_huhdr, ls_quancla, ls_mat_uom, ls_zhu_pmat.
    ENDWHILE.
  ENDLOOP.

ENDMETHOD.
```

Listing 4.1 Coding of HU_PROPOSAL Method

Switch on Automatic Packing

In IMG activity **EWM • Goods Receipt Process • Inbound Delivery • Manual Settings • Define Document Types for Inbound Delivery Process**, choose document type INB for document category PDI, change the following settings, and save:

- **Packaging Material Proposal Procedure: OIBD**
  This packaging specification procedure entry is required to switch on the automatic packing in general. We enter a procedure, although we will not use packaging specifications. Make sure you enter a procedure for which you do not use packaging specifications in your project.

- **No Automatic Packing: Yes**
  With this setting, we switch off the automatic packing during inbound delivery creation. As in our process variant, we first want the user to verify the quantity and then create the handling unit labels in the office. We want the user to start the automatic packing manually when he is done with checking.

Create a Condition Record

As we want the system to print the labels automatically when the user creates the handling units, check and create new condition records in SAP menu **EWM • Work Scheduling • Print • Settings • Create Condition Records for Printing (HUs)**. Enter application and maintenance group PHU and select existing condition records for condition type OHU1. Check the results list. If one does not exist yet, create one entry for each packaging material you use as in Figure 4.6 with the following values:

- **Condition Type**: OHU1
- **Warehouse**: 1710
- **HU Step**: I—Create
- **Packaging Material**: for example, EWMS4-STOCON00 (EWM Default Storage Container/Box)
- **HU Type**: for example, YN02 (EWM Carton/Box)
- **Form**: /SCWM/HU_CONTENT
- **Printer**: for example, LP01
- **Spool**: 01
- **Action**: HU_LABEL_GENERAL_AND_RF

Testing of Process 1FSa

You can now test the handling unit creation and handling unit printing (see Table 4.6). In Figure 4.7, you can see the result of test step 4.1. For an inbound delivery quantity of 40 EA, the system created five handling units. All were created as boxes of 8 EA.

Step	Step Description	Input Data and Expected Results
4.2	Create EWM Inbound Delivery	Use Transaction /SCWM/GR (Goods Receipt).
		Search for the inbound delivery using the PO number or using the ASN number.
		Check the delivery data against the revised delivery note and adapt the quantities if necessary.
		Use the **Pack** button to navigate to the **Work Center Packing for Inbound Delivery** screen for inbound deliveries, select the delivery items, and use the **Pack Automatically** button (see Figure 4.7).
		Navigate back and use the **Post Goods Receipt** button.
		Expected results:
		The system generates handling units.
		The system prints handling unit labels.

Table 4.6 Test Steps for Enhancement 1FSa

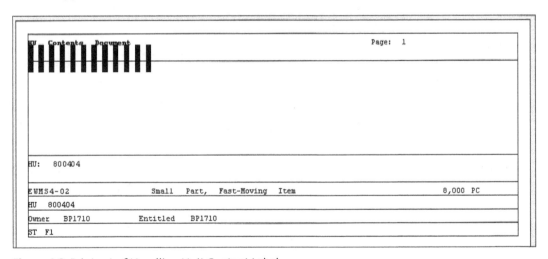

Warehouse/HU/Item	Product	PckQty AUn	Alt. Unit
☐ ⌄ 🏠 1710			
☑ 🛒 Small Part, Fast-Moving Item	EWMS4-02	40	PC
☐ ⌄ 🏷 800380	EWMS4-STOCON00		
☐ 🛒 Small Part, Fast-Moving Item	EWMS4-02	8	PC
☐ ⌄ 🏷 800381	EWMS4-STOCON00		
☐ 🛒 Small Part, Fast-Moving Item	EWMS4-02	8	PC
☐ ⌄ 🏷 800382	EWMS4-STOCON00		
☐ 🛒 Small Part, Fast-Moving Item	EWMS4-02	8	PC
☐ ⌄ 🏷 800383	EWMS4-STOCON00		
☐ 🛒 Small Part, Fast-Moving Item	EWMS4-02	8	PC
☐ ⌄ 🏷 800384	EWMS4-STOCON00		
☐ 🛒 Small Part, Fast-Moving Item	EWMS4-02	8	PC

Figure 4.7 Automatic Packing in Inbound Deliveries

After the user saves the results of automatic packing, the system will automatically print the handling unit labels, shown in Figure 4.8. The standard form shows a barcode, but it is very likely that you will have to adjust this form to your printer size and your barcode type.

```
HU  Contents  Document                                   Page:  1
▐█▌▐█▌▐█▌▐█▌▐█▌▐█▌




HU:    800404

EWMS4-02              Small   Part,  Fast-Moving  Item            8,000  PC
HU    800404
Owner    BP1710        Entitled    BP1710
ST  F1
```

Figure 4.8 Printout of Handling Unit Content Label

For the putaway step 4 of the test case, you have now two options: either execute the step as described in the standard process, or continue with the information in the next section to use enhancement 1FSb.

4.2.3   Enhancement 1FSb: Simplify the Screen Flow for Radio Frequency Putaway

In enhancement 1FSb, we will change step 7, Put Away the Goods, of process 1FS. The changes are described in Table 4.7. In the standard process, the putaway is paper-driven and without RF support. The warehouse operators move the pallets to the final bins and hand over the papers to the office clerk. Several times per day, the office clerk confirms the warehouse orders in the system based on the returned papers. This way, the stock increases and becomes available for sale. In process variant 1FSb, the warehouse operators will use RF devices and confirm each move of stock in the system immediately.

In this section, we give an instruction on how to simplify the Putaway by Warehouse Order RF transaction (logical RF Transaction PTWOSI). With an adjustment in the RF framework, we reduce the number of UIs and eliminate one RF screen. So for each pallet the user scans, there is a warehouse order barcode from the paper and the destination bin barcode.

Step	Physical Activity	System Activity
4.6.5: Move Products from Clarification Zone to Mezzanine	The warehouse worker takes the warehouse order printouts and sticks one printout on the goods. The warehouse worker moves the goods from the clarification zone to the final storage in the mezzanine.	The warehouse operator confirms each putaway via RF.

Table 4.7 Process Steps with Deviation for Enhancement 1FSb

To realize the variant 1FSb, Simplify the Screen Flow for RF Putaway, you have to do the following steps:

1. Create RF presentation profile 1710 and copy the standard menu.
2. Change the RF step flow for logical Transaction PTWOSI and presentation profile 1710 such that the first screen is skipped.

The details for these two steps are described in the following sections. As usual, we will begin by discussing the prerequisites and end by discussing testing of this enhancement.

Prerequisites for Enhancement 1FSb

Enhancement 1FSb has the following prerequisites:

- Wi-Fi and mobile devices are supported in the warehouse
- Warehouse order barcode is on the printout of the warehouse order

Create the Presentation Profile

Now create a new presentation profile (see also Chapter 3, Section 3.3) to make warehouse-specific changes in the RF framework Customizing in the next step:

- Create a new presentation and personalization profile. This is done in the **EWM • Mobile Data Entry • Define Steps in Logical Transactions** IMG activity. In the **Define Presentation Profiles** folder, create a new entry, "1710", by copying the existing **** entry.

- In the **RF Menu Manager** IMG activity, keep the default values on the entry screen and use the **Copy Menu** function. In the popup, enter presentation profile 1710, then continue and save.

- Assign the new presentation profile 1710 to warehouse number 1710. This is done in IMG activity **Assign Presentation Profile to Warehouse**.

Change the RF Step Flow

We now change one entry in the RF framework Customizing so that the system will skip the putaway source screen.

Go to IMG activity **EWM • Mobile Data Entry • Define Steps in Logical Transactions**. In the **Define Logical Transactions** folder, select logical Transaction PTWO** and navigate to subfolder **Define Logical Transaction Step Flow**. Select and copy the entry with the following keys:

- **Presentation profile:** ****
- **Logical transaction:** PTWO**
- **Step:** PTHUSC
- **Function code:** PBO1

Before you save, change the following fields:

- **Presentation profile:** 1710
- **Next step:** PTHUDS
- **Processing mode:** 1—Background
- **Function code background:** PBO1

With the changed settings, the system will skip the screen for step PTHUSC and immediately continue with step PTHUDS.

> **Copy Instead of Change**
>
> We recommend not changing settings for presentation profile ****. For each project/template project, create a separate presentation profile as shown in step 3 and copy the standard settings from profile **** to your own profile before changing them. You can then use the unchanged settings for profile **** as reference. If there is a problem in RF, you can change back to **** before you ask SAP Support for help.

Testing of Enhancement 1FSb

Start your test with test steps 1 to 5 from process 1FS. Then replace step 6 with the test described in Table 4.8.

Step	Step Description	Input Data and Expected Results
4.6.5	Move Products from Clarification Zone to Mezzanine—Choose Menu	■ Use Transaction /SCWM/RFUI (Log onto RF Environment) and log onto warehouse 1710 with resource YREC-1 and presentation device YE00. ■ Navigate to menu item **03 Inbound Process • 03 Putaway • 03 Putaway by WO** (fast access via 333). ■ Scan the warehouse order barcode. ■ Scan the destination bin. *Expected result:* The warehouse order is confirmed, and the stock is available for sale.

Table 4.8 Test Steps for Enhancement 1FSb

In Figure 4.9, we want to show you how the RF transaction works for standard presentation profile ****, as follows:

In the RF menu, the user chooses **03 Putaway by WO**.

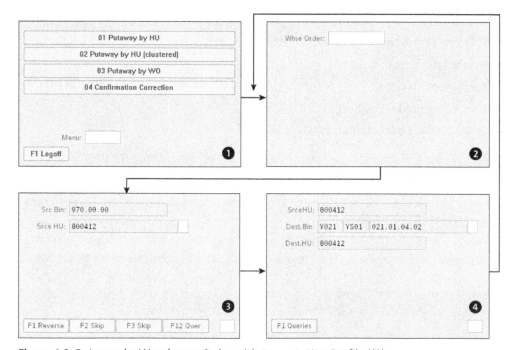

Figure 4.9 Putaway by Warehouse Order with Presentation Profile ****

On the entry screen, the user scans the barcode for the warehouse order (RF step PTWOSL).

On the source screen (RF step PTHUSC), the user confirms the pickup of the stock with several presses of ⌈Enter⌉.

On the destination screen (RF step PTHUDS), the user scans the destination bin after he puts the stock there.

When using the new presentation profile 1710, you'll see that step PTHUSC is skipped by the system. The flow of screens is shown in Figure 4.10. So for each putaway transaction, the user will save one screen and one ⌈Enter⌉ press. There is also a difference in the number of warehouse tasks: the system will not use two tasks (one for posting stock from the source bin to the resource and another for posting stock from the resource to the destination bin). It will post only one task—that is, the moment the user confirms the destination bin.

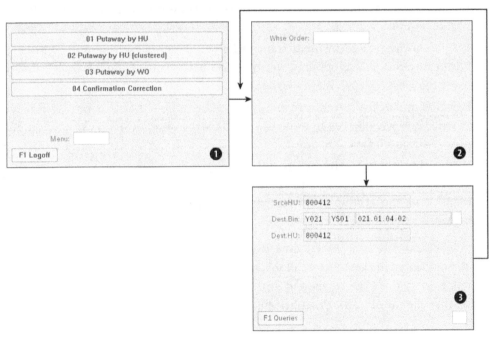

Figure 4.10 Putaway by Warehouse Order with Presentation Profile 1710

To have only one instead of two warehouse tasks at the end of the transaction is also a benefit in case the user changes his mind and steps back with ⌈F7⌉ on the destination screen (step PTHUDS). With the standard settings, the stock would stay on the resource and hence no other resource would be able to perform this warehouse order. If you work with high-level forklifts and low-level forklifts, it can happen quite often that only after seeing the destination screen can the operator decide if he is capable of doing the putaway at that destination bin.

In this section, you learned how to skip screens in RF and how to process steps in background mode without coding adjustments. There are more RF transactions in the standard where you might have the need to skip a screen if the screen does not provide valuable information to your users.

4.3   Warehouse Inbound Processing from Supplier with Batch Management: 1V5

In this section, we will introduce inbound scope item 1V5 (Warehouse Inbound Processing from Supplier with Batch Management). We will ensure that we create two variants of this process by adding custom developments and Customizing settings:

- **1V5a: Permit activation of the transportation unit only after entering the license plate and pager**
  We will show how you can realize additional checks during the activation of transportation units.

- **1V5b: Putaway depending on quarantine period**
  With this custom development, we show you how to affect the putaway strategy using the /SCWM/EX_CORE_PTS_TYPSQ BAdI.

- **1V5c: Enhancing the warehouse monitor**
  We will show you how to place your own node in the warehouse management monitor for advanced data selection.

- **1V5d: Delay inbound delivery with missing batch**
  You will learn to recognize an opportunity by using the /SCWM/EX_ERP_INT_CONF BAdI to influence the creation of the inbound delivery notification during batch capturing within inbound processing.

Both process variants start in the same way: an inbound delivery without packing information is created in EWM. The vendor is not labeling the pallets in such a way that the warehouse can reuse the labels, and furthermore, no label information is passed electronically to EWM. All of the described enhancements are independent of each other.

4.3.1   Process Description of Scope Item 1V5

In Table 4.9, you will find in an overview of the steps for process 1V5, Warehouse Inbound Processing from Supplier with Batch Management. We list the physical activities and the system activities in separate columns. The process steps in SAP S/4HANA are skipped, and we start with the description of the EWM steps. A purchase order and inbound delivery (optional) were created in the SAP S/4HANA system as preparation steps.

Steps 2, 4, and 6 are completed by a goods receipt office clerk with system access. The warehouse operators who are physically moving the pallets from the truck to the final bin are without system access. They use the printouts of the office clerk to find out which pallet needs to be moved to which bin. When they are done with the physical work, they hand the printouts back to the clerk, who then confirms the work in the system.

We have extended the scope item with incoming truck handling using the shipping and receiving module of EWM. Be aware that this module falls under the advanced features of embedded EWM and might require additional licensing. The extended steps will work out of the box in the respective SAP Best Practices processes however, so no additional configuration will be required.

Step	Physical Activity	System Activity
1: A truck arrives at the checkpoint and drives to the door.	A truck arrives. A checkpoint clerk communicates the door to the truck driver. The truck drives to the door.	*Scope item extension:* A checkpoint clerk creates a transportation unit, assigns the transportation unit to a door, and confirms the arrival of the truck at the door.
		Scope item extension: A goods receipt office clerk assigns the inbound delivery items to the transportation unit.
2: Check the delivery note and find or create an inbound delivery.		A good receipt office clerk finds or creates an inbound delivery.
3: Unload the truck and check the goods.	A warehouse worker unloads the truck. A warehouse clerk checks the goods against the delivery note.	
4: Post the good receipt and create put-away warehouse orders.		The goods receipt office clerk checks the quantities and posts the goods receipt. The system creates and prints warehouse orders.
5: The truck leaves.	The truck leaves.	*Scope item extension:* The goods receipt office clerk confirms the departure of the truck.

Table 4.9 Process Description of Inbound Process 1V5

Step	Physical Activity	System Activity
6: Putaway the goods.	The warehouse worker takes the warehouse order printouts and sticks one printout to the goods. The warehouse worker moves the goods to the final bin or to the clarification zone (exceptional case).	The warehouse clerk confirms the warehouse order.

Table 4.9 Process Description of Inbound Process 1V5 (Cont.)

The process description of scope item 1V5 can also be found in the flow chart and test script of the scope item.

4.3.2   Enhancement 1V5a: Permit Activation of the Transportation Unit Only after Entering the License Plate and Pager

In variant 1V5a, we will show you how you can realize additional checks during the activation of transportation units. With this custom development, you can ensure that during the creation of the transportation units or, at the latest, during the posting of the **Arrival at Checkpoint** transportation unit action, a license plate of the truck and a pager number have to be entered.

Quite often it is the case in larger warehouse facilities that a truck driver has to register first at a central check-in point of the plant in order to pick up or deliver goods. Now the truck is being maintained in the EWM system via Transaction /SCWM/TU (Maintain Transportation Unit). For the sake of traceability and facility protection, the license plate number is also retained. At this time, however, the corresponding door does not necessarily need to be assigned. This may be because another department does the door assignment (e.g., the goods receipt office). Therefore, the project requirement might be that if the truck driver is provided with the door, he should go to it at any time after check-in. The following custom development ensures that the employee at the plant cannot forget to retain the pager number and license plate of the truck.

To perform enhancement 1V5a, the following steps are necessary:

1. Define an identification type in the IMG to collect the pager number.
2. Create three messages in the ZEWMDEVBOOK_1V5A message class.
3. Implement the BEFORE_SAVE method of BAdI /SCWM/EX_SR_SAVE.

Next, we explain in detail how to proceed with each of these steps before finishing with information on testing this enhancement.

Define an Identification Type

To create the identification type for collecting the pager number, follow these steps:

1. Navigate to IMG activity **EWM • Cross-Process Settings • Shipping and Receiving • Define Identification Type for Transportation Unit/Vehicle**.

2. Under identification types, in the **IDTpe** column, retain the abbreviation P and assign a description ("Pager"; see Figure 4.11).

3. Save your entries.

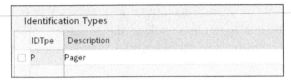

Figure 4.11 Identification Type for Pager Number

Create Three Messages

To create the three new messages, follow these steps:

1. Start Transaction SE91 (Message Maintenance).

2. Create three new messages in the ZEWMDEVBOOK_1V5A message class, as shown in Figure 4.12.

3. Save your entries.

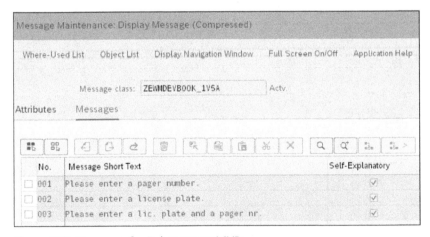

Figure 4.12 Messages for Enhancement 1V5a

Implement the BEFORE_SAVE Method

To implement the BEFORE_SAVE method of the /SCWM/EX_SR_SAVE BAdI, proceed as follows:

1. Start the BAdI builder (Transaction SE19) and create an enhancement implementation (e.g., ZEWM_EI_SR_SAVE) for enhancement spot /SCWM/ES_SR_READ_SAVE.

2. Then create a BAdI implementation (e.g., ZEX_SR_SAVE) for BAdI definition /SCWM/EX_ SR_SAVE and an implementing class (e.g., ZCL_IM_SR_SAVE).

3. Now you can program the /SCWM/IF_EX_SR_SAVE~BEFORE_SAVE method with the sample code from Listing 4.2:

   - In our example, we first check whether the transportation unit is currently being changed. This we determine based on the *changing indicator* of the business object (wmesr_objstate_new or wmesr_objstate_chg).

   - Next, we must determine which business process for the transportation unit is currently running. Our check should only be carried out in the case of activating the transportation unit. The BAdI, and thus our sample implementation, however, is executed for each action of the transportation unit (on creation, change, save, delete, cancel, etc.).

   - After verifying that all requirements are met, we can now check if the user actually entered a license plate and a pager number. At this point, we would like to accurately determine which entry may be missing in order to be able to issue a specific error message. If a value has not been entered, we write the corresponding message in the log object (coding section "6) and trigger the /SCWM/CX_SR_ ERROR exception. With the exception, the save operation is canceled, and a popup will display the respective error context for the user.

```
METHOD /scwm/if_ex_sr_save~before_save.

    BREAK-POINT ID zewmdevbook_1v5a.

    LOOP AT it_bo_tu ASSIGNING FIELD-SYMBOL(<fs_bo_tu>).
      IF <fs_bo_tu>-bo_ref IS BOUND.
        TRY.
            <fs_bo_tu>-bo_ref->get_data(
              IMPORTING
                ev_objstate = DATA(lv_state)
                et_ident    = DATA(lt_ident) ).
          CATCH /scwm/cx_sr_error.
            CONTINUE.
        ENDTRY.
        "1. Check changing indicator of object
        CHECK lv_state = wmesr_objstate_new
        OR    lv_state = wmesr_objstate_chg.
        "2. Determine context
        CHECK <fs_bo_tu>-bo_ref->get_sr_act_state( ) =
        wmesr_act_state_active.
        CHECK <fs_bo_tu>-bo_ref->get_status_change_by_id(
        wmesr_status_check_in ) = abap_true.
        "3. Check for pager
```

```
    TRY.
        DATA(ls_ident) = lt_ident[ idart = 'P' ].
      CATCH cx_sy_itab_line_not_found.
        DATA(lv_check) = 1.
    ENDTRY.
    IF ls_ident-ident IS INITIAL.
      lv_check = 1. "no pager
    ENDIF.
    "4. Check for lic_plate
    <fs_bo_tu>-bo_ref->get_data(
        IMPORTING es_bo_tu_data = DATA(ls_bo_tu_data) ).
    IF ( ls_bo_tu_data-lic_plate         = ''
    OR   ls_bo_tu_data-lic_plate_country = '' )
    AND  lv_check = 1.
      lv_check = 3. "no pager and no lic_plate
    ELSEIF ( ls_bo_tu_data-lic_plate         = ''
    OR        ls_bo_tu_data-lic_plate_country = '' ).
      lv_check = 2. "no lic_plate
    ENDIF.
    "5. Raise message
    CASE lv_check.
      WHEN 1. "no pager
        MESSAGE e001(zewmdevbook_1v5a) INTO DATA(lv_msg).
      WHEN 2. "no lic_plate
        MESSAGE e002(zewmdevbook_1v5a) INTO lv_msg.
      WHEN 3. "no pager and lic_plate
        MESSAGE e003(zewmdevbook_1v5a) INTO lv_msg.
    ENDCASE.
    "6. add message to current log and raise exception
    IF NOT lv_check IS INITIAL.
      /scwm/cl_sr_bom=>so_log->add_message( ).
      RAISE EXCEPTION TYPE /scwm/cx_sr_error.
    ENDIF.
    ENDIF.
    CLEAR: lv_msg, lv_check.
  ENDLOOP.

ENDMETHOD.
```

Listing 4.2 Sample Code for BAdI /SCWM/EX_SR_SAVE

[«]

MESSAGE Statement

Make sure that you *never* use the MESSAGE statement without the INTO addition in your own BAdI implementations (see coding section "5 in Listing 4.2).

Testing Enhancement 1V5a

To test enhancement 1V5a, add the steps in Table 4.10 to the preparation of the test case, using the test instructions provided in the table.

Step	Step Description	Input Data and Expected Results
1	A truck arrives at the check-point and drives to the door (EWM).	
1.1	Create a transportation unit and assign it to a free door.	Start Transaction /SCWM/TU (Maintain Transportation Unit) and choose **Create**. Enter the data as stated in the test case description. On the **Assigned Doors** tab, choose **Add Door Assignment** and enter warehouse number 1710 and an empty door. Save your entries. *Expected result:* The transportation unit has been created and is assigned to a door.
1.2: Variant A	Confirm the arrival of the truck at the door.	Now select the transportation unit in Transaction /SCWM/TU and choose menu path **Action • Door • Arrival at Door**. Then save your action. *Expected result:* You receive an error message stating that the action was canceled because you did not enter a pager number and a license plate number.
1.2: Variant B	Confirm the arrival of the truck at the door.	Now select the transportation unit in Transaction /SCWM/TU. Switch to form view and enter the following data: ■ **License Plate Number** ■ **Country of Registration Number** ■ **Identification Type**: P ■ **Pager Number** (alternative transportation unit identification) Then choose the menu path **Action • Door • Arrival at Door** and save your action. *Expected result:* The transportation unit has both the status **Arrival at Checkpoint** and **Docked at Door**.

Table 4.10 Additional Test Steps for Enhancement 1V5a

Figure 4.13 shows an example of how you can enter the license plate and the pager number in Transaction /SCWM/TU.

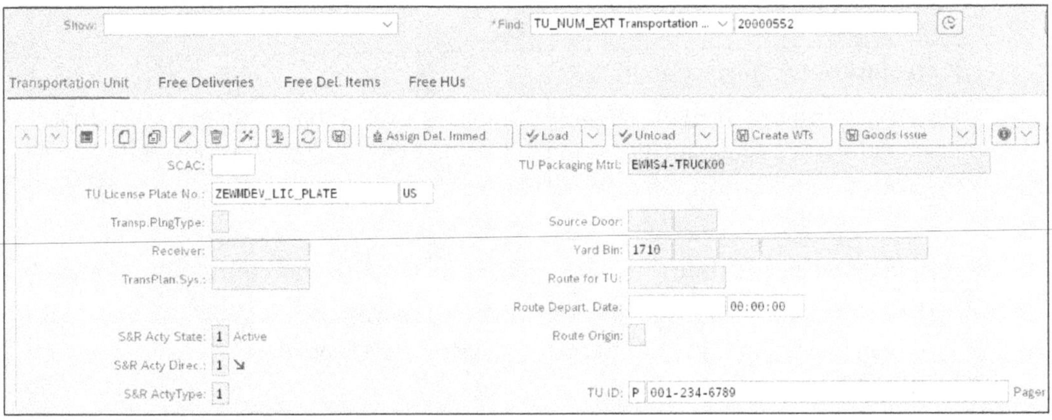

Figure 4.13 Sample for 1V5a

4.3.3   Enhancement 1V5b: Putaway Depending on Quarantine Period

With this custom development, we want to influence the putaway strategy. It often happens in projects that products must be stored separately. Normally such product-specific settings are controlled via master data attributes of the warehouse product (e.g., putaway control indicator, storage section indicator). However, if a product is to be treated more flexibly—for example, due to technical production requirements—it might make sense to use a case distinction. In our example, the product is stored under normal conditions in the storage type that was determined during the putaway strategy based on the putaway control indicator. In the event that a quarantine period is set for the product, it should be different from the normal case and moved into a different storage type for maturation. The enhancement contains this as a rather simple extension to the standard provided putaway strategy and highlights the ease of integrating custom messages into the warehouse task creation log, which allows the business user to understand why certain destination bins might have been (sometimes unexpectedly) determined in a specific situation.

Enhancement 1V5b, Putaway Depending on Quarantine Period, requires the following steps:

1. Define new storage type search sequences in the IMG and assign corresponding storage types.

2. Create the ZEWMDEVBOOK_1V5B message class and add a new message.

3. Implement the STORAGE_TYPE_SEQ method of the /SCWM/EX_CORE_PTS_TYPSQ BAdI.

4. Create the C_PTS_TYPSQ constant in the implementing class.

Next, we will explain in detail how to proceed with each of these steps. As usual, we will begin by discussing the prerequisites and end by discussing testing of this enhancement.

Prerequisites for Enhancement 1V5b

The prerequisite for the successful implementation of enhancement 1V5b is that you have maintained a quarantine period in the corresponding **Quarantine Period** field on the **WM Execution** tab of the material master.

> **Field Quarantine Period**
>
> The **Quarantine Period** field is not used within EWM standard (SAP S/4HANA 2022). You can maintain the field in the material master (**WM Execution** tab). Note for decentralized EWM that the field is part of the MATMAS IDoc and will hence be distributed during the master data transfer from SAP S/4HANA to EWM.

Define and Assign Storage Type and Search Sequences

To create the new storage type, search sequences, and assign a storage type, follow these steps:

1. In the **EWM • Goods Receipt Process • Strategies • Storage Type Search • Define Storage Type Search Sequence for Putaway** IMG activity, create the entry in Table 4.11 by copying the existing storage type search sequences (e.g., YE02) and prefix them with a *Q* instead of a *Y*. Feel free to add more storage type search sequences to your liking in a similar fashion.

Warehouse Number	Storage Type Search Sequence	Description
1710	QE02	Bin Determination in Mezzanine for Q

Table 4.11 Storage Type Search Sequence for Enhancement 1V5b

2. Now assign the appropriate storage types (e.g., storage type Y970, Clarification Zone) to the new search sequences in the **EWM • Goods Receipt Process • Strategies • Storage Type Search • Assign Storage Types to Storage Type Search Sequence** IMG activity. Feel free to create new storage types if you prefer; for our demo and test purposes, using the clarification zone seems sufficient.

Create the Message Class

To create the message, start Transaction SE91 (Message Maintenance) and type in the ZEWMDEVBOOK_1V5B message class. Create the new message 001. As a short text message, enter "Storage type search sequence & 1 changed to & 2".

Implement the STORAGE_TYPE_SEQ Method

To make the BAdI implementation, proceed as follows:

1. Start the BAdI builder (Transaction SE19) and create an enhancement implementation (e.g., ZEWM_EI_CORE_PTS_TYPSQ) for enhancement spot /SCWM/ES_CORE_PTS.

2. Then create a BAdI implementation (e.g., ZEX_CORE_PTS_TYPSQ) for BAdI definition /SCWM/EX_CORE_PTS_TYPSQ and an implementing class (e.g., ZCL_IM_CORE_PTS_TYPSQ).

3. Now program the /SCWM/IF_EX_CORE_PTS_TYPSQ~STORAGE_TYPE_SEQ method with the sample code from Listing 4.3:

   - Begin to take over the transferred storage type search sequence (IV_PUT_SSEQ) and the storage control (IV_PUT_RULE) as a return parameter.

   - Next check if the quarantine period is maintained in the product master and whether a storage type search sequence has already been determined. You can assume that this is the case because the putaway strategy in the SAP Best Practices warehouse scenario is based entirely on the fact that for all products a corresponding putaway control indicator is maintained.

   - Then change the storage type search sequence so that the putaway strategy later finds the other storage types based on the Customizing; for example, search sequence YE02 is changed into QE02.

   - Finally, document your changes in the application log by writing a message as information in table ET_BAPIRET. This is very important so that the user can also understand the system behavior.

```
METHOD /scwm/if_ex_core_pts_typsq~storage_type_seq.

  BREAK-POINT ID zewmdevbook_1v5b.
  "1 Set return values
  ev_put_sseq = iv_put_sseq.
  ev_put_rule = iv_put_rule.
  "2 Changing the stor.type search seq.
  IF  NOT is_mat_global-qqtime IS INITIAL
  AND NOT ev_put_sseq IS INITIAL.
    REPLACE SECTION LENGTH '1' OF ev_put_sseq
    WITH c_pts_typsq.
    "3 Raise message
    MESSAGE i001(zewmbookdev_1v5b)
    WITH iv_put_sseq ev_put_sseq INTO DATA(message).
    DATA(ls_bapiret) = VALUE bapiret2( type       = sy-msgty
                                       id         = sy-msgid
                                       number     = sy-msgno
                                       message_v1 = sy-msgv1
```

```
                                        message_v2 = sy-msgv2
                                        message_v3 = sy-msgv3
                                        message_v4 = sy-msgv4 ).
        APPEND ls_bapiret TO et_bapiret.
      ENDIF.


    ENDMETHOD.
```

Listing 4.3 Sample Coding for BAdI /SCWM/EX_CORE_PTS_TYPSQ

Create the C_PTS_TYPSQ Constant

Create the new static constant C_PTS_TYPSQ on the **Attributes** tab in the implementing class tab of the BAdI with type CHAR1 and assign the initial value Q.

Testing the Enhancement 1V5b

To test enhancement 1V5b, run the 1V5 test case with material EWMS4-01 for direct put-away to the mezzanine storage type. Ensure that the quarantine period is set for material EWMS4-01 on the **Warehouse Execution** tab of the material master. At step 4.3.2, use the test instructions in Table 4.12.

Step	Step Description	Input Data and Expected Results
4.3.1	Process Goods Receipt (creating the final putaway warehouse orders)	Trigger putaway warehouse task while receiving the newly created handling units.
4.3.2	Check Warehouse Orders	*Expected result:* Warehouse orders for putaway have been created. In contrast to the normal case of putaway to the mezzanine, the warehouse tasks point to the destination bins of your alternative Q storage type (e.g., 970.00.00 in destination storage type Y970).

Table 4.12 Test Steps for Enhancement 1V5b

After a successful test, you should see the custom message for changing the storage type search sequences come up in the message log. In addition, the mezzanine destination storage type should be replaced by the defined quarantine storage type from the storage type search strategy—in our case, clarification zone Y970. See Figure 4.14 for successful testing results.

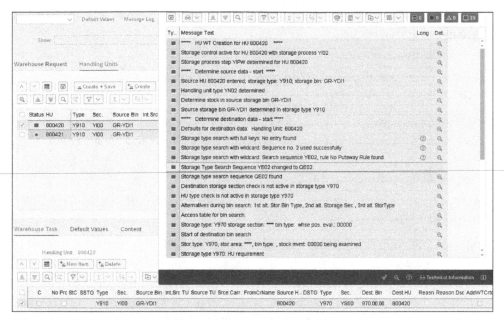

Figure 4.14 Successful Testing Results of Enhancement 1V5b

4.3.4   Enhancement 1V5c: Enhancing the Warehouse Monitor

With the help of variant 1V5c, we want to show you how you can place your own node into the warehouse management monitor for advanced data selection using a detailed guide. The SAP Best Practices scope items are also completely executable without batch functionality.

In practice, however, most warehouses handle batch stocks at least partially. Because these batches are generally classified—that is, batch characteristics (production date, vendor batch, etc.) are included—we want to display the selection of the available stock in the warehouse management monitor in addition to the **Production Date** and **Vendor Batch** batch characteristics.

We implement our new node and the necessary ABAP logic based on the standard functions that are behind the **Available Stock** monitor node. These standard functions can be found primarily in the /SCWM/AVLSTOCK_NO_BINS_MON function module and in the includes of the associated function group, /SCWM/STOCK_OVERVIEW_MON. Here, however, exists a variety of embedded monitor nodes that might seem a little confusing at first. Therefore, we copy some coding sections particularly for this enhancement.

Custom development 1V5c, Enhancing the Warehouse Management Monitor, requires the following steps:

1. Enhance the /SCWM/INCL_EEW_AQUA extension structure with structure ZEWM_S_AQUA_ALL_MON (with fields ZZ_PROD_DAT and ZZ_VEND_BATCH).

2. Create the Z_OVERVIEW_MONITOR function group and implement the includes.

3. Implement the Z_YEWM_AVLSTOCK_NO_BINS_MON function module within function group Z_OVERVIEW_MONITOR.

4. Create the text elements.

5. Define a new **Available Stock (1710)** node in the IMG and assign function module Z_YEWM_AVLSTOCK_NO_BINS_MON.

Next, we explain in detail how to proceed with each of these steps. As usual, we will begin by discussing the prerequisites and end by discussing testing of this enhancement.

Prerequisites for Enhancement 1V5c

For the realization of enhancement 1V5c, the following prerequisites must be fulfilled with respect to the master data:

■ At least one product is managed in batches (e.g., EWMS4-20 large part, fast-moving item, batches).

■ You use the standard *production date* (LOBM_HSDAT) and *vendor batch* (LOBM_LICHA) characteristics as class characteristics. As an example, your batch class in EWM could look like the image in Figure 4.15 (class YN_EWM01). Feel free to extend the SAP Best Practices–provided batch class or create a new class and assign it to your newly created batch-managed material.

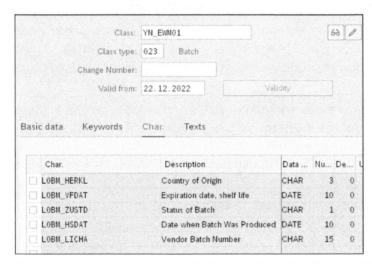

Figure 4.15 SAP Best Practices Batch Class YN_EWM01, Extended with Characteristics for Enhancement 1V5c

We will not describe how to set up the batch management required for a product or how to create batch classes and their validations at this point. There is plenty of information available on this subject, as well as several SAP Notes (SAP Note 990638, SAP Note 1305698, etc.) on the SAP Support Portal (*https://support.sap.com*).

■ These characteristics are recorded during the goods receipt process.

Enhance the Extension Structure

To create the new append structure, proceed as follows:

1. First, extend the standard structure that displays available stock in the warehouse management monitor. Start Transaction SE11 (ABAP Dictionary Maintenance) and select structure /SCWM/INCL_EEW_AQUA.

2. Click the **Append Structure** button and create the new append structure, ZEWM_S_ AQUA_ALL_MON.

3. Declare two fields, ZZ_PROD_DAT (data element /SCWM/DE_BPROD_DATE) and ZZ_VEND_ BATCH (data element /SCWM/DE_VENDOR_BATCHNO). The structure can be enhanced (character-type or numeric).

4. Activate your append structure.

Create the Function Group

To create and implement the master program, proceed like this:

1. Start the ABAP workbench (Transaction SE80) and choose your development package. Create function group Z_OVERVIEW_MONITOR using the context menu. If you want to create more project-specific monitor nodes, we recommend that you also embed the needed function modules in this function group.

2. Next, declare in the LZ_OVERVIEW_MONITORTOP TOP include of the function group the global variables and then make the selection screen 100 (see Listing 4.4), which appears when you select the monitor node in Transaction /SCWM/MON by double-clicking. You can see that for the image design, neither the screen painter nor any other settings or logic (process after input [PAI], process before output [PBO]) need to be considered. Our selection screen will end up looking like the one in Figure 4.16.

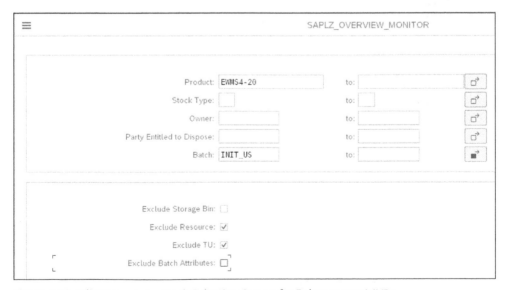

Figure 4.16 Adjustments to Stock Selection Screen for Enhancement 1V5c

3. Finally, include two standard includes as most form routines, which we use for our example, are included there.

```
FUNCTION-POOL z_overview_monitor.            "MESSAGE-ID ..

* INCLUDE LZ_OVERVIEW_MONITORD...           " Local class definition

"1. Global data
TYPE-POOLS: rsds, wmegc, abap, icon.
TABLES: sscrfields, /scwm/s_ui_mon_suom_change.
TYPES:
  BEGIN OF lsty_btch_val,
    matid         TYPE /scwm/de_matid,
    batchid       TYPE /scwm/de_batchid,
    zz_vend_batch TYPE /scwm/de_charg,
    zz_prod_dat   TYPE /scwm/de_bprod_date,
  END OF lsty_btch_val,
  ltty_btch_val TYPE STANDARD TABLE OF lsty_btch_val.
CONSTANTS: gc_vbtch TYPE atnam VALUE 'LOBM_LICHA',
           gc_hsdat TYPE atnam VALUE 'LOBM_HSDAT'.
DATA:
  functxt        TYPE smp_dyntxt,
  gs_tabname     TYPE /scwm/s_tabname_alias,
  gt_tabname     TYPE /scwm/tt_tabname_alias,
  gt_wherecl_tab TYPE rsds_twhere,
  gt_whereclause TYPE rsds_where_tab,
  gv_matnr_sel   TYPE /scwm/s_lagp_mon_f4-matnr,
  gv_matid_sel   TYPE /scwm/de_matid,
  gv_stcat_sel   TYPE /scwm/s_lagp_mon_f4-stcat,
  gv_entit_sel   TYPE /scwm/s_lagp_mon_f4-entitled,
  gv_owner_sel   TYPE /scwm/s_lagp_mon_f4-owner,
  gv_batch_sel   TYPE /scwm/s_lagp_mon_f4-charg,
  gv_free_sel    TYPE char255,
  go_mon_stock   TYPE REF TO /scwm/cl_mon_stock,
  gt_btchval     TYPE ltty_btch_val.
"Additional declarations S4
DATA gv_txt02.
DATA p_altme.
DATA p_quana.
DATA p_meins.
DATA p_quan.
"2. Build selection screen 100
SELECTION-SCREEN BEGIN OF SCREEN 100 AS WINDOW.
  SELECTION-SCREEN BEGIN OF BLOCK warehouse.
    PARAMETERS:
```

```
    p_lgnum TYPE /scwm/s_lagp_mon_f4-lgnum NO-DISPLAY.
  SELECTION-SCREEN END OF BLOCK warehouse.
  SELECTION-SCREEN BEGIN OF BLOCK stock_batch WITH FRAME TITLE TEXT-001.
    SELECT-OPTIONS:
    s_matnr FOR gv_matnr_sel,
    s_stcat FOR gv_stcat_sel,
    s_owner FOR gv_owner_sel,
    s_entit FOR gv_entit_sel,
    s_batch FOR gv_batch_sel,
    s_matid FOR gv_matid_sel NO-DISPLAY.
  SELECTION-SCREEN END OF BLOCK stock_batch.
  SELECTION-SCREEN BEGIN OF BLOCK exclude
    WITH FRAME TITLE TEXT-002.
    PARAMETERS:
      p_lgpla TYPE xfeld,
      p_rsrc  TYPE xfeld,
      p_tu    TYPE xfeld,
      p_ybtch TYPE xfeld.
  SELECTION-SCREEN END OF BLOCK exclude.
  SELECTION-SCREEN BEGIN OF BLOCK free.
    SELECT-OPTIONS:
    s_free FOR gv_free_sel NO-DISPLAY.
  SELECTION-SCREEN END OF BLOCK free.
  SELECTION-SCREEN: FUNCTION KEY 1.
  SELECTION-SCREEN: FUNCTION KEY 2.
  SELECTION-SCREEN: FUNCTION KEY 3.
SELECTION-SCREEN END OF SCREEN 100.
"3. Include of standard routines
INCLUDE:
/scwm/lstock_overview_monf01,
/scwm/lstock_overview_monf02.
```

Listing 4.4 TOP Include

4. Insert the LZ_OVERVIEW_MONITORS01 include by copying the /SCWM/LSTOCK_OVERVIEW_ MONS01 include from the /SCWM/STOCK_OVERVIEW_MON function group. The logic in this part of the source code (Listing 4.5) is responsible for the screen controller of the selection screen.

5. Adjust the standard logic in the following section (see Listing 4.5):

   – Change the code within the CASE statement for image number 100. The other distinctions you can remove because we only use one screen in our example.

   – If you want to use several different selection screens in the project environment due to several individual monitor nodes, you can add case distinctions at this point.

```
CASE sy-dynnr.
  WHEN '0100'.
* Fill alias table
    PERFORM aqua_alias.
ENDCASE.
* Display dynamic selections dialog
* (and take S_FREE into account)
CALL FUNCTION '/SCWM/DYN_SEL4MON'
  EXPORTING
    it_tabname     = gt_tabname
    it_selopt      = s_free[]
  IMPORTING
    et_wherecltab  = gt_wherecl_tab
    et_whereclause = gt_whereclause.
```

Listing 4.5 Sample for LZ_OVERVIEW_MONITORS01

6. Next define two form routines, BATCH_VAL and YBTCH_MAPPING, within in the new LZ_OVERVIEW_MONITORF01 include:

   – In the BATCH_VAL subroutine (see Listing 4.6), first determine if the call mode is a refresh of the screen or whether it is a new selection. So long as the user does not enter new select conditions, we hold the already determined batch characteristics in the buffer (gt_btchval).

   – Then build a table containing the required product-batch combinations. Products without batches and multiple entries are sorted out. If we do not have a matching record in the buffer already, we read the entire batch master for each of the product-batch combinations using the GET_BATCH method. With this feature, you can also determine other batch attributes. For our custom development, we use only the production date and the vendor batch.

   – We need the second YBTCH_MAPPING subroutine (see Listing 4.6) for the fielded control for our selection screen. We use an additional parameter (p_ybtch), which we will use later to give the end users the opportunity to decide for themselves whether the batch characteristics are to be read or not.

   – In Chapter 3, Section 3.1, we indicated the importance of performance within the warehouse management monitor. The additional reading of several hundred batch master records costs a lot of time. Through our control parameter, the user decides whether to take a longer runtime behavior into account.

   – Thus, the control parameters during the initialization of the screen do not retain their assigned values. We need to extend table LT_MAPPING accordingly.

```
*&---------------------------------------------------------------------*
*& Include           LZ_OVERVIEW_MONITORF01
*&---------------------------------------------------------------------*
```

```
*&---------------------------------------------------*
*& Form BATCH_VAL
*&---------------------------------------------------*
FORM batch_val USING
     it_stock_mon TYPE /scwm/tt_stock_mon
     iv_mode      TYPE /scwm/de_mon_fm_mode.
  DATA:
    lt_whbatch    TYPE /scwm/tt_batch,
    lo_batch_appl TYPE REF TO /scwm/cl_batch_appl.

  "1 Clear buffers
  /scwm/cl_batch_appl=>cleanup( ).
  "2 Check for REFRESH-Mode
  IF iv_mode NE 4.
    CLEAR gt_btchval.
  ENDIF.
  LOOP AT it_stock_mon ASSIGNING FIELD-SYMBOL(<ls_stock_mon>).
    DATA(ls_whbatch) = VALUE /scwm/s_batch( lgnum   = <ls_stock_mon>-lgnum
                                            batchid = <ls_stock_mon>-batchid
                                            matid   = <ls_stock_mon>-matid ).
    APPEND ls_whbatch TO lt_whbatch.
  ENDLOOP.
  SORT lt_whbatch BY lgnum batchid matid.
  DELETE ADJACENT DUPLICATES FROM lt_whbatch.
  CLEAR ls_whbatch.
  LOOP AT lt_whbatch INTO ls_whbatch
    WHERE matid   IS NOT INITIAL
    AND   batchid IS NOT INITIAL.
    "3 If we have the record in buffer, we use it
    IF iv_mode EQ 4.
      READ TABLE gt_btchval TRANSPORTING NO FIELDS
        WITH KEY matid   = ls_whbatch-matid
                 batchid = ls_whbatch-batchid
      BINARY SEARCH.
      CHECK NOT sy-subrc = 0.
    ENDIF.
    "4 Get instance
    TRY.
        lo_batch_appl ?= /scwm/cl_batch_appl=>get_instance(
        iv_productid = ls_whbatch-matid
        iv_batchid   = ls_whbatch-batchid
        iv_lgnum     = ls_whbatch-lgnum ).
      CATCH /scwm/cx_batch_management.
        CONTINUE.
```

```
    ENDTRY.
    "5 Get batch and values
    TRY.
        lo_batch_appl->get_batch(
        EXPORTING
          iv_no_classification = abap_true "remove if necessary
          IMPORTING
            es_batch    = DATA(ls_batch)
            et_val_num  = DATA(lt_val_num)
            et_val_char = DATA(lt_val_char)
            et_val_curr = DATA(lt_val_curr) ).
      CATCH /scwm/cx_batch_management.
    ENDTRY.
    "6 Fill global table
    READ TABLE lt_val_char ASSIGNING FIELD-SYMBOL(<val_char>)
      WITH KEY charact = gc_vbtch.
    IF sy-subrc = 0.
      DATA(ls_btchval) = VALUE lsty_btch_val( zz_vend_batch = <val_char>-
value_char ).
    ENDIF.
    IF ls_batch-vendrbatch_used = abap_true.
      ls_btchval-zz_vend_batch = ls_batch-vendrbatch.
    ENDIF.
    READ TABLE lt_val_num ASSIGNING FIELD-SYMBOL(<val_num>)
      WITH KEY charact = gc_hsdat.
    IF sy-subrc = 0.
      ls_btchval-zz_prod_dat = CONV date( <val_num>-value_from ).
    ENDIF.
    IF ls_batch-prod_date_used = abap_true.
      ls_btchval-zz_prod_dat = ls_batch-prod_date.
    ENDIF.
    ls_btchval = CORRESPONDING #( BASE ( ls_btchval ) ls_batch ).

    APPEND ls_btchval TO gt_btchval.

  ENDLOOP.
ENDFORM. " BATCH_VAL
*&---------------------------------------------------*
*& Form YBTCH_MAPPING
*&---------------------------------------------------*
FORM ybtch_mapping
CHANGING ct_mapping TYPE /scwm/tt_map_selopt2field.
  DATA: ls_mapping TYPE /scwm/s_map_selopt2field.
  MOVE: '/SCWM/AQUA' TO ls_mapping-tablename,
```

```
          'P_YBTCH'     TO ls_mapping-selname,
          'X_BTCH'      TO ls_mapping-fieldname.
    APPEND ls_mapping TO ct_mapping.
ENDFORM. " YBTCH_MAPPING
```

Listing 4.6 Sample Coding for Include LZ_OVERVIEW_MONITORF01

Implement the Function Module

To implement the advanced function module, do the following:

1. Mark the function group in the ABAP workbench and create a function module via the context menu. Here we use the standard /SCWM/AVLSTOCK_NO_BINS_MON function module as the template for our new function module, Z_YEWM_AVLSTOCK_NO_BINS_MON.

2. In Chapter 3, Section 3.1, we briefly presented the rough structure that you should consider when creating your own function module for the warehouse management monitor. Based on the Z_YEWM_AVLSTOCK_NO_BINS_MON function module, we show this structure in an example. The numbered code sections (see Listing 4.7) serve the following purposes:

   – "1: Check if selection variant is used
   – "2: Clear screen elements
   – "3: Map select options and parameters to database tables and fields
   – "4: Fill selection criteria based on the selection variant, if used
   – "5: Check if selection screen is to be displayed
   – "6: Pass selection criteria
   – "7: Convert selection results to UI appearance; selection will be carried out completely by method GET_AVAILABLE_STOCK

3. Following the selection of the available stock, we determine the batch characteristics for the selection result, if necessary, using the batch_val form routine. We set control parameter p_ybtch by default to "X." This facilitates fast selection for the user without batch characteristics.

4. Finally, we bring the available stocks and the corresponding batch characteristics together in the return table ET_DATA. This table refers to the declaration of the /SCWM/S_AQUA_ALL_MON structure that we have extended in the first step.

```
FUNCTION z_ewm_avlstock_no_bins_mon.
*"----------------------------------------------------------------------
*"*"Local Interface:
*"  IMPORTING
*"     REFERENCE(IV_LGNUM) TYPE  /SCWM/LGNUM
*"     REFERENCE(IV_VARIANT) TYPE  VARIANT OPTIONAL
*"     REFERENCE(IV_MODE) TYPE  /SCWM/DE_MON_FM_MODE DEFAULT '1'
*"  EXPORTING
```

```
*"      REFERENCE(ET_DATA) TYPE   /SCWM/TT_AQUA_ALL_MON
*"      REFERENCE(EV_RETURNCODE) TYPE   XFELD
*"      REFERENCE(EV_VARIANT) TYPE   VARIANT
*"   CHANGING
*"      REFERENCE(CT_TAB_RANGE) TYPE   RSDS_TRANGE OPTIONAL
*"   RAISING
*"      /SCWM/CX_MON_NOEXEC
*"----------------------------------------------------------------------

  DATA:
    lv_repid   TYPE sy-repid,
    lt_mapping TYPE /scwm/tt_map_selopt2field.

  lv_repid = sy-repid.
  CLEAR gt_tabname.
  "1 Only display popup and exit
  IF iv_mode = '3'.
    CALL FUNCTION 'RS_VARIANT_CATALOG'
      EXPORTING
        report               = lv_repid
        dynnr                = '0100'
      IMPORTING
        sel_variant          = ev_variant
      EXCEPTIONS
        no_report            = 1
        report_not_existent  = 2
        report_not_supplied  = 3
        no_variants          = 4
        no_variant_selected  = 5
        variant_not_existent = 6
        OTHERS               = 7.
    IF sy-subrc <> 0.
      MESSAGE ID sy-msgid TYPE sy-msgty NUMBER sy-msgno
      WITH sy-msgv1 sy-msgv2 sy-msgv3 sy-msgv4.
    ENDIF.
    RETURN.
  ENDIF.
  "2 Initialization (clear screen elements)
  PERFORM initialization
    USING
      iv_lgnum
      lv_repid
    CHANGING
      et_data.
  "3 Fill mapping table
```

```abap
PERFORM aqua_mapping    CHANGING lt_mapping.
PERFORM bin_ind_mapping CHANGING lt_mapping.
PERFORM ybtch_mapping   CHANGING lt_mapping.
IF iv_variant IS NOT INITIAL.
  "4 Use selection criteria
  CALL FUNCTION 'RS_SUPPORT_SELECTIONS'
    EXPORTING
      report               = lv_repid
      variant              = iv_variant
    EXCEPTIONS
      variant_not_existent = 1
      variant_obsolete     = 2
      OTHERS               = 3.
  IF sy-subrc <> 0.
    MESSAGE ID sy-msgid TYPE sy-msgty NUMBER sy-msgno
    WITH sy-msgv1 sy-msgv2 sy-msgv3 sy-msgv4.
  ENDIF.
ENDIF.
IF lines( ct_tab_range ) > 0.
  CALL FUNCTION '/SCWM/RANGETAB2SELOPT'
    EXPORTING
      iv_repid    = lv_repid
      it_mapping  = lt_mapping
    CHANGING
      ct_tab_range = ct_tab_range.
ELSEIF iv_variant IS INITIAL.
  p_rsrc  = 'X'.
  p_tu    = 'X'.
  p_ybtch = 'X'.
ENDIF.
IF iv_mode = '1'.
  "5 Show selection screen
  p_lgnum = iv_lgnum.
  CALL SELECTION-SCREEN '0100' STARTING AT 10 10
  ENDING AT 130 30.
  IF sy-subrc <> 0.
    ev_returncode = 'X'.
    RETURN.
  ENDIF.
ENDIF.
"Prepare WHERECLAUSE
CLEAR gt_tabname.
PERFORM aqua_alias.
"Convert free select options to where clause
CALL FUNCTION '/SCWM/SFREE2WHERE4MON'
```

4

```
    EXPORTING
      it_tabname      = gt_tabname
      it_selopt       = s_free[]
    IMPORTING
      et_whereclause = gt_whereclause.
"Export selection criteria
CALL FUNCTION '/SCWM/SELOPT2RANGETAB'
  EXPORTING
    iv_repid      = lv_repid
    it_mapping    = lt_mapping
  IMPORTING
    et_tab_range = ct_tab_range.
"6. Select the data according to selection criteria
"7. Convert UI fields
CALL METHOD go_mon_stock->get_available_stock
  EXPORTING
    iv_skip_bin      = p_lgpla
    iv_skip_resource = p_rsrc
    iv_skip_tu       = p_tu
    it_matnr_r       = s_matnr[]
    it_cat_r         = s_stcat[]
    it_owner_r       = s_owner[]
    it_entitled_r    = s_entit[]
    it_charg_r       = s_batch[]
    it_whereclause   = gt_whereclause
  IMPORTING
    et_stock_mon     = DATA(lt_stock_mon)
    ev_error         = ev_returncode.
"Fill extensions (1V5c)
CHECK NOT lt_stock_mon IS INITIAL.
IF p_ybtch IS INITIAL.
  PERFORM batch_val USING lt_stock_mon iv_mode.
  SORT gt_btchval BY matid batchid.
ENDIF.
"Fill exporting table
LOOP AT lt_stock_mon ASSIGNING FIELD-SYMBOL(<fs_stock_mon>).
  DATA(ls_data) = CORRESPONDING /scwm/s_aqua_all_mon(
                    <fs_stock_mon> MAPPING
                    unit       = meins
                    cat_txt    = cat_text
                    doccat     = stref_doccat
                    stock_docno = stock_docno_ext ).
  READ TABLE gt_btchval ASSIGNING FIELD-SYMBOL(<fs_batch>)
    WITH KEY matid   = <fs_stock_mon>-matid
             batchid = <fs_stock_mon>-batchid
```

```
      BINARY SEARCH.
    IF sy-subrc EQ 0.
      ls_data = CORRESPONDING #( BASE ( ls_data ) <fs_batch> ).
    ELSE.
      CLEAR: ls_data-zz_prod_dat, ls_data-zz_vend_batch.
    ENDIF.
    APPEND ls_data TO et_data.
  ENDLOOP.
ENDFUNCTION.
```

Listing 4.7 Function Module Z_YEWM_AVLSTOCK_NO_BINS_MON

Create Text Elements

To create the new text elements, navigate to the selection texts and text symbols via **Go to • Text Elements**. The text elements you should create here can be found in Table 4.13 and Table 4.14.

Text Symbols	Text
001	Stock Attributes
002	Exclude Stock and Additional Info
DYN	Filled

Table 4.13 Text Symbols

Selection Texts	Text	Dictionary Reference
P_LGPLA	Exclude Storage Bin	
P_RSRC	Exclude Resource	
P_TU	Exclude TU	
P_YBTCH	Exclude Batch Attributes	
S_BATCH	Batch	X
S_ENTIT	Party Entitled to Dispose	X
S_MATNR	Product	X
S_OWNER	Owner	X
S_STCAT	Stock Type	X

Table 4.14 Selection Texts

Define a New Node

To define the new monitor node in Customizing, proceed as follows:

1. In Chapter 3, Section 3.1, we described how you can create a new monitor in Customizing and how to get along in the node hierarchy. Now place the new node profile ZAQUA018 in the IMG under **EWM • Monitoring • Warehouse Management Monitor • Define Nodes • Define Node Profiles** as a copy of the existing P0000018 profile.

2. Replace in the **List Funct. Module** field the function module /SCWM/AVLSTOCK_NO_BINS_MON with the new function module Z_YEWM_AVLSTOCK_NO_BINS_MON. Also change the following values:
   - **Dynpro Program**: SAPLZ_OVERVIEW_MONITOR (name of the master program of the function group)
   - **Dynpro No.**: 0100
   - **Text**: Available Stock (1710)

3. Now select the **Define node** point in the same IMG activity and create the new ZAQUAALL18 node using node profile ZAQUA018. Save your settings.

4. Now go to the **EWM • Monitoring • Warehouse Management Monitor • Define Monitor** IMG activity. Select the monitor you would like to enhance, such as **SAP**, and then jump by double-clicking in the left dialog structure to **Define Node Hierarchy**. Our node should be placed under the main **Stock and Bin** node. Click the **Position** button and look for the parent node C000000011 (**Stock and Bin**). You will notice that there are exactly 11 subnodes. Now put in the 16th sequence by using the following values:
   - **Higher Node**: C000000011
   - **Lower Node**: ZAQUAALL18
   - **Sequence**: 16
   - Leave both checkboxes empty.

5. At last, save your entries.

Testing Enhancement 1V5c

To test enhancement 1V5c, run the 1V5 test case with a batch-managed material for which the **Production Date** (LOBM_HSDAT) and **Vendor Batch** (LOBM_LICHA) batch characteristics are maintained. Then use the test instructions in Table 4.15 to test the custom development.

After the selection, the result of the custom development may look like the image in Figure 4.17.

Step	Step Description	Input Data and Expected Results
1	Selection of the available stock	■ Start Transaction /SCWM/MON (Warehouse Management Monitor) and navigate to monitor node **Stock and Bin • Available Stock (1710)**. ■ Open the selection screen by double-clicking this node, enter the batch managed product, and choose **Execute** F8. *Note:* Make sure that you have unchecked the **Exclude Batch Attributes** checkbox.
		Expected result: Both batch characteristics are displayed in the selection result.

Table 4.15 Test Steps for Enhancement 1V5c

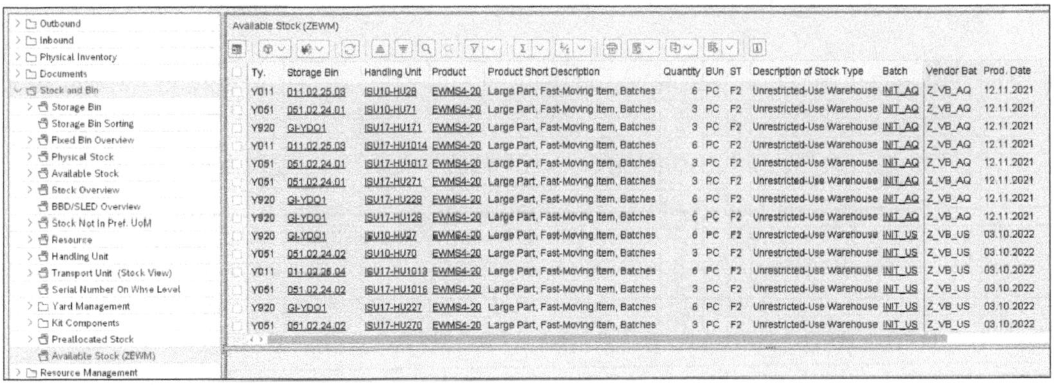

Figure 4.17 Monitor Available Batch Stock Enhancement 1V5c

4.3.5   Enhancement 1V5d: Delay Inbound Delivery with Missing Batch

The following custom development shows a way to influence the creation of the inbound delivery notification when entering the batch during inbound delivery processing in SAP ERP or SAP S/4HANA. This scenario might only occur in decentral EWM, where replication of batches from SAP ERP or SAP S/4HANA to EWM is still necessary. However, we still mention it here in context of the SAP Best Practices for embedded EWM, in case you might find yourself in a decentral EWM scenario and will specifically not be able to turn on direct batch replication in the **Define Enhanced Settings for Transfer to Decentralized EWM** Customizing transaction (view /SPE/V_EWM_DEST).

For example, it may happen that a truck delivers goods for which a purchase order indeed exists, but no inbound delivery has yet been created in the SAP ERP or SAP S/4HANA system. The employee in the goods receipt office creates an inbound delivery in the SAP ERP or SAP S/4HANA system with reference to the purchase order using

Transaction VL31N (Create Inbound Delivery) based on the supplier's delivery note. In this transaction, the employee can also create a batch for each delivery item that holds a batch-managed product. Because the distributions of the inbound delivery and the batch are carried out asynchronously and separately, the inbound delivery may be created in decentral EWM before the batch. The activation of the inbound delivery document will fail, and the document will remain in status *inactive*. With the help of the enhancement 1V5d, the creation of the inbound delivery document is delayed so that this situation does not occur.

[»]

Alternative Solutions

SAP Notes 1344366 and 2863720 describe in detail other ways you can work around the problem of inactive inbound delivery documents due to batch data missing during the inbound delivery processing. They might try to activate inactive documents once missing batches arrive in EWM instead of delaying inbound delivery document creation until batch data becomes available.

Enhancement 1V5d, Delay Inbound Delivery with Missing Batch, requires the following steps:

1. Implement the DET_DOCTYPE method of BAdI /SCWM/EX_ERP_INT_CONF.

2. Create a remote-enabled function module in SAP ERP or SAP S/4HANA.

Next, we explain in detail how to proceed with each of these steps. As usual, we will begin by discussing the prerequisites and end by discussing testing of this enhancement.

Prerequisites for Enhancement 1V5d

To achieve enhancement 1V5d, three requirements must be met:

- You are using decentralized EWM and transfer of batches via ALE.
- You must use SAP batch management. At this point, we will not describe how to set up the batch management required for a product and how to create batch classes and their validations. On this subject, there is plenty of information available, including several SAP Notes, on the SAP Support Portal (*http://support.sap.com*).
- You must not use automatic batch creation in EWM.
- Similar to the SAP Best Practices scope item, you must use alphanumeric product numbers.

Implement the DET_DOCTYPE Method

To create a BAdI implementation, proceed as follows:

1. Start the BAdI builder (Transaction SE19) and create an enhancement implementation (e.g., ZEWM_EI_ERP_INT_CONF) for enhancement spot /SCWM/ES_ERP_INT_CONF.

4

2. Then create a BAdI implementation (e.g., ZEX_ERP_INT_CONF) for BAdI definition /SCWM/EX_ERP_INT_CONF and an implementing class (e.g., ZCL_IM_ERP_INT_CONF).

3. Program the /SCWM/IF_EX_ERP_INT_CONF~DET_DOCTYPE method with the sample code from Listing 4.8:

   – First you integrate the standard logic of the /SCWM/IF_EX_ERP_INT_CONF~DET_DOC-TYPE method of the /SCWM/CL_DEF_IM_ERP_INT_CONF fallback class.

BAdI /SCWM/EX_ERP_INT_CONF   [«]

Once you create an implementation for BAdI /SCWM/EX_ERP_INT_CONF, the default implementation of the /SCWM/CL_DEF_IM_ERP_INT_CONF fallback class is no longer executed. The methods of this class are responsible for document/item type determination in delivery documents. If you only want to substitute one of these determinations or none of them, you should first implement all three methods—DET_DOCTYPE, DET_ITEMTYPE, and DET_ERP_DLVTYPE—and call the corresponding standard methods of the fallback class. After the standard logic, you can then deploy and execute your own ABAP logic in one of the methods.

   – Then determine, based on the business system group (IV_ERPBSKEY), the logical system and the corresponding RFC connection to the SAP ERP or SAP S/4HANA system from which the current inbound delivery has been distributed to EWM (coding sections "1 and "2).

   – Then call the SAP ERP or SAP S/4HANA system by RFC to receive all material/batch combinations of the inbound delivery (coding section "3).

   – Unless you get a return value (LT_MATBTCH), convert the SAP ERP or SAP S/4HANA material number in the technical key of SAP Supply Chain Management.

   – With the product ID and the batch, check whether the batch master has already been created in EWM. If the batch master of the current material/batch combination exists, the entry of LT_INTKEY is deleted. This routine is repeated for all items. If there is still one entry in LT_INTKEY available at the end of the loop, wait for two seconds and start the checks for the remaining entries again (coding section "5).

   – With the DO statement, we avoid an endless loop, if, for example, an error occurs during a specific batch distribution or creation.

```
METHOD /scwm/if_ex_erp_int_conf~det_doctype.

    DATA lo_std TYPE REF TO /scwm/cl_def_im_erp_int_conf.

    CREATE OBJECT lo_std.
    CALL METHOD lo_std->/scwm/if_ex_erp_int_conf~det_doctype
      EXPORTING
        iv_lgnum              = iv_lgnum
```

```
     iv_erpbskey          = iv_erpbskey
     it_bapidlvpartner    = it_bapidlvpartner
     it_header_deadlines  = it_header_deadlines
     is_header            = is_header
     it_extension1        = it_extension1
     it_extension2        = it_extension2
     iv_doccat            = iv_doccat
   RECEIVING
     ev_doctype           = ev_doctype.


************* Enhancement 1V5d ******************

   TYPES:
     BEGIN OF lsty_mat_btch,
       matnr TYPE matnr,
       werks TYPE werks_d,
       charg TYPE /scwm/de_charg,
     END OF lsty_mat_btch.


   DATA:
     lt_matbtch           TYPE STANDARD TABLE OF lsty_mat_btch,
     lo_send_to_bussys    TYPE REF TO /scmb/cl_business_system,
     ls_receiving_system  TYPE /scwm/s_recieving_system,
     ls_extkey            TYPE /scmb/mdl_ext_matnr_str,
     lt_extkey            TYPE /scmb/mdl_ext_matnr_tab,
     lt_extprod           TYPE /scmb/mdl_extprod_key_tab,
     ls_intkey            TYPE /scwm/dlv_matid_batchno_str,
     lt_intkey            TYPE /scwm/dlv_matid_batchno_tab,
     lo_stock_fields      TYPE REF TO /scwm/cl_ui_stock_fields.


   BREAK-POINT ID zewmdevbook_1v5d.


   CLEAR ls_receiving_system.


   "1. Get business object with receiver info
   ls_receiving_system-bskey = iv_erpbskey.
   TRY.

       lo_send_to_bussys =
       /scmb/cl_business_system=>get_instance( iv_erpbskey ).
     CATCH /scmb/cx_business_system. "#ec no_handler
       EXIT.
   ENDTRY.
   ls_receiving_system-logsys = lo_send_to_bussys->m_v_logsys.
   "2. Get RFC destination
```

```abap
TRY.
    CALL METHOD /scwm/cl_mapout=>get_rfc_destination
      EXPORTING
        iv_erplogsys       = ls_receiving_system-logsys
      IMPORTING
        ev_rfc_destination = ls_receiving_system-rfc_destination.
  CATCH /scwm/cx_mapout. "#ec no_handler
    EXIT.
ENDTRY.


"3. RFC call: get product + batch from ERP delivery
CALL FUNCTION 'Z_EWM_GET_BATCH_FROM_DLV'
  DESTINATION ls_receiving_system-rfc_destination
  EXPORTING
    iv_vbeln               = is_header-deliv_numb
  IMPORTING
    et_matnr_charg         = lt_matbtch
  EXCEPTIONS
    communication_failure = 1
    system_failure        = 2
    OTHERS                = 3.
IF sy-subrc <> 0 OR lt_matbtch IS INITIAL.
  EXIT.
ENDIF.


"4. Convert matnr to matid (prefetch)
LOOP AT lt_matbtch ASSIGNING FIELD-SYMBOL(<matbtch>).
  CLEAR ls_extkey.
  ls_extkey-ext_matnr = <matbtch>-matnr.
  COLLECT ls_extkey INTO lt_extkey.
ENDLOOP.
TRY.
    CALL FUNCTION '/SCMB/MDL_EXTPROD_READ_MULTI'
      EXPORTING
        iv_logsys = ls_receiving_system-logsys
        it_extkey = lt_extkey
      IMPORTING
        et_data   = lt_extprod.
  CATCH /scmb/cx_mdl. "#ec no_handler
    EXIT.
ENDTRY.

LOOP AT lt_matbtch ASSIGNING <matbtch>.
  "lt_extprod is sorted
```

313

```
      READ TABLE lt_extprod ASSIGNING FIELD-SYMBOL(<extprod>)
              WITH KEY ext_matnr = <matbtch>-matnr
    BINARY SEARCH.
    IF sy-subrc = 0.
      ls_intkey-productid = <extprod>-matid.
      ls_intkey-batchno = <matbtch>-charg.
      APPEND ls_intkey TO lt_intkey.
    ENDIF.
ENDLOOP.

IF lt_intkey[] IS INITIAL.
  EXIT.
ENDIF.

IF NOT lo_stock_fields IS BOUND.
  CREATE OBJECT lo_stock_fields.
ENDIF.

"5. Check if batch master exists
DO 10 TIMES.
  CALL METHOD lo_stock_fields->prefetch_batchid_by_no
    EXPORTING
      it_matid_charg    = lt_intkey
    IMPORTING
      et_batchid_extkey = DATA(lt_batch).
  SORT lt_batch BY batchno productid.
  LOOP AT lt_intkey ASSIGNING FIELD-SYMBOL(<intkey>).
    READ TABLE lt_batch ASSIGNING FIELD-SYMBOL(<batch>)
              WITH KEY batchno = <intkey>-batchno
                       productid = <intkey>-productid
              BINARY SEARCH.
    IF sy-subrc IS INITIAL AND
    <batch>-batchid IS NOT INITIAL. "batch exists
      DELETE lt_intkey.
    ENDIF.
  ENDLOOP.
  "Every batch exists -> lt_inkey is empty
  IF lt_intkey[] IS INITIAL.
    EXIT.
  ENDIF.
  WAIT UP TO 2 SECONDS.
  "Reset buffer for batches
  /scwm/cl_batch_appl=>cleanup( ).
  CLEAR lt_batch.
```

```
ENDDO.

ENDMETHOD.
```

Listing 4.8 Sample Code for BAdI /SCWM/EX_ERP_INT_CONF

Create a Remote-Enabled Function Module

To implement the RFC function module in the SAP ERP or SAP S/4HANA system, proceed as follows:

1. Create a function group (e.g., Z_EWM_MISSING_BATCH) in the SAP ERP or SAP S/4HANA system that is connected to the EWM. To do this, start Transaction SE37 (Function Builder) and select the menu path **Goto • Function Groups • Create Group**.

2. Then create in this function group a new function module (e.g., Z_EWM_GET_BATCH_FROM_DLV) and implement the coding from Listing 4.9. Make sure that you choose, on the **Attributes** tab, the setting **Remote-Enabled Module** for the function module as the processing type:

   – First, set the read options for determining the delivery and then call the BAPI_DELIVERY_GETLIST function module with your SAP ERP or SAP S/4HANA delivery number.

   – Coding section "3 checks for which delivery items a batch has been entered and fills the appropriate material batch combination in the return table ET_MATNR_CHARG.

```
FUNCTION z_ewm_get_batch_from_dlv.
*"----------------------------------------------------------------------
*"*"Local Interface:
*"  IMPORTING
*"     REFERENCE(IV_VBELN) TYPE  VBELN
*"  EXPORTING
*"     REFERENCE(ET_MATNR_CHARG) TYPE  MCHA_KEY_TABLE
*"----------------------------------------------------------------------
  DATA:
    ls_vbeln        TYPE bapidlv_range_vbeln,
    lt_vbeln        TYPE STANDARD TABLE OF bapidlv_range_vbeln,
    ls_dlv_item     TYPE bapidlvitem,
    lt_dlv_item     TYPE bapidlvitem_t,
    ls_dlv_control  TYPE bapidlvbuffercontrol,
    ls_matnr_charg  TYPE mcha_key,
    lv_lines        TYPE i.

  "1. Set read options
  ls_dlv_control-bypassing_buffer = abap_true.
  ls_dlv_control-item = abap_true.
```

```
ls_vbeln-sign = 'I'.
ls_vbeln-option = 'EQ'.
ls_vbeln-deliv_numb_low = iv_vbeln.
APPEND ls_vbeln TO lt_vbeln.

"2. Get delivery
CALL FUNCTION 'BAPI_DELIVERY_GETLIST'
  EXPORTING
    is_dlv_data_control = ls_dlv_control
  TABLES
    it_vbeln            = lt_vbeln
    et_delivery_item    = lt_dlv_item.

"3. Fill return table
LOOP AT lt_dlv_item INTO ls_dlv_item.
  MOVE-CORRESPONDING ls_dlv_item TO ls_matnr_charg.

  CHECK NOT ls_matnr_charg-charg IS INITIAL.

  READ TABLE et_matnr_charg TRANSPORTING NO FIELDS
  WITH KEY matnr = ls_matnr_charg-matnr
  charg = ls_matnr_charg-charg.
  IF sy-subrc NE 0.
    DESCRIBE TABLE et_matnr_charg LINES lv_lines.
    ADD 1 TO lv_lines.
    INSERT ls_matnr_charg INTO et_matnr_charg
    INDEX lv_lines.
  ENDIF.
ENDLOOP.
ENDFUNCTION.
```

Listing 4.9 Example SAP ERP or SAP S/4HANA Function Module

[»]

Dynamic Processing

In our coding example (see Listing 4.9), we have done a rather lean implementation. You can use this code and adjust it according to your project requirements; for example, you can make the check depending on the warehouse number (IV_LGNUM). It may also be advantageous if the number of loops and the waiting time are determined dynamically. You can achieve this by reading, for example, a custom parameter at the beginning. This allows you also to regulate the delay in a production system without having to change the code.

Testing Enhancement 1V5d

To test enhancement 1V5d, run this technical test case first. Then you will be able to test the process using the 1V5 test case as outlined in Table 4.16.

Step	Step Description	Input Data and Expected Results
1	Deregister the EWM inbound queues for delivery processing.	Start Transaction SMQR (Registration of Inbound Queues) and deregister the queues. The first three characters of the queue name are DLV*.
2	Turn off immediate processing for BATMAS IDocs in EWM.	In Transaction WE20 set inbound processing for message type BATMAS to **Background Report**.
3	Activate checkpoint group in EWM.	Start Transaction SAAB (Checkpoints that Can Be Activated) and activate the breakpoints of checkpoint group ZEWMDEVBOOK_1V5D.
4	Create an inbound delivery with reference to a purchase order in SAP ERP or SAP S/4HANA.	■ Start Transaction VL31N (Create Inbound Delivery). ■ Enter the data (e.g., as stated in the test case description). ■ Enter a batch for a batch-managed item. ■ Press **Save**. *Expected result:* The inbound delivery was distributed to EWM.
5.1	Start the waiting queue for the inbound delivery in EWM.	Start Transaction SMQ2 (QRFC Monitor, Inbound Queue) and search for all queues. You will find a new queue: DLV* (contains the inbound delivery). Activate the queue of the inbound delivery. You will be holding in the debugger at statement BREAK-POINT ID ZEWMDEVBOOK_1V5D. *Expected result:* You will not receive the required batch ID via export table LT_BATCH from method prefetch_batchid_by_no.
5.2	Trigger BATMAS IDoc processing in EWM	■ Start a second mode and process the BATMAS IDoc containing the batch master record in Transaction BD87. Trigger batch replication from SAP ERP or SAP S/4HANA via IDoc using Transaction BD90 if no IDoc has been received yet. ■ Now you can start another round of the DO statement in the first mode. *Expected result:* You will receive the required batch ID via export table LT_BATCH from method prefetch_batchid_by_no.

Table 4.16 Test Steps for Enhancement 1V5d

4.4   Outbound Process Using Pick Handling Units as Shipping Handling Units: 1G2

In this section, we will look at the first outbound scope item of the SAP Best Practices for embedded EWM, which focuses on functions of warehouse request management and handling units for warehousing and shipping. After the presentation of the business process, we will describe the following custom developments:

- **1G2a: Enhancing the delivery interface by custom data**
  Learn how to transfer custom data from SAP S/4HANA to EWM via the delivery interface.

- **1G2b: Transfer of custom data from the outbound delivery order to the warehouse task**
  Learn how to transfer custom data from the outbound delivery order to the picking warehouse task.

- **1G2c: Showing custom data in the form view of the outbound delivery order item**
  Learn how to enhance the form view of the EWM delivery to display custom field information.

- **1G2d: Determination and transfer of a handling unit type from the packaging specification to the pick warehouse task**
  Learn how to determine the handling unit type of a pick handling from the packaging specification at warehouse order creation.

- **1G2e: Determination of the operative UOM by packaging specification of goods receipt**
  Learn how to determine the operative UOM for a pick warehouse task from a packaging specification used at goods receipt.

- **1G2f: Prohibit goods issue for incomplete packing**
  Learn how to implement a custom check for completed packing or an outbound delivery at the time of goods issue.

4.4.1   Process Description of Scope Item 1G2

Upon outbound delivery order creation, the system automatically assigns the outbound delivery orders to routes. The system then creates warehouse tasks and warehouse orders automatically, and the warehouse activities begin.

The warehouse orders are printed as a work list for paper-based picking. A warehouse worker takes the printout of a warehouse order and prepares a pick handling unit to be used for the picking of the products listed on the warehouse order printout. The worker then takes two labels with the same external handling unit identifiers and sticks one to the physical handling unit and the other to the printout of the warehouse order. The warehouse worker carries out the picking for one or several pick handling units and then brings the goods to the staging area. The warehouse worker then hands over the printouts of the warehouse orders to the warehouse clerk responsible for the confirmation of the picking. With the confirmation of the warehouse orders, the pick handling units are created in the system.

In the staging area, a warehouse worker weighs and labels the handling units with the shipping label and creates an outbound delivery for each handling unit. This triggers the printout of a delivery note, which is put into the handling unit before the handling unit is physically closed.

When the truck arrives, it checks in and the checkpoint clerk directs it to a door. Once the truck arrives at the door, the warehouse worker commences the physical loading of the handling units. After the physical loading of all handling units for the route has been finished, a shipping office clerk posts the goods issue, prints a second delivery note for each outbound delivery, and hands the delivery notes over to the truck driver. The truck leaves the premises. Table 4.17 summarizes the process steps.

Step	Physical Activity	System Activity
0: Create SAP S/4HANA outbound delivery without sales order reference		SAP S/4HANA outbound delivery is created and replicated to EWM when saved.
1: Assign route to outbound delivery order		The system automatically determines and assigns a route to the outbound delivery order.
2: Create pick warehouse orders		The system automatically creates and prints out pick warehouse orders.
3: Pick the goods	A warehouse worker prepares a pick handling unit, labels the pick handling unit, and puts the pick handling unit onto a resource. The warehouse worker picks the goods into the pick handling unit and moves the pick handling unit to the staging area.	
		A warehouse clerk creates the pick handling unit and confirms the warehouse order.

Table 4.17 Steps in Outbound Scope Item 1G2

Step	Physical Activity	System Activity
4: Label the handling units and prepare the loading		A warehouse worker weighs the pick handling unit and prints shipping handling unit labels.
	The warehouse worker labels the shipping handling unit.	
		The warehouse worker creates an outbound delivery for the shipping handling unit. The system prints the delivery note.
	The warehouse worker puts the delivery note into the shipping handling unit and closes the shipping handling unit.	
5: A truck arrives at the checkpoint and drives to the door	A truck arrives. The checkpoint clerk communicates the door to the truck driver. The truck drives to the door.	
6: Load the truck	A warehouse worker moves the shipping handling units to the truck.	
7: Post the goods issue and print the loading list		The shipping office clerk posts the good issue. The system prints the loading list.
	The shipping office clerk hands over the loading list to the truck driver.	
8: The truck leaves	The truck leaves.	

Table 4.17 Steps in Outbound Scope Item 1G2 (Cont.)

You can find further details in the process description of scope item 1G2.

4.4.2 Enhancement 1G2a: Extending the Delivery Interface by Custom Data

The following enhancement shows how you can transfer additional data from SAP S/4HANA to EWM via the delivery interface and use this data in the warehouse order creation. In this example, a handling code that has been defined in the SAP S/4HANA system on the outbound delivery item level as a custom field can be passed into the outbound delivery order item. The following two BAdI implementations and two structure enhancements will be required to get this to work, which we will demonstrate in a detailed way. We are assuming that the custom data field already exists in the outbound delivery item of the SAP S/4HANA system:

- Passing custom data from SAP S/4HANA into the delivery interface (BAdI SMOD_ V50B0001).
- Enhancing the data object of the outbound delivery request (EWM). This step will only be applicable in a decentralized EWM setup in case the outbound delivery request will not be skipped. Embedded EWM does not use delivery request documents anymore. (Enhancement of structure /SCDL/INCL_EEW_DR_ITEM_STR.)
- Passing custom data from the delivery interface to the outbound delivery request (EWM). Also, this step is only relevant for decentral EWM with outbound delivery request used (BAdI /SCWM/EX_MAPIN_OD_SAVEREPL).
- Enhancing the data object of the outbound delivery order (EWM; enhancement of structure /SCDL/INCL_EEW_DLV_ITEM_STR).

The description for scope item 1G2a will only change in step 0, as outlined in Table 4.18.

Step	Physical Activity	System Activity
0: Create SAP S/4HANA outbound delivery without sales order reference	N/A	<ul><li>SAP S/4HANA outbound delivery is created and replicated to EWM when saved.</li><li>Replicating the delivery will include a custom data field that will be passed to EWM and stored in the outbound delivery request and outbound delivery order on the item level.</li></ul>

Table 4.18 Process Steps with Deviation for Variant 1G2a

The custom development will require that the following activities are performed step by step:

1. Providing custom data from SAP S/4HANA
2. Enhancing the structure for the outbound delivery request
3. Passing the custom data into the outbound delivery request
4. Passing the custom data from the outbound delivery request into the outbound delivery order

We will now explain in detail which activities you will need to perform in the individual steps. We will also discuss what is required to test this enhancement.

Provide Custom Data

Let's start with the first step in the SAP S/4HANA system, using Transaction SE19 (BAdI Builder). You have to supply a value to the custom field in method EXIT_SAPLV50K_007 of BAdI definition SMOD_V50B0001—for example, by reading it from the SAP S/4HANA delivery item and passing it to the ET_EXTENSION2 output parameter. This table is suitable for transferring customer-specific data that is structured. The other output parameter, ET_EXTENSION1, is available in the method and can be used for unstructured data. In our case, we have set up a fixed value to the field so as not to overly extend this example (see Listing 4.10). You may certainly provide your own logic to enhance or replace the example, potentially using further custom fields and selecting data appropriately. For our example data, add two private constants (C_FIELDNAME of type NAME_FELD with initial value 'ZZFIELD1' and C_FIELDVALUE of type CHAR255 with initial value 'A') as attributes in the implementing class of your BAdI implementation—for example, ZCL_IM_EI_ODLV_EXTEND.

```
METHOD if_ex_smod_v50b0001~exit_saplv50k_007.

    "Fill delivery interface extension structure from SAP S/4HANA
    "Simple example with one field per item only
    BREAK-POINT ID zewmdevbook_1g2a.

    LOOP AT it_lips ASSIGNING FIELD-SYMBOL(<fs_lips>).
      DATA(ls_bapiext) = VALUE bapiext( param = <fs_lips>-vbeln
                                        row   = <fs_lips>-posnr
                                        field = c_fieldname
                                        value = c_fieldvalue ).
      APPEND ls_bapiext TO et_extension2.
      CLEAR ls_bapiext.
    ENDLOOP.

ENDMETHOD.
```

Listing 4.10 Example Implementation of BAdI SMOD_V50B0001

Transfer of Custom Data via Delivery Interface

You can find further information and a sample implementation for sending custom data by BAPI structure EXTENSION1 in SAP Note 351303. The sample implementation is still based on the former user exit. In addition, the note contains a list of the individual methods of the BAdI that explains their use in either inbound or outbound message processing.

Enhancing the Structure

Before handling the custom data in EWM, you need to enhance data dictionary structure /SCDL/INCL_EEW_DR_ITEM_STR for the outbound delivery request with the additional field ZZFIELD1. To do so, we will select the structure in Transaction SE11 (Data Dictionary) and enhance it with an append structure that contains the custom field with the corresponding field definition (see Figure 4.18).

By checking the activation log, you can view the transparent tables, table types, and views that were adjusted, with the changes being dependent objects of the enhancement structure.

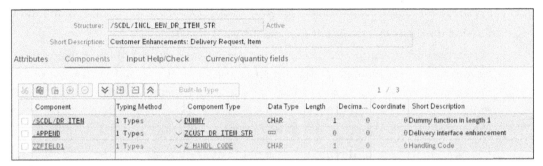

Figure 4.18 Enhancing the Delivery Request Item Structure

Passing the Custom Data into the Outbound Delivery Request

The third step consists of passing the value of the custom field from the extension structure of the interface to the outbound delivery request item into EWM. To do so, we will implement BAdI /SCWM/EX_MAPIN_OD_SAVEREPL, which is included in enhancement spot /SCWM/ES_ERP_MAPIN, as shown in Listing 4.11.

```
METHOD /scwm/if_ex_mapin_od_saverepl~mapin.

    BREAK-POINT ID zewmdevbook_1g2a.

    LOOP AT ct_dlv_request
    ASSIGNING FIELD-SYMBOL(<fs_dlv_req>).
      LOOP AT <fs_dlv_req>-t_item
      ASSIGNING FIELD-SYMBOL(<fs_item>).
        DATA(ls_keymap) = VALUE #( <fs_item>-t_keymap_item[ 1 ] ).
        CHECK sy-subrc IS INITIAL.
        DATA(lv_vbeln) = ls_keymap-docno.
        DATA(lv_posnr) = ls_keymap-itemno.
        TRY.
            DATA(ls_bapiext) = VALUE #( it_bapi_extension2[ param = lv_vbeln
                                                            row   = lv_posnr
                                                            field = c_
```

```
fieldname ] ).
        CATCH cx_sy_itab_line_not_found.
          CONTINUE.
      ENDTRY.
      MOVE ls_bapiext-value TO <fs_item>-s_eew-zzfield1.
    ENDLOOP.
  ENDLOOP.

  ENDMETHOD.
```

Listing 4.11 Example Implementation of BAdI /SCWM/EX_MAPIN_OD_SAVEREPL

Passing the Custom Data into the Outbound Delivery Order

Before the custom data can be passed from the delivery request to the delivery order, we must enhance the data dictionary structure /SCDL/INCL_EEW_DLV_ITEM_STR of the delivery order by the custom field. To do so, select the structure in Transaction SE11 and enhance it. The field definition should be identical to the previously created append structure in step 2. The procedure is also the same as in step 2.

Because the transfer of the custom data of the delivery request to the delivery order works automatically for identically named fields in both structures, you do not need to implement the /SCDL/TS_DATA_COPY BAdI definition of the transition service. This would only be required in the case of differently named fields, because the automatic transfer is executed via the move-corresponding command.

When you replicate an outbound delivery from SAP S/4HANA to EWM, you should already see the custom field filled in with the outbound delivery request and the outbound delivery order. You can find it at the end of the item display structure of the list view, as shown in Figure 4.19.

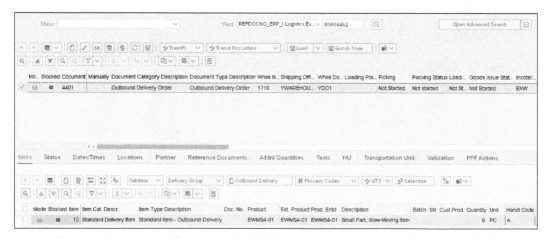

Figure 4.19 Custom Delivery Item Field in the List View of Outbound Delivery Order (Bottom Right Corner)

Testing Enhancement 1G2a

To test the enhancement, run the test case for scope item 1G2. Note the change in the test instructions in Table 4.19.

Step	Description	User Input and Expected Results
4.2	Create Delivery	Create an outbound delivery in SAP S/4HANA that will be replicated to EWM when saved. *Expected result:* The outbound delivery order has been created in EWM containing the custom data in the additional field as supplied from the SAP S/4HANA side.

Table 4.19 Test Steps for Enhancement 1G2a

4.4.3   Enhancement 1G2b: Transfer of Custom Data from Outbound Delivery Order to Warehouse Task

Our example is not yet complete. The custom field passed from SAP S/4HANA to the outbound delivery order item is now to be passed further into the picking warehouse task. The field could then, for example, be used in the warehouse order creation. A potential use case could be to determine the queue based on the custom **Handling Code** field.

Enhancement 1G2b, Transfer of Custom Data from Outbound Delivery Order to Warehouse Task, will require us to perform the following steps:

1. Enhancing the warehouse task data object via enhancement of structures /SCWM/INCL_EEW_S_ORDIM and /SCWM/INCL_EEW_S_WT_CREA.

2. Pass custom data from the outbound delivery order item to the warehouse task. BAdI /SCWM/EX_TOWHR_PTO_CREA will be implemented to pass our custom field value from the outbound delivery order item to the warehouse task.

You can find the change process description in Table 4.20.

Step	Physical Activity	System Activity
2: Create Pick Warehouse Orders	N/A	▪ The system automatically creates and prints out pick warehouse orders. ▪ The custom **Handling Code** field is passed from the outbound delivery order item to the warehouse task.

Table 4.20 Process Steps with Deviation for Enhancement 1G2b

Enhancing the Warehouse Task Data Object

Do the following in order to enhance warehouse task structures. First use an append in order to include the custom field (ZZFIELD1 type Z_HANDL_CODE) in enhancement structures /SCWM/INCL_EEW_S_ORDIM and /SCWM/INCL_EEW_S_WT_CREA of the warehouse task. Table 4.21 tells you under which conditions a custom field should be included in the two structures.

EEW Structure	Where Used	Recommendation
Custom data for warehouse task creation (/SCWM/INCL_EEW_S_WT_CREA)	Internal structure for the creation of warehouse tasks/warehouse orders (/SCWM/S_TO_CREATE_INT).	Use this structure for data that you would like to use during warehouse task creation but will not require to be stored persistently.
Custom data for the warehouse task (/SCWM/INCL_EEW_S_ORDIM)	Structure /SCWM/S_ORDIM_ATT is used in the /SCWM/ORDIM* database tables. Structure /SCWM/S_TO_DET_MON* is used in the monitor nodes for warehouse tasks.	Use this structure for data that you would like to use after warehouse task creation in follow-on processes or that you would like to see in reporting, such as the warehouse monitor. This data will be present in the warehouse monitor and the database and will have an influence on performance.

Table 4.21 Field Enhancement Options for Warehouse Tasks

Passing the Custom Data to the Warehouse Task

Implement BAdI /SCWM/EX_DLV_TOWHR_PTO_CREA (enhancement spot /SCWM/ES_DLV_TOWHR), which is specifically designed for data transfer from delivery documents to referenced product warehouse tasks. Listing 4.12 shows such an implementation (e.g., named Z_EI_DLV_TOWHR). Because of the identical naming of the custom fields, the warehouse task creation automatically moves field content from structure /SCWM/INCL_EEW_S_WT_CREA to structure /SCWM/INCL_EEW_S_ORDIM. In our example, we assume for simplicity reasons that the field value can be copied from the outbound delivery order to the warehouse task. For your project implementation, you should remember that you can access the data of the delivery item in BAdIs through the reference of the outbound delivery order item in the warehouse task at any time. Preferably, use the BAdI and the enhancement structures for new fields in the warehouse task creation that you determine indirectly from the outbound delivery order item and that should be visible to the user further in the process flow.

To verify the successful data transfer, you can use a technical test and check the existence of the custom data in a warehouse task by looking at the database table of open warehouse tasks, /SCWM/ORDIM_O (e.g., in Transaction SE16).

```
METHOD /scwm/if_ex_dlv_towhr_pto_crea~get_additional_whr_data.

    BREAK-POINT id zewmdevbook_1g2b.

    "Transfer custom data to warehouse task structure
    MOVE is_whr_item-eew-zzfield1 TO es_prod_wt_crea_cust-zzfield1.

ENDMETHOD.
```

Listing 4.12 Example Implementation of BAdI /SCWM/EX_DLV_TOWHR_PTO_CREA

Testing Enhancement 1G2b

To test the custom development, execute scope item 1G2 of the SAP Best Practices for embedded EWM. For step 4.3, use the updated test description as shown in Table 4.22.

Step	Description	User Input and Expected Results
4.3	Create Warehouse Tasks Manually	Call the warehouse monitor and find the pick warehouse task created in the Run Outbound Process—Deliveries app, in the **Documents • Warehouse Task** node. Include the custom field in the display structure for the list view. *Expected result:* The warehouse task contains the custom field with the value passed from the outbound delivery order item.

Table 4.22 Test Steps for Enhancement 1G2b

Figure 4.20 shows the extended warehouse task, including the custom **Handling Code** field.

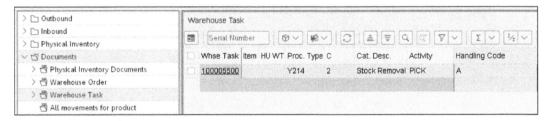

Figure 4.20 Custom Field for Warehouse Task Shown in Warehouse Monitor

4.4.4   Enhancement 1G2c: Showing Custom Data in the Form View of the Outbound Delivery Order Item

We will now show the custom field in the form view of the outbound delivery order item. Such an enhancement is generally possible for the delivery header, delivery item, and handling unit data.

The following activities are required for enhancement 1G2c, Showing Custom Data in the Form View of the Outbound Delivery Order Item:

1. **Creating a function group**
   A new function group will be created with PBO and PAI modules.

2. **Creating Dynpros and subscreens**
   A new Dynpro and subscreen will be created containing the custom field.

3. **Displaying the custom field in the UI of the outbound delivery order**
   BAdI /SCWM/EX_DLV_UI_SCREEN will be used to display the custom field in the UI.

We will now explain in detail which activities you will need to perform in the individual steps. We will also discuss what is required to test this enhancement.

Creating a Function Group

Create a new function group (e.g., Z_DLV_UI) and include a new PBO and PAI module in it, as shown in Listing 4.13 and Listing 4.14.

```
MODULE output OUTPUT.
  CALL METHOD /scwm/cl_dlv_ui_badi_mgmt=>pbo_item
    EXPORTING
      iv_transaction = /scwm/if_ex_dlv_ui_screen=>sc_ta_prdo.
ENDMODULE.
```

Listing 4.13 Example PBO Module for Form View of Outbound Delivery Order Item

```
MODULE input INPUT.
  CALL METHOD /scwm/cl_dlv_ui_badi_mgmt=>pai_item
    EXPORTING
      iv_transaction = /scwm/if_ex_dlv_ui_screen=>sc_ta_prdo.

ENDMODULE.
```

Listing 4.14 Example PAI Module for Form View of Outbound Delivery Order Item

Creating Dynpros and Subscreens

Now we need to create a Dynpro (e.g., 1000) of type **Subscreen**. This subscreen should include our custom field that we want to display in form view. Use the /SCDL/INCL_EEW_DLV_ITEM_STR enhancement structure for the definition of the field in the screen painter. You can read about the procedure in more detail in the BAdI documentation of the **Business Add-Ins (BAdIs) for Extended Warehouse Management • Cross-Process Settings • Delivery—Warehouse Request • BAdI: Screen Enhancements for Customer Enhancement Structures** IMG node.

Displaying the Custom Field

Finally, you still need to implement the DEFINE_ITEM_EXTENSION method of BAdI /SCWM/ EX_DLV_UI_SCREEN, which is assigned to enhancement spot /SCWM/ES_DLV_UI_SCREEN in a new enhancement implementation (e.g., Z_EI_DLV_UI_SCREEN). You might name the new implementing class ZCL_IM_DLV_UI_SCREEN. Add two private constants to the class: c_repid_ewm_dlv_ui of type SYREPID with initial value 'SAPLZ_EWM_DLV_UI', and C_DYNNR_ 1000 of type SYDYNNR with initial value '100'. The newly created function group and subscreen need to be set in the BAdI method. Listing 4.15 can serve as an example.

```
METHOD /scwm/if_ex_dlv_ui_screen~define_item_extension.

    BREAK-POINT ID zewmdevbook_1g2c.

    "Set constants as declared in class attributes
    ev_repid = c_repid_ewm_dlv_ui. "'SAPLZ_EWM_DLV_UI'
    ev_dynnr = c_dynnr_1000.          "'1000'

ENDMETHOD.
```

Listing 4.15 Example Implementation of BAdI /SCWM/EX_DLV_UI_SCREEN

As a result, you should see the custom field in the form view of the outbound delivery order item, as shown in Figure 4.21.

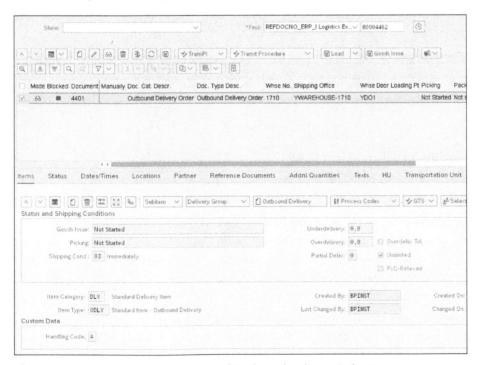

Figure 4.21 Custom Data in Form View of Outbound Delivery Order Item

Testing Enhancement 1G2c

To test enhancement 1G2c, select a newly created outbound delivery and display the form view of the outbound delivery order item (Transaction /SCWM/PRDO) that should contain the custom field. You have already checked the existence of the field value in enhancement 1G2a. Now ensure that field and value are correctly showing.

4.4.5   Enhancement 1G2d: Determination and Transfer of Handling Unit Type from Packaging Specification to Pick Warehouse Task

The automatic creation of pick handling units is controlled by the pack profile assigned to the warehouse order creation rule determined at warehouse order creation. With this pack profile, a packaging specification is determined that contains a handling unit type that can control the putaway or printing behavior. The standard SAP S/4HANA system uses the standard handling unit type from the product master of the packaging material for the automatic creation of pick handling units. An alternative and more flexible approach would be to determine the handling unit type from the packaging specification independent of the settings in the product master of the packaging material.

Enhancement 1G2d, Determination and Transfer of Handling Unit Type from Packaging Specification to Pick Warehouse Task, requires the following activities:

1. Implementation of method SORT in BAdI /SCWM/EX_WHO_SORT.
2. Creation of method GET_WCR_TO and the static attribute SS_WCR in the implementing class.
3. Implementation of method CHANGE in BAdI /SCWM/EX_HU_BASICS_HUHDR.

Next, we explain in detail how to proceed with each of these steps. As usual, we will begin by discussing the prerequisites and end by discussing testing of this enhancement.

Prerequisites for Enhancement 1G2d

Enhancement 1G2d is based on the following three assumptions regarding master data and Customizing settings:

1. Because the outbound scope item 1G2 does not foresee an automatic creation of pick handling units, you need to add the following Customizing settings: call the IMG activity **Cross-Process Settings • Warehouse Order • Define Packing Profile for Warehouse Order Creation** and set the **Create HUs** indicator for the **YP02 (Picking onto Pallet)** pack profile.
2. Define a bin on which the pick handling unit is to be created via Transaction /SCWM/SEBA (Assign Start/End Storage Bin for Activity Area) using activity area YN01 and activity PICK, setting the starting point (e.g., storage bin GI-YDO1).

3. In Transaction /SCWM/PACKSPEC (Maintain Packaging Specification), change the packaging specification for the packaging materials for large parts (description: Picking onto Pallet), which controls the determination of the pick handling unit for large parts. On the **Warehouse** tab, exchange the handling unit type YNO1 (EWM Pallet) for another, possibly newly created, handling unit type (e.g., YNO3—EWM US Pallet). This handling unit type should be differently defined than the standard type of handling unit contained in the packaging product master.

In enhancement 1G2d, you can determine a handling unit type for the pick handling unit that deviates from the handling unit type of the packing material but will instead be drawn from the packaging specification. Table 4.23 shows the custom development in process step 2.

In addition, in this example, we show how to use local buffers in the interaction of two BAdI implementations. Because the pick handling units are created toward the end of the warehouse order creation, we will also use another BAdI implementation for buffering of data that is required for the determination of the handling unit type.

Step	Physical Activity	System Activity
2: Create Pick Warehouse Orders	N/A	■ The system automatically creates and prints out pick warehouse orders. ■ Customizing: For picking from defined storage type, pick handling units will be automatically created. ■ Custom development: The pick handling units will be created with the handling unit type determined from the corresponding packaging specification.

Table 4.23 Process Steps with Deviation for Enhancement 1G2d

Implementing the SORT Method

To create the BAdI implementation, follow these steps:

1. Start the BAdI builder (Transaction SE19) and create an implementation for enhancement spot /SCWM/ES_WHO.

2. Then create an implementation and an implementing class for BAdI definition /SCWM/EX_WHO_SORT.

3. Use method SORT to fill the local buffer with input parameters of the method—here, the warehouse order creation rule (IS_WCR), programmed as shown in Listing 4.16.

```
METHOD /scwm/if_ex_who_sort~sort.

  BREAK-POINT ID zewmdevbook_1g2d.
```

```
        "If a packaging profile is supplied fill the buffer
        CHECK NOT is_wcr-packprofile IS INITIAL.
        ss_wcr = is_wcr.

    ENDMETHOD.
```

Listing 4.16 Example Implementation of BAdI /SCWM/EX_WHO_SORT

Creating of GET_WCR_TO Method

Furthermore, you need to create a new static and public GET_WCR_TO method in the implementing class for BAdI /SCWM/EX_WHO_SORT (see Listing 4.17). We will use this method later on to read the necessary data to the buffer.

```
METHOD get_wcr_to.

    BREAK-POINT ID zewmdevbook_1g2d.
    es_wcr = ss_wcr.

ENDMETHOD.
```

Listing 4.17 Example Method for Providing Buffered Data

Before you can activate the method correctly, you still have to define the ss_wcr public static attribute for the implementing class, as shown in Figure 4.22.

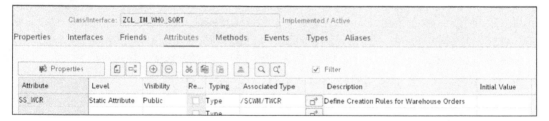

Figure 4.22 Defining Static Attribute

Implementing the CHANGE Method

Finally, restart the BAdI builder (Transaction SE19) and create an implementation for method CHANGE of BAdI /SCWM/EX_HU_BASICS_HUHDR, assigned to enhancement spot /SCWM/ES_HU_BASICS. Use the coding shown in Listing 4.18:

- At the beginning of the method, we read the buffered data of the warehouse order creation rule as well as settings for the warehouse number (scheme for pack profile determination and supply chain unit for the warehouse number). This data is used for determining the packaging specification based on condition technique.
- Furthermore, we compare the packaging material of the pick handling unit and the determined packaging specification. If they are identical, the handling unit type of

the packaging material will be overwritten with the handling unit type from the packaging specification.

```
METHOD /scwm/if_ex_hu_basics_huhdr~change.

  DATA: ls_t340d     TYPE /scwm/t340d,
        ls_t300md    TYPE /scwm/s_t300_md,
        lt_packspec TYPE /scwm/tt_guid_ps,
        lt_pscont   TYPE /scwm/tt_packspec_nested.
```

```
  BREAK-POINT ID zewmdevbook_1g2d.

  "Get WCR from buffer
  DATA(ls_wcr) = zcl_im_who_sort=>get_wcr_to( ).
  "Check if buffer is filled
  CHECK NOT ls_wcr IS INITIAL.
  "Get warehouse settings
  CALL FUNCTION '/SCWM/T340D_READ_SINGLE'
    EXPORTING
      iv_lgnum   = cs_huhdr-lgnum
    IMPORTING
      es_t340d   = ls_t340d
    EXCEPTIONS
      not_found = 1
      OTHERS    = 2.
  IF sy-subrc <> 0.
    EXIT.
  ENDIF.
  "Get warehouse assignment
  CALL FUNCTION '/SCWM/T300_MD_READ_SINGLE'
    EXPORTING
      iv_lgnum   = cs_huhdr-lgnum
    IMPORTING
      es_t300_md = ls_t300md
    EXCEPTIONS
      not_found  = 1
      OTHERS     = 99.
  IF sy-subrc <> 0.
    EXIT.
  ENDIF.
  "Build up field catalog
  DATA(ls_fields) = VALUE /scwm/pak_com_i( pak_locid = ls_t300md-scuguid
                                           pak_rule  = ls_wcr-packprofile ).
```

```abap
"Get packaging specification
CALL FUNCTION '/SCWM/PS_FIND_AND_EVALUATE'
  EXPORTING
    is_fields        = ls_fields
    iv_procedure     = ls_t340d-whoctlist
    i_data           = ls_wcr-packprofile
  IMPORTING
    et_packspec      = lt_packspec
  EXCEPTIONS
    determine_error = 1
    read_error       = 2
    OTHERS           = 99.
IF sy-subrc <> 0.
  EXIT.
ENDIF.
"Determine HU type from packspec
LOOP AT lt_packspec INTO DATA(lv_guid_ps).
  CLEAR: lt_pscont.
  CALL FUNCTION '/SCWM/PS_PACKSPEC_GET'
    EXPORTING
      iv_guid_ps            = lv_guid_ps
      iv_read_elements      = abap_true
      iv_read_dyn_attributes = abap_true
    IMPORTING
      et_packspec_content    = lt_pscont
    EXCEPTIONS
      error                  = 1
      OTHERS                 = 99.
  IF sy-subrc <> 0.
    EXIT.
  ENDIF.
  SORT lt_pscont BY content-content_seq DESCENDING.
  TRY.
      DATA(pscont) = VALUE #( lt_pscont[ 1 ] ).
    CATCH cx_sy_itab_line_not_found.
      CONTINUE.
  ENDTRY.
  SORT pscont-levels BY display_seq DESCENDING.
  DATA(level) = VALUE #( pscont-levels[ 1 ] OPTIONAL ).
  IF level-hu_matid IS INITIAL.
    CONTINUE.
  ENDIF.
  "Set handling unit type from packaging specification
```

```
"Only if packmat of handling unit and packspec is the same
IF level-hu_matid EQ cs_huhdr-pmat_guid
AND NOT level-hutyp IS INITIAL.
  cs_huhdr-letyp = level-hutyp.
ELSE.
  CONTINUE.
ENDIF.
ENDLOOP.
ENDMETHOD.
```

Listing 4.18 Example Implementation of BAdI /SCWM/EX_HU_BASICS_HUHDR

Testing Enhancement 1G2d

To test enhancement 1G2d, run the SAP Best Practices test case for scope item 1G2 with product PROD-L01. For step 2, use the changed test instructions as shown in Table 4.24.

Step	Description	User Input and Expected Results
4.3	Create Warehouse Tasks Manually	Call the warehouse monitor and find the warehouse order for the created warehouse task in node **Documents • Warehouse Order**. Branch to the pack proposals created for the warehouse order to check the created pick handling units. *Expected result:* ■ Pick handling units have automatically been created for the warehouse order. ■ The pick handling units have been created with the handling unit type from the packaging specification.

Table 4.24 Test Steps for Enhancement 1G2d

4.4.6   Enhancement 1G2e: Determination of the Operative Unit of Measure by Packaging Specification of Goods Receipt

Enhancement 1G2e also deals with an enhancement to step 4.3 of scope item 1G2. In this scenario, a picking warehouse task is created with a unique operative UOM that is determined on the basis of the stock to be picked from certain storage types. It is assumed that all stock of a product in a certain storage type will carry the same UOM. With this enhancement, we determine the alternative UOM for the warehouse task depending on the operative UOM maintained in the packaging specification of the source handling unit as created in the goods receipt process. The second goal of this enhancement is to explain the possibilities of the BAdI used. Table 4.25 shows the enhancements in process step 2.

Step	Physical Activity	System Activity
4.3: Create Warehouse Tasks Manually	N/A	■ The warehouse clerk manually creates and prints out pick warehouse orders. ■ The warehouse tasks are created with the operative UOM from the packaging specification by which the source handling unit was created.

Table 4.25 Process Steps with Deviation for Enhancement 1G2e

Prerequisites for Enhancement 1G2e

For this enhancement to work, we need to set up automatic packing by supplier-dependent packaging specification during good receipt. The warehouse may receive product A from two suppliers who send the goods in different UOMs—for example, in boxes of ten pieces from supplier 1 and boxes of six pieces from supplier 2. Enhancement 1G2e is based on the following assumptions:

■ Several packaging specifications exist for each product, which differ in operative UOM assignments.

■ In goods receipt, an automatic handling unit creation is executed by packaging specification depending on the vendor (with different packaging quantities per supplier).

■ Complete handling units are put away in the warehouse as initially received from supplier.

Operative Unit of Measure

Let us briefly explain the determination of the operative UOM by standard processing.

The quantity classification specifies the packaging specification level by which products will be putaway to or removed from a storage type. An example of quantity classification would be different packaging units, such as cartons, boxes, or pallets. Each of these is then represented by different packaging specification levels. During picking warehouse task creation, a packaging specification is determined for the requested product with condition type OWHT. The warehouse task is created with the operative UOM of the packaging specification level matching the quantity classification of the storage type. If the system cannot determine a packaging specification for the product, the warehouse task will be created with the base UOM.

The standard system behavior assumes that there is only one UOM for each product for a quantity classification and that this unit is maintained in the packaging specification. However, if you receive different carton quantities from your suppliers and do not want to repack these before putaway, the warehouse task may show a different operational UOM than the one by which the product was actually stored in the warehouse.

Realization of Enhancement 1G2e

For the realization of enhancement 1G2e, we need to implement method OPUNIT of BAdI /SCWM/EX_CORE_RMS_OPUNIT, which is assigned to enhancement spot /SCWM/EX_CORE_RMS. We use the coding as shown in Listing 4.19, which includes the following logic:

- The custom coding first takes over the operative UOM, which already exists in the warehouse task. This ensures that the operative unit does not change in case the implementation cannot determine a better result.

- The program further checks whether it deals with a product-based picking warehouse task and reads the packaging specification by which the handling unit was originally created.

- Another check clarifies whether the warehouse task removes the complete quantity of a handling unit or whether a partial quantity is to be picked. In the case of complete quantity removal, the operative UOM will be determined from the handling unit. Otherwise, the highest packaging specification level will be used for which the requested quantity will be less than the total quantity.

- In case the program successfully determines an operative unit from the packaging specification, this unit will be taken over into the warehouse task as an alternative UOM.

```abap
METHOD /scwm/if_ex_core_rms_opunit~opunit.

    DATA: lt_cont  TYPE /scwm/tt_packspec_nested.

    BREAK-POINT ID zewmdevbook_1g2e.
    "Set standard value
    ev_opunit = is_ltap-altme.
    "Check context; only pick warehouse tasks are considered
    CHECK is_ltap-trart CA wmegc_trart_pick. "'2'
    "Source-HU must be supplied
    IF is_ltap-vlenr IS INITIAL OR
    is_ltap-flghuto = abap_true.
      RETURN.
    ENDIF.
    "Get data of source handling unit
    /scwm/cl_wm_packing=>set_global_fields( iv_lgnum = is_ltap-lgnum ).
    DATA(lo_pack) = NEW /scwm/cl_wm_packing( ).
    lo_pack->get_hu(
      EXPORTING
        iv_guid_hu = is_ltap-sguid_hu
      IMPORTING
        es_huhdr = DATA(ls_huhdr) ).
    IF NOT sy-subrc IS INITIAL.
```

```
        io_log->add_message( ip_row   = iv_row
                             ip_field = 'ALTME' ).
      RETURN.
   ENDIF.
   "Handling unit must contain a packaging specification
   IF ls_huhdr-ps_guid IS INITIAL.
      RETURN.
   ENDIF.
   "Get packaging specification
   CALL FUNCTION '/SCWM/PS_PACKSPEC_GET'
      EXPORTING
         iv_guid_ps          = ls_huhdr-ps_guid
      IMPORTING
         et_packspec_content = lt_cont
      EXCEPTIONS
         OTHERS              = 99.
   IF NOT sy-subrc IS INITIAL.
      io_log->add_message( ip_row   = iv_row
                           ip_field = 'ALTME' ).
      RETURN.
   ENDIF.
   DATA(pscont) = VALUE #( lt_cont[ 1 ] OPTIONAL ).
   IF pscont IS INITIAL.
      RETURN.
   ENDIF.
   SORT pscont-levels BY level_seq.
   LOOP AT pscont-levels
   ASSIGNING FIELD-SYMBOL(<pslevel>).
      IF is_ltap-vsolm < <pslevel>-total_quan.
         EXIT.
      ENDIF.
      CHECK NOT <pslevel>-operat_unit IS INITIAL.
      "Set operative unit of measure
      ev_opunit = <pslevel>-operat_unit.
      "Operative unit of measure &1 set.
      MESSAGE s001(zewmdevbook_1g2e) WITH ev_opunit
      INTO DATA(lv_msg).
   ENDLOOP.
   IF NOT lv_msg IS INITIAL.
      io_log->add_message( ip_row = iv_row ).
   ENDIF.

ENDMETHOD.
```

Listing 4.19 Example Implementation of BAdI /SCWM/EX_CORE_RMS_OPUNIT

Testing Enhancement 1G2e

You should now test the determination of the operative UOM within scope item 1G2. Check the results of step 4.3 as described in Table 4.26.

Step	Description	User Input and expected Results
4.3	Create Warehouse Tasks Manually	Call the warehouse monitor and find the warehouse task in node **Documents • Warehouse Task** with reference to the outbound delivery order and check the operative UOM.
		Expected result:
		The pick warehouse task shows the UOM of the packaging specification by which the handling unit was created in good receipt as an alternative UOM.

Table 4.26 Test Steps for Enhancement 1G2e

4.4.7 Enhancement 1G2f: Prohibit Goods Issue for Incomplete Packing

In this enhancement, we will show you a simple implementation through which you can prevent the goods issue posting of not completely packaged outbound deliveries. If you use deliveries for which an advanced shipping notification with packaging information would be sent alongside the goods issue posting, the posting reported to SAP S/4HANA should also include this complete packaging information, especially if you activated the packaging requirement for the delivery item category in SAP S/4HANA Customizing. In case not all packaging information is sent, the SAP S/4HANA inbound message processing will return an error (message VL615: Delivery item is not or only partially packed). With this custom development in place, you can avoid such errors by validating the goods issue posting in EWM and preventing it if necessary. The enhancement will be relevant in step 4.12 of the scope item 1G2, as Table 4.27 shows.

Step	Physical Activity	System Activity
4.12: Post Goods Issue for Outbound Delivery Order	The shipping office clerk hands over the loading list to the truck driver.	The shipping office clerk posts the goods issue while the system checks if the outbound deliveries have been completely packed. The system prints the loading list.

Table 4.27 Process Steps with Deviation for Enhancement 1G2f

Enhancement 1G2f, Prohibit Goods Issue for Incomplete Packing, requires the following steps to be performed:

1. **Implementation of the check logic**
   Create an implementation of BAdI /SCWM/EX_DLV_GM, which will be called at the time of goods issue for an outbound delivery order.

2. **Creation of a custom message**

   Create a new message 001 in a custom message class called zewmdevbook_1g2f.

Next, we explain in detail how to proceed with each of these steps. As usual, we will begin by discussing the prerequisites and end by discussing testing of this enhancement.

Prerequisites for Enhancement 1G2f

We assume for this enhancement that no batch split items will be used. If batch split items will be used, the enhancement would need to be extended accordingly.

Implementing the Check Logic

Create an implementation in method CHECK_DOCUMENT of BAdI /SCWM/EX_DLV_GM, which is assigned to enhancement spot /SCWM/ES_DLV_GM using the example coding shown in Listing 4.20.

```
METHOD /scwm/if_ex_dlv_gm_process~check_document.

    BREAK-POINT ID zewmdevbook_1g2f.

    "Check if goods issue is being processed
    CHECK iv_gmcat = /scwm/if_docflow_c=>sc_gi.
    LOOP AT it_dlv_item
    ASSIGNING FIELD-SYMBOL(<item>).
      "Check if current item is completely packed
      DATA(ls_status) = VALUE #( <item>-status[
        status_type = /scdl/if_dl_status_c=>sc_t_packing ] OPTIONAL ).
      IF ls_status IS INITIAL
      OR ls_status-status_value NE /scdl/if_dl_status_c=>sc_v_finished.
        "Delivery &1 item &2 not fully packed. GM not allowed.
        MESSAGE e001(zewmdevbook_1g2f)
        WITH <item>-docno <item>-itemno INTO DATA(lv_msg).
        DATA(ls_symsg) = /scwm/cl_dm_message_no=>get_symsg_fields( ).
        "Issue message
        co_message->add_message(
          iv_msgcat = /scdl/cl_dm_message=>sc_mcat_bus
          iv_doccat = <item>-doccat
          iv_docid  = <item>-docid
          iv_itemid = <item>-itemid
          is_symsg  = ls_symsg ).
      ENDIF.
    ENDLOOP.

  ENDMETHOD.
```

Listing 4.20 Example Implementation of BAdI /SCWM/EX_DLV_GM

Creating a Custom Message

Create a new message class `zewmdevbook_1g2f` and message 001 in Transaction SE91. Use a message text such as "Delivery &1 item &2 not fully packed. GM not allowed." The message should be self-explanatory.

Testing Enhancement 1G2f

Execute the test case for scope item 1G2 running step 4.12, as outlined in Table 4.28. We will use a negative test and unpack the outbound delivery before attempting to post goods issue. Next, you'll want to remove the handling unit requirement from storage type Y920 to allow for unpacked stock on the outbound staging area.

Step	Description	User Input and Expected Results
4.12	Post Goods Issue for Outbound Delivery Order	■ Call the pack dialog for the outbound delivery order. ■ Delete an handling unit or unpack a stock item contained in an handling unit by dragging it onto the storage bin. ■ Save the changes and return to the delivery maintenance. *Expected result:* An error message pops up explaining that goods issue is not allowed based on incomplete packing.

Table 4.28 Test Steps for Enhancement 1G2f

Figure 4.23 shows in an example of how the error message could look.

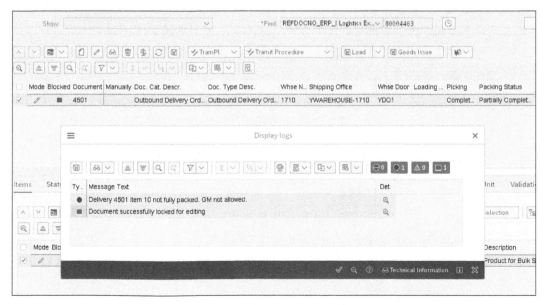

Figure 4.23 Error Message for Goods Issue with Incomplete Packing

4.5   Outbound Process Using Wave, Pick Handling Units, Packing, Staging, and Loading: 1V7

In this section, we'll introduce you to scope item 1V7. We will create two variants of this process by adding custom developments:

- **1V7a: Take over transportation unit after unloading**
  Here you will learn how to develop a PPF action with a schedule condition.

- **1V7b: Print picking labels on a mobile printer**
  The condition technique will be enhanced by a new field. You will get familiar with the BAdIs for printing in EWM.

4.5.1   Process Description of Scope Item 1V7

For scope item 1V7, Outbound Process Using Wave, Pick Handling Unit, Packing, Staging, and Loading, you will find an overview of the steps in Table 4.29. The physical activities and system activities are listed in separate columns. The process steps in the SAP S/4HANA system are skipped, and we start with the description of the EWM steps. In the SAP S/4HANA system, a sales order and outbound delivery were created as preparation.

Step	Physical Activity	System Activity
1: Route determination		The system determines a route for each outbound delivery.
2: Create waves		The system builds picking waves.
3: Create a transportation unit	The shipping office clears orders' transportation capacity.	
	The shipper confirms the transportation capacity and communicates an external identifier.	The shipping office clerk creates a transportation unit with the external identifier and the route.
4: Release the waves		The system releases the waves, creates warehouse orders, and assigns them to queues.

Table 4.29 Steps in Outbound Scope Item 1V7

Step	Physical Activity	System Activity
5: Pick the goods		A warehouse worker logs on as a resource in the RF environment. The system proposes the next warehouse order in the queue to be processed.
	The warehouse worker puts a wire basket onto the resource.	The warehouse worker creates the pick handling unit.
	The warehouse worker picks the goods into the pick handling unit and moves the pick handling unit to the packing station.	The warehouse worker confirms the warehouse task and warehouse order.
6: Pack the goods		A packer logs on as a resource in the RF environment. The packer scans the pick handling unit.
	The packer prepares an empty pallet for each ship-to.	The packer creates the shipping handling unit. The system prints preliminary handling unit labels.
	The packer applies the labels to the shipping handling units and repacks the goods from the pick handling unit into the shipping handling units.	The packer confirms the repacking.
		The packer weighs and closes the shipping handling unit. The system prints the final shipping handling unit labels and creates a warehouse order to the staging area.
	The packer applies the labels to the shipping handling unit.	

Table 4.29 Steps in Outbound Scope Item 1V7 (Cont.)

Step	Physical Activity	System Activity
7: Stage the goods		A warehouse worker logs on as a resource. The warehouse worker scans the shipping handling unit. The system determines the open warehouse order for the shipping handling unit.
	The warehouse worker moves the shipping handling unit to the staging area.	The warehouse worker confirms the warehouse order.
8: A truck arrives at the checkpoint and drives to the door	A truck arrives.	The checkpoint clerk determines the door and confirms the arrival of the truck.
	The checkpoint clerk communicates the door to the truck driver. The truck drives to the door.	
9: Load the truck		A warehouse worker logs on as a resource. The warehouse worker scans the shipping handling unit. The system determines the door for loading.
	The warehouse worker moves the shipping handling unit to the truck.	The warehouse worker confirms the loading of the shipping handling unit.
10: Post the goods issue and print the delivery notes and road waybill		The shipping office clerk posts the goods issue. The system prints the delivery notes and the road waybill.
	The shipping office clerk hands over the delivery notes and the road waybill to the truck drive.	
11: The truck leaves the warehouse	The truck leaves.	The shipping office clerk confirms the departure of the truck.

Table 4.29 Steps in Outbound Scope Item 1V7 (Cont.)

You can find more details in the process description of scope item 1V7.

4.5.2   Enhancement 1V7a: Take Over Transportation Unit after Unloading

In enhancement 1V7a, Take over Transportation Unit after Unloading, we will connect the inbound scope item 1V5 with the outbound scope item 1V7 by using the same transportation unit. After the swap trailer of a truck is unloaded at the warehouse door (1V5), it will be used for loading in the outbound process (1V7) at the same door. This process can be used in warehouses where the same doors are used for loading and unloading.

The reuse of a transportation unit is supported in EWM (see Figure 4.24). In Transaction /SCWM/TU (Process TU), a user can use the **Copy** and **Activate** buttons to take over a transportation unit after unloading.

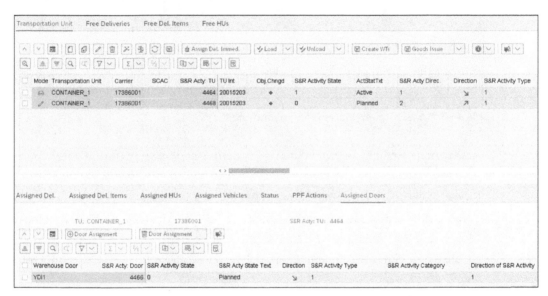

Figure 4.24 Reuse Transportation Unit for Inbound Process after Unloading (Manual Approach)

The system will close the receiving activity and will create a new shipping activity for the transportation unit. So the transportation unit with its attributes carrier, license plate, and so on will stay in the system and can be used for the outbound process.

In enhancement 1V7a, we will develop a PPF action, Z_TU_COPY, for the object transportation unit. The goal is that the system will automatically do the two earlier user steps (copy and activate) the moment the unloading is completed. To make sure the PPF action runs at the correct point of time, we will also develop a schedule condition, Z_TU_COPY_CHECK.

In Table 4.30, you will find the deviations in processes 1V5 and 1V7. All steps that are not listed in the table stay unchanged but are still required (see Table 4.3 in Section 4.2.1 and Table 4.29).

Step	Physical Activity	System Activity
1: A truck arrives at the checkpoint and drives to the door	The checkpoint clerk advises the truck driver that this swap trailer is planned first for unloading and then for loading at a special door.	The checkpoint clerk creates a transportation unit with the means-of-transport swap trailer. Then he assigns a special door to the transportation unit and confirms the arrival of the truck at the door.
5: Unloading is finished	Truck stays at the door.	The good receipt office confirms that unloading of the truck is finished.
3: Create a transportation unit		System creates a transportation unit for the outbound.

Table 4.30 Process Step Deviations for Enhancement 1V7a

To realize enhancement 1V7a in your EWM system, you have to perform the following four steps:

1. Create a new door in IMG that allows unloading and loading.
2. Create a new PPF execution method, such as Z_TU_COPY for classic BAdI EXEC_METHOD-CALL_PPF, in the BAdI builder (Transaction SE19).
3. Create a new PPF scheduling method, such as Z_TU_COPY_SCHED for classic BAdI EVAL_SCHEDCOND_PPF.
4. Create IMG entries for the new ZSR_TU_COPY_ACTIVATE PPF action.

Next, we explain in detail how to proceed with each of these steps. As usual, we will begin by discussing the prerequisites and end by discussing testing of this enhancement.

Prerequisites for Enhancement 1V7a

To make use of enhancement 1V7a in your warehouse, the following two prerequisites must be fulfilled:

- You have warehouse doors that can be used for loading and unloading.
- You do not use yard management functions in EWM.

Create a New Door

To create a new door in IMG that allows unloading and loading, follow these steps:

1. Create a new entry in the **EWM • Master Data • Warehouse Door • Define Warehouse Door** IMG activity for warehouse number 1710. The loading direction of the new door (e.g., YDX1) must have option **B—Inbound and Outbound**. For the other attributes, keep the same values as the other existing doors:
   - **Number Range**: 01
   - **Default Staging Area Group**: Y930
   - **Default Staging Area**: YS00

2. Create a new storage bin (e.g., DOOR-YDX1) and assign it to the new door YDX1. Use Transactions /SCWM/LS01 (Create Storage Bins) and /SCWM/DOOR_SCU (Assignments of Warehouse Door to SCU).

3. Create a new entry ZSWAP (Description: Swap Trailer) in the **EWM • Master Data • Shipping and Receiving • Define Means of Transport** IMG activity. Take over the attributes from existing entry 0001 (Truck).

4. Create a new entry in the **EWM • Cross-Process Settings • Shipping and Receiving • General Settings • Define Control Parameters for Forming Vehicles/Transportation Units** IMG activity. Use the following attributes:
   - **Means of Transport**: ZSWAP
   - **Vehicle/Transportation Unit**: TU
   - **Number Range**: 01
   - **Action Profile**: /SCWM/TU

5. In the SAP menu, start Transaction /SCWM/PM_MTR (Link Between Packaging Material (TU) and Means of Transport) and create a new entry. Enter "ZSWAP" for **Means Of Transport** and "EWMS4-TRUCK00" for **Packaging Material**. Also, set the checkboxes for **Optional packaging material** and **Packaging material has character of container**.

6. After completing these settings, you should be able to create a new transportation unit in Transaction /SCWM/TU with means of transport ZSWAP.

Create a New PPF Execution Method

Create a new implementation, such as Z_TU_COPY, in the BAdI builder (Transaction SE19) for the classic EXEC_METHODCALL_PPF BAdI. Enter a filter value method, like Z_TU_COPY (see Figure 4.25).

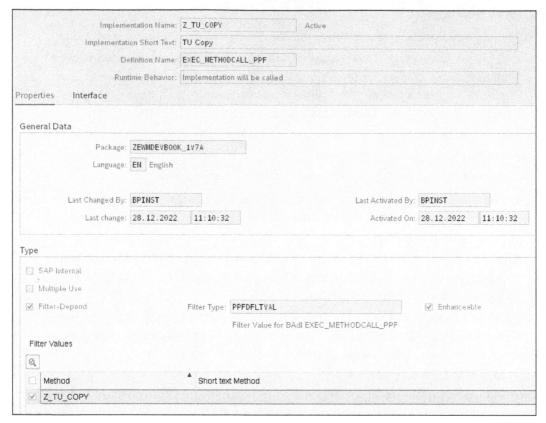

Figure 4.25 Create Implementation for BAdI EXEC_METHODCALL_PPF

If you navigate via double-click to the execute method of the ZCL_IM__TU_COPY implementing class, you can enter the coding (see Listing 4.21). Activate the class and the BAdI implementation. A few notes on the code:

- In the coding, we first take over the generic application object from the PPF (see paragraph "1) and cast it to the transportation unit object (class /SCWM/CL_SR_TU_PPF).

- In the following paragraph "2, we look up the business object for this transportation unit from the database or buffer (method get_bo_tu_by_key).

- To prepare the copying of the transportation unit, we look up the actual door of the transportation unit and take over plan times and warehouse number from this door (see paragraph "3).

- In coding paragraphs "4 and "5, the transportation unit is first copied and then activated (method switch_tu_active).

- At last, the changes are committed to the database (see "6), and the return parameter for successful processing (parameter RP_status) is set.

```abap
METHOD if_ex_exec_methodcall_ppf~execute.

  DATA: lt_tu_key TYPE /scwm/tt_aspk_tu.

  BREAK-POINT ID zewmdevbook_1v7a.

  rp_status = sppf_status_error.
  "1) Cast imported PPFf-object to get the TU-key:
  DATA(lo_tu_ppf) = CAST /scwm/cl_sr_tu_ppf( io_appl_object ).
  DATA(ls_key) = VALUE /scwm/s_tu_sr_act_num(
    tu_num       = lo_tu_ppf->get_tu_num( )
    tu_sr_act_num = lo_tu_ppf->get_tu_sr_act_num( ) ).
  IF ( ls_key-tu_num IS INITIAL ) OR ( ls_key-tu_sr_act_num IS INITIAL ).
    MESSAGE e136(/scwm/shp_rcv) WITH flt_val INTO DATA(msg).
    CALL METHOD cl_log_ppf=>add_message
      EXPORTING
        ip_problemclass = wmegc_log_vip "'1' very important
        ip_handle       = ip_application_log.
    EXIT.
  ENDIF.
  TRY.
      "2) Get the bo for the inbound TU
      DATA(lo_bom) = /scwm/cl_sr_bom=>get_instance( ).
      DATA(lo_tu)  = lo_bom->get_bo_tu_by_key(
        EXPORTING
          is_tu_sr_act_num = ls_key ).
      "3) Get active door of the inb TU
      lo_tu->get_tu_door(
        EXPORTING
          iv_get_executed = space
        IMPORTING
          et_bo_tu_door   = DATA(lt_door) ).
      LOOP AT lt_door ASSIGNING FIELD-SYMBOL(<ls_door>)
      WHERE start_actual IS NOT INITIAL
      AND end_actual IS INITIAL.
        EXIT. "active door found
      ENDLOOP.
      IF <ls_door> IS NOT ASSIGNED.
        RETURN.
      ENDIF.
      lo_tu->get_data(
        IMPORTING
          es_act = DATA(ls_act) ).
```

```
      "4) Create a new outbound TU (copy from inbound)
      DATA(ls_tu_new) = CORRESPONDING /scwm/s_bo_tu_new( <ls_door> ). "times
      ls_tu_new-yard = <ls_door>-lgnum.
      ls_tu_new-act_dir = /scdl/if_dl_doc_c=>sc_procat_out.
      lo_bom->create_new_bo_tu(
        EXPORTING
          is_bo_tu_new    = ls_tu_new
          is_tu_sr_act_num = ls_key
        IMPORTING
          eo_bo_tu        = DATA(lo_tu_new) ).
      ls_key = lo_tu_new->get_num( ).
      /scwm/cl_tm=>set_lgnum( iv_lgnum = ls_act-yard ).
      "5) Activate the outbound TU
      APPEND ls_key TO lt_tu_key.
      /scwm/cl_sr_my_service=>switch_tu_active(
        EXPORTING
          iv_lgnum   = ls_act-yard
          it_aspk_tu = lt_tu_key ).
      "6) Save
      lo_bom->save( ).
    CATCH /scwm/cx_sr_error .
      CALL METHOD cl_log_ppf=>add_message
        EXPORTING
          ip_problemclass = wmegc_log_vip "'1' very important
          ip_handle       = ip_application_log.
      /scwm/cl_tm=>cleanup( ).
      EXIT.
  ENDTRY.
  /scwm/cl_tm=>cleanup( ).
  rp_status = sppf_status_processed.

ENDMETHOD.
```

Listing 4.21 Coding for Execute Method

Create a New PPF Scheduling Method

Create a new implementation, such as Z_TU_COPY_SCHED, in the BAdI builder (Transaction SE19) for the classic EVAL_SCHEDCOND_PPF BAdI. Enter a filter value schedule condition, like Z_TU_COPY_SCHED.

Navigate to the EVALUATE_SCHEDULE_CONDITION method of the implementing ZCL_IM__TU_COPY_SCHED class and enter the coding in Listing 4.22.

Activate the class and the BAdI implementation (see Figure 4.26).

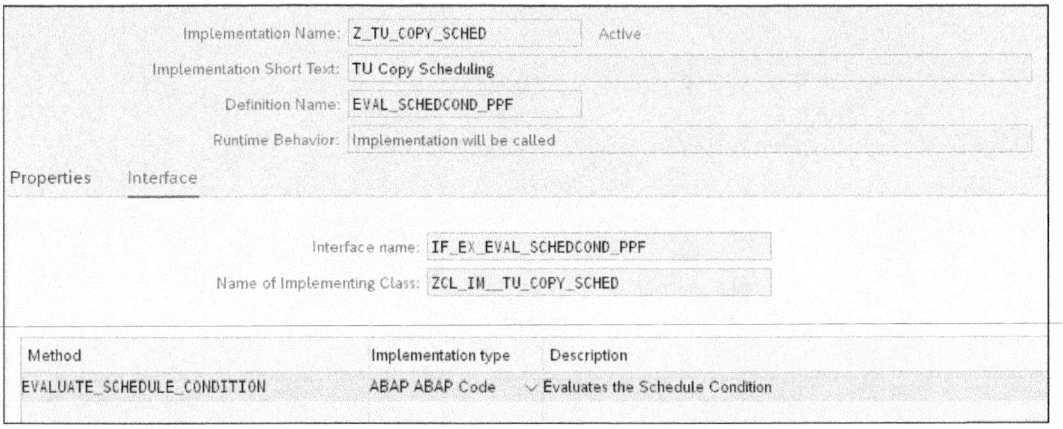

Figure 4.26 Activate BAdI for PPF

Within the BAdI implementation (see Listing 4.22), we first make sure that we are in the right context. The PPF action is called during the saving of a transportation unit and again during the synchronization of deliveries with a transportation unit. So we make sure that this coding does not run during delivery synchronization (see the only_synch method call).

Similar to the coding of method execute (see Listing 4.21), we take over the application object in paragraphs "1 and "2. In paragraphs "3 to "6, the system will do several checks:

- Does the transportation unit have the direction "inbound"?
- Does the transportation unit switch to status "Unloading completed"?
- Does the transportation unit have the status "Posted GR"?
- Does the transportation unit have means of transport ZSWAP?

```
METHOD if_ex_eval_schedcond_ppf~evaluate_schedule_condition.

  BREAK-POINT ID zewmdevbook_1v7a.

  ep_rc = 1. "Condition not fulfilled
  DATA(lo_context) = CAST /scwm/cl_sr_context_tuppf( io_context ).
  IF lo_context->only_sync = abap_true.
    RETURN.
  ENDIF.
  "1) Cast imported PPF-object to get the TU-key:
  DATA(lo_tu_ppf) = CAST /scwm/cl_sr_tu_ppf( io_context->appl ).
  DATA(ls_key) = VALUE /scwm/s_tu_sr_act_num(
    tu_num        = lo_tu_ppf->get_tu_num( )
    tu_sr_act_num = lo_tu_ppf->get_tu_sr_act_num( ) ).
  IF ( ls_key-tu_num IS INITIAL ) OR
  ( ls_key-tu_sr_act_num IS INITIAL ).
```

```abap
      MESSAGE e136(/scwm/shp_rcv) WITH flt_val
      INTO DATA(msg).
      CALL METHOD cl_log_ppf=>add_message
        EXPORTING
          ip_problemclass = wmegc_log_vip "'1' very important
          ip_handle       = ip_protocol.
      EXIT.
    ENDIF.
  IF lo_tu_ppf->get_deleted( ) = abap_true.
    "Undefined side effects may occur.
    EXIT.
  ENDIF.
  TRY.
      "2) Get the bo for the inbound TU
      DATA(lo_bom) = /scwm/cl_sr_bom=>get_instance( ).
      DATA(lo_tu)  = lo_bom->get_bo_tu_by_key(
        EXPORTING
          is_tu_sr_act_num = ls_key ).
      "3) Check direction of the TU
      CALL METHOD lo_tu->get_sr_act_dir
        RECEIVING
          ev_sr_act_dir = DATA(lv_dir).
      IF lv_dir <> wmesr_sr_act_dir_inb .
        EXIT. "no inbound tu
      ENDIF.
      "4) Check the status "unloading end"
      DATA(lv_status) = wmesr_status_unload_end.
      DATA(lv_tu_status) =
      lo_tu->get_status_by_id( lv_status ) .
      IF lv_tu_status = abap_false.
        EXIT. "not unloaded yet
      ENDIF.
      IF lo_tu->get_status_change_by_id(
      lv_status ) = abap_false.
        EXIT. "not the correct point of time
      ENDIF.
      "5) Check status "goods receipt" if dlvs are assigned
      lo_tu->get_tu_dlv(
        EXPORTING
          iv_dlv_data_retrieval = abap_true
        IMPORTING
          et_bo_tu_dlv          = DATA(lt_bo_tu_dlv) ).
      IF lt_bo_tu_dlv IS NOT INITIAL.
        CLEAR lv_tu_status.
```

```
         lv_status = wmesr_status_goods_receipt.
         lv_tu_status =
         lo_tu->get_status_by_id( lv_status ) .
         IF lv_tu_status = abap_false.
           EXIT. "not unloaded yet
         ENDIF.
       ENDIF.
       "6) Check the means of transport
       DATA(lv_mtr) = lo_tu->get_mtr( ).
       IF lv_mtr = c_mtr_zswap. "'ZSWAP'
         ep_rc = 0.
       ENDIF.
     CATCH /scwm/cx_sr_error .
       CALL METHOD cl_log_ppf=>add_message
         EXPORTING
           ip_problemclass = wmegc_log_vip "'1' very important
           ip_handle       = ip_protocol.
       EXIT.
   ENDTRY.

 ENDMETHOD.
```

Listing 4.22 Coding for EVALUATE_SCHEDULE_CONDITION Method

Create IMG Entries

In the **EWM • Cross-Process Settings • Shipping and Receiving • Message Processing • Define Action Profiles for Transportation Units** IMG activity, choose the action profile **/SCWM/TU** and navigate to the **Action Definition** subfolder. In change mode, create a new entry (e.g., ZSR_TU_COPY_ACTIVATE) and enter the following settings:

- **Processing At**: Choose option **4—Processing when saving document**.
- **Processing Times Not Permitted**: Choose option **X00X0—Immediate Processing**. This is necessary as we use method save to update the transportation unit object in the PPF action.
- **Schedule Automatically**: Set this checkbox.
- **Determination Technology**: Keep the default.
- **Rule type**: Change to option **COD—Conditions Using BAdI**.
- **Action Merging**: Change to option **EWM: Max. 1 Unprocessed Action for each Action Definition**.
- **Description** and **Action Description**: Enter, for example, "TU Copy & Activate".

Now navigate to the **Processing Type** subfolder and use the **New Entries** button. You can enter a new line with value "Method Call" using the F4 value help in the **Permitted**

Processing Types of Action table (see Figure 4.27). In the field method, you can enter value Z_TU_COPY using the F4 value help. Note that neither field appears open for input; you can enter values, but by using value help only. Save your entries.

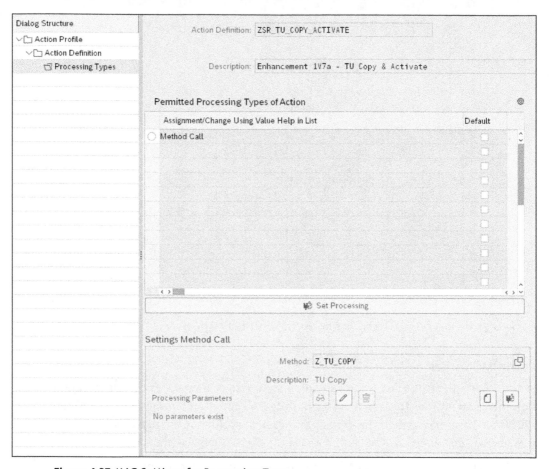

Figure 4.27 IMG Settings for Processing Type

Next, we create a new condition for the just created action. To do so, leave the previous IMG activity and choose the **Define Action Conditions for Transportation Units** IMG activity. Within this screen (see Figure 4.28), select the **Transportation Unit** action profile in the tree control on the left side. On the right side, use the **Create** button and choose the **Copy & Activate TU** entry from the dropdown list.

In the lower part of the screen, choose the **Schedule Condition** tab and enter the value Z_TUCOPY_SCHED by using the F4 value help; see Figure 4.29. Save your entry.

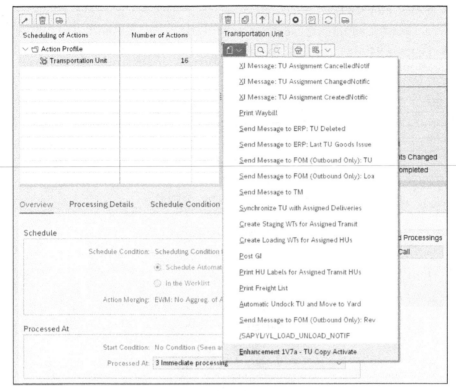

Figure 4.28 Create New Condition, Copy & Activate TU

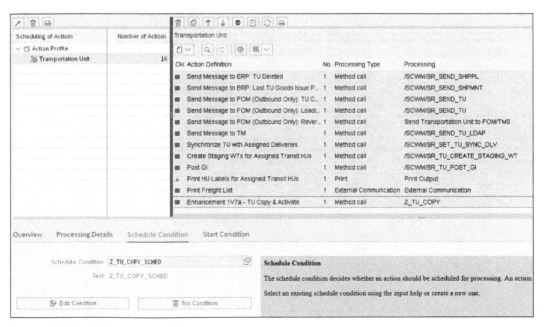

Figure 4.29 Add Schedule Condition

Testing of Enhancement 1V7a

Now you can test the automatic copying and activating of a transportation unit. In Table 4.31, you will find the test steps. We simplified the test in order to focus on the custom development.

Step	Step Description	Input Data and Expected Results
1	Create a transportation unit and assign it to a door.	Use Transaction /SCWM/TU (Process Transportation Unit). On the **Transportation Unit** tab, choose the **Create** button. In the popup, enter the following values: ■ **TU**: for example, Container ■ **Means of transport**: ZSWAP ■ **Packaging Material**: MTR ■ **S&R Activity Direction**: Inbound On the **Assigned Doors** tab, use the **Add Door Assignment** button and choose warehouse door YDX1 and warehouse number 1710. Now select the **Action • Door • Arrival at Door** menu entry. Save and refresh the display. *Expected result:* The transportation unit is created, and a door is assigned. On the **Status** tab, you will see the status value **Docked at Door** (DD) with a green icon for status set.
5	Unloading of truck is finished.	After you post the goods receipt for the assigned inbound deliveries, select the transportation unit in Transaction /SCWM/TU (Process Transportation Unit). Use the **Unload** button and save. *Expected result:* On the **Status** tab, you'll find the **Unloading Completed** (UC) status and **Departure from Checkpoint** (CHKO) with the green icon. On the **PPF** tab, you'll find your PPF action in the table, showing a green traffic light for successful processing (see Figure 4.30).
6	No departure from checkpoint.	In this test variant, the truck stays at the door, so no departure from the checkpoint is posted at this point in time in the system.

Table 4.31 Test Steps for Enhancement 1V7a

Step	Step Description	Input Data and Expected Results
7	Select the transportation unit and assign a route.	Select the transportation unit in Transaction /SCWM/TU (Process Transportation Unit). As the system shows two entries, select the active transportation unit with direction outbound. *Expected result:* On the **Assigned Doors** tab, you will find the active door YDX1, and on the **Status** tab, you will find the **Docked at Door** (DD) status with a green icon for status set.
8	No truck arrival.	In this variant, this step is skipped.
11	Truck is leaving the warehouse.	Select the transportation unit in Transaction /SCWM/TU (Process Transportation Unit). Select the menu entry **Action • Checkpoint • Departure + Save**. *Expected result:* The transportation unit is completed.

Table 4.31 Test Steps for Enhancement 1V7a (Cont.)

In Figure 4.30, you will see the result after test step 3 (1V7): two S&R activities exist for the Container transportation unit 7302 and 7304. The first line shows the completed transportation unit with direction inbound. For this line, you see the Copy & Activate TU PPF action. The second line is the transportation unit with direction outbound.

Figure 4.30 Reuse Transportation Unit for Outbound Process after Unloading (Automatic Approach)

4.5.3   Enhancement 1V7b: Print Picking Labels on a Mobile Printer

In Enhancement 1V7b, we will extend the printing in order to print picking labels on a mobile printer. Step 5, Pick the Goods in the outbound scope item 1V7 (refer back to Table 4.29) will be augmented. During the picking process, the warehouse operator moves from bin to bin (e.g., using a forklift) and removes the requested items. The user confirms each removal/pick in the system, and at that point the system will print a picking label. The assumption is that the operator has a mobile printer on his resource. The picking label could look like the image in Figure 4.31, containing product information ❹, the customer ❶, the route ❸, and a barcode for the stock identification ❷ ❺. The operator attaches the picking label to the just removed stock. After the operator drops the wire basket with all picking items at the packing station, another operator will use the barcode on the picking label to repack the stock into the ship handling unit.

Figure 4.31 Picking Label Example

To make sure that the picking label is only printed for partial quantities and not for full pallet removals, we will add a HU-Flag field to the field catalog for printing in this custom development. Thus, if the operator has to do a handling unit removal, the system will not print a picking label; the existing handling unit label will be used instead.

In Table 4.32, you will find the deviation in scope item 1V7 for enhancement 1V7b. All of the steps that are not listed in the table stay unchanged but are still required (refer back to Table 4.29).

Step	Physical Activity	System Activity
5: Pick the goods		A warehouse worker logs on as a resource in the RF environment. The system proposes the next warehouse order in the queue to be processed.
	The warehouse worker puts a wire basket onto the resource.	The warehouse worker creates the pick handling unit.

Table 4.32 Process Steps with Deviation for Enhancement 1V7b

Step	Physical Activity	System Activity
	The warehouse worker picks and labels the goods, puts them into the wire basket, and moves the wire basket to the packing station.	The warehouse worker confirms the warehouse tasks and warehouse order. For each confirmed picking task, the system prints a picking label. The warehouse worker confirms the drop of the pick handling unit at the packing station.
6: Pack the goods		A packer logs on as a resource in the RF environment. The packer scans the pick handling unit.
	The packer prepares an empty pallet for each ship-to.	The packer creates the shipping handling unit. The system prints preliminary handling unit labels.
	The packer applies the preliminary labels to the shipping handling units and repacks the goods from the pick handling unit into the shipping handling units.	The packer scans each picking label barcode and confirms the repacking into the correct ship handling unit by scanning the ship handling unit as well.
		The packer weighs and closes the shipping handling unit. The system prints the final shipping handling unit labels and creates a warehouse order for the staging area.
	The packer applies the final labels to the shipping handling unit.	

Table 4.32 Process Steps with Deviation for Enhancement 1V7b (Cont.)

To realize enhancement 1V7b in your EWM system, you have to perform the following four steps:

1. Create a new ZDO_HUFLAG domain and a new ZDE_HUFLAG data element.
2. Add the new ZHUFLG field to the field catalog for warehouse order printing. Create a new condition record table and complete the condition record Customizing.
3. Implement BAdI /SCWM/EX_PRNT_CCAT_WO so that the value for the new ZHUFLG field is determined.
4. Create a new condition record for your resource and your printer such that you can test the variant.

Next, we explain in detail how to proceed with each of these steps. As usual, we will begin by discussing the prerequisites and end by discussing testing of this enhancement.

Prerequisites for Enhancement 1V7b

This enhancement is feasible for your warehouse if the resources (e.g., forklifts) are equipped with a mobile printer and you want to increase stock accuracy in the outbound process by using picking labels.

Create a New Domain

Start the ABAP Dictionary (Transaction SE11) and create a new ZDO_HUFLAG domain with description "Warehouse Task: HU or Product." On the **Definition** tab, enter data type "CHAR" and number of characters "1." On the **Value Range** tab, enter two fixed values: H for "HU Warehouse Task" and P for "Product Warehouse Task" (see Figure 4.32). Activate the domain.

Figure 4.32 Domain ZDO_HUFLAG

Create a new ZDE_HUFLAG data element with the same description as the domain and reference the new ZDO_HUFLAG domain on tab **Data Type**. On the **Field Label** tab, enter the description "WT HU/Prod." Activate the data element.

Add New Field to Field Catalog

In the **EWM • Cross-Process Settings • Warehouse Order • Print** IMG folder, you will now enter the settings for the following eight IMG activities:

1. **IMG activity Create Field Catalog**
   In change mode, create a new entry with the field name ZHUFLAG and the following attributes (see Figure 4.33):
   - **Field Type**: choose option **I—Item Field**
   - **Implementation Type**: enter value "1 – Default Implementation"
   - **Virtual**: enter value "C – Internal and external usage"
   - **Selection Type**: choose option **B—Individual Values without Operator**
   - **Data Element**: ZDE_HUFLAG

Save the entry and the system will automatically generate some condition record Customizing and database entries.

			Header Flds	Item Fields	Header and Item Fields	All Fields					
Fields(EWM - Print Warehous)											
	D...	Fie...	I...	Field name		Vir...	V...	S...	A...	Data element	
☐	🔍	I	2	PWO_RSRC		C		B	☐	/SCWM/DE_PRSRC	
☐	🔍	I	1	ZHUFLAG		C		B	☐	ZDE_HUFLAG	

Figure 4.33 New Entry ZHUFLAG in Warehouse Order Field Catalog

2. **IMG activity Define Condition Tables**
   Create a new condition record CUS_RES1 and select the following fields:
   - PWO_LGNUM: Warehouse Number/Warehouse Complex
   - PWO_TOSTEP: WT Event (Create/Confirm)
   - PWO_RSRC: Executing Resource (Means of Transport or User)
   - ZHUFLAG: WT HU or Product

   Save and activate the table. Note that the prefix CUS is mandatory for condition tables and that you need a development package where the name starts with Z* or Y*. The system will use this development package to generate the new condition table.

3. **IMG activity Define Access Sequences**
   Create a new access sequence entry (e.g., ZARF) and enter condition record CUS_RES1. Navigate to the **Fields** folder and check that all fields are listed (see Figure 4.34). Save your entries.

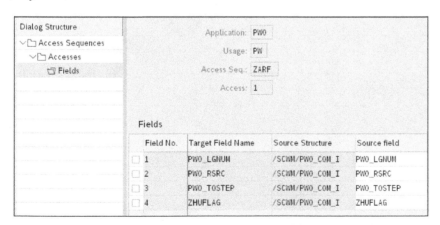

Figure 4.34 Access Sequence ZARF with Four Source Fields

4. **IMG activity Define Condition Types**
   Create a new condition type, ZCRF, and add your access sequence ZARF to this new condition type.

5. **IMG activity Define Determination Procedure**
   Create a new entry, ZPRF, and add the condition type ZCRF.

6. **IMG activity Assign Determination Procedure**
   Add the determination procedure ZPRF to the existing warehouse process type Y214 for warehouse 1710.

7. **IMG activity Create Condition Maintenance Group**
   Select the maintenance group PWO and open the **Condition Maintenance Group: Detail** folder. Create a new entry with counter 1 and enter the condition type ZCRF and condition table CUS_RES1, as shown in Figure 4.35. Use the F4 value help. When you save, the system will generate the required view maintenance coding automatically.

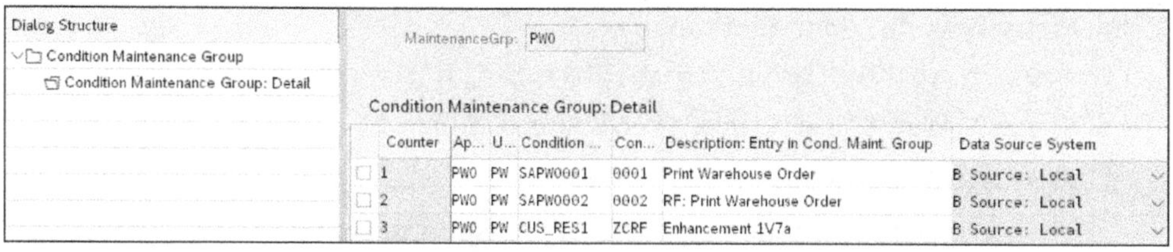

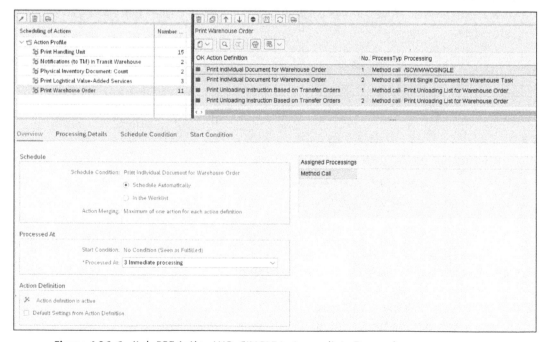

Figure 4.35 Condition Maintenance Group PWO with New Condition Table CUS_RES1

8. **IMG activity Define PPF Conditions**
   Select the existing WO_SINGLE condition for action profile **/SCWM/WO**. Unset the **Default Settings from Action Definition** checkbox and change the value in field **Processed at** to **3 Immediate processing**, as shown in Figure 4.36.

Figure 4.36 Switch PPF Action WO_SINGLE to Immediate Processing

[«]

Special Cases for Printing Warehouse Orders

In SAP Note 1344974, you will find a lot of information about warehouse order printing. This consulting note describes the necessary settings for different print scenarios. The **3—Immediate Printing** setting mentioned in step 2 is described for the Printing of Single Warehouse Tasks scenario.

The last required Customizing setting in step 2 needs to be done in IMG activity **Define Warehouse Process Type** in folder **EWM • Cross-Process Settings • Warehouse Task.** For existing warehouse process type P211, change the setting for field **Stock ID Control** to value **C—Always Assign Stock Identification Anew.** Based on this new setting, the system will generate a stock identification for each picking warehouse task. The generated stock identification number is usually created by combining the warehouse number and the warehouse task number.

Implement BAdI /SCWM/EX_PRNT_CCAT_WO

Create a new enhancement implementation Z_EI_PRNT_CCAT in the BAdI builder (Transaction SE19) for enhancement spot /SCWM/ES_PRNT_CCAT. Choose the /SCWM/EX_PRNT_CCAT_WO BAdI and enter an implementation name (e.g., ZEX_PRNT_CCAT_WO) and the name of the implementing class (e.g., ZCL_IM_PRNT_CCAT_WO).

You will find the sample coding for the change method in Listing 4.23:

- In coding paragraph "1, we check if the new ZHUFLAG field is in the condition technique request.
- In paragraph "2, the current warehouse task is read from the memory.
- Finally, in paragraph "3, the value is determined based on the FLGHUTO warehouse task attribute (flag handling unit warehouse task).

As the CT_REQUEST BAdI interface parameter is using a sorted table item_attributes, we have to first delete the existing entry (without value) and add a new entry (with value).

```
METHOD /scwm/if_ex_prnt_ccat_wo~change.

  DATA: lt_ordim_o   TYPE /scwm/tt_ordim_o,
        ls_attribute TYPE /sapcnd/det_attrib_value.

  BREAK-POINT ID zewmdevbook_453.

  DATA(lo_appl) = CAST /scwm/cl_wo_ppf( io_context_wo->appl ).
  DATA(lv_tanum) = lo_appl->get_tanum( ).
  IF lv_tanum IS INITIAL.
    RETURN.
  ENDIF.
```

```abap
"1 See if field ZHUFLAG is in request
READ TABLE ct_request
ASSIGNING FIELD-SYMBOL(<fs_request>) INDEX 1.
READ TABLE <fs_request>-item_attributes
ASSIGNING FIELD-SYMBOL(<fs_attribute>)
WITH KEY fieldname = cv_fieldname. "'ZHUFLAG'
IF sy-subrc = 0 AND <fs_attribute>-value IS INITIAL.
  DELETE <fs_request>-item_attributes INDEX sy-tabix.
ELSE.
  RETURN. "field is not in condition table, so value is not required
ENDIF.
"2 Get the WT from memory
DATA(lv_who) = lo_appl->get_who( ).
IF lv_who IS NOT INITIAL.
  TRY.
      CALL FUNCTION '/SCWM/WHO_GET'
        EXPORTING
          iv_lgnum  = iv_lgnum
          iv_whoid  = lv_who
          iv_to     = abap_true
        IMPORTING
          et_ordim_o = lt_ordim_o.
    CATCH /scwm/cx_core.
      "no error
  ENDTRY.
ENDIF.
"3 Determine if it is a product or HU task
READ TABLE lt_ordim_o ASSIGNING FIELD-SYMBOL(<ordim_o>)
WITH KEY tanum = lv_tanum.
IF sy-subrc IS INITIAL.
  CASE <ordim_o>-flghuto.
    WHEN space.
      ls_attribute-value = 'P'.
    WHEN abap_true.
      ls_attribute-value = 'H'.
  ENDCASE.
ENDIF.
"4 Return the value
ls_attribute-fieldname = cv_fieldname. "'ZHUFLAG'
TRANSLATE ls_attribute-value TO UPPER CASE.
INSERT ls_attribute INTO TABLE <fs_request>-item_attributes.

ENDMETHOD.
```

Listing 4.23 Coding for BAdI "/SCWM/EX_PRNT_CCAT_WO"

Create a New Condition Record

Start Transaction /SCWM/PRWO6 (Create Condition Records for Printing—WO) in the SAP menu and enter the maintenance group PWO.

Create a new entry for condition type ZCRF and enter **Warehouse Number** (e.g., 1710), **Resource** (e.g., YALL-1), **WT Event** (choose value **2**, warehouse task confirm), and for the new field **WT HU/Prod** the value "P", as shown in Figure 4.37.

Figure 4.37 Maintain Condition Record

Testing of Enhancement 1V7b

In the last part of this section, we will test the printing of picking labels during RF picking. Execute the test case of scope item 1V7 with the changes in steps 5 and 6 (see Table 4.33). In step 5 (pick the goods), you'll test the enhancement for warehouse order printing, which we just completed. If your warehouse order consists of multiple picks, make sure the system prints after each pick. The system will not print a picking label if a warehouse task is a full pallet pick. In step 6 (pack the goods), you can test RF Transaction ZSORT, which is described in Chapter 3, Section 3.3.6.

Step	Step Description	Input Data and Expected Results
5	Pick the goods	▪ Use Transaction/SCWM/RFUI (Log on to RF Environment). ▪ Log onto warehouse 1710, resource YALL-1, and use presentation device YE00. Make sure you entered the resource for which you maintained a condition record (see Figure 4.37). ▪ Choose the RF picking (e.g., system-guided picking). ▪ On the picking entry screen, scan the permanent handling unit barcode of the wire basket as the pick handling unit number and choose F2 (**HU Create**). ▪ On the picking confirmation screen, confirm the requested quantity and scan the pick handling unit. ▪ On the handling unit confirmation screen, confirm the drop of the pick handling unit to the destination bin. *Expected result:* After each picking confirmation screen, the system automatically prints a picking label. Check this in the spool (Transaction SP01).

Table 4.33 Test Steps for Enhancement 1V7b

Step	Step Description	Input Data and Expected Results
6	Pack the goods	■ Use Transaction/SCWM/RFUI (Log on to RF Environment). ■ Log onto warehouse 1710, resource YALL-1, and use presentation device YE00. ■ Choose RF Transaction ZSORT from Chapter 3, Section 3.3.6. ■ Scan the stock identification of the first item in the pick handling unit. ■ Scan the ship handling unit. *Expected result*: After each pair of scans (pick label barcode, ship handling unit barcode), the system automatically repacks the item from the pick handling unit into the ship handling unit.

Table 4.33 Test Steps for Enhancement 1V7b (Cont.)

In Figure 4.38, notice the RF picking screens ❶ ❷ ❸ as described in step 5 (pick the goods) in Table 4.33. The printout you find in the spool will not look like the picking label shown earlier (see Figure 4.31). Adjusting the default standard label (/SCWM/WO_SIN-GLE) cannot be a part of this development, as doing so would depend significantly on the project, warehouse, and physical printer.

Figure 4.38 RF Picking with Entry, Confirmation, and Destination Screen

4.6 Physical Inventory in Warehouse: 1FW

This section deals with the procedure of physical inventory in the warehouse. The scope item available in the SAP Best Practices for Embedded EWM will be enhanced in the following way:

■ **1FWa: Enhancing the goods movement interface by additional data**
You will learn about the enhancement of the goods movement interface by implementing BAdI /SCWM/EX_ERP_GOODSMVT_EXT.

4.6.1   Process Description of Scope Item 1FW

Performing physical inventory is a common and necessary procedure to control the stock in your warehouse and comply with legal requirements. In this process, you regularly create inventory documents for a select number of storage bins or products in order to distribute the workload of inventory counting throughout the year. This procedure is also known as *permanent inventory*. It starts with the creation of physical inventory documents on behalf of which the counting of stock is either paper-based or completed using a mobile device. The system will also create a warehouse order with reference to a physical inventory document so that documents can either be printed or executed via RF based on such a warehouse order. Next, posting of inventory documents will adjust the book inventory in EWM. Detected differences will be communicated to the SAP S/4HANA system, where stock will be written off accordingly.

During the inventory process, you can make progress using the warehouse monitor. If you mainly work with product-specific inventory counting, you should also consider using the inventory procedures of putaway inventory and low stock check in your warehouse, thereby reducing the counting effort. These inventory procedures are available in EWM alongside the periodic or annual physical inventory. The process of physical inventory will run as shown in Table 4.34.

Step	Physical Activity	System Activity
4.1: Create physical inventory documents and warehouse orders		▪ The warehouse clerk monitors the physical inventory progress and creates physical inventory documents. ▪ The warehouse clerk prints the warehouse orders (paper-based). ▪ The system assigns the warehouse orders to a queue (RF-based).
4.2: Count the bins or products	▪ The counter counts the bin or product.	▪ A counter logs on as a resource (RF-based). ▪ The system proposes the next bin or product to be counted (RF-based). ▪ The warehouse clerk (paper based) or the counter (RF-based) enter the count results.
4.3: Post the physical inventory documents	▪ A supervisor posts the remaining physical inventory documents. ▪ The supervisor reviews and posts the remaining differences.	▪ The system posts physical inventory documents according to tolerance settings. ▪ The system posts the differences according to tolerance settings.

Table 4.34 Steps of SAP Best Practices Scope Item 1FW, Physical Inventory in Warehouse

You can find more details in the process description of scope item 1FW.

4.6.2 Enhancement 1FWa: Enhancing the Goods Movement Interface by Additional Data

With the following custom development, we will show you how the goods movement interface from EWM to SAP S/4HANA can be enhanced. As an example, the **Reference** field will be handed over from the physical inventory document in EWM to the material document in the SAP S/4HANA system. This data is not passed by default. It is therefore advisable to fill the **Item Text** field with this data in the SAP S/4HANA material document. On the part of SAP S/4HANA materials management, the **Item Text** can even be passed from the material document to the accounting document and thus be used for evaluation purposes. The **Reference** field can be used as a single-line, shortened text field, which makes a good counterpart to the **Item Text** field of the material document.

Figure 4.39 shows the fields when creating an EWM physical inventory document.

Figure 4.39 Reference in EWM Physical Inventory Document

Our sample custom development takes place in steps 4.1 and 4.3 of the inventory process, as shown in Table 4.35. The activities that are different from the standard process are highlighted in italics.

Step	Physical Activity	System Activity
4.1: Create physical inventory documents and warehouse orders	N/A	■ The warehouse clerk monitors the physical inventory progress and creates physical inventory documents. ■ *The warehouse clerk will additionally input references while creating physical inventory documents.*
4.3: Post the differences	N/A	■ The system posts the differences according to tolerance settings. ■ The supervisor reviews and posts the remaining differences. ■ *The field reference can be found back in the SAP S/4HANA material document as item text (Transaction MIGO).*

Table 4.35 Steps Changed with Custom Development for Reference

In the following, we'll discuss how to implement and test this enhancement.

Realization of Enhancement 1FWa

To implement enhancement 1FWa, proceed as follows. Start with the implementation of the BAdI in the goods movement interface /SCWM/EX_ERP_GOODSMVT_EXT, which is assigned to enhancement spot /SCWM/ES_ERP_GOODSMVT. This BAdI is called in the outbound message processing for SAP S/4HANA–relevant goods movements created in EWM. Within the BAdI, the data of the corresponding EWM goods movement documents (confirmed warehouse tasks) are available as input parameters. The data relevant for the creation of the SAP S/4HANA material document have already been generated and are also available. This can be changed inside the BAdI.

However, you must note that the items between the EWM goods movement and the SAP S/4HANA material document are not necessarily mapped one to one. This is especially true for the scenario of cumulated difference postings triggered from the EWM difference analyzer, where the number of line items posted back to SAP S/4HANA is reduced. For an EWM goods movement, there will be one item for each difference. Each warehouse task item could reference an item of a PID. However, when cumulative posting is requested, the associated SAP S/4HANA material document will contain one item for each stock characteristic with cumulated quantities and will carry a reference to the corresponding EWM goods movement document at the header level (parameter CS_GOODSMVT_REF_EWM). As mentioned earlier, the EWM difference analyzer offers individual and collective postings of difference items, as shown in Figure 4.40.

For our example, it is therefore important to note that when posting differences cumulatively, there is no item reference available that will allow tracing back **the Reference**

field of the underlying physical inventory documents. Note that this will also be true for posting differences periodically in background mode through Transaction /SCWM/ WM_ADJUST (Automatic Posting of Differences).

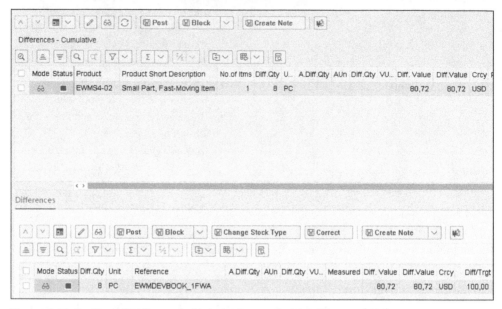

Figure 4.40 Posting of Differences to SAP S/4HANA with Difference Analyzer

For the **Reference** field, you should also note that in case of recounts, its value will not be transferred from the original to the new physical inventory document. However, original and recount documents will reference each other, which should generally allow you to trace the value from the original document. For our simplified example, we assume that neither cumulative postings nor recounting will be used. Thus, the line items for the EWM goods movement and the SAP S/4HANA material document should be identical in number and sorting and there can be a clear reference to the linked inventory document item to trace the **Reference information**.

Listing 4.24 shows the corresponding example code for the custom development.

```
METHOD /scwm/if_ex_erp_goodsmvt~change_matdoc.

    "Reference to be found in text type scwm_refui
    DATA: lt_item_pi TYPE /lime/pi_t_guid,
          ls_item_pi TYPE /lime/pi_guid.

    "Set BreakPointID
    BREAK-POINT ID zewmdevbook_1fwa.
* Assumptions:
* 1.NO cumulative posting!
```

```
* 2.NO recounts!
* 3.Entries of ordim_c = entries of goodsmvt_item
    DATA(lv_erplines) = lines( ct_goodsmvt_item ).
    DATA(lv_ewmlines) = lines( it_ordim_c ).
    IF lv_erplines <> lv_ewmlines.
      RETURN.
    ENDIF.
    LOOP AT it_ordim_c ASSIGNING FIELD-SYMBOL(<fs_ordim_c>).
      DATA(lv_tabix) = sy-tabix.
      "Is predecessor pi document?
      IF <fs_ordim_c>-qdoccat <> wmegc_doccat_wi1
      AND <fs_ordim_c>-qdocid IS INITIAL.
        CONTINUE.
      ENDIF.
      CLEAR: lt_item_pi, ls_item_pi.
      MOVE <fs_ordim_c>-qdocid TO ls_item_pi-guid.
      APPEND ls_item_pi TO lt_item_pi.
      CALL METHOD me->z_pi_item_get(
        EXPORTING
          is_pi_item_guid         = ls_item_pi
        IMPORTING
          et_pi_item_read_single = DATA(lt_item_read) ).

      "Get reference for physical inventory document
      DATA(ls_item_read) = VALUE #( lt_item_read[ 1 ] ).
      IF sy-subrc <> 0.
        CONTINUE.
      ENDIF.
      DATA(ls_logitem) = VALUE #( ls_item_read-t_logitem[ ref_doc_type = c_doc_
type ] ).
      DATA(lv_reference) = ls_logitem-ref_doc_id.
      "Move reference into material document
      READ TABLE ct_goodsmvt_item
      ASSIGNING FIELD-SYMBOL(<fs_gm_item>) INDEX lv_tabix.
      IF  <fs_gm_item> IS ASSIGNED
      AND <fs_gm_item>-item_text IS INITIAL.
        MOVE lv_reference TO <fs_gm_item>-item_text.
      ENDIF.
      CLEAR lv_tabix.
    ENDLOOP.

  ENDMETHOD.
```

Listing 4.24 Example Implementation of BAdI /SCWM/EX_ERP_GOODSMVT_EXT

[»]

Debugging of the BAdI

To debug BAdI /SCWM/EX_ERP_GOODSMVT_EXT, you should set and activate a checkpoint group at the beginning of the BAdI method. Also, be sure to activate update debugging.

Within the example implementation, we use a proprietary static method for reading the PID data that is assigned to the BAdI implementing class. You can find its content in Listing 4.25.

```
METHOD z_pi_item_get.

  DATA:
    lt_item_key  TYPE /lime/pi_t_item_key,
    lt_item_read TYPE /lime/pi_t_item_read_getsingle,
    lt_item_pi   TYPE /lime/pi_t_guid,
    lt_item_guid TYPE /lime/pi_t_guid_item.

  CLEAR lt_item_pi.
  APPEND is_pi_item_guid TO lt_item_pi.
  "Get key of physical inventory document
  CALL FUNCTION '/LIME/PI_DOCUMENT_GET_ITEM_KEY'
    EXPORTING
      it_line_guid = lt_item_pi
    IMPORTING
      et_item_key  = lt_item_key.
  IF sy-subrc = 0.
    "Get physical inventory document
    DATA(ls_item_key) = VALUE #( lt_item_key[ 1 ] ).
    DATA(ls_head) = VALUE /lime/pi_head_attributes(
      process_type = ls_item_key-process_type
      lgnum        = ls_item_key-lgnum ).
    CLEAR lt_item_guid.
    DATA(ls_item_guid) = VALUE /lime/pi_s_guid_item(
      guid_doc = ls_item_key-guid_doc ).
    APPEND ls_item_guid TO lt_item_guid.
    CALL FUNCTION '/LIME/PI_DOCUMENT_READ_SINGLE'
      EXPORTING
        is_head     = ls_head
        it_guid_doc = lt_item_guid
      IMPORTING
        et_item_read = lt_item_read.
    IF sy-subrc = 0.
      et_pi_item_read_single = lt_item_read.
    ENDIF.
```

```
ENDIF.

ENDMETHOD.
```

Listing 4.25 Method for Reading Physical Inventory Document Data

As part of this example custom development, we have shown you how to use the BAdI to influence the goods movement interface to the SAP S/4HANA system. At the same time, we have enhanced the transfer of the additional **Reference** field to the SAP S/4HANA material document while posting stock differences. We have, however, made a number of strong assumptions. You could further strengthen these by adding additional checks for the posting of physical inventory documents or eliminate them by adding additional logic.

Testing Enhancement 1FWa

To test the custom development, run the test case for scope item 1FW of SAP Best Practices warehouse 1710. Table 4.36 shows the relevant part of steps 4.1 and 4.3.3 of the test instructions.

In Figure 4.41, you will see a material document in SAP S/4HANA with the field item text (ERP), which was transferred from the EWM physical inventory document into the SAP S/4HANA material document by means of the custom development. In the **Material Slip** field, you can find the standard reference made up from the associated EWM warehouse number and goods movement warehouse task—for example, 171010000004801.

Step	Description	User Input and Expected Results
4.1	Manual creation of one or multiple PIDs	■ Call Transaction /SCWM/PI_DOC_CREATE or use the Create Physical Inventory Documents app (SAP Fiori app F3197). ■ Provide values for the field reference and choose a reason that is known in SAP S/4HANA as well.
4.3.3	Post differences to SAP S/4HANA	■ Call Transaction /SCWM/DIFF_ANALYZER and select physical inventory documents by the reason used when creating physical inventory documents. ■ In SAP S/4HANA, select the material document for difference postings by product or EWM warehouse task (material slip) in Transaction MIGO. *Expected result:* In the SAP S/4HANA material document, you can find the reference as item text.

Table 4.36 Testing Enhancement 1FWa

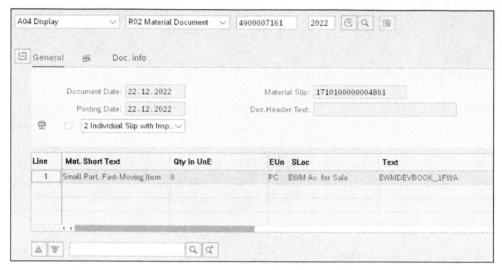

Figure 4.41 Transaction MIGO: Material Document with Item Text

4.7   Summary

In this chapter, we described several development enhancements in the context of the main processes of the SAP Best Practices scope items for embedded EWM. In your project, SAP Best Practices warehouse 1710 could be the foundation from which you extend step by step, using the EWM BAdIs and frameworks in order to implement additional customer requirements that cannot be met by standard functionality. In Section 4.2 and Section 4.3, you found examples of how to extend the inbound processes in a warehouse using BAdIs, the warehouse monitor, and RF framework extensions. Section 4.4 and Section 4.5 showed you how to use PPF, condition techniques, and BAdIs to extend the warehouse outbound processes. In Section 4.6, we described a useful physical inventory extension realized within a BAdI.

In Chapter 5, you will get an overview of the most common function modules and methods that you might reuse in your custom developments.

Chapter 5

Function Modules, Methods, and APIs for Extended Warehouse Management

In this chapter, you will learn how to make use of EWM core function modules, methods, and APIs. Use this chapter as the starting point for your technical design and programming in EWM.

In this chapter, you will find a collection of central function modules and methods from EWM. The use of functions in EWM and their calls in possible customer developments are explained using short coding examples.

The functions are described according to the following pattern:

- **Technical name**
  The following are possible subsections:
  - Function module(s)
  - Class(es)
  - Method(s)
  - Type group(s)
  - Interface(s)

- **Program logic**
  We roughly describe the program flow within a method or a function module.

- **Documentation**
  If a supplementary official documentation is available for the feature, we mention it in this section.

- **Use in EWM**
  This section explains where the function is used in EWM. Thus, you will have the opportunity to examine this feature for an example in more detail, before using it in a separate customer development.

- **Recommended use for custom development**
  Here you will find recommendations and tips for using a feature in your custom development.

- **Sample coding**
  In some cases, we have created sample code that demonstrates how to use the function via an example.

[»]

Minimizing Risk

Your custom developments can, with proper use of EWM capabilities, be more specific, more stable, and less time-consuming. Misuses, though, can result in performance problems and database inconsistencies. Only sufficient testing of all possible scenarios and mass tests can minimize these risks.

[»]

Testing

Very few of the function modules and methods listed herein have been officially released for customers so far. Thus, interfaces or functions could be incompatibly changed, and official documentation is missing. Therefore, we strongly encourage you to test your custom developments, particularly after a release or support package upgrade.

5.1   Transaction Manager for a Logical Unit of Work in Extended Warehouse Management

The EWM transaction manager coordinates central tasks and provides services to pull information about global data. Be sure to understand its concept before creating custom applications in EWM:

Class

- /SCWM/CL_TM

Methods

- CLEANUP (static)
- SET_LGNUM (static)

Program Logic

- The CLEANUP method sets back the local and global memory area for registered EWM objects and removes locks. This method is a mandatory addition to the COMMIT and ROLLBACK ABAP commands in the EWM environment.
- The SET_LGNUM method sets the warehouse number for EWM objects whose storage area is being held for each warehouse number.

Documentation

In SAP Notes 1414179 and 3140915, you will find documents attached or linked that deal with technical transaction handling and delivery processing in SAP EWM and EWM with SAP S/4HANA. For developing your own reports/transactions in the EWM environment, you will find many important fundamentals explained in these documents.

Use in Extended Warehouse Management

The central function groups/classes for the handling unit, delivery, warehouse task, goods movement, and other EWM objects register on method REGISTER_CLEANUP_XX in the transaction manager, once global tables and structures of each function group/class are filled. Calling the CLEANUP method causes the global tables/parameters of registered function groups and classes to be initialized.

If a user starts, for example, an EWM dialog transaction and processes an object, CLEANUP will be performed on user command SAVE or CANCEL; that is, the object and, if appropriate, dependent items are removed from memory. The user can remain in the dialog transaction and process the next object without having the changes to the first object lead to unwanted side effects in the memory.

Recommended Use for Custom Development

If you develop a new (RF) transaction or a new program, use the /SCWM/CL_TM=>SET_LGNUM() method in your program logic at the beginning and the /SCWM/CL_TM=>CLEANUP() method when you exit or cancel. If you are unsure whether an earlier logical unit of work is correctly terminated or if the users in your application can change the selection of the objects again, call the /SCWM/CL_TM=>CLEANUP() method again.

[«]

> **Warning**
>
> Do not use these methods in BAdI implementations in any way, because you would reset the global tables of the standard processing by doing so.

The IV_REASON import parameter is preassigned with the /SCDL/IF_SP1_TRANSACTION=>SC_CLEANUP_END constant. This value is recommended and ensures a complete cleanup, which means that EWM objects are then no longer in memory and locks are removed.

In very rare cases (e.g., for performance reasons in time-critical applications), you should make use of the /SCDL/IF_SP1_TRANSACTION=>SC_CLEANUP_COMMIT constant, which ensures that storage and the database have the same status and that you can continue working on the same objects.

[+]

> **COMMIT and AND WAIT**
>
> It is also recommended to use the COMMIT command with the AND WAIT addition, as many EWM objects (handling unit, warehouse task, warehouse order, etc.) use the update task for complex processing.

Sample Coding

At the beginning of an independent customer development, add the following:

```
/scwm/cl_tm=>set_lgnum( lv_lgnum )
```

As of SAP S/4HANA 2020, you should use the statement in Listing 5.1 instead, which includes value validation.

```
DATA: lo_tm TYPE REF TO /scwm/if_tm.
lo_tm ?= /scwm/cl_tm_factory=>get_service( /scwm/cl_tm_factory=>sc_manager ).
TRY.
    lo_tm->set_whno_w_check( p_lgnum ).
  CATCH /scwm/cx_tm_check INTO DATA(lx_lgnum).
    MESSAGE lx_lgnum TYPE 'E'.
ENDTRY.
```

Listing 5.1 Using EWM Transaction Manager

At the end, as an addition to the ROLLBACK or COMMIT command, implement the code in Listing 5.2.

```
IF lv_rejected = abap_true.
  ROLLBACK WORK.
  /scwm/cl_tm=>cleanup( ).
ELSE.
  COMMIT WORK AND WAIT.
  /scwm/cl_tm=>cleanup( ).
ENDIF.
```

Listing 5.2 CLEANUP Method

5.2   EWM API Concept

EWM provides a list of APIs as ABAP object-oriented interfaces, which can be consumed in custom developments.

Interfaces

- /SCWM/IF_API

Use in Extended Warehouse Management

Each available EWM-based API starts with prefix /SCWM/IF_API in the technical interface name. Class /SCWM/CL_API_FACTORY takes care of instance creation for the API implementations. All API interfaces and their implementations can be found in database table /SCWM/TAPI_IMPL.

For the full list of available APIs, see SAP Notes 3115182 and 3078938. Each interface includes dedicated technical documentation that can be accessed in the ABAP development environment, such as by using Transaction SE24. As all API interfaces include interface /SCWM/IF_API, you can easily get an overview of available APIs in your system by displaying this interface with its implementing classes in Transaction SE80.

Recommended Use for Custom Development

We generally recommend using the EWM-provided APIs for leaner and more harmonized, meaning ABAP Objects–based, programming. However, be aware that the APIs are provided by SAP without an official stability contract, different to the stability contract provided with BAPIs or released function modules. Therefore, these APIs are not guaranteed to stay fully upward compatible in future software versions. Nevertheless, SAP attempts to keep them compatible as much as possible.

Sample Coding

For most APIs, sample code should be included in their technical interface documentation alongside further information. However, find a quick example for reading preallocated stock in Listing 5.3.

```
REPORT z_pas_read.

PARAMETERS: p_lgnum TYPE /scwm/lgnum.
DATA pas_api TYPE REF TO /scwm/if_api_pre_allocated.

TRY.
    /scwm/cl_api_factory=>get_service( IMPORTING eo_api = pas_api ).
    CHECK pas_api IS BOUND.
    pas_api->read(
      EXPORTING
        iv_whno                 = p_lgnum
      IMPORTING
        eo_message              = DATA(lo_pas_message)
        et_pre_allocated_stock  = DATA(pre_allocated_tab) ).

  CATCH /scwm/cx_api_pre_allocated INTO DATA(lo_pas_exception).
    MESSAGE ID sy-msgid TYPE /scwm/if_api_message=>sc_msgty_error
         NUMBER sy-msgno INTO DATA(error_message)
            WITH sy-msgv1 sy-msgv2 sy-msgv3 sy-msgv4.
    WRITE error_message.   "e.g. warehouse not does not exist
    RETURN.
ENDTRY.

WRITE: 'Number of Preallocated Stock in Warehouse', p_lgnum, ':',
     lines( pre_allocated_tab ).
```

Listing 5.3 Service Consumption Example for Reading Preallocated Stock

5.3   External APIs

In addition to the more internally used APIs described in the previous sections, EWM also provides APIs intended for external use, meaning across systems.

Use in Extended Warehouse Management

Standard EWM provides some OData APIs for custom developments. These were designed for warehouse management in SAP S/4HANA Cloud only. You can find the OData APIs available in your system in package WME_ODATA_API using ABAP Workbench (Transaction SE80). Alternatively, check the subpackages of package /SCWM/ODATA_MAIN for backend implementations of the APIs. Most API methods implement checkpoint group /SCWM/ODATA_API_DEBUG, which you can activate in Transaction SAAB and use for debugging.

Recommended Use for Custom Development

The external APIs can be made available for use in embedded or decentralized EWM, such as when building sidecar apps on SAP Business Technology Platform (SAP BTP) or building custom SAP Fiori apps for handling warehouse tasks and orders. You should check SAP Note 3078938 for more details on how to make them available. Also consider that the APIs might not fit the scope of functionality you require, given that they were built to focus on the potentially reduced scope of cloud warehouse management. Therefore, we recommend checking the scope before using an external API.

Sample Coding

The full list of OData APIs can be found at the SAP API Business Hub (*https://api.sap.com/*). Each API is explained in detail, and there should be code snippets provided.

5.4   Service Class for Filling Stock Fields

EWM requires technical key conversion of EWM stock-related objects, which can be done using the class in this section.

Class

- /SCWM/CL_UI_STOCK_FIELDS

Methods

- GET_XX_BY_YY
- PREFETCH_XX_BY_YY

Program Logic

- The GET methods of the class convert a technical value of a stock field—product, batch, and so on—to a user-readable name or vice versa.
- The PREFETCH_XX_BY_YY method essentially corresponds to the GET method, but in contrast, a table of values is converted.

Use in Extended Warehouse Management

In EWM, the technical keys (usually the code and the global unique identifier [GUID]) are used for the system internal processing. By using this service class, the technical values will be converted prior to the output on the screen. A user input is converted to the technical value before the internal processing is called.

Recommended Use for Custom Development

We recommend that you use the GET methods for individual accesses and PREFETCH methods for mass access and better performance. Also, use the methods to prepare outputs for the user or user inputs and to avoid your own transformations or database access. Only work with the technical values internally.

Sample Coding

Listing 5.4 shows a short example of technical material key conversion in EWM.

```
DATA(go_stock) = NEW /scwm/cl_ui_stock_fields( ).
go_stock->get_matkey_by_id(
   EXPORTING iv_matid = p_matid
   IMPORTING ev_matnr = DATA(matnr) ).
```

Listing 5.4 Convert Technical Product Key to Readable Product Number

5.5   Date and Time for Time Zone of Warehouse Number

EWM allows for assignment of time zones to warehouse numbers, as there might be warehouses of different time zones run on the same system. Ensure that you consider date and time conversions in your custom code using the function modules in this section.

Function Modules

- /SCWM/CONVERT_DATE_TIME
- /SCWM/CONVERT_TIMESTAMP

Program Logic

- In function module /SCWM/CONVERT_DATE_TIME, the input from the user time interval (from date/time to until date/time) is converted into two reference time stamps (UTC), considering the time zone of the warehouse number.
- In function module /SCWM/CONVERT_TIMESTAMP, a reference time stamp (UTC) is converted into the date/time of the warehouse number time zone.

Use in Extended Warehouse Management

Time stamps are stored in the EWM databases as UTC reference time stamps. When a user enters a date and time in a selection screen (e.g., in the warehouse management monitor), the time stamp for the database selection will be calculated using the /SCWM/CONVERT_DATE_TIME function module, considering the time zone of the warehouse number. All time stamps that are displayed in EWM transactions (e.g., changing date of an handling unit, confirmation date of the warehouse task), have been previously converted into the time zone of the warehouse number by using the /SCWM/CONVERT_TIMESTAMP function module.

Recommended Use for Custom Development

Once the date and time in your customer developments play a role, you should use the two function modules to convert user inputs in reference time stamps. If there are new database tables with time stamps in your customer development, you should also save the reference time stamp. Do not take the user's time zone as a reference; use the time zone of the warehouse number.

Sample Coding

See Listing 5.17 for instructions on how to use the /SCWM/CONVERT_DATE_TIME function module.

5.6   Cross-Application Constants

This section discusses the most used EWM cross-application constants, those that are frequently used in standard code and can similarly be used in custom code to allow for common readability and reuse of objects.

Type Groups

- WMEGC
- WMESR

Interfaces

- /SCWM/IF_DL_C
- /SCDL/IF_DL_C

Use in Extended Warehouse Management

Most objects, such as warehouse task, handling unit, storage bin, goods movement, transportation unit, and so on, have deposited constants in type groups. Often, they are the only overarching constants. That means that almost any object also has its own local constants defined in an interface or in a function group. The delivery object has deposited constants in interfaces. The earlier mentioned interfaces are only the best known. For more delivery constants, search in Transaction SE24 (Class Builder) for "/SCDL/IF*DL*C" or "/SCWM/IF*DL*C".

Recommended Use for Custom Development

Of course, you can also use the constants of the EWM standard type groups and interfaces in your customer developments. Be aware that you should not only choose the fixed value but also the corresponding data element.

Sample Coding

You can find a short example use of a cross-application constant in Listing 5.5. The constant is used to declare and set the document category PDI for inbound delivery.

```
TYPE-POOLS: wmegc.
DATA(doccat) = wmegc_doccat_pdi.
```

Listing 5.5 Use of WMEGC Constant

5.7   Create and Extend Application Log

The well-known application log is frequently used in EWM standard and often implemented in custom code to log all kinds of messages and information.

Class

- /SCWM/CL_LOG

Method

- ADD_MESSAGE
- CREATE_LOG
- DISPLAY_LOG

Program Logic

Wrapping of the function modules of the central application log from the SAP base.

Use in Extended Warehouse Management

Many of the function modules, methods, and BAdIs have a parameter for an instance of the /SCWM/CL_LOG class. The functions collect all occurring success, warnings, and error messages as a record over several caller steps.

The EWM UIs feature the ability to display the log (exception: RF environment). Transaction /SCWM/ACTLOG (Activate Application Log) controls per subobject of the /SCWM/WME object whether or not the protocol of the instance /SCWM/CL_LOG is written as an application log to the database. In this case, a user or SAP support can make use of it in Transaction SLG1 later on to carry out an analysis.

For the object warehouse order, there are additional log settings in Transaction /SCWM/WOLOG (Set Up Control Parameters for Warehouse Order Creation).

Recommended Use for Custom Development

If you decide to use a BAdI that has an import parameter for a /SCWM/CL_LOG instance, you can use it to write your own messages in the standard log. A success message per return parameter in the BAdI can be very useful for an analysis during a test phase. Using BAdIs within the creation and confirmation of warehouse tasks, you can use function module /SCWM/TO_LOG_GET_INSTANCE to get access to the log instance.

Thus, it is possible to mix project-specific customer messages and standard messages in the very same protocol. To make it clear and quickly recognizable—for example, to the support employees—which message of one protocol is SAP standard and which message is customized, simply add at the beginning or end of each message text a constant, such as "(ZBADI)", to make the message look like this: "amount to 20 reduced (ZBADI)".

Sample Coding

The sample code in Listing 5.6 shows a typical usage of the /SCWM/CL_LOG class in EWM. First, the actual error message is raised with the MESSAGE statement in the string variable. Subsequently, the filled system fields for messages (e.g., sy-msgid) are passed to the protocol using the ADD_MESSAGE method. This approach has the advantage, among others, that the *where-used* reference works for the error message.

```
/scwm/cl_log=>get_instance( IMPORTING eo_instance = DATA(lo_log) ).
MESSAGE e042(/scwm/wmebasics) INTO DATA(string).
lo_log->add_message( ).
```

Listing 5.6 Pass Error Message to the Log Instance

Custom Development with Your Own Protocol

Maintain your own subobject (e.g., ZE_123) in the object or work area /SCWM/WME in the view V_BALSUB (using Transaction SM31). Then you can also manage this subobject via Transaction /SCWM/ACTLOG (Activate Application Log). The current settings for your subobject will then have to be read by the /SCWM/LOG_ACT_READ_SINGLE function module within your customer coding.

We recommend that you save the application log with the /SCWM/APP_LOG_WRITE_V2 function module using a V2 update task with low priority. A good template, where the validity of protocol settings also is considered, provides the /SCWM/MFS_WRITE_LOG function module.

5.8   Read EWM Deliveries and Warehouse Requests

Reading data of EWM warehouse requests or deliveries can be a bit difficult due to the nature of the objects' architecture. Study this section's methods and their respective documentation to better understand how to access EWM delivery data.

Class

- /SCWM/CL_DLV_MANAGEMENT_PRD

Related Classes

- /SCWM/CL_DLV_MANAGEMENT_DR
- /SCWM/CL_DLV_MANAGEMENT_FD

Method

- QUERY

Program Logic

Warehouse requests or deliveries will be partially or completely read according to preset selections (parameters IT_DOCID, IT_DOCNO, IT_SELECTION). The IS_READ_OPTIONS, IS_EXCLUDE_DATA, and IS_INCLUDE_DATA parameters control whether or not the delivery object has to be fully instantiated and which attributes of the object have to be read. Keep in mind that you are not to use the IS_EXCLUDE_DATA parameter; use IS_INCLUDE_DATA instead.

Documentation

Start Transaction SE24 (Class Builder) and navigate to the **Documentation** function of the QUERY method. The method is documented on about 10 pages in great detail. With the proper use of this method, you will minimize the performance risk of your custom development.

Use in Extended Warehouse Management

The more than 300 usages within the EWM coding show that this is the central method to read a warehouse request.

Recommended Use for Custom Development

If you need reading access to a warehouse request within your custom development, use this method. The other methods of the /SCWM/CL_DLV_MANAGEMENT_PRD class are not recommended for use.

Sample Coding

The code example in Listing 5.7 contains a report to output the route from an outbound delivery order.

```
REPORT z_query_odo.

PARAMETERS: p_docid  TYPE /scdl/dl_docid.

DATA:       lt_docid TYPE /scwm/dlv_docid_item_tab.

DATA(ls_incl_data) = VALUE /scwm/dlv_query_incl_str_prd( head_transport = abap_
true ).

DATA(ls_read_options) = VALUE /scwm/dlv_query_contr_str(
  data_retrival_only      = abap_true
  mix_in_object_instances = abap_true
  head_part_select        = abap_true ).

DATA(ls_docid) = VALUE /scwm/dlv_docid_item_str(
  docid = p_docid
  doccat = /scdl/if_dl_doc_c=>sc_doccat_out_prd ).
APPEND ls_docid TO lt_docid.

DATA(lo_bom_prd) = /scwm/cl_dlv_management_prd=>get_instance( ).
TRY.
    CALL METHOD lo_bom_prd->query
      EXPORTING
        it_docid        = lt_docid
        is_include_data = ls_incl_data
        is_read_options = ls_read_options
```

```
     IMPORTING
        et_headers        = DATA(lt_prd_hdr).
  CATCH /scdl/cx_delivery.
    MESSAGE ID sy-msgid TYPE sy-msgty NUMBER sy-msgno
    WITH sy-msgv1 sy-msgv2 sy-msgv3 sy-msgv4
    RAISING error.
ENDTRY.
DATA(ls_prd_hdr)   = lt_prd_hdr[ 1 ].
DATA(ls_transport) = ls_prd_hdr-transport[ 1 ].
WRITE: ls_prd_hdr-docno, ls_transport-route_id.
```

Listing 5.7 Read Warehouse Request Using Query Method

5.9   Change EWM Deliveries or Warehouse Requests

Changing an EWM warehouse request or delivery can be similarly difficult as reading one. Study this section's mentioned classes and additional documentation to better understand how to change EWM delivery data in your custom code.

Classes

- /SCDL/CL_SP_PRD_OUT
- /SCDL/CL_BO_MANAGEMENT

Documentation

To edit an inbound delivery or an outbound delivery order, see SAP Notes 1414179 and 1064376 for detailed information.

Use in Extended Warehouse Management

The classes are used, among others, in the delivery processing transactions (e.g., /SCWM/PRDI, /SCWM/PRDO).

Recommended Use for Custom Development

If you edit warehouse requests within a BAdI implementation and the technical keys of the warehouse requests are available, you can go directly for the classes of the delivery service provider layer (see the sample coding in SAP Note 1064376).

If you edit warehouse requests in a separate custom development (e.g., a report with a UI), make sure to use the class for the service provider (/SCDL/CL_SP_PRD_OUT). See SAP Note 1414179 for details, and check the DelivServiceProviderCallExamples.pdf attachment.

Sample Coding

In the sample code in Listing 5.8, the project-specific my_own_field field will be set to the my_own_value value for a delivery item. The technical keys of the outbound delivery order (iv_docid) and of the item to be changed (iv_itemid) are passed to the method. The sample code can be used within a BAdI of the delivery processing. It therefore does not set any locks or cause any SAVE action.

```
REPORT z_change_odo.

PARAMETERS: p_doccat TYPE /scwm/de_doccat,
            p_docid  TYPE /scdl/dl_docid,
            p_itemid TYPE /scdl/dl_itemid.

"1. Get business object manager (BOM)
CHECK p_doccat = wmegc_doccat_out_pdo.
DATA(lo_bom) = /scdl/cl_bo_management=>get_instance( ).
"2. Get business object (BO)
DATA(lo_bo) = lo_bom->get_bo_by_id( iv_docid = p_docid ).
IF lo_bo IS NOT BOUND.
  RETURN. "Add error handling
ENDIF.

"3. Get current custom extension for ODO item
DATA(lo_item_prd) = CAST /scdl/cl_dl_item_prd(
lo_bo->get_item( iv_itemid = p_itemid ) ).
DATA(ls_eew) = lo_item_prd->get_eew( ).
"4. Update custom fields
ls_eew-zzactivity = '1'. "Custom field
"5. Write changes to item
lo_item_prd->set_eew( ls_eew ).

"Add error handling and saving
```

Listing 5.8 Change Delivery Item

5.10   Read Warehouse Product Master

Using warehouse product master data in your custom code is a frequent requirement. The function modules and sample code offer examples for reading global and warehouse-related product data.

Function Modules

- /SCWM/MATERIAL_READ_SINGLE
- /SCWM/MATERIAL_READ_MULTIPLE
- /SCWM/MATERIAL_READ_RANGE

Program Logic

The product master is read for one or more product numbers. Access to the necessary database tables (e.g., global or warehouse-specific product attributes) is optimized, and the results are buffered. The generic service function modules of the master data layer are optimally used.

Use in Extended Warehouse Management

Access on the product master in EWM is done exclusively via these function modules and not via direct database access.

Recommended Use for Custom Development

We encourage that you use these function modules and avoid your own database access on the product master. If you have extended the product master with your own customer attributes, these function modules will also return the extension fields. For performance reasons, only implement the export parameters of the function modules that you actually need in the calling program.

Sample Coding

The example in Listing 5.9 shows the reading of the global product master attributes.

```
REPORT z_read_product.

PARAMETERS: p_lgnum TYPE /scwm/lgnum,
            p_matnr TYPE /scwm/de_matnr,
            p_prod  TYPE abap_bool AS CHECKBOX.

DATA: lv_matid      TYPE /scwm/de_matid,
      ls_mat_global TYPE /scwm/s_material_global,
      ls_mara       TYPE mara,
      ls_makt       TYPE makt.

IF p_prod = abap_true. "Read Product
  TRY.
      CALL FUNCTION 'CONVERSION_EXIT_MDLPD_INPUT'
        EXPORTING
          input  = p_matnr
        IMPORTING
          output = lv_matid.

      CALL FUNCTION '/SCWM/MATERIAL_READ_SINGLE'
        EXPORTING
          iv_matid      = lv_matid
          iv_lgnum      = p_lgnum
```

```
      IMPORTING
        es_mat_global = ls_mat_global.
    CATCH /scwm/cx_md.
      MESSAGE ID sy-msgid TYPE sy-msgty NUMBER sy-msgno
      WITH sy-msgv1 sy-msgv2 sy-msgv3 sy-msgv4
      RAISING error.
  ENDTRY.
ELSE. "Read Material Global Data (MARA)
  CALL FUNCTION 'MARA_READ'
    EXPORTING
      i_matnr    = p_matnr
      i_sprache = sy-langu
    IMPORTING
      e_makt     = ls_makt
      e_mara     = ls_mara
    EXCEPTIONS
      no_entry  = 1
      OTHERS    = 2.
  IF sy-subrc <> 0.
* Implement suitable error handling here
  ENDIF.

ENDIF.
IF p_prod = abap_true.
  WRITE: ls_mat_global-maktx.
ELSE.
  WRITE: ls_makt-maktx.
ENDIF.
```

Listing 5.9 Read Product Master

5.11   Create/Change Warehouse Product Master Records

Get to know the central function module for creating and changing EWM warehouse product data.

Function Module

- /SCWM/MATERIAL_WHST_MAINT_MULT

Program Logic

The function module creates a warehouse product for a product and the entitled. Also, this function enables the changing routines of a warehouse product. The function module is suitable to read many products with a single call.

Use in Extended Warehouse Management

Report /SCWM/R_CCIND_MAINTAIN (Transaction /SCWM/CCIND_MAINTAIN) determines the cycle-counting indicator from SAP Advanced Planning and Optimization for all warehouse products and changes the warehouse products using the /SCWM/MATERIAL_WHST_MAINT_MULT function module.

Recommended Use for Custom Development

You can use this function module for your own migration report of warehouse-specific attributes (e.g., *putaway control indicator* and *stock removal control indicator*). As of SAP EWM release 7.0 EHP 2, you can use the existing migration report.

> **Locks**
>
> The /SCWM/MATERIAL_WHST_MAINT_MULT function module will not set any database locks. However, if you want to set locks, you must implement the /SCWM/MATERIAL_WHST_ENQ function module. To delete locks, use the /SCWM/MATERIAL_WHST_DEQ_ALL function module.

Sample Coding

The sample code in Listing 5.10 shows a report that creates warehouse products for a product master. The user just enters the product and the entitled.

```
REPORT z_create_whse_product.

DATA: lt_mat_lgnum TYPE /scwm/tt_material_lgnum_maint,
      lt_matmap    TYPE /scwm/tt_matid_matnr,
      lt_bapiret   TYPE bapirettab.

PARAMETERS:
  p_lgnum  TYPE /scwm/lgnum MEMORY ID /scwm/lgn OBLIGATORY,
  p_entitl TYPE /scwm/de_entitled,
  p_matnr  TYPE /scwm/de_matnr.

START-OF-SELECTION.
  "1. Convert product into GUID
  DATA(lo_stock) = NEW /scwm/cl_ui_stock_fields( ).
  DATA(lo_log)   = NEW /scwm/cl_log( ).
  DATA(ls_mat_lgnum) = VALUE /scwm/s_material_lgnum_maint(
    matid    = lo_stock->get_matid_by_no(
                 iv_matnr = p_matnr )
    entitled = p_entitl ).
  APPEND ls_mat_lgnum TO lt_mat_lgnum.
```

```
DATA(ls_matmap) = VALUE /scwm/s_matid_matnr(
  matid = ls_mat_lgnum-matid ).
APPEND ls_matmap TO lt_matmap.
"2. Lock product
CALL FUNCTION '/SCWM/MATERIAL_WHST_ENQ'
  EXPORTING
    iv_lgnum      = p_lgnum
    iv_entitled   = p_entitl
  CHANGING
    ct_matid_matnr = lt_matmap.
"3. Create warehouse product
TRY.
    CALL FUNCTION '/SCWM/MATERIAL_WHST_MAINT_MULT'
      EXPORTING
        it_mat_lgnum = lt_mat_lgnum
        iv_lgnum     = p_lgnum
        iv_commit    = abap_true
      IMPORTING
        et_bapiret   = lt_bapiret.
    lo_log->add_log( it_prot = lt_bapiret ).
  CATCH /scwm/cx_md_lgnum_locid.
  CATCH /scwm/cx_md_interface.
    "Add error handling
ENDTRY.
"4. Unlock product
CALL FUNCTION '/SCWM/MATERIAL_WHST_DEQ_ALL'.
```

Listing 5.10 Warehouse Product Creation

5.12   Service Class Batch Management

Get familiar with how to programmatically work with batches in EWM.

Class

- /SCWM/CL_BATCH_APPL

Methods

- GET_INSTANCE
- GET_BATCH (Instance Method)
- PRODUCT_GET_CLASS
- GET_BATCH_ATTR_BY_CLASS

Program Logic

- To retrieve the details of a batch, first create an instance of the /SCWM/CL_BATCH_APPL class per each product/batch combination using method GET_INSTANCE.

- With the GET_BATCH instance method, you can then read the details of the batch: class, status, the standard characteristics, and so on. This class has a buffer for batches; that is, not each call will result in a database access.

- The static PRODUCT_GET_CLASS and GET_BATCH_ATTR_BY_CLASS methods determine the class and the characteristics for a product.

Use in Extended Warehouse Management

This class is used in EWM, among others, to display batch details in the warehouse monitor (Transaction /SCWM/MON).

Recommended Use for Custom Development

If batch details are needed in your custom development, use the GET_BATCH method in order to use the buffer and avoid your own database selections. Listing 5.11 provides an example for reading a batch.

```
REPORT z_get_batch.

PARAMETERS:
  p_matnr TYPE /scwm/de_matnr,
  p_charg TYPE /scwm/de_charg.

TRY.
    DATA(lo_batch) = /scwm/cl_batch_appl=>get_instance(
     iv_productno = p_matnr
     iv_batchno   = p_charg ).
    lo_batch->get_batch( IMPORTING es_batch = DATA(ls_batch) ).
  CATCH /scwm/cx_batch_management.
    MESSAGE ID sy-msgid TYPE sy-msgty NUMBER sy-msgno
    WITH sy-msgv1 sy-msgv2 sy-msgv3 sy-msgv4.
ENDTRY.
WRITE: ls_batch-charg, ls_batch-coo.
```

Listing 5.11 Reading Batch

5.13   Read Warehouse Task

Working with warehouse tasks is certainly most often required in custom enhancements of EWM. This section contains function modules for reading warehouse task data.

Function Modules

- /SCWM/TO_GET_WIP: Read warehouse tasks (using selection conditions)
- /SCWM/TO_READ_SINGLE: Read warehouse task (single access)
- /SCWM/TO_READ_MULT: Read warehouse tasks (mass access)

Use in Extended Warehouse Management

- The /SCWM/TO_GET_WIP function module is used in the monitor and allows selection of warehouse tasks based on attributes (product, source bin, etc.).
- The /SCWM/TO_READ_SINGLE and /SCWM/TO_READ_MULT function modules allow the reading of one or more warehouse tasks via a key (warehouse task number and warehouse number).

Recommended Use for Custom Development

For customer reports, monitor nodes, and so on, the use of function module /SCWM/TO_GET_WIP is preferred instead of direct database access. The /SCWM/TO_READ_xxx function modules can be used only if the warehouse task number is available.

5.14   Create/Confirm and Cancel Warehouse Task

This section discusses function modules for any actions performed on warehouse tasks.

Function Modules

- /SCWM/TO_CREATE
- /SCWM/TO_CREATE_MOVE_HU
- /SCWM/TO_CANCEL
- /SCWM/TO_CONFIRM

Program Logic

- The function module /SCWM/TO_CREATE is used to create product warehouse tasks.
- The function module /SCWM/TO_CREATE_MOVE_HU is used to create handling unit warehouse tasks.
- The function module /SCWM/TO_CANCEL is used to cancel warehouse tasks.
- The function module /SCWM/TO_CONFIRM is used to confirm warehouse tasks.

Use in Extended Warehouse Management

These function modules are especially used in RF transactions.

Recommended Use for Custom Development

These function modules are suitable for standalone customer developments, such as programs and (RF) transactions. Per each logical unit of work, only one of these function modules may be called as the first step within the function modules to initialize the internal memory.

In BAdI implementations, you should therefore not use these function modules directly. However, you can use the function modules with the as separate unit addition and send them via qRFC in a separate logical unit of work.

Sample Coding

The sample code in Listing 5.12 shows how a warehouse task is created with the /SCWM/ TO_CREATE function module using a separate queue. For the queue name, the prefix WMZZ is proposed here. The EWM standard uses the queue prefixes WMTH, WMTR, WMTP, and so on. An entire list can be found in the WMEGC type group. In rare cases, it may make sense to use a standard queue prefix for your custom implementation. If you decide to use your own prefix, either use WM*, or check in the queue monitor (Transaction SMQR) to determine whether your queue prefix is registered.

```
REPORT z_move_hu.

PARAMETERS: p_lgnum TYPE /scwm/lgnum,
            p_hu    TYPE /scwm/de_huident.

DATA:  lt_create_hu TYPE /scwm/tt_to_crea_hu.

"1. Set HU WT data (assumption HU moved by next process step)
DATA(ls_create_hu) = VALUE /scwm/s_to_crea_hu( huident = p_hu ).
APPEND ls_create_hu TO lt_create_hu.
"2. Set queue name
CONCATENATE 'WMZZ' p_lgnum p_hu INTO DATA(queue).
DATA(ls_queue) = VALUE /scwm/s_rfc_queue(
  queue = queue
  mandt = sy-mandt ).
"3. Create queue
CALL FUNCTION 'TRFC_SET_QIN_PROPERTIES'
  EXPORTING
    qin_name = ls_queue-queue.
"4. Create HU WT
CALL FUNCTION '/SCWM/TO_CREATE_MOVE_HU'
  IN BACKGROUND TASK
  AS SEPARATE UNIT
  EXPORTING
    iv_lgnum      = p_lgnum
```

```
       iv_commit_work = abap_true
       iv_bname       = sy-uname
       is_rfc_queue   = ls_queue
       it_create_hu   = lt_create_hu.

COMMIT WORK.
```

Listing 5.12 Create Handling Unit Warehouse Task via qRFC

5.15   Select Handling Units from Database

Handling units are core objects in warehouse management. Consider the function module in this section for reading handling unit data in your project.

Function Module

- /SCWM/HU_SELECT_GEN

Program Logic

With about 60 selection criteria for the handling unit, the function module interface is very powerful. Depending on the selection conditions being supplied by the caller, the number of hits for the handling units will be determined by complex database selections. With the IV_FILTER parameter, you can control whether the exact number of hits or, alternatively, the entire handling unit is expected in your export parameters.

Documentation

The IV_HIERARCHY import parameter is documented in Transaction SE37 (Function Builder).

Use in Extended Warehouse Management

The function module is called among others from the warehouse management monitor and the work center transactions. The function module selects the handling units from the database and fills the global handling unit memory.

Recommended Use for Custom Development

The function module is suitable for your own customized reports to select handling units or stocks. In particular, if the handling units are to be determined based on an attribute (e.g., warehouse process or stock identification), then this function module offers numerous possibilities. Check if the function module is suitable for your requirements and avoid programming your own database selections. For simple reading of handling units (e.g., in a BAdI implementation), the function module is not recommended, because the handling unit memory is bypassed.

Sample Coding

In the sample code (see Listing 5.13) the user enters a consolidation group number. According to the entered value, handling units are determined via the /SCWM/HU_ SELECT_GEN function module.

```
REPORT z_select_hu.

TABLES: /scwm/s_quan_att.

PARAMETERS: p_lgnum TYPE /scwm/lgnum
            MEMORY ID /scwm/lgn OBLIGATORY.
SELECT-OPTIONS: sr_dgrp FOR /scwm/s_quan_att-dstgrp.

DATA: lt_huhdr TYPE /scwm/tt_huhdr_int,
      lt_huitm TYPE /scwm/tt_huitm_int,
      lr_dgrp  TYPE rseloption.

/scwm/cl_tm=>set_lgnum( p_lgnum ).
APPEND LINES OF sr_dgrp TO lr_dgrp.

CALL FUNCTION '/SCWM/HU_SELECT_GEN'
  EXPORTING
    iv_lgnum        = p_lgnum
    ir_dstgrp       = lr_dgrp
    iv_filter_items = abap_true
  IMPORTING
    et_huitm        = lt_huitm
    et_huhdr        = lt_huhdr
  EXCEPTIONS
    wrong_input     = 1
    not_possible    = 2
    error           = 3
    OTHERS          = 99.
IF sy-subrc <> 0.
  MESSAGE ID sy-msgid TYPE sy-msgty NUMBER sy-msgno
  WITH sy-msgv1 sy-msgv2 sy-msgv3 sy-msgv4.
ENDIF.

LOOP AT lt_huhdr ASSIGNING FIELD-SYMBOL(<huhdr>).
  WRITE:/ 'HU: ', <huhdr>-huident, 'HU GUID: ', <huhdr>-guid_hu.
ENDLOOP.
```

Listing 5.13 Determine Handling Unit by Consolidation Group

5.16   Create and Change Handling Units

Use the central class in this section for custom creation and change of handling units.

Class

- /SCWM/CL_WM_PACKING

Methods

- GET_INSTANCE (static)
- SET_GLOBAL_FIELDS (static)
- INIT
- GET_HU
- CHANGE_HUHDR
- CREATE_HU
- PACK_HU
- MOVE_HU
- REPACK_STOCK
- SAVE

Program Logic

The methods include simple interfaces. Handling units can be read (GET_HU), created (CREATE_HU), and changed (CHANGE_HUHDR). Stock items can be repacked from the source handling unit or from the storage bin into the destination handling unit (REPACK_STOCK). Handling units, on the other hand, can be nested into other handling units (PACK_HU) or disbanded (MOVE_HU). The methods use the global handling unit memory and access the database only if necessary.

Use in Extended Warehouse Management

The methods are used for packing processes in the work center and in the RF environment.

Recommended Use for Custom Development

Use these methods in BAdIs, reports, as well as in RF transactions. You will receive a separate instance of the class via method GET_INSTANCE. This should be the preferred choice for performance reasons, instead of creating a separate instance on your own. If you are not in a BAdI implementation, begin each logical unit of work with the INIT method and finish it with the SAVE method. Within a BAdI implementation, you should be calling method SET_GLOBAL_FIELDS once at the beginning and passing the warehouse number (see Listing 5.14).

```
/scwm/cl_wm_packing=>set_global_fields(
              iv_lgnum = iv_lgnum ).
/scwm/cl_wm_packing=>get_instance(
  IMPORTING eo_instance = DATA(lo_pack) ).
lo_pack->get_hu(
            EXPORTING
              iv_guid_hu = iv_guid_hu
            IMPORTING
              es_huhdr = DATA(ls_huhdr) ).
IF NOT sy-subrc IS INITIAL.
  io_log->add_message( ).
  RETURN.
ENDIF.
```

Listing 5.14 Read Handling Unit within BAdI Implementation

5.17   Get Stock

This section discusses a class for any custom stock selection requirements in your project.

Class

- /SCWM/CL_MON_STOCK

Methods

- GET_AVAILABLE_STOCK
- GET_STOCK_OVERVIEW
- GET_PHYSICAL_STOCK
- GET_HU
- GET_PHYSICAL_STOCK_ON_HU

Program Logic

Based on various selection options (storage bin, stock, handling unit), the physical or available stock is determined. Depending on the selection conditions supplied by the caller, the stock will be determined via complex database selections (e.g., inner joins).

Use in Extended Warehouse Management

The methods are used in the warehouse management monitor (Transaction /SCWM/ MON) for stock display. Table 5.1 shows the methods used in specific monitor nodes.

Method	Monitor Node
GET_AVAILABLE_STOCK	**Stock and Bin • Available Stock**
GET_PHYSICAL_STOCK	**Stock and Bin • Physical Stock**
GET_STOCK_OVERVIEW	**Stock and Bin • Stock Overview**
GET_HU	**Stock and Bin • Handling Unit**
GET_PHYSICAL_STOCK_ON_HU	**Stock and Bin • HU • Physical Stock**

Table 5.1 Usage of Methods in Warehouse Management Monitor

Recommended Use for Custom Development

If you need to determine stocks in your customer developments, first check if these methods are sufficient for your purposes. The performance of these methods relies on how the selection conditions are used by the caller. This means that the better you restrict the number of hits on a selection, the faster a method provides the results. To increase the performance, it could be helpful to create new indices for the selections. Avoid developing your own selections on the database tables.

Sample Coding

The sample code in Listing 5.15 selects the available stock for a product. Product and warehouse numbers in this example have to be entered by the user.

```
REPORT z_get_avail_stock.

TABLES: /scwm/s_matnr_r.

PARAMETERS: p_lgnum TYPE /scwm/lgnum
            MEMORY ID /scwm/lgn OBLIGATORY.
SELECT-OPTIONS: sr_matnr FOR /scwm/s_matnr_r-low.

DATA(go_mon_stock) = NEW /scwm/cl_mon_stock( iv_lgnum = p_lgnum ).

CALL METHOD go_mon_stock->get_available_stock
  EXPORTING
    iv_skip_bin      = abap_false
    iv_skip_resource = abap_true
    iv_skip_tu       = abap_true
    it_matnr_r       = sr_matnr[]
  IMPORTING
    et_stock_mon     = DATA(gt_stock_mon).

LOOP AT gt_stock_mon ASSIGNING FIELD-SYMBOL(<stock_mon>).
```

```
  WRITE:/ 'MATNR: ', <stock_mon>-matnr,
          'QUAN : ', <stock_mon>-quana,
          'UoM :',   <stock_mon>-altme.
ENDLOOP.
```

Listing 5.15 Determine Available Stock for Product

5.18   Posting Change of Stock

Stock is frequently changed in custom requirements. The function module in this section should be considered for any requirements of stock changes in your project.

Function Module

- /SCWM/STOCK_CHANGE

Program Logic

A posting change can be performed for one or more stock items; for example, a stock type for a product can be changed from **Blocked** (B6) to **Unrestricted-use** (F2). If you are familiar with inventory management in SAP ERP or SAP S/4HANA, this function module can be compared to the BAPI_GOODSMVT_CREATE BAPI there.

Use in Extended Warehouse Management

Transaction /SCWM/POST (Posting Change for Product) shows you the possibilities to change the stock attributes of a product: batch, product, stock type, owner, usage, and so on. After pressing the **Create Posting Change** button, the user input for the posting will be converted to the technical values and passed to the /SCWM/STOCK_CHANGE function module.

Recommended Use for Custom Development

You can use this function module for your own posting changes in the warehouse management monitor in your programs or in RF transactions. We do not recommend using this function module within a BAdI implementation.

Enable the breakpoints for checkpoint group /SCWM/GM in order to understand the usage of function module /SCWM/STOCK_CHANGE in Transaction /SCWM/POST (Posting Change for Product) or to find out which parameters or fields of the interface are to be filled in the respective posting change scenarios.

Sample Coding

The sample code in Listing 5.16 reads a handling unit with item data and posts the determined stock to the new stock type. For the posting change, you must set the source data (see parameter ls_item-source_s) and the destination data (see parameter ls_item-dest_s) properly.

```abap
REPORT z_change_stock.

PARAMETERS: p_lgnum TYPE /scwm/lgnum
              MEMORY ID /scwm/lgn OBLIGATORY,
            p_hu    TYPE /scwm/huident OBLIGATORY,
            p_cat   TYPE /scwm/de_cat OBLIGATORY.

DATA: lt_huitm    TYPE /scwm/tt_huitm_int,
      lt_sitem    TYPE /scwm/tt_spitem,
      lv_severity TYPE bapi_mtype,
      lt_bapiret  TYPE TABLE OF bapiret2,
      lv_item_id  TYPE /lime/line_item_id.

/scwm/cl_tm=>cleanup( EXPORTING iv_lgnum = p_lgnum ).
"1. Read HU Data
CALL FUNCTION '/SCWM/HU_READ'
  EXPORTING
    iv_appl    = wmegc_huappl_wme
    iv_lgnum   = p_lgnum
    iv_huident = p_hu
  IMPORTING
    et_huitm   = lt_huitm
  EXCEPTIONS
    deleted    = 1
    not_found  = 2
    error      = 3.
IF sy-subrc <> 0.
  "Add error handling
ENDIF.
"2. Fill posting change header data
DATA(ls_header) = VALUE /scwm/s_gmheader(
  lgnum      = p_lgnum
  created_by = sy-uname
  code       = '/SCWM/MON' "example tx
  compl      = abap_true
  post       = abap_true ).
GET TIME STAMP FIELD ls_header-created_at.
"3. Fill Pposting change item data
LOOP AT lt_huitm INTO DATA(ls_huitem).
  DATA(ls_sitem) = CORRESPONDING /scwm/s_spitem( ls_huitem ).
  lv_item_id = lv_item_id + 1.
```

```
    ls_sitem-id = lv_item_id.
    ls_sitem-id_group = '000001'.
    ls_sitem-direction = wmegc_lime_post_transfer. "Movement: Transfer 'T'
    ls_sitem-squant_set = abap_true.
    ls_sitem-guid_hu = ls_huitem-guid_parent.
    "Quantities
    IF NOT ls_huitem-quan_t IS INITIAL.
      ls_sitem-t_quan = ls_huitem-quan_t.
    ELSE.
      DATA(ls_quan) = VALUE /scwm/s_quan(
          unit = ls_huitem-meins
          quan = ls_huitem-quan ).
      APPEND ls_quan TO ls_sitem-t_quan.
      CLEAR ls_quan.
    ENDIF.
    ls_sitem-t_serid = ls_huitem-serid.
    MOVE-CORRESPONDING ls_huitem TO ls_sitem-source_s.
    MOVE-CORRESPONDING ls_huitem TO ls_sitem-dest_s.
    "Stock Type
    ls_sitem-dest_s-cat = p_cat.
    "Clear destination data
    CLEAR ls_sitem-dest_s-idx_stock.
    CLEAR ls_sitem-dest_s-guid_stock.
    CLEAR ls_sitem-dest_s-guid_stock0.
    APPEND ls_sitem TO lt_sitem.
ENDLOOP.
"4. Change stock
CALL FUNCTION '/SCWM/STOCK_CHANGE'
  EXPORTING
    is_header    = ls_header
    it_item      = lt_sitem
  IMPORTING
    et_bapiret   = lt_bapiret
    ev_severity  = lv_severity.
IF lv_severity CA wmegc_severity_ea.
  ROLLBACK WORK.
  /scwm/cl_tm=>cleanup( EXPORTING iv_lgnum = p_lgnum ).
  "Add error handling
ELSE.
  COMMIT WORK AND WAIT.
  /scwm/cl_tm=>cleanup( EXPORTING iv_lgnum = p_lgnum ).
ENDIF.
```

Listing 5.16 Posting Change into New Stock Type

5.19   Select, Release, Split, and Merge Waves

Learn how to programmatically work with waves in EWM.

Function Modules

- /SCWM/WAVE_SELECT_EXT
- /SCWM/WAVE_RELEASE_EXT
- /SCWM/WAVE_MERGE_EXT
- /SCWM/WAVE_SPLIT_EXT

Program Logic

- The /SCWM/WAVE_SELECT_EXT function module has over 30 selection criteria as parameters to determine waves and wave items.
- With the /SCWM/WAVE_MERGE_EXT and /SCWM/WAVE_SPLIT_EXT function modules, you can merge or split waves.
- The wave release can be triggered by the /SCWM/WAVE_RELEASE_EXT function module.

Use in Extended Warehouse Management

In the warehouse management monitor, you will find a number of methods for the **Wave** node that use the function modules provided within the /SCWM/WAVE_MGMT_EXT function group.

Recommended Use for Custom Development

The function modules of the /SCWM/WAVE_MGMT_EXT function group are particularly suitable for standalone developments—for example, for your own reports. They should not be used in BAdI implementations, as the function modules all call the /SCWM/CL_TM=>CLEANUP method.

Sample Coding

In Listing 5.17, with Z_WAVE_REPEAT, items of already released waves will be selected and then released again. The report is suitable for scheduling as a background job.

For performance reasons, the report has a limitation on the entry screen regarding the release date as well as a limitation parameter for wave items (see Figure 5.1). If the report is run in a productive system and releases all (faulty) waves again without limitations, the lock table may overflow. The report may be started directly, or it may be scheduled regularly in the background only with very restrictive selection criteria. It is recommended that the **WT Creation** parameter be set to **B** to select only wave items with missing warehouse tasks. We strongly encourage you also to set the release date to no more than three days in the past.

The IV_RELEASE_SINGLE parameter of the /SCWM/WAVE_RELEASE_EXT function module can have a great impact. This parameter controls whether the warehouse order creation runs per wave or for all selected waves.

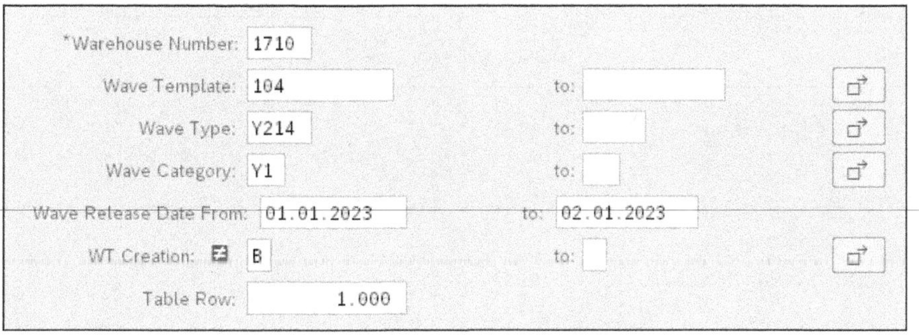

Figure 5.1 Entry Screen for Report Z_WAVE_REPEAT

```
REPORT z_wave_repeat.

TYPE-POOLS wmegc.
DATA: lt_so_stat_cr   TYPE rseloption,
      lt_so_tmplt     TYPE rseloption,
      lt_so_wvtyp     TYPE rseloption,
      lt_so_wvcat     TYPE rseloption,
      lt_so_rlsdt     TYPE rseloption,
      lt_wave_itm     TYPE /scwm/tt_waveitm_int,
      ls_wave_itm     TYPE /scwm/s_waveitm_int,
      lt_bapiret      TYPE bapirettab,
      lt_ordim_o      TYPE /scwm/tt_ordim_o_int,
      lv_wave         TYPE /scwm/de_wave,
      ls_wave_int     TYPE /scwm/s_wavehdr_int,
      lt_wave_itm_ext TYPE /scwm/tt_wave_itm,
      ls_timestamp_r  TYPE /scwm/s_timestamp_r.

"1. Selection Screen
PARAMETERS:
  p_lgnum TYPE /scwm/lgnum MEMORY ID /scwm/lgn OBLIGATORY.
SELECT-OPTIONS:
  so_tmplt FOR ls_wave_int-tmplt,
  so_wvtyp FOR ls_wave_int-wave_type,
  so_wvcat FOR ls_wave_int-wave_cat.

SELECTION-SCREEN BEGIN OF LINE.
  SELECTION-SCREEN COMMENT 1(34) TEXT-001 FOR FIELD p_wrdtf.
  PARAMETERS: p_wrdtf TYPE /scwm/de_rls_date. "Rel. Date from
```

```abap
  SELECTION-SCREEN COMMENT 52(5) TEXT-002 FOR FIELD p_wrdtt.
  PARAMETERS: p_wrdtt TYPE /scwm/de_rls_date. "Rel. Date to
SELECTION-SCREEN END OF LINE.

SELECT-OPTIONS: so_stcr FOR ls_wave_itm-stat_cr.
PARAMETERS: p_thresh TYPE sy-tabix DEFAULT '1000'.

START-OF-SELECTION.
  CLEAR: lt_so_tmplt, lt_so_wvtyp, lt_so_wvcat,
         lt_so_stat_cr, lt_so_rlsdt, lt_wave_itm_ext,
         ls_timestamp_r.
  APPEND LINES OF so_tmplt TO lt_so_tmplt.
  APPEND LINES OF so_wvtyp TO lt_so_wvtyp.
  APPEND LINES OF so_wvcat TO lt_so_wvcat.
  APPEND LINES OF so_stcr TO lt_so_stat_cr.
  "Convert date & time to time stamp
  IF p_wrdtf IS NOT INITIAL OR
     p_wrdtt IS NOT INITIAL.
    DATA(ls_dattim_from) = VALUE /scwm/s_date_time( date = p_wrdtf ).
    DATA(ls_dattim_to)   = VALUE /scwm/s_date_time( date = p_wrdtt ).
    CALL FUNCTION '/SCWM/CONVERT_DATE_TIME'
      EXPORTING
        iv_lgnum          = p_lgnum
        is_dattim_from    = ls_dattim_from
        is_dattim_to      = ls_dattim_to
      IMPORTING
        es_timestamp_range = ls_timestamp_r
      EXCEPTIONS
        input_error       = 1
        data_not_found    = 2
        OTHERS            = 3.
    IF sy-subrc > 0.
      MESSAGE ID sy-msgid TYPE sy-msgty NUMBER sy-msgno
        WITH sy-msgv1 sy-msgv2 sy-msgv3 sy-msgv4.
    ENDIF.
    DATA(ls_so) = CORRESPONDING rsdsselopt( ls_timestamp_r ).
    APPEND ls_so TO lt_so_rlsdt.
  ENDIF.

  IF lt_so_stat_cr IS INITIAL AND
     lt_so_rlsdt IS INITIAL.
    RETURN. "input missing
  ENDIF.
  "2. Select failed wave items up to threshold
```

```
CALL FUNCTION '/SCWM/WAVE_SELECT_EXT'
  EXPORTING
    iv_lgnum       = p_lgnum
    iv_rdoccat     = wmegc_doccat_pdo
    ir_tmplt       = lt_so_tmplt
    ir_wave_type   = lt_so_wvtyp
    ir_wave_cat    = lt_so_wvcat
    ir_stat_cr     = lt_so_stat_cr
    ir_released_at = lt_so_rlsdt
  IMPORTING
    et_waveitm     = lt_wave_itm.
SORT lt_wave_itm BY wave wave_itm ASCENDING.
LOOP AT lt_wave_itm ASSIGNING FIELD-SYMBOL(<wave_itm>).
  DATA(lv_tabix) = sy-tabix.
  IF lv_wave <> <wave_itm>-wave AND
  lv_tabix > p_thresh.
    EXIT.
  ENDIF.

  DATA(ls_wave_itm_ext) = CORRESPONDING /scwm/s_wave_itm( ls_wave_itm ).
  APPEND ls_wave_itm_ext TO lt_wave_itm_ext.
  lv_wave = ls_wave_itm-wave.
  CLEAR ls_wave_itm_ext.
ENDLOOP.
"3. Release waves again
CALL FUNCTION '/SCWM/WAVE_RELEASE_EXT'
  EXPORTING
    iv_lgnum       = p_lgnum
    iv_rdoccat     = wmegc_doccat_pdo
    it_wave_itm    = lt_wave_itm_ext
    iv_immediate   = abap_true
    iv_update_task = abap_true
    iv_commit_work = abap_true
  IMPORTING
    et_ordim_o     = lt_ordim_o
    et_bapiret     = lt_bapiret.
"4. Write messages for batch job output in spool
WRITE: / 'Wave-items released: ', lv_tabix.
LOOP AT lt_ordim_o ASSIGNING FIELD-SYMBOL(<ordim_o>).
  WRITE: / 'Warehouse Task ' ,
  <ordim_o>-tanum , ' created'.
ENDLOOP.
LOOP AT lt_bapiret ASSIGNING FIELD-SYMBOL(<bapiret>) WHERE type CA 'EAX'.
  MESSAGE ID <bapiret>-id TYPE <bapiret>-type
```

```
  NUMBER <bapiret>-number WITH <bapiret>-message_v1
  <bapiret>-message_v2 <bapiret>-message_v3
  <bapiret>-message_v4 INTO DATA(lv_msgtxt).
  WRITE:/ 'Error ' , lv_msgtxt.
ENDLOOP.
```

Listing 5.17 Wave Release via Report Z_WAVE_REPEAT

5.20 Get Transportation Units

Consider the classes and example code in this section when reading transportation units.

Classes

- /SCWM/CL_SR_TU_QUERY
- /SCWM/CL_SR_DB_TU

Program Logic

The selection conditions (handling unit, door, etc.) are passed via the methods of class /SCWM/CL_SR_TU_QUERY to a query instance. This query instance then has to be passed as a parameter to the /SCWM/CL_SR_DB_TU=>READ_SR_ACTIVITY database selection method. Then you get a table of transportation units, including the unique key (internal transportation unit number, shipping and receiving activity number). If you already know the unique key of a transportation unit, you can call the /SCWM/CL_SR_DB_TU=>READ_SR_ACT_BY_NUM method. This method searches the transportation unit first in the buffer before a database selection is performed.

Use in Extended Warehouse Management

The methods are used, among other options, for the selection of transportation units in the EWM monitor.

Recommended Use for Custom Development

The selection of transportation units can be used in customized reports as well as in BAdI implementations. Make sure when using the /SCWM/CL_SR_DB_TU=>READ_SR_ACTIVITY method that the selection is limited in an optimal way; that is, the number of hits is small. Listing 5.18 shows an example of a transportation unit query.

Transportation units are groupings of handling units. Handling unit items reference delivery items. Thus, the selection of a transportation unit can result in a selection of all dependent objects.

```abap
REPORT z_read_tu.

DATA: ls_sel_hu         TYPE /scwm/s_sel_huident.

PARAMETERS:     p_lgnum TYPE /scwm/lgnum OBLIGATORY.
SELECT-OPTIONS: s_hu    FOR  ls_sel_hu-low.

"1. Create query instance for warehouse and HU
DATA(lo_log)      = NEW /scwm/cl_log( ).
DATA(lo_tu_query) = NEW /scwm/cl_sr_tu_query(
  iv_sel_start = wmesr_ass_start_min
  iv_sel_end   = wmesr_ass_end_max
  io_log       = lo_log ).
DATA(ls_sel_whse) = VALUE /scwm/s_sel_whse(
  sign   = wmesr_sel_include
  option = wmesr_sel_equal
  low    = p_lgnum ).
lo_tu_query->add_whse( is_whse = ls_sel_whse ).
LOOP AT s_hu.
  CLEAR: ls_sel_hu.
  ls_sel_hu = CORRESPONDING #( s_hu ).
  lo_tu_query->add_huident( is_sel_huident = ls_sel_hu ).
ENDLOOP.

"2. Select transportation units from database
TRY.
    /scwm/cl_sr_db_tu=>read_sr_activity(
      EXPORTING
        io_tu_query = lo_tu_query
        io_log = lo_log
      IMPORTING
        et_tu_sr_act = DATA(lt_tu_sr_act) ).
  CATCH /scwm/cx_sr_error .
    MESSAGE e524(/scwm/shp_rcv).
ENDTRY.

LOOP AT lt_tu_sr_act ASSIGNING FIELD-SYMBOL(<tu_sr_act>).
  WRITE:/ <tu_sr_act>-tu_num,
          <tu_sr_act>-tu_sr_act_num.
ENDLOOP.
```

Listing 5.18 Determine Transportation Unit Based on Assigned Handling Unit

5.21   Change Transportation Unit

Consider the methods in this section for your custom changes to transportation units.

Classes

- /SCWM/CL_SR_BO
- /SCWM/CL_SR_BOM

Methods

- GET_DATA
- SET_*
- SAVE

Program Logic

The methods of these classes read a transportation unit from the database or from the buffer. Attributes of the transportation unit can be changed in the SET_* methods.

Use in Extended Warehouse Management

The methods are used, for example, in Transaction /SCWM/TU (Maintain Transportation Unit) and in the RF environment (load/unload).

Recommended Use for Custom Development

Use these methods in your own customized reports or RF applications, similar to the example in Listing 5.19. Within a BAdI implementation, the SAVE method should not be called.

```
REPORT z_change_tu.

PARAMETERS: p_tu_sr TYPE /scwm/de_tu_sr_act_num OBLIGATORY.

TRY.
    "1. Get TU
    DATA(lo_bom) = /scwm/cl_sr_bom=>get_instance( ).
    DATA(lo_bo_tu) = lo_bom->get_bo_tu_by_act_id( p_tu_sr ).
    CALL METHOD lo_bo_tu->get_data
      IMPORTING
        es_bo_tu_data = DATA(ls_tu).
    "2. Change TU license plate
    ls_tu-lic_plate = '1234'.
    CALL METHOD lo_bo_tu->set_tu_data
      EXPORTING
        is_bo_tu_data = ls_tu.
    lo_bom->save( ).
```

```
  CATCH /scwm/cx_sr_error.
    ROLLBACK WORK.
    /scwm/cl_tm=>cleanup( ).
    RETURN.
ENDTRY.
COMMIT WORK AND WAIT.
/scwm/cl_tm=>cleanup( ).
```

Listing 5.19 Change Custom Transportation Unit Fields

5.22 Read and Determine Packaging Specifications

Packaging specifications are frequently used in EWM processes to determine packaging materials or container quantities. The function modules in this section can be used for these purposes.

Function Modules

- /SCWM/API_PACKSPEC_GETLIST
- /SCWM/API_PACKSPEC_READ
- /SCWM/PS_FIND_EVALUATE_MULTI

Program Logic

- The /SCWM/API_PACKSPEC_GETLIST function module determines a list of packaging specification keys upon different selection criteria (packaging specification identification, status, packaging specification group, etc.) from the database.
- The /SCWM/API_PACKSPEC_READ function module reads complete packaging specifications from memory or from the database and buffers, if necessary.
- The /SCWM/PS_FIND_EVALUATE_MULTI function module determines valid packaging specifications upon a scheme of the condition technique and the fields from the field catalog (product, warehouse number, ship-to party, etc.).

Use in Extended Warehouse Management

The API function modules are used in Transaction /SCWM/PACKSPEC (Maintain a Pack Specification) on the entry screen for determining the packaging specifications. To locate the packaging specification (automatic packaging, warehouse task, slotting, etc.), function module /SCWM/PS_FIND_EVALUATE_MULTI is recommended.

Recommended Use for Custom Development

The function modules are suitable for your own customized programs, as well as to realize your own determination of packaging specifications upon a new scheme.

5.23 Create/Change/Copy/Delete Packaging Specifications

Consider the function modules in this section for working with packaging specifications programmatically.

Function Modules

- /SCWM/API_PACKSPEC_CREATE
- /SCWM/API_PACKSPEC_CHANGE
- /SCWM/API_PACKSPEC_COPY
- /SCWM/API_PACKSPEC_DELETE

Program Logic

This API function modules can create packing specifications as well as modify, copy, and delete them.

Use in Extended Warehouse Management

These API function modules are, among others, used in the report for initial upload of packaging specifications using Transaction /SCWM/IPU.

Recommended Use for Custom Development

The function modules are suitable for your own programs.

5.24 Service Class for Radio Frequency Framework

Consider a closer look at the class in this section when doing customizations of the mobile transactions of the RF framework.

Class

- /SCWM/CL_RF_BLL_SRVC

Methods

- GET_ACT_FIELD
- SET_FCODE
- SET_SCRELM_INPUT_OFF
- SET_SCRELM_INPUT_ON

Program Logic

The methods of this service class provide simple interfaces and enable you to intervene in the process and in the presentation of the RF transactions:

- The GET_ACT_FIELD method returns the field name of the current user-processed input field.
- Use the SET_SCRELM_INPUT_OFF and SET_SCRELM_INPUT_ON methods to control whether certain fields are ready for input or not.
- With the SET_FCODE method, it is possible to overrule the Customizing setting for the follow-up function.

Use in Extended Warehouse Management

The methods are used within both the RF framework and the RF applications for putaway, picking, and so on.

Recommended Use for Custom Development

Simple RF transactions go without these methods so long as the application function modules are used properly. However, if you face the limits of RF Customizing, you can use these methods.

5.25 Summary

In this chapter, we provided an overview of the central function modules and methods used in EWM. This should give you a good understanding of the use of these functions in EWM and their calls in possible custom developments. We also provided various coding examples and some hints of what to keep in mind during the implementation.

In the next chapter, we will introduce a list of selected BAdIs within the core applications of EWM.

Chapter 6
Useful Business Add-Ins within Extended Warehouse Management

Most EWM implementations make use of Business Add-Ins. This chapter provides information on selected BAdIs within the core modules of EWM.

In the previous chapters, you learned about the usage of frequently available elements of the SAP Enhancement Framework, called Business Add-Ins (BAdIs). In this chapter, we provide a list of additional BAdIs available in EWM. Due to the large number of BAdIs available, we cannot present a complete list of all BAdIs and will therefore limit ourselves to some focus areas around delivery processing and core warehouse logistics. These include the following:

- Delivery processing (Section 6.1)
- Waves (Section 6.2)
- Warehouse tasks (Section 6.3)
- Warehouse orders (Section 6.4)
- Exception handling (Section 6.5)

If you are already using other SAP products, such as SAP S/4HANA, you have certainly gained experience with BAdI-based enhancements. EWM, however, might surprise you with its well-structured BAdI search option and documentation. The BAdIs are not only clearly assigned to meaningful enhancement spots, but also mostly documented in much detail. You can find this documentation in the IMG under **Extended Warehouse Management Business Add-Ins (BAdIs) for Extended Warehouse** or in the interface associated with the BAdI (Transaction SE24). Occasionally, there might even be sample implementations available.

[«]

Overview of Available Business Add-Ins in Extended Warehouse Management

In addition to the view of the IMG, we recommend getting an overview of available BAdIs by taking a look at enhancement spots for EWM. Call Transaction SE20 and select the composite enhancement spot, /SCWM/ESC_MAIN. This composite enhancement spot again consists of an additional level of composite enhancement spots, which are broken down by functional areas or development packages. By double-clicking one of these composite enhancement spots, you will be presented with a list of included enhancement spots on the next level. With another double-click, you will then be taken to the BAdI definitions contained in the selected enhancement spot.

In EWM, there are no user exits used. Custom enhancements are only possible through BAdIs as part of the Enhancement Framework.

Introduction to Business Add-In Implementation

We assume that you have already implemented one or more BAdIs. Therefore, we do not introduce working with BAdIs at this point. A good introduction to the implementation of BAdIs can be found in the SAP Help documentation under **Enhancement Framework** (see *http://help.sap.com*).

In the following sections, we will describe the BAdIs using this common scheme:

- **Composite Enhancement Spot <Name>**
  You can find a BAdI in Transaction SE20 linked to an enhancement spot that is assigned to this composite enhancement spot.

- **Enhancement Spot <Name>**
  You can find the BAdI in Transaction SE18 while selecting by this enhancement spot.

- **BAdI <Name>**
  You can find the BAdI by this name in Transaction SE18.

- **Functional Description**
  The function of the BAdI will be summarized in this paragraph. This should help you understand if the BAdI is applicable to your planned enhancement. If available, you can find additional details on the BAdI in its own documentation within the Customizing documentation or in the technical documentation of the underlying interface.

- **Methods <Name>**
  The name of the methods included in the BAdI will likely already give some idea of what it is to be used for. This can be of some help when searching for the right enhancement option.

- **Calling Spot**
  Here you will find applications or development objects that will call the BAdI, similar to a where-used list.

- **Customizing Path <Path>**
  For most BadIs, there will be a Customizing node available that might contain further information for the BAdI itself and that can be used to start its implementation.

6.1   Delivery Processing

Figure 6.1 shows the use of the selected enhancement spots in the flow of the delivery (or warehouse request) processing. The enhancement spots are listed chronologically according to the document flow of the delivery (or warehouse request) document in EWM from one to ten, corresponding to Section 6.1.1 through Section 6.1.10.

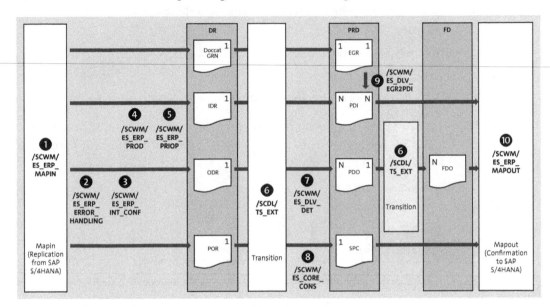

Figure 6.1 Selected Enhancement Spots in Delivery Processing

The document flow starts with the replication of the document from SAP ERP or SAP S/4HANA in the EWM inbound processing (MAPIN), passes through one or two follow-up documents (transition) depending on its category, and extends toward the confirmation back to SAP ERP or SAP S/4HANA (MAPOUT). The available enhancement spots are based on the respective processing times of the delivery request, the processing delivery, and the confirmed or final delivery.

The enhancement spots in this section belong to the /SCWM/ESC_ERP and /SCWM/ESC_DLV composite enhancement spots.

6.1.1   Enhancement Spot /SCWM/ES_ERP_MAPIN

BAdIs for incoming messages from the SAP S/4HANA system (customer exits) are as follows:

- /SCWM/EX_ERP_MAPIN_ID_REPLACE
- /SCWM/EX_ERP_MAPIN_ID_SAVEREPL
- /SCWM/EX_ERP_MAPIN_OD_SAVEREPL
- /SCWM/EX_ERP_MAPIN_OD_CHANGE

- `/SCWM/EX_ERP_MAPIN_MFG`
- `/SCWM/EX_ERP_MFG_DATE_CMP`

In these BAdIs, you can influence the mapping of SAP S/4HANA delivery and manufacturing order data to EWM delivery and production material request data. You can pass, for example, custom data from the extension structures to customer-specific fields of the EWM delivery and production material request or determine dates for staging of components using custom logic.

The important methods of these BAdIs are as follows:

- `MAPIN`: Serves customer changes
- `GET_STAGING_DATE`: Dates for staging of components (in `/SCWM/EX_ERP_MFG_DATE_CMP`)

The BAdIs will be called in inbound message processing shortly before handing over the SAP S/4HANA delivery data to EWM delivery processing. This will happen in method `CALL_MAPIN_BADI` of the following classes:

- `/SCWM/CL_MAPIN_ID_REPLACE`
- `/SCWM/CL_MAPIN_ID_SAVEREPLICA`
- `/SCWM/CL_MAPIN_OD_SAVEREPLICA`
- `/SCWM/CL_MAPIN_OD_CHANGE`

For production material requests, the following methods are used:

- `/SCWM/CL_MAPIN_PRODUCTION~CREATE_WHR`
- `/SCWM/CL_MAPIN_PRODUCTION~MAP_COMP_DATES`

The relevant Customizing paths are as follows:

- **Interfaces • ERP Integration • Inbound Messages from ERP System to EWM**
- **Interfaces • ERP Integration • Production**

6.1.2   Enhancement Spot /SCWM/ES_ERP_ERROR_HANDLING

This enhancement spot uses the `/SCWM/EX_ERP_ERROR_QUEUE` BAdI (Additional Functions Error in qRFC). With this BAdI, you can add additional functions due to an incorrect processing of inbound messages in EWM. You can, for example, implement a function to trigger an alert or workflow that will promptly inform the administrator of an unprocessed message, similar to the standard available message processing alerting. Note that hanging queue entries can also be displayed in the warehouse monitor.

The important method of this BAdI is `PUBLISH_Q_ERROR` (reaction to errors in processing inbound RFC delivery).

This BAdI is called for an error processed in the message handling in method `CREATE_APPL_LOG` of class `/SCWM/CL_MESS_MAPIN`.

The relevant Customizing path is **Interfaces • ERP Integration • Delivery Processing • BAdI: Additional Functions Error in qRFC**.

How-to Guide on qRFC Message Alerting

For more information on how to set up the EWM standard available qRFC message alerting, check the EWM how-to guide named *How to Configure Email Alerting for qRFC: Simplified qRFC Monitoring*. You can find it in the list of EWM how-to guides from the SAP Support Wiki at *https://wiki.scn.sap.com/wiki/display/SCM/How-To+Guides+for+SAP+EWM*.

6.1.3 Enhancement Spot /SCWM/ES_ERP_INT_CONF

This enhancement spot uses the /SCWM/EX_ERP_INT_CONF BAdI (ERP-WME Integration Document and Item Types). This BAdI is used for mapping the document and item types of the SAP S/4HANA delivery to the EWM delivery or warehouse request. By default, the /SCWM/CL_DEF_IM_ERP_INT_CONF BAdI implementation is active. The default code is automatically executed. Either a customer implementation or the default implementation will be run through. This is why you should include the standard processing logic within your implementation in case your custom logic will not return any document or item type.

The important methods of these BAdIs are as follows:

- DET_DOCTYPE (determine document type for delivery from SAP S/4HANA system)
- DET_ITEMTYPE (determine item type for delivery from SAP S/4HANA system)
- DET_ERP_DLVTYPE (determine SAP S/4HANA delivery type for EWM document type)

The DET_DOCTYPE and DET_ITEMTYPE methods are called sequentially during inbound processing of delivery messages from SAP S/4HANA to EWM. They are run through once for each item. The DET_ERP_DLVTYPE method is called during replication of EWM-created deliveries to SAP S/4HANA and is used for the determination of document and item types.

The relevant Customizing path is **Interfaces • ERP Integration • BAdI: ERP–EWM Integration for the Delivery**.

6.1.4 Enhancement Spot /SCWM/ES_ERP_PROD

This enhancement spot uses the /SCWM/EX_ERP_PROD BAdI (Create Product Master Anew in Mapping Inbound Processing). With this BAdI, you can create a product master record within inbound message processing of an inbound delivery. It includes example implementation /SCWM/CL_EI_ERP_PROD for your reference.

The important methods of this BAdI are as follows:

- PRODUCT_ADD (collect data for creating product)
- PRODUCT_CREATE (create products)

The BAdI is called during inbound message processing in method CREATE_DR of class /SCWM/CL_MAPIN_ID_SAVEREPLICA.

The relevant Customizing path is **Interfaces • ERP Integration • Inbound Messages from ERP System to EWM • BAdI: Handle Missing Product Master Data in Mapping Inbound Processing**.

6.1.5   Enhancement Spot /SCWM/ES_ERP_PRIOP

This enhancement spot uses the /SCWM/EX_ERP_PRIOP BAdI (Update PrioP on Subsequent Documents). With this BAdI, you can change the priority points in the follow-on documents of the inbound warehouse request—for example, the warehouse task or handling unit.

The important method of this BAdI is SAVE (saves priority points on subsequent documents).

The BAdI is run when an SAP S/4HANA inbound delivery subsequently receives a priority points update from SAP Advanced Planning and Optimization (SAP APO) and will generate update message processing for the corresponding inbound warehouse request in EWM. The BAdI is called in method CALL_BADI of class /SCWM/CL_MAPIN_ID_PRIOP.

The relevant Customizing path is **Interfaces • ERP Integration • Inbound Messages from ERP System to EWM • BAdI: Update Priority on Follow-On Documents**.

6.1.6   Enhancement Spot /SCDL/TS_EXT

This enhancement spot uses the following BAdIs:

- /SCDL/TS_DATA_COPY (Inbound Warehouse Request)
- /SCDL/TS_DATA_COPY_O (Outbound Warehouse Request)

With these BAdIs, you can control the transfer of data between the delivery document types. You will need to implement the methods of the respective aspects. An implementation is only necessary when the custom fields of subsequent document types carry different naming. The data exchange between fields with identical naming is automatically done. An example case would be the transfer of customer-specific data from warehouse request notifications to processing documents for header data (MODIFY_EEW_HEAD) or item data (MODIFY_EEW_ITEM). Be aware that these BAdIs will only be called in message inbound processing if delivery requests are not skipped, meaning you are using decentralized EWM and have not activated the skip request in Customizing.

The important methods of these BAdIs are as follows:

- MODIFY_DATE_HEAD
- MODIFY_REFDOC_HEAD
- MODIFY_PARTYLOC_HEAD
- MODIFY_INCOTERMS_HEAD
- MODIFY_TRANSP_HEAD
- MODIFY_DATE_ITEM
- MODIFY_REFDOC_ITEM
- MODIFY_STOCK_ITEM
- MODIFY_PARTYLOC_ITEM
- MODIFY_PRODUCT_ITEM
- MODIFY_DELTERM_ITEM
- MODIFY_HU
- MODIFY_PRCODES_ITEM
- MODIFY_EEW_HEAD
- MODIFY_EEW_ITEM
- MODIFY_PRODUCT_ITEM_EXT
- MODIFY_ADDMEAS_HEAD
- MODIFY_ADDMEAS_ITEM

The BAdIs are run through in the transition service called at creation of follow-on documents in warehouse request processing. The BAdI methods are called in the corresponding methods of classes /SCDL/CL_TS_DT*.

The relevant Customizing path is **Cross-Process Settings • Delivery – Warehouse Request • BAdI: Data Transfer from Source to Destination Object (Inbound Process)** and **BAdI: Data Transfer from Source to Destination Object (Outbound Process)**.

6.1.7   Enhancement Spot /SCWM/ES_DLV_DET

This enhancement spot uses the following BAdIs:

- /SCWM/EX_DLV_AVAIL_CHECK (Availability Check Processing of Input and Output Data)
- /SCWM/EX_DLV_DET_ADDMEAS (Processing of Additional Quantities)
- /SCWM/EX_DLV_DET_AFTER_CHANGE (Determination According to Timespot Create/Change)
- /SCWM/EX_DLV_DET_AFTER_SAVE (Timespot after Transfer of Delivery to Update Task)
- /SCWM/EX_DLV_DET_AT_SAVE (Determination at Timespot Saving)
- /SCWM/EX_DLV_DET_GM_BIN (Determination of Goods Movement Bin)

- /SCWM/EX_DLV_DET_HIER_CORR (Determination of Delivery Quantity Correlation in Hierarchies)

- /SCWM/EX_DLV_DET_LOAD (Determinations According to Timespot Loading (Fields Still Changeable))

- /SCWM/EX_DLV_DET_POD_REL (BAdI: Determine POD Relevance for Delivery Item Created in EWM)

- /SCWM/EX_DLV_DET_PROCTYPE (Determination of Warehouse Process Type)

- /SCWM/EX_DLV_DET_REJ (Scheduling of Job to Set Status DWM)

- /SCWM/EX_DLV_DET_ROUTE (Route Determination and Validation)

With these BAdIs, you can influence different determinations in the warehouse request processing, mostly in the transition from notification to processing document. You can, for example, overwrite the determination of the route, the warehouse process type, or the goods movement bin by custom logic. You may check SAP Note 1064376 for details and example implementations of BAdIs /SCWM/EX_DLV_DET_AFTER_CHANGE and /SCWM/EX_DLV_VAL_VALIDATE.

[»]

> **Method**
>
> See the respective BAdI or interface documentation for further method analysis—specifically, for understanding input and output parameters.

The BAdIs will be called at creation or change of warehouse requests.

The relevant Customizing path is **Cross-Process Settings • Delivery–Warehouse Request • Determinations**.

6.1.8   Enhancement Spot /SCWM/ES_CORE_CONS

For enhancement spot /SCWM/ES_CORE_CONS, we will look at two BAdIs: /SCWM/EX_CORE_CONS and /SCWM/EX_CORE_CONS_ST.

BAdI /SCWM/EX_CORE_CONS

The first BAdI we will look at is /SCWM/EX_CORE_CONS (Determine Consolidation Group). With this BadI, you can determine the consolidation group for an outbound delivery item by your own logic. Besides the default parameters of warehouse number, ship-to, route, priority, and door, you can query additional warehouse request data for the determination of the consolidation group.

The important method of this BAdI is DSTGRP (consolidation group).

The BadI is called at the creation of an outbound warehouse request processing document in function module /SCWM/DSTGRP_OUTB_DET.

The relevant Customizing path is **Goods Issue Process • BadI: Define Consolidation Group**.

BadI /SCWM/EX_CORE_CONS_ST

The second BadI we'll look at is /SCWM/EX_CORE_CONS_ST (Definition of Consolidation Group for Stock Transfer). With this BadI, you can determine the consolidation group for a stock transfer delivery item by your own logic. Besides the default parameters of warehouse number, priority, warehouse process type, and document category, you can query additional delivery data for the determination of the consolidation group. Customizing and number ranges for consolidation group determination are available as well. Set changing parameter CV_DSTGRP in your custom implementation following your custom logic.

The important method of this BAdI is DSTGRP (consolidation group).

The BAdI is called at the creation of a stock transfer delivery processing document in local class lcl_st_doc of include /SCWM/LDSTGRPF03, with method call_badi.

The relevant Customizing path is **Internal Warehouse Processes • Stock Transfer • BAdI: Definition of Consolidation Group for Stock Transfer.**

6.1.9 Enhancement Spot /SCWM/ES_DLV_EGR2PDI

This enhancement spot contains the following BAdIs:

- /SCWM/EX_DLV_EGR2PDI_AFTERCOPY (Copy Additional Data from Expected GR to Inbound Delivery)
- /SCWM/EX_DLV_EGR2PDI_COMPARE (Fill Additional Fields for Comparing Expected GR/ Inbound Delivery)
- /SCWM/EX_DLV_EGR2PDI_TEXT (Manipulate Texts from Expected Goods Receipt During Inbound Delivery Creation)
- /SCWM/EX_DLV_EGR2PDI_VAL (Validate Expected GR/Inbound Delivery before Creation of Inbound Delivery from Expected GR)

With these BAdIs, you can copy additional data from an expected goods receipt document to an inbound warehouse request and control the transfer of custom fields as well as the usage of texts.

> **Method**
>
> See the respective BAdI or interface documentation for further method analysis—specifically, for understanding input and output parameters.

The BAdIs are called when transferring an expected goods receipt document to an inbound warehouse request in the corresponding methods of class /SCWM/CL_DLV_ EGR2PDI.

The relevant Customizing path is **Goods Receipt Process • Expected Goods Receipt.**

6.1.10 Enhancement Spot /SCWM/ES_ERP_MAPOUT

All of the BAdIs discussed in this section are called when saving the respective warehouse request document. The relevant Customizing path for these BAdIs is **Interfaces • ERP Integration • Outbound Messages from EWM to ERP System**.

We'll look at three specific BAdIs (/SCWM/EX_ERP_MAPOUT_DELINFO, /SCWM/EX_MSL_MESSAGE_SORT, /SCWM/EX_VAL_PROD_REF) as well as two groups of BAdIs in the following sections.

BAdI /SCWM/EX_ERP_MAPOUT_DELINFO

The first BAdI we'll look at is /SCWM/EX_ERP_MAPOUT_DELINFO (Assigns a Message to a Treatment Class). This BAdI can be used to assign a processing class to a custom message type in the integration of EWM with an SAP S/4HANA system. New message types are determined through the corresponding BAdIs named /SCWM/EX_MSL_FILL_*. You can assign a processing class that is available by standard means or one that you have created. The custom class must implement the interface /SCWM/IF_MAPOUT_DELINFO. For the assignment of a class, see examples in method PROCESS_MESSAGES of class /SCWM/CL_MAPOUT_MSG_DELINFO.

The important method of this BAdI is ASSIGN_CLASS (assigns a message to a treatment class).

BAdI /SCWM/EX_MSL_MESSAGE_SORT

Next, let's look at the BAdI /SCWM/EX_MSL_MESSAGE_SORT (Sorts Determined Messages). You can use this BAdI to sort the custom message types. You determine one or more message types in the /SCWM/CL_DLV_MSL_FILL BAdI. In addition to these custom message types, you can also determine standard message types. These are sorted in method SORT_INSERT_MESSAGES of class /SCWM/CL_DLV_MSG_LOG. The sorting will follow a ranking of the time_stamp field. You will need to assign a rank to your message type, which should be made up from a whole (positive) number. If you do not assign a rank, the system will assign rank 999 to your message type. The message types (standard and custom) will be sorted according to their rank. The associated SAP S/4HANA messages will be sent out to the SAP S/4HANA system in exactly this order.

The important method of this BAdI is SORT (sorts determined messages).

BAdI /SCWM/EX_VAL_PROD_REF

Finally, let's look at the /SCWM/EX_VAL_PROD_REF BAdI (Production Data Validation). This BAdI is called when saving a manually created inbound warehouse request. The BAdI checks if the reference for production is valid. The validation can be carried out within EWM or in SAP S/4HANA. During the EWM-based validation, a search is carried out in the database for warehouse request items with the same reference for production. If this reference exists, the validation has been successful. For SAP S/4HANA–based validation, the /SPE/INB_GR_PROD_CHECK function module is called in the SAP S/4HANA system. This function module checks whether a reference for production exists and compares the open SAP S/4HANA quantities with the EWM warehouse request quantities. If the validation in SAP S/4HANA is not successful, SAP S/4HANA sends detailed information back to EWM.

The important method of this BAdI is CHECK_REFERENCE (checks production reference).

BAdIs to Influence the Data Transfer of Messages

The /SCWM/ES_ERP_MAPOUT enhancement spot contains two main groups of BAdIs. With the first group of BAdIs (MAPOUT), you can influence the data transfer of the messages from EWM to SAP S/4HANA, as follows:

- /SCWM/EX_ERP_MAPOUT_ID_CONFDEC (BAdI for GR of Inbound Deliveries)
- /SCWM/EX_ERP_MAPOUT_ID_REPLACE (BAdI for ID REPLACE)
- /SCWM/EX_ERP_MAPOUT_ID_REPLICA (BAdI for ID REPLICA)
- /SCWM/EX_ERP_MAPOUT_ID_SPLIT (BAdI for ID SPLIT DEC)
- /SCWM/EX_ERP_MAPOUT_OD_CHANGE (BAdI for OD CHANGE)
- /SCWM/EX_ERP_MAPOUT_OD_CONFDEC (BAdI for OD CONF DEC)
- /SCWM/EX_ERP_MAPOUT_OD_REPLICA (BAdI for OD REPLICA)
- /SCWM/EX_ERP_MAPOUT_OD_SPLIT (BAdI for OD SPLIT DEC)

All BAdIs include a method named MAPOUT.

BAdIs to Fill the Message Log with Custom Logic

The other group of BAdIs (MSL_FILL) allows you to fill the message log by custom logic. Messages to SAP S/4HANA are planned in the message log from where the sending will be controlled. The following individual BAdIs relate to the various document types and are defined by the same interface, /SCWM/IF_EX_MSL_FILL:

- /SCWM/EX_MSL_FILL_FD (BAdI for FD Message Log Determination)
- /SCWM/EX_MSL_FILL_PRD_INB (BAdI for PRDI Message Log Determination)
- /SCWM/EX_MSL_FILL_PRD_OUTB (BAdI for PRDO Message Log Determination)
- /SCWM/EX_MSL_FILL_SPC (BAdI for SPC Message Log Determination)

This interface includes the DET_ERP_MESSAGES method.

6.2   Waves

Automatic wave planning can perform a wave determination and group outbound delivery orders, posting changes, or stock transfer items optimally into waves as wave items following the rules defined in the so-called wave templates. Next to extensive Customizing options you can use two BAdIs in wave planning to tailor this process to your own needs, as shown in Figure 6.2. The three BAdI methods that are generally available for wave processing can be found in two of three processing blocks of wave management.

Warehouse request line items can be automatically assigned to waves. The wave template, determined based on condition technique, defines the respective rules for this grouping. The values of additional fields that should be used in the condition technique may be determined using a BAdI. Next to this, you can influence the result of automatic wave assignment. Finally, you can change wave header and item fields at the time of saving the wave. While debugging wave management, activation of the /SCWM/ WAVE checkpoint group can be helpful. Enhancement spot /SCWM/ES_WAVE belongs to composite enhancement spot /SCWM_ESC_CORE.

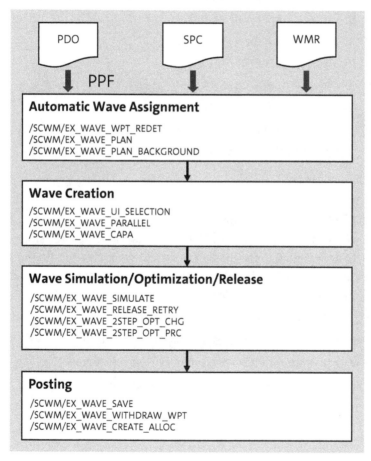

Figure 6.2 BAdIs in Wave Management

6.2.1   Enhancement Spot /SCWM/ES_WAVE

In the following sections, we'll discuss 13 BAdIs that are contained within enhancement spot /SCWM/ES_WAVE.

BAdI /SCWM/EX_WAVE_WPT_REDET

Let's start by looking at the /SCWM/EX_WAVE_WPT_REDET BAdI (Activation of Warehouse Process Type Redetermination before Wave Determination). With this BAdI, you can trigger a redetermination of the warehouse process type before delivery items are added to a wave. The redetermination is performed only if the wave determination takes place in the Post Processing Framework (PPF). You can use method IS_REDETERMI-NATION_REQUIRED to check the header and item information of the delivery and to decide whether the redetermination will be performed. If it will, the warehouse process type will be cleared to initiate a new determination. You can also implement BAdI /SCWM/EX_DLV_DET_PROCTYPE (Determination of Warehouse Process Type) to derive a new warehouse process type based on custom logic. It is required to enable automatic wave creation for the new warehouse process type; otherwise an error is raised.

The important method of this BAdI is IS_REDETERMINATION_REQUIRED; it decides if the warehouse process type redetermination is required.

The BAdI is called during automatic wave determination and assignment in class /SCWM/CL_PROCTY_REDETERMINE.

The relevant Customizing path is **Goods Issue Process • Wave Management • BAdI: Warehouse Process Type Redetermination before Wave Determination**.

BAdI /SCWM/EX_WAVE_PLAN

Now let's look at the /SCWM/EX_WAVE_PLAN BAdI. With this BAdI, you can influence the automatic assignment of warehouse request items to waves.

The important methods of this BAdI are as follows:

- FILL_FIELDS (fill field values)
  With this BAdI method, you can supply values for custom-defined fields of the field catalog for condition techniques used at automatic wave assignment. The CS_FIELD-NAME_VALUE changing parameter has two fields. In field FIELDNAME, the field name of the additionally defined field from the field catalog is supplied. Field VALUE should then contain the appropriate value for the field in order to influence the wave template determination.

- CHANGE_WAVES (change automatic wave assignment)
  The proposed waves are passed into the BAdI method in table CT_WHRITEM_WAVE. Header and item data of the warehouse request and the data of valid wave templates are available as import parameters as well. After the BAdI has been run through, the further wave processing logic tries to assign the warehouse request items to waves from table CT_WHRITEM_WAVE.

The BAdIs are called during automatic wave determination and assignment as performed in methods FILL_FIELDS and ASSIGN_WHR_TO_WAVE of class /SCWM/CL_WAVE_PLAN.

The relevant Customizing path is **Goods Issue Process • Wave Management • BAdI: Wave Planning**.

BAdI /SCWM/EX_WAVE_PLAN_BACKGROUND

With the /SCWM/EX_WAVE_PLAN_BACKGROUND BAdI, you can enhance the selection screen and the logic of report /SCWM/R_WAVE_PLAN_BACKGROUND (Background Wave Generation). An example implementation is available in class /SCWM/CL_EI_WAVE_PLAN_BG. It demonstrates how to enhance the selection of both the warehouse request and the just-in-time (JIT) call. The class also contains example coding for a report that contains the required subscreen for the additional fields in method SCREEN_ENHANCEMENT_EXAMPLE. In the example, the **Priority** and **Control Cycle** fields are added to the selection screen as custom fields. They are ready for input when the document category is WMR (stock transfer delivery); otherwise they are read-only. When the user runs the report, the selections from the custom fields are stored in the instance of /SCWM/CL_EI_WAVE_PLAN_BG. Report /SCWM/R_WAVE_PLAN_BACKGROUND then calls this instance of the BAdI implementation, which adapts the selection criteria to consider the custom fields.

The important methods of this BAdI are as follows:

- CHANGE_WHR_SELECTION (change warehouse request selection-table)
- AT_SELECTION_SCREEN_OUTPUT (handle at selection screen output)
- CHANGE_JIT_SELECT_REQUIRED (change whether JIT call selection is needed)
- CHANGE_JIT_SELECTION (change JIT call selections)
- GET_VARIANT_DATA (get selection data as XString to save it in report variants)
- SET_VARIANT_DATA (set selection data from XString loaded in report variant)

The BAdI methods are called during different stages of report /SCWM/R_WAVE_PLAN_BACKGROUND.

There is no Customizing path for this BAdI.

BAdI /SCWM/EX_WAVE_UI_SELECTION

Next, let's look at the /SCWM/EX_WAVE_UI_SELECTION BAdI (Enhancement of Selection of WRs in Wave UI). With this BAdI, you can enhance the selection screens with custom-specific fields for the selection of warehouse requests in Transaction /SCWM/WAVE (Maintain Waves).

The important method of this BAdI is MODIFY_SELECTIONS (modify selection table).

The BAdI is called in method WHR_QUERY of class /SCWM/CL_WVMGT_SP.

The relevant Customizing path is **Goods Issue Process • Wave Management • BAdI: Enhancement of Selection of WHRs in Waves**.

BAdI /SCWM/EX_WAVE_PARALLEL

Let's look at the /SCWM/EX_WAVE_PARALLEL BAdI (Influence on Parallelization of Waves). With this BAdI, you can change the parallelization settings of wave Customizing more flexibly. You can influence whether the creation and posting of the warehouse tasks will be executed with parallel processes or not. You cannot influence the parallel creation of warehouse orders, however. This can be set in Transaction /SCWM/WOLOG. Check out implementation example class /SCWM/CL_EI_WAVE_PARALLEL.

The important method of this BAdI is CHANGE_PARALLELIZATION (deactivate wave parallelization).

The BAdI is called during the wave release and wave release simulation within function module /SCWM/WAVE_CREATE_TO_1ST_STEP and include /SCWM/LWAVE_MGMT_BASICSF32, subroutine TO_CREATE_WAVE.

The relevant Customizing path is **Goods Issue Process • Wave Management • BAdI: Influence on Parallelization of Waves**.

BAdI /SCWM/EX_WAVE_CAPA

Next is the /SCWM/EX_WAVE_CAPA BAdI (Capacity Check for Waves). With this BAdI, you can influence and change the capacity check during the assignment of delivery items to waves. The BAdI is called for waves that have a wave capacity profile in the following situations:

- Wave creation
- Assignment or reassignment of items to existing waves
- Automatic wave assignment (precheck)
- Changes to wave attributes

The important method of this BAdI is CHECK_CAPA (check capacity of wave).

The BAdI is called within include /SCWM/LWAVE_MGMT_BASICSF43, subroutine CHECK_CAPA.

The relevant Customizing path is **Goods Issue Process • Wave Management • BAdI: Capacity Check for Waves**.

BAdI /SCWM/EX_WAVE_SIMULATE

Now let's look at the /SCWM/EX_WAVE_SIMULATE BAdI (Processing after Wave Simulation). With this BAdI, you can add additional messages in the wave simulation log and influence the simulation status of the wave header. You can also use this BAdI to trigger follow-on actions after the wave simulation. Check example implementation /SCWM/CL_EI_WAVE_SIMULATE. You can use this example implementation to unassign unfulfilled wave items—that is, any wave item without the simulation status **Wave Can Be Fulfilled**. Only successfully simulated wave items remain in the wave. The wave header simulation status is set to green.

The important method of this BAdI is AFTER_SIMULATION (method to change simulation status and add log messages).

The BAdI is called when saving waves within include /SCWM/LWAVE_MGMT_BASICSF24, subroutine WAVE_UPDATE.

The relevant Customizing path is **Goods Issue Process • Wave Management • BAdI: Processing After Wave Simulation**.

BAdI /SCWM/EX_WAVE_RELEASE_RETRY

Let's look at the /SCWM/EX_WAVE_RELEASE_RETRY BAdI (Control of Automatic Wave Release Retry). With this BAdI, you can control if the system should automatically try to release a wave again based on the wave's header and item data. When a wave is released with errors, the system can try to release the wave again automatically at a later point in time. In the standard system, you can define one retry interval per wave template. With this BAdI, it is possible to define whether the wave release should be retried automatically and the period of time the system should wait before retrying.

The important method of this BAdI is CHANGE_RETRY_CONTROL (control automatic wave release retry).

The BAdI is called when saving waves within include /SCWM/LWAVE_MGMT_BASICSF52, subroutine SCHEDULE_RELEASE_RETRY.

The relevant Customizing path is **Goods Issue Process • Wave Management • BAdI: Control of Automatic Wave Release Retry**.

BAdI /SCWM/EX_WAVE_2STEP_OPT_CHG

Let's look at the /SCWM/EX_WAVE_2STEP_OPT_CHG BAdI (Change of Optimization for Two-Step Picking). With this BAdI, you can influence the optimization of two-step picking. Method DISABLE_OPTIMIZATION allows you to skip the optimization for a wave, to provide a list of products that should not be optimized, and to filter the units of measure (UOMs) that can be used in optimization. *Note:* Do not add additional UOMs to changing parameter CT_UOMS_PER_PRODUCT.

Method CHANGE_TWO_STEP_PICKING allows you to change the two-step picking status for each wave item after optimization as well as to set or reset the optimization status of the wave. Changing parameter CV_WAVE_OPTIMIZATION_STATUS must be set to abap_true to take over the changes to the two-step picking indicator in changing parameter CT_WAVE_ITEM_TWO_STEP.

If you clear changing parameter CV_WAVE_OPTIMIZATION_STATUS, all updates in changing parameter CT_WAVE_ITEM_TWO_STEP are disregarded. This method is called even if the optimization from the first method is skipped. Therefore, you can implement a simple optimization algorithm with this BAdI by always skipping the optimization and programming-specific logic in method CHANGE_TWO_STEP_PICKING. Example implementation class /SCWM/CL_EI_WAVE_2STEP_OPT_CHG is available for your further reference.

The important methods of this BAdI are as follows:

- DISABLE_OPTIMIZATION (disable optimization or filter products and units of measure)
- CHANGE_TWO_STEP_PICKING (change two-step picking status of wave items)

The BAdI is called in class /SCWM/CL_WAVE_2STEP_OPTIMIZE.

The relevant Customizing path is **Goods Issue Process • Wave Management • Two-Step Picking • BAdI: Change of Optimization for Two-Step Picking**.

BAdI /SCWM/EX_WAVE_2STEP_OPT_PRC

Let's look at the /SCWM/EX_WAVE_2STEP_OPT_PRC BAdI (Implementation of Optimization Algorithm for Two-Step Picking). With this BAdI, you can implement a custom optimization algorithm in a two-step picking scenario. In the standard system, fallback class /SCWM/CL_EI_WAVE_2STEP_OPT_PRC is called, which contains the standard logic for the optimization of two-step picking. The goal of this logic is to pick larger UOMs. The BAdI includes the following methods:

- SKIP_OPTIMIZATION
  You can skip the entire optimization process. This allows you to ignore the persisted optimization status.

- FILTER_OPTIMIZATION_CANDIDATES
  You can choose which products to ignore, which products are to be picked directly, and whether to filter the UOMs. It is also possible to skip the optimization after the UOMs have been determined by the system. Note that the fallback class calls the DISABLE_OPTIMIZATION method of BAdI SCWM/EX_WAVE_2STEP_OPT_CHG. If you create your own implementation, this BAdI might no longer be called.

- GROUP_WAVE_ITEMS
  You can split table CT_WITHDRAWAL_REQUEST into additional entries, which are then used as input for simulating the creation of withdrawal tasks. Each wave item must be assigned to one withdrawal group. The quantity of the withdrawal group must match the cumulative quantities of the wave items assigned to the withdrawal group. Thus, when you split wave items from the withdrawal group, you must reduce the quantity of the original withdrawal group accordingly, while also increasing the quantity of the new withdrawal group. In addition, you must update the WITHDRAWAL_GROUP field of the wave items. Do not update other fields of the wave items.

- DETERMINE_2STEP_PICKING
  You can evaluate the simulated withdrawal tasks and choose which wave items should use two-step picking and which should use direct picking.

If you want to implement an optimization logic that does not require simulated withdrawal tasks, it is probably simpler to implement only BAdI /SCWM/EX_WAVE_2STEP_OPT_CHG.

The BAdI is called in class /SCWM/CL_WAVE_2STEP_OPTIMIZE.

The relevant Customizing path is **Goods Issue Process • Wave Management • Two-Step Picking • BAdI: Implementation of Optimization Algorithm for Two-Step Picking**.

BAdI /SCWM/EX_WAVE_SAVE

With the /SCWM/EX_WAVE_SAVE BAdI, you can control if the system should automatically try to release a wave again based on the wave's header and item data. When a wave is released with errors, the system can try to release the wave again automatically at a later point in time. In the standard system, you can define one retry interval per wave template.

The important method of this BAdI is SAVE. When saving waves, you can use this BAdI for changes of noncritical data of the wave header and wave items. The system transfers the tables of wave header and wave items. With the EV_CHANGED export parameter, you should inform the system that you have made changes within the BAdI.

The BAdI is called when saving waves within include /SCWM/LWAVE_MGMT_BASICSF24, subroutine WAVE_UPDATE.

The relevant Customizing path is **Goods Issue Process • Wave Management • BAdI: Change Wave Data when Saving.**

BAdI /SCWM/EX_WAVE_WITHDRAW_WPT

Let's look at the /SCWM/EX_WAVE_WITHDRAW_WPT BAdI (Change of Warehouse Process Type for Withdrawal Task).

With this BAdI, you can change the warehouse process type for the warehouse tasks that are created for the withdrawal step of the two-step picking process. The BAdI is called during wave release for the withdrawal step, during wave simulation for waves that are relevant for two-step picking, and during the optimization of two-step picking. Example class /SCWM/CL_EI_WAVE_WITHDRAW_WPT is available for your reference.

The important method of this BAdI is CHANGE_WITHDRAWAL_WPT (change warehouse process type of withdrawal task).

The BAdI is called when saving waves within include /SCWM/LWAVE_MGMT_BASICSP13, local class method CALL_BADI_CHANGE_WITHDRAW_WPT.

The relevant Customizing path is **Goods Issue Process • Wave Management • Two-Step Picking • BAdI: Change of Warehouse Process Type for Withdrawal Task.**

BAdI /SCWM/EX_WAVE_CREATE_ALLOC

Finally, let's look at the /SCWM/EX_WAVE_CREATE_ALLOC BAdI (Automatic Creation of Allocation Task). With this BAdI, you can control the automatic creation of warehouse tasks for the allocation step of the two-step picking process in wave management. The BAdI is called during the update phase of the commit for the warehouse task confirmation, if the confirmed warehouse task is a withdrawal task for two-step picking. The system determines the related wave items for the withdrawal task to create the necessary allocation tasks. With this BAdI, this automatic task creation can be enabled or disabled per withdrawal group. If the automatic creation of allocation tasks is enabled, the system starts the warehouse task creation using a queued RFC (qRFC).

Note that in some cases, the system cannot identify the related wave items that are to be released and automatic task creation does not occur. This can happen if warehouse task confirmation to the intermediate bin is more complex, such as when layout-oriented storage control is used. In this case, the BAdI is not called. Therefore, once all withdrawal tasks are confirmed, we recommend that you plan to release the wave for allocation, either manually or automatically, to ensure that all warehouse tasks are created.

The important method of this BAdI is CREATE_ALLOC_TASKS (create allocation warehouse tasks during confirmation of withdrawal warehouse tasks).

The BAdI is called during warehouse task confirmation update within include /SCWM/LHU_TO_UPDF71 in the subroutine WAVE_TRIGGER_ALLOCATION_TASK.

The relevant Customizing path is **Goods Issue Process • Wave Management • Two-Step Picking • BAdI: Automatic Creation of Allocation Task**.

6.3   Warehouse Tasks

The creation and confirmation of warehouse tasks is certainly the centerpiece of EWM. It controls warehousing and goods movement activities. A huge variety of enhancement options are available, through which you can influence the creation, validation, determination, and strategies for source and destination bins as well as the posting of warehouse tasks. Figure 6.3 shows the BAdIs that will be presented in more detail, grouped into individual processing blocks (1–8).

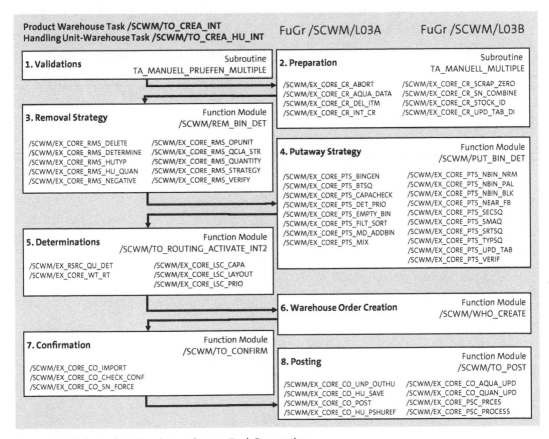

Figure 6.3 Selected BAdIs of Warehouse Task Processing

The available BAdIs are listed in chronological order of their calls, grouped into the given processing blocks. In the upper-right corners of the blocks, you can find the subroutines and function modules that represent the entry points of each processing block. The function groups /SCWM/L03A and /SCWM/L03B listed at the top-right corner of Figure 6.3 contain these objects.

The following enhancement spots belong to composite enhancement spot /SCWM/ESC_CORE.

6.3.1   Enhancement Spot /SCWM/ES_CORE_CR

For enhancement spot /SCWM/ES_CORE_CR (Create Warehouse Task), we will look at eight different BAdIs in the following sections.

BAdI /SCWM/EX_CORE_CR_ABORT

Let's start by looking at the /SCWM/EX_CORE_CR_ABORT BAdI (Terminate WT Creation). With this BAdI, you can cancel the warehouse task creation process for one task, such as in case of an insufficient available quantity that would trigger an underdelivery scenario. For an example implementation, see class /SCWM/CL_EI_WT_CR_ABORT_PACK.

The important method of this BAdI is ABORT (terminate warehouse task creation for underdelivery).

The BAdI is called in the warehouse task creation processing within function module /SCWM/BADI_TO_CREATE_ABORT.

The relevant Customizing path is **Cross-Process Settings • Warehouse Task • Creation of Warehouse Tasks • BAdI: Termination of Warehouse Task Creation.**

BAdI /SCWM/EX_CORE_CR_AQUA_DATA

Let's look at the /SCWM/EX_CORE_CR_AQUA_DATA BAdI (Fill Data for Available Quantity). In this BAdI, you can fill custom-specific fields in table /SCWM/AQUA, which represents the available quantities.

The important method of this BAdI is CHANGE_DATA (change data in Aqua Data Studio).

The BAdI is called in the warehouse task creation processing within function module /SCWM/AQUA_DATA_DETERMINE.

The relevant Customizing path is **Cross-Process Settings • Warehouse Task • Creation of Warehouse Tasks • BAdI: Data for Available Quantity.**

BAdI /SCWM/EX_CORE_CR_DEL_ITM

Let's look at the /SCWM/EX_CORE_CR_DEL_ITM BAdI (Prevent Deletion of Items). With this BAdI, you can prevent the deletion of temporarily created warehouse tasks at runtime. You can update your own temporary table if required or reset updates that have already occurred when creating the temporary warehouse task. Preventing deletion is useful, for example, if due to other BAdI methods several warehouse tasks have been created that are internally consistent, and the deletion of a dependent warehouse task must not be carried out. If this BAdI method refuses to delete a warehouse task, you should put a message from the BAdI method into table ET_BAPIRET to inform the user accordingly.

The important method of this BAdI is DEL_ITM (prevent deletion of warehouse tasks).

The BAdI is called in the warehouse task creation processing within function module /SCWM/BADI_TO_CREATE_DEL_ITM.

The relevant Customizing path is **Cross-Process Settings • Warehouse Task • Creation of Warehouse Tasks • BAdI: Prevention of Deletion of Items**.

BAdI /SCWM/EX_CORE_CR_INT_CR

Let's look at the /SCWM/EX_CORE_CR_INT_CR BAdI (Create a WT Internally). This BAdI enables you to influence the creation of a warehouse task specifically to update custom-specific fields at the warehouse task level. The BAdI method is executed when a warehouse task is transiently created. You can update custom data fields in the CS_LTAP_CUST_S4 structure, which is included in the extension structure of the /SCWM/INCL_EEW_S_ORDIM_PS warehouse task.

The important method of this BAdI is INSERT (update of custom tables).

The BAdI is called in the warehouse task creation processing within include /SCWM/LL03AF87 in the TAPOS_HINZUFUEGEN subroutine.

The relevant Customizing path is **Cross-Process Settings • Warehouse Task • Creation of Warehouse Tasks • BAdI: Internal Warehouse Task Creation**.

BAdI /SCWM/EX_CORE_CR_SCRAP_ZERO

Let's look at the /SCWM/EX_CORE_CR_SCRAP_ZERO BAdI (Create WTs for Scrapping without Picking Quantity). The important method of this BAdI is SCRAP_ZERO (create warehouse tasks for scrapping without picking quantity).

With this BAdI, you can create warehouse tasks for scrapping without picking quantity. Thus, the nonscrapping quantity of a product can be inspected in a storage bin. This BAdI method is run through when a warehouse task is created transiently. First you create a warehouse task for scrapping a product. You then enter an amount that is to be retained. The available quantity in a storage bin or in a handling unit is less than or equal to the quantity that you want to keep.

The BAdI is called in the warehouse task creation processing within function module /SCWM/BADI_TO_CREATE_SCRAP_ZER.

The relevant Customizing path is **Cross-Process Settings • Warehouse Task • Creation of Warehouse Tasks • BAdI: Creation of Warehouse Tasks for Scrapping without Pick Quantity.**

BAdI /SCWM/EX_CORE_CR_SN_COMBINE

Let's look at the /SCWM/EX_CORE_CR_SN_COMBINE BAdI (Combine Quants for Serial Numbers According to Available Quantity). You can use this BAdI when searching for predefined serial numbers. If the system finds stock items for the predefined serial numbers, this BAdI enables you to combine the quants corresponding to the level of available quantity (storage bin or handling unit) as set up in the storage type or as available quantity for batches (batch-specific or batch-neutral).

The important method of this BAdI is SN_COMBINE.

The BAdI is called in the warehouse task creation processing within include /SCWM/LREM_BIN_DETF42, subroutine QMAT_CREATE_SN.

The relevant Customizing path is **Cross-Process Settings • Warehouse Task • Creation of Warehouse Tasks • BAdI: Combine Quants for Serial Numbers Corresponding to Available Quantity.**

BAdI /SCWM/EX_CORE_CR_STOCK_ID

Let's look at the /SCWM/EX_CORE_CR_STOCK_ID BAdI (Number Assignment for SI). With this BAdI, you can influence the number assignment of the stock identification. EWM standard will create the stock identification from the warehouse number and the current warehouse task number, or a warehouse task number drawn from a number range. You can use this BAdI to make your own number assignments (e.g., an SSCC number). Enter the result of your determination within the BAdI method in parameter CV_IDPLATE. The data of the warehouse task is available inside the BAdI method.

The important method of this BAdI is STOCK_ID (custom number assignment for stock identification).

The BAdI is called in the warehouse task creation processing within include /SCWM/LL03AF31, subroutine STOCK_ID_GET.

The relevant Customizing path is **Cross-Process Settings • Warehouse Task • Creation of Warehouse Tasks • BAdI: Number Assignment Stock Identification.**

BAdI /SCWM/EX_CORE_CR_UPD_TAB_DI

Finally, let's look at the /SCWM/EX_CORE_CR_UPD_TAB_DI BAdI (Update Tables at Internal WT Deletion). This BAdI enables you to update custom-specific data for the warehouse task in case of deletion of a temporarily created warehouse task at runtime. Ensure changing parameter CS_ORDIM_CUST_S4 is set accordingly inside the BAdI method.

The important method of this BAdI is UPD_TABLES_DEL_ITEM (update tables when deleting a warehouse task created internally).

The BAdI is called in the warehouse task creation processing within function module /SCWM/BADI_TO_CREATE_UPD_DEL.

The relevant Customizing path is **Cross-Process Settings • Warehouse Task • Creation of Warehouse Tasks • BAdI: Table Update During Deletion of an Item**.

6.3.2   Enhancement Spot /SCWM/ES_CORE_RMS

For enhancement spot SCWM/ES_CORE_RMS (Stock Removal Strategy), we will look at 10 different BAdIs in the following sections.

BAdI /SCWM/EX_CORE_RMS_DELETE

Let's start by looking at the /SCWM/EX_CORE_RMS_DELETE BAdI (Delete Quant Buffer). With this BAdI, you can delete the quant buffer for available stock. To do so, set the EV_DELETE export parameter to ABAP_TRUE. The BAdI is run during warehouse task creation—more specifically, at the beginning of quant determination. The BAdI also allows you to update custom-specific fields added as an append to structure /SCWM/INCL_EEW_S_ORDIM_PS.

The important method of this BAdI is DELETE (delete quant buffer).

The BAdI is called at the start of quant determination within include /SCWM/LREM_BIN_DETF35, subroutine BADI_REM_BIN_DET_DELETE and include /SCWM/LREM_BIN_DETF13, subroutine QMAT_CREATE.

The relevant Customizing path is **Goods Issue Process • Strategies • Stock Removal Strategies • BAdI: Deletion of Quant Buffer**.

BAdI /SCWM/EX_CORE_RMS_DETERMINE

Let's look at the /SCWM/EX_CORE_RMS_DETERMINE BAdI (Filter and/or Sort Quants). With this BAdI, you can filter and sort available quants according to your custom logic to finally determine the removal bin to be used. The BAdI is always called after the standard stock determination and sorting, so it's possible to predict what the standard stock removal strategies would have done and influence the strategy results when needed. The BAdI also allows you to update custom-specific fields added as an append to structure /SCWM/INCL_EEW_S_ORDIM_PS. Be aware that fallback class /SCWM/CL_EI_CORE_RMS_DET is defined, which runs if no implementation for this BAdI exists. When creating a custom implementation, the fallback class and method should be called at the beginning or at the end of it. The BAdI includes several implementation example classes that you can check out or copy over for your own implementation.

The important method of this BAdI is DETERMINE (filter and/or sort quants).

The BAdI will be called in removal bin determination within include /SCWM/LREM_BIN_DETF12, subroutine SRC_BIN_DET.

The relevant Customizing path is **Goods Issue Process • Strategies • Stock Removal Strategies • BAdI: Filtering and/or Sorting of Quants**.

BAdI /SCWM/EX_CORE_RMS_HUTYP

Let's look at the /SCWM/EX_CORE_RMS_HUTYP BAdI (Change HU Type). With this BAdI, you can implement custom logic for handling unit type determination in warehouse task creation processing. Set your custom determined handling unit type accordingly in export parameter EV_HUTYP. The BAdI also allows you to update custom-specific fields added as an append to structure /SCWM/INCL_EEW_S_ORDIM_PS.

The important method of this BAdI is HUTYP (change handling unit type).

The BAdI is called during removal strategy processing within include /SCWM/LREM_BIN_DETF39, subroutine BADI_REM_BIN_DET_HUTYP and include /SCWM/LREM_BIN_DETF02, subroutine SRC_QUANTITY_DET.

The relevant Customizing path is **Goods Issue Process • Strategies • Stock Removal Strategies • BAdI: Change of HU Type**.

BAdI /SCWM/EX_CORE_RMS_HU_QUAN

Let's look at the /SCWM/EX_CORE_RMS_HU_QUAN BAdI (Change Quantity of a HU). With this BAdI, you can change the quantity of a handling unit, the alternative UOM of a warehouse task, and the rounding level within the removal strategy. It is also possible to decide to skip the current quant. The quantity for the handling unit is used only to round the quantity of the warehouse task accordingly. The BAdI also allows you to update custom-specific fields added as an append to structure /SCWM/INCL_EEW_S_ORDIM_PS.

The important method of this BAdI is HU_QUAN (change quantity in a handling unit).

The BAdI is called in include /SCWM/LREM_BIN_DETF02, subroutine SRC_QUANTITY_DET.

The relevant Customizing path is **Goods Issue Process • Strategies • Stock Removal Strategies • BAdI: Change of HU Quantity**.

BAdI /SCWM/EX_CORE_RMS_NEGATIVE

Let's look at the /SCWM/EX_CORE_RMS_NEGATIVE BAdI (Allow Negative Quantities). With this BAdI, you can allow picking tasks to be created that cause negative stock. This will allow you to define a more granular logic for negative stock options as offered by Customizing. Set changing parameter CV_NEGAT to A (allow available negative stock), X (allow negative stock), or blank (do not allow negative stock). The BAdI also allows you to update user-defined fields added as an append to structure /SCWM/INCL_EEW_S_ORDIM_PS.

The important method of this BAdI is NEGATIVE (allow negative quantities).

The BAdI is called during removal strategy processing within include /SCWM/LREM_BIN_DETF61, subroutine BADI_REM_BIN_DET_NEGATIVE and include /SCWM/LREM_BIN_DETF12, subroutine SRC_BIN_DET.

The relevant Customizing path is **Goods Issue Process • Strategies • Stock Removal Strategies • BAdI: Allowance of Negative Quantities**.

BAdI /SCWM/EX_CORE_RMS_OPUNIT

Let's look at the /SCWM/EX_CORE_RMS_OPUNIT BAdI (Change Operative Unit of Measure). This BAdI will allow you to change the operative or alternative UOM to be used in the picking warehouse task. Set export parameter EV_OPUNIT accordingly. The BAdI also allows you to update custom-specific fields added as an append to structure /SCWM/INCL_EEW_S_ORDIM_PS.

The important method of this BAdI is OPUNIT (change operative unit of measure).

The BAdI is called in function module /SCWM/TO_OPUNIT_DET.

The relevant Customizing path is **Goods Issue Process • Strategies • Stock Removal Strategies • BAdI: Change of Operative Unit of Measure**.

BAdI /SCWM/EX_CORE_RMS_QCLA_STR

Let's look at the /SCWM/EX_CORE_RMS_QCLA_STR BAdI (Change Quantity Classifier for Storage Type Search Sequence). The BAdI allows you to change the quantity determination classifier to be used for storage type search sequence determination by your custom logic. Set changing parameter CV_QUANCLA accordingly. The BAdI also allows you to update custom-specific fields added as an append to structure /SCWM/INCL_EEW_S_ORDIM_PS.

The important method of this BAdI is CHANGE (change the quantity classification).

The BAdI is called in include /SCWM/LREM_BIN_DETF11, subroutine SRC_TYPE_DET.

The relevant Customizing path is **Goods Issue Process • Strategies • Stock Removal Strategies • BAdI: Change of Quantity Classifier for Storage Type Search Sequence**.

BAdI /SCWM/EX_CORE_RMS_QUANTITY

Let's look at the /SCWM/EX_CORE_RMS_QUANTITY BAdI (Change Requested Quantity). With this BAdI, you can change the requested quantity (for underdeliveries and overdeliveries), the handling unit type, and the alternative UOM in the picking warehouse task. Make sure to set the EV_SET export parameter to ABAP_TRUE to communicate your changes. For example, if a warehouse task for stock removal is created for a small quantity and a source pallet is determined in a rack, you can use this BAdI to increase the quantity to be removed in specific business conditions so that the whole handling unit is picked. However, consider that the corresponding outbound delivery order item should allow the overpicking scenario. The BAdI also allows you to update custom-specific fields added as an append to structure /SCWM/INCL_EEW_S_ORDIM_PS.

The important method of this BAdI is QUANTITY (change requested quantity).

The BAdI is called in include /SCWM/LREM_BIN_DETF02, subroutine SRC_QUANTITY_DET.

The relevant Customizing path is **Goods Issue Process • Strategies • Stock Removal Strategies • BAdI: Change of Requested Quantity**.

BAdI /SCWM/EX_CORE_RMS_STRATEGY

Let's look at the /SCWM/EX_CORE_RMS_STRATEGY BAdI (Change Storage Type Search Sequence and Stock Removal Rule). With this BAdI, you can change the storage type search sequence and the removal rule. Set export parameters EV_REM_SSEQ and EV_REM_RULE accordingly. To apply the stock removal rule, parameter EV_REM_RULE_SET must be set to ABAP_TRUE. The BAdI also allows you to update custom-specific fields added as an append to structure /SCWM/INCL_EEW_S_ORDIM_PS.

The important method of this BAdI is STRATEGY (change search sequence and stock removal rule).

The BAdI is called in include /SCWM/LREM_BIN_DETF11, subroutine SRC_TYPE_DET.

The relevant Customizing path is **Goods Issue Process • Strategies • Stock Removal Strategies • BAdI: Change of Search Sequence and Stock Removal Rule**.

BAdI /SCWM/EX_CORE_RMS_VERIFY

Finally, let's look at the /SCWM/EX_CORE_RMS_VERIFY BAdI (Check Storage Bin). With this BAdI, you can run a last additional check on the removal storage bin that has been determined by the removal strategy. You can influence and monitor the warehouse task creation process via additional messages and message types. It is possible to prevent the system from using this storage bin for stock removal. For this purpose, you should include a message in table ET_BAPIRET and set parameter EV_SEVERITY to E or A. The system will then continue with the next available quantity.

The important methods of this BAdI are as follows:

- VERIFY (check proposed bin)
- ADJ_SRC_BIN_CHECK (adjust source bin checks)

The BAdI is called in include /SCWM/LREM_BIN_DETF08 in the subroutine SRC_QUANT_DET.

The relevant Customizing path is **Goods Issue Process • Strategies • Stock Removal Strategies • BAdI: Check of Specified Bin**.

6.3.3   Enhancement Spot /SCWM/ES_CORE_PTS

For enhancement spot /SCWM/ES_CORE_PTS (Putaway Strategies), we will look at 18 different BAdIs in the following sections.

BAdI /SCWM/EX_CORE_PTS_BINGEN

Let's start by looking at the /SCWM/EX_CORE_PTS_BINGEN BAdI (Change Generic Destination Storage Bin Search During WT Creation). The BAdI allows you to overrule the **WT Generic** Customizing setting, which is set on the storage type level, when creating warehouse tasks. The BAdI is called during the creation of every single warehouse task to allow you to influence the Customizing setting for every warehouse task individually. Usage of this BAdI depends on the storage-type-specific Customizing setting for **WT Generic**, as follows:

- If the warehouse task creation is generic (Customizing setting value **1—Storage Type and Storage** or **2—Only Storage Type**), you can use this BAdI to deactivate this setting to execute a search for a specific destination storage bin.

- If the warehouse task creation is not generic (value is **<blank>—Not Generic (Storage Type, Storage Section, and Storage Bin)**), you can use this BAdI to activate a generic warehouse task creation for a destination storage type.

Set changing parameter CV_PARTDET accordingly in your implementation.

The important method of this BAdI is CHANGE (change generic bin determination).

The BAdI is called at the beginning of destination bin determination in the putaway strategy—specifically, in include /SCWM/LPUT_BIN_DETF96, subroutine DET_BINGEN.

The relevant Customizing path is **Goods Receipt Process • Strategies • Putaway Strategies • BAdI: Change Search for Generic Destination Storage Bin During WT Creation**.

BAdI /SCWM/EX_CORE_PTS_BTSQ

Let's look at the /SCWM/EX_CORE_PTS_BTSQ BAdI (BAdI: Search Sequence of Bin Type). This BAdI allows you to determine the search sequence of the bin type for putaway bin determination by your custom logic.

The important method of this BAdI is STORAGE_BINTYPE_SEQ (search sequence of bin type).

The BAdI is called in include /SCWM/LPUT_BIN_DETF19, subroutine BINTYPES_DETERMINE.

The relevant Customizing path is **Goods Receipt Process • Strategies • Putaway Strategies • BAdI: Change Storage Bin Type Search Sequence**.

BAdI /SCWM/EX_CORE_PTS_CAPACHECK

Let's look at the /SCWM/EX_CORE_PTS_CAPACHECK BAdI (BAdI: Determination of Capacity Check Result (for Whse Task)). This BAdI allows you to execute a custom capacity check. Capacity evaluation is a widely used functionality that is applied during creation or change of a warehouse task to determine whether the destination bin or destination handling unit has enough free capacity. The capacity can be evaluated considering weight, volume, and capacity factor. The early capacity check is used to search for possible storage bin types before the actual storage bin is determined. We recommend reading the further documentation provided for the BAdI's interface methods:

- CUSTOM_CAPA_CHECK (influence result of capacity check)
- CANCEL_BUFFERED_WT (remove internally created warehouse task from buffer)

The BAdI is called in include /SCWM/LHUFUNCF29, subroutine CAPA_CHECK_BADI. This BAdI is called when the following occurs:

- Capacity check is completed, and after a decision is reached on whether capacity on the destination is sufficient for creation of the warehouse task
- Capacity check is successful, and the warehouse task can be created, and when the standard logic decides that there is not enough capacity available on the bin/handling unit (method CUSTOM_CAPA_CHECK)
- The created warehouse task is confirmed with changes (method CUSTOM_CAPA_CHECK)
- The early capacity check against storage bin types is performed (method CUSTOM_CAPA_CHECK)
- Transaction /SCWM/TODLV_I calculates the information on the **Stock Can Be Added** tab (method CUSTOM_CAPA_CHECK)
- An internal warehouse task that was created but not saved is canceled (method CANCEL_BUFFERED_WT)

This BAdI is not called when the following occurs:

- Capacity check fails due to violation of mix bin restrictions
- Capacity check terminates due to foreign locks, data inconsistencies, and other situations of exception
- The capacity of a bin is calculated (Transaction /SCWM/LS03) and no check for putaway is performed, just calculation of dynamic bin capacity
- A generic warehouse task is created because there is no known storage bin at the time and, when the warehouse task is later confirmed with the actual destination bin, the standard capacity check is executed (method CUSTOM_CAPA_CHECK)

The implementation of this BAdI affects whether the capacity check passes or fails. This is decided via changing parameter CV_CAPA_OK. This decision is considered during the creation of warehouse tasks, as follows:

- If the BAdI implementation decides that there is enough capacity, then the warehouse task can be created (according to standard capacity check).
- If the BAdI implementation decides that there is not enough capacity, the warehouse task will not be created with the destination bin/handling unit. You can make settings in Customizing to allow warehouse task splitting.

The relevant Customizing path is **Goods Receipt Process • Strategies • Putaway Strategies • BAdI: Determination of Capacity Check Result (for WhseTask)**.

BAdI /SCWM/EX_CORE_PTS_DET_PRIO

Let's look at the /SCWM/EX_CORE_PTS_DET_PRIO BAdI (Specify Priority of Storage Type/StorageSection/StorageBin Type). With this BAdI, you can set the priority of the storage type, storage section, and storage bin type within the putaway bin determination. By setting the priority, you can influence the sequence by which the organizational elements are to be considered for bin determination.

The important method of this BAdI is DET_PRIORITIES (specify priority of storage type/storage section/storage bin type).

The BAdI is called in include /SCWM/LPUT_BIN_DETF78, subroutine DET_ENTRANCE_TABLE.

The relevant Customizing path is **Goods Receipt Process • Strategies • Putaway Strategies • BAdI: Determine Priority of Storage Type/Storage Area/Storage Bin Type.**

BAdI /SCWM/EX_CORE_PTS_FILT_SORT

Let's look at the /SCWM/EX_CORE_PTS_FILT_SORT BAdI (Filter and Sort Possible Storage Bins). With this BAdI, you can filter and sort destination bin candidates for storage types in different contexts. This BAdI is called with normal or bulk storage behavior when the system searches for bins for additional quantities. In this case, you can sort or filter the available stock that was found in storage bin candidates. You cannot append additional destination data in this context.

This BAdI is also called when searching for empty destination bins, to sort or filter the list of candidates based on data that was selected either from the database or from a buffered table if multiple requests are handled within the same logical unit of work.

In both cases, you can sort or filter the candidates; you cannot append additional destination data in this context, however.

When using a near fixed bin scenario, the BAdI is called to allow you to sort or filter storage bin candidates that are located in the reserve storage type of the putaway strategy used. You can append additional destination data in this context. For example, this can be used to assign a reserve bin in an aisle that differs from the aisle of the related fixed bin.

The different contexts can be distinguished by the changing parameters provided. The system runs this BAdI when a warehouse task is created. When searching for empty bins, the system uses a buffer when calling the BAdI for identical destination data multiple times in the same logical unit of work. As a result, any filtered candidates that were removed in a BAdI implementation will not be provided again in the next calls in the same logical unit of work.

The BAdI includes example implementation /SCWM/CL_EI_CORE_PTS_FILT_SORT for equal distribution of products over multiple aisles.

The important method of this BAdI is FILT_SORT (filter and sort possible storage bins).

The BAdI is called in include /SCWM/LPUT_BIN_DETF17, subroutine BIN_DETERMINATION_1 as well as include /SCWM/LPUT_BIN_DETF92, subroutine NEARFIXBIN_SEARCH and include /SCWM/LPUT_BIN_DETF75, subroutine NEARFIXBIN_SEARCH.

The relevant Customizing path is **Goods Receipt Process • Strategies • Putaway Strategies • BAdI: Filter and Sort Possible Storage Bins**.

BAdI /SCWM/EX_CORE_PTS_MIX

Let's look at the /SCWM/EX_CORE_PTS_MIX BAdI (Mixed Storage). With this BAdI, you can define an additional check for allowing mixed storage. For example, when dealing with additional custom stock attributes at the quant level, this BAdI can be used to compare the attributes in source and destination data. This avoids mixing stock with different properties. When adding a quant to an existing quant, the custom attributes are not relevant for keeping the quants separated, and the additional attributes might be lost due to the merging of the quants.

The important methods of this BAdI are as follows:

- MIX_ALLOWED (allow mixed storage despite Customizing)
- MIX_CHECK (forbid mixed storage; Customizing allowed)

The BAdI is called in include /SCWM/LHUFUNCF23, subroutine MIX_CHECK_HUITM.

The relevant Customizing path is **Goods Receipt Process • Strategies • Putaway Strategies • BAdI: Mixed Storage**.

BAdI /SCWM/EX_CORE_PTS_NBIN_NRM

Let's look at the /SCWM/EX_CORE_PTS_NBIN_NRM BAdI (Determine Destination Storage Bin: Putaway Behavior: Normal). With this BAdI, you can influence the destination bin determination for normal storage procedure.

The important method of this BAdI is DET_DEST_BIN_NORMAL (determine destination storage bin: putaway behavior: normal).

The BAdI is called in include /SCWM/LPUT_BIN_DETF17, subroutine BIN_DETERMINATION_1.

The relevant Customizing path is **Goods Receipt Process • Strategies • Putaway Strategies • BAdI: Destination Bin Determination: Storage Behavior Normal**.

BAdI /SCWM/EX_CORE_PTS_NBIN_PAL

Let's look at the /SCWM/EX_CORE_PTS_NBIN_PAL BAdI (Determine Destination Bin: Putaway Behavior: Pallet). With this BAdI, you can influence the destination bin determination for pallet storage procedure.

The important method of this BAdI is DET_DEST_BIN_PALLET (determine destination bin: putaway behavior: pallet).

The BAdI is called in include /SCWM/LPUT_BIN_DETF17, subroutine BIN_DETERMINATION_1.

The relevant Customizing path is **Goods Receipt Process • Strategies • Putaway Strategies • BAdI: Destination Bin Determination: Storage Behavior Pallet**.

BAdI /SCWM/EX_CORE_PTS_NBIN_BLK

Let's look at the /SCWM/EX_CORE_PTS_NBIN_BLK BAdI (Determine Destination Bin: Putaway Behavior: Bulk Storage). With this BAdI, you can influence the destination bin determination for bulk storage procedure.

The important method of this BAdI is DET_DEST_BIN_BULK (determine destination bin: putaway behavior: bulk storage).

The BAdI is called in include /SCWM/LPUT_BIN_DETF33, subroutine CALL_BADI_CORE_PTS_NBIN_BLK.

The relevant Customizing path is **Goods Receipt Process • Strategies • Putaway Strategies • BAdI: Destination Bin Determination: Storage Behavior Block**.

BAdI /SCWM/EX_CORE_PTS_NEAR_FB

Let's look at the /SCWM/EX_CORE_PTS_NEAR_FB BAdI (Near Fix Bin—Determine Fix Bin). This BAdI enables you to influence the "near fix bin" putaway behavior by considering the spatial distance to identify vacant bins. The /SCWM/CORE_PTS_NEAR_FB_IMPL sample implementation can be helpful when using the BAdI.

The important method of this BAdI is DET_NEAR_FB.

The BAdI is called in include /SCWM/LPUT_BIN_DETF74, subroutine NEARFIXBIN_INIT.

The relevant Customizing path is **Goods Receipt Process • Strategies • Putaway Strategies • BAdI: Near to Fixed Bin: Determine Fixed Bin**.

BAdI /SCWM/EX_CORE_PTS_SECSQ

Let's look at the /SCWM/EX_CORE_PTS_SECSQ BAdI (Change Storage Section Search Sequence). With this BAdI, you can change the storage section search order by influencing which storage sections are considered for destination bin determination during warehouse task creation.

The important method of this BAdI is STORAGE_SECTION_SEQ (change storage section search sequence).

The BAdI is called in include /SCWM/LPUT_BIN_DETF18, subroutine STORAGESECTIONS_DETERMINE.

The relevant Customizing path is **Goods Receipt Process • Strategies • Putaway Strategies • BAdI: Change Storage Area Search Sequence**.

BAdI /SCWM/EX_CORE_PTS_SMAQ

Let's look at the /SCWM/EX_CORE_PTS_SMAQ BAdI (Decide whether Maximum Storage Type Quantity Is Considered).

The important methods of this BAdI are as follows:

- `DECIDE_SMAQ_USE` (decide whether maximum storage type quantity is considered)
- `CHECK_SMAQ_LGTYPG` (checks maximum quantity of storage type group)

The BAdI is called in include /SCWM/LPUT_BIN_DETF81, subroutine `BIN_DETRERMINATION_SINGLE`.

The relevant Customizing path is **Goods Receipt Process • Strategies • Putaway Strategies • BAdI: Consider Maximum Quantity in Storage Type**.

BAdI /SCWM/EX_CORE_PTS_SRTSQ

Let's look at the /SCWM/EX_CORE_PTS_SRTSQ BAdI (Change Putaway Search Sequences). With this BAdI, you can change the putaway search sequences by controlling the order in which storage types, storage sections, and storage bin types are searched in the destination bin determination. You must accept the contents of the import table IT_SORT-TAB in the export table ET_SORTTAB and assign a priority for each entry via the EVALPOS field.

The important method of this BAdI is `SORT_SEQUENCE` (change putaway search sequences).

The BAdI is called in include /SCWM/LPUT_BIN_DETF78, subroutine `DET_ENTRANCE_TABLE`.

The relevant Customizing path is **Goods Receipt Process • Strategies • Putaway Strategies • BAdI: Change Putaway Search Sequences**.

BAdI /SCWM/EX_CORE_PTS_TYPSQ

Let's look at the /SCWM/EX_CORE_PTS_TYPSQ BAdI (Change Storage Type Search Sequence and Putaway Rule). In this BAdI, you can change the storage type search sequence and putaway rule.

The important method of this BAdI is `STORAGE_TYPE_SEQ` (change storage type search sequence and putaway rule).

The BAdI is called in include /SCWM/LPUT_BIN_DETF03, subroutine `DEST_TYPE_DET`.

The relevant Customizing path is **Goods Receipt Process • Strategies • Putaway Strategies • BAdI: Change Storage Type Search Sequence and Putaway Rule**.

BAdI /SCWM/EX_CORE_PTS_UPD_TAB

Let's look at the /SCWM/EX_CORE_PTS_UPD_TAB BAdI (Update Tables when Creating a Fixed Bin). This BAdI enables you to update custom tables during the determination of a fixed bin. It will be run through when assigning a product to a bin. The BAdI is run for all processes that can create a fixed storage bin (warehouse task creation, slotting, manual table maintenance for fixed bins). The BAdI does not provide any export or changing parameters, but it can be used to, for example, trigger custom-specific actions or update custom-specific tables during warehouse task creation.

The important method of this BAdI is UPDATE_TABLES (update user-defined tables).

The BAdI is called in function module /SCWM/FB_UPDATE_VB.

The relevant Customizing path is **Goods Receipt Process • Strategies • Putaway Strategies • BAdI: Update of Tables When Creating Fixed Storage Bin**.

BAdI /SCWM/EX_CORE_PTS_VERIF

Let's look at the /SCWM/EX_CORE_PTS_VERIF BAdI (Check Given Storage Bin). With this BAdI, you can check a manually provided destination storage bin in warehouse task creation. Consider providing additional warning or error messages to the user in case your custom check fails for usage of a certain bin. The BAdI also allows you to update custom-specific fields added as an append to structure /SCWM/INCL_EEW_S_ORDIM_PS.

The important method of this BAdI is VERIFY (check given storage bin). The BAdI is called in include /SCWM/LPUT_BIN_DETF52, subroutine DEST_BIN_CHECK.

The relevant Customizing path is **Goods Receipt Process • Strategies • Putaway Strategies • BAdI: Check Storage Bin Entered**.

BAdI /SCWM/EX_CORE_PTS_EMPTY_BIN

Let's look at the /SCWM/EX_CORE_PTS_EMPTY_BIN BAdI (BAdI: Empty Bin Determination). This BAdI can be used to determine empty bins according to custom requirements.

The important methods of this BAdI are as follows:

- DELETE_EMPTY_BIN_BUFFER (delete internal empty bin buffer)
- DETERMINE_EMPTY_BINS (determine empty bins using custom criteria)

The BAdI is called in include /SCWM/LPUT_BIN_DETA03, subroutines CALL_BADI_EMPTY_BIN_1 and CALL_BADI_EMPTY_BIN_2.

The relevant Customizing path is **Goods Receipt Process • Strategies • Putaway Strategies • BAdI: Empty Bin Determination**.

BAdI /SCWM/EX_CORE_PTS_MD_ADDBIN

Let's look at the /SCWM/EX_CORE_PTS_MD_ADDBIN BAdI (BAdI: Multi–Depth Bin Determination for Addition to Stock). With this BAdI, you can determine a storage bin to which the current warehouse task should add the handling unit. The handling unit is then placed in front of the last handling unit in the storage bin.

The important method of this BAdI is DETERMINE_BIN (determine storage bin).

The BAdI is called in include /SCWM/LPUT_BIN_DETF17, subroutine CALL_BADI_MD_ADDBIN.

The relevant Customizing path is **Goods Receipt Process • Strategies • Putaway Strategies • BAdI: Multi-Depth Bin Determination for Addition to Stock**.

6.3.4   Enhancement Spot /SCWM/ES_RSRC_QU

This enhancement spot uses the /SCWM/EX_RSRC_QU_DET BAdI (RF: Queue Determination During WO Creation). With this BAdI, you can determine a queue in the warehouse task creation. The BAdI is run through for each warehouse task. Custom fields are available for the queue determination logic inside the BAdI.

The important method of this BAdI is DETERMINE (queue determination at WO creation).

The BAdI is called in include /SCWM/LCORE_CUST_SELF03, subroutine BADI_TO_CREATE_QUEUE.

The relevant Customizing path is **Internal Warehouse Processes • Resource Management • Queue Determination.**

6.3.5   Enhancement Spot /SCWM/ES_CORE_WT_RT

This enhancement spot uses the /SCWM/EX_CORE_WT_RT BAdI (Extract Time Determination in Warehouse Task). An extract time will be calculated during warehouse task creation in accordance with the Customizing settings. The extract time indicates how much time is required to pick or place the product in the warehouse task. With this BAdI, you can change the determined time during the creation or activation of the warehouse task according to your specifications.

The important method of this BAdI is REACHTIME_OVERWRITE (overwrite extract time determined for each warehouse task).

The BAdI is called in include /SCWM/LTO_REACHTIMEF06, subroutine REACHTIME_DET_BADI.

The relevant Customizing path is **Cross-Process Settings • Warehouse Task • BAdI: Extract Time Determination in Warehouse Task.**

6.3.6   Enhancement Spot /SCWM/ES_CORE_LSC

For enhancement spot /SCWM/ES_CORE_LSC (Layout-Oriented Storage Control), we will look at three different BAdIs in the following sections.

BAdI /SCWM/EX_CORE_LSC_CAPA

Let's start by looking at the /SCWM/EX_CORE_LSC_CAPA BAdI (Capacity Check in Layout-Oriented Storage Control). With this BAdI, you can conduct a capacity check in layout-oriented storage control. For example, in the context of a material flow system (but not for case conveyor logic), before the warehouse task creation for the next communication point, the system checks the capacity of the segment and communication point. You can perform a custom-specific capacity check for the segment determined by layout-oriented storage control and exclude it when creating a warehouse task for the next communication point so that the system searches for alternative routes.

The important method of this BAdI is CHECK (check capacity).

The BAdI is called in function module /SCWM/MFS_WT_R2S_CHK.

The relevant Customizing path is **Cross-Process Settings • Warehouse Task • Layout-Oriented Storage Control • BAdI: Capacity Check in Layout-Oriented Warehouse Management.**

BAdI /SCWM/EX_CORE_LSC_LAYOUT

Let's look at the /SCWM/EX_CORE_LSC_LAYOUT BAdI (Layout-Oriented Storage Control). With this BAdI, you can change the determined destination data or prevent the redirection of the warehouse task to an intermediate point in the context of layout-oriented storage control. To prevent the usage of an intermediate bin, clear changing parameters CV_ILTYP, CV_ILBER, and CV_ILPLA.

The important method of this BAdI is LAYOUT (layout-oriented storage control).

The BAdI is called in function module /SCWM/BADI_STORAGE_CTRL_LAYOUT.

The relevant Customizing path is **Cross-Process Settings • Warehouse Task • Layout-Oriented Storage Control • BAdI: Layout-Oriented Storage Control.**

BAdI /SCWM/EX_CORE_LSC_PRIO

Finally, let's look at the /SCWM/EX_CORE_LSC_PRIO BAdI (Extract Time Determination in Warehouse Task). With this BAdI, you can determine a segment from all suitable segments before the system creates a warehouse task for the next communication point in the context of a material flow system.

The important methods of this BAdI are as follows:

- SORT (sorting of segments)
- SORT_NOFIT (sorting of inactive segments)

The BAdI is called in function module /SCWM/TROUTL_DET.

The relevant Customizing path is **Cross-Process Settings • Warehouse Task • Layout-Oriented Storage Control • BAdI: Prioritizing in Layout-Oriented Warehouse Control.**

6.3.7 Enhancement Spot /SCWM/ES_CORE_PSC

For enhancement spot /SCWM/ES_CORE_PSC (Layout-Oriented Storage Control), we will look at two BAdIs: /SCWM/EX_CORE_PSC_PRCES and /SCWM/EX_CORE_PSC_PROCESS.

BAdI /SCWM/EX_CORE_PSC_PRCES

First, let's look at BAdI /SCWM/EX_CORE_PSC_PRCES (Set Process Profile). With this BAdI, you can influence the determination of a process profile. It runs if the storage control of all packed stock of a handling unit is not the same. The standard system determines the storage control for a handling unit from the first stock item in it. You can overrule this behavior by your custom logic, setting exporting parameter EV_PRCES accordingly.

The important method of this BAdI is HUHDR_PRCES (set process profile).

The BAdI is called in include /SCWM/LLO3AF37, subroutine ROUTING_SET_HU_ATT. It will also be called during packing for inbound delivery and customer returns.

The relevant Customizing path is **Cross-Process Settings • Warehouse Task • Process-Oriented Storage Control • BAdI: Set Process Profile**.

BAdI /SCWM/EX_CORE_PSC_PROCESS

Next, let's look at BAdI /SCWM/EX_CORE_PSC_PROCESS (Process-Oriented Storage Control). With this BAdI, you can change the standard determined destination data and warehouse process type in the context of process-oriented storage control. It will also allow you to skip the intended process step or to abort warehouse task creation.

The important method of this BAdI is PROCESS (process-oriented storage control).

The BAdI is called in function module /SCWM/BADI_STORAGE_CTRL_PROCES.

The relevant Customizing path is **Cross-Process Settings • Warehouse Task • Process-Oriented Storage Control • BAdI: Process-Oriented Storage Control**.

6.3.8   Enhancement Spot /SCWM/ES_CORE_CO

For enhancement spot /SCWM/ES_CORE_CO (Confirmation of Warehouse Task), we will look at nine different BAdIs in the following sections.

BAdI /SCWM/EX_CORE_CO_CHECK_CONF

Let's start by looking at the /SCWM/EX_CORE_CO_CHECK_CONF BAdI (Check During Confirmation). With this BAdI, you can extend the checks at confirmation of a warehouse task and refuse the confirmation if necessary.

The important method of this BAdI is CHECK_CONF (check during confirmation).

The BAdI is called in function module /SCWM/BADI_TO_CONFIRM_CHECK.

The relevant Customizing path is **Cross-Process Settings • Warehouse Task • Confirmation of Warehouse Task • BAdI: Check During Confirmation**.

BAdI /SCWM/EX_CORE_CO_HU_SAVE

Let's look at the /SCWM/EX_CORE_CO_HU_SAVE BAdI (HU Updates when Saving). This BAdI allows you to change the handling unit data when saving the handling unit at warehouse task confirmation.

The important method of this BAdI is CONF (confirm warehouse tasks).

The BAdI is called in include /SCWM/LHU_TO_UPDF12, subroutine UPDATE_HU.

The relevant Customizing path is **Cross-Process Settings • Warehouse Task • Confirmation of Warehouse Task • BAdI: HU Updates in Saving.**

BAdI /SCWM/EX_CORE_CO_IMPORT

Let's look at the /SCWM/EX_CORE_CO_IMPORT BAdI (Change Import Parameters when Confirming WT). This BAdI allows changing import parameters for warehouse task confirmation.

The important method of this BAdI is CHANGE (change import parameters).

The BAdI is called in include /SCWM/LL03BF53, subroutine BADI_IMPORT.

The relevant Customizing path is **Cross-Process Settings • Warehouse Task • Confirmation of Warehouse Task • BAdI: Changing the Import Parameters When Confirming the WT.**

BAdI /SCWM/EX_CORE_CO_POST

Let's look at the /SCWM/EX_CORE_CO_POST BAdI (Update Confirmed WTs). With this BAdI, you can save your custom data at warehouse task confirmation or initiate follow-up actions. All other database updates of warehouse task creation have already been made. The BAdI runs in the update processing.

The important method of this BAdI is POST (update confirmed warehouse tasks).

The BAdI is called in function module /SCWM/BADI_TO_CONFIRM_POST.

The relevant Customizing path is **Cross-Process Settings • Warehouse Task • Confirmation of Warehouse Task • BAdI: Posting of Confirmed Warehouse Tasks.**

BAdI /SCWM/EX_CORE_CO_SN_FORCE

Let's look at the /SCWM/EX_CORE_CO_SN_FORCE BAdI (Force Serial Number Input during Confirmation). With this BAdI, you can force the input of serial numbers during warehouse task confirmation.

The important method of this BAdI is FORCE (force entry of serial numbers).

The BAdI is called in include /SCWM/LL03BF70, subroutine SN_CHECK_DATA.

The relevant Customizing path is **Cross-Process Settings • Warehouse Task • Confirmation of Warehouse Task • BAdI: Mandatory Serial Number Entry when Confirming.**

BAdI /SCWM/EX_CORE_CO_UNP_OUTHU

Let's look at the /SCWM/EX_CORE_CO_UNP_OUTHU BAdI (Unpack Outer HU at WT Confirmation). With this BAdI, you can unpack the higher-level handling unit during warehouse task confirmation. The system unpacks as many higher levels as you return to the EV_DEL_LEVEL parameter. The BAdI includes the sample implementation /SCWM/CL_EI_CORE_CO_UNP_OUTHU.

The important method of this BAdI is UNPACK_OUTER_HU (unpack outer handling unit).

The BAdI is called in include /SCWM/LL03AF13, subroutine OUTER_HU_UNPACK_DET.

The relevant Customizing path is **Cross-Process Settings • Warehouse Task • Confirmation of Warehouse Task • BAdI: Unpack Higher-Level Handling Unit at Warehouse Task Confirmation.**

BAdI /SCWM/EX_CORE_CO_HU_PSHUREF

Let's look at the /SCWM/EX_CORE_CO_HU_PSHUREF BAdI (Control Planned HU Reference for Full Pallet Withdrawal). With this BAdI, you can overrule the standard check for the decision to add the reference of the planned shipping handling unit to the handling unit being withdrawn. The standard check happens at full pallet withdrawal. The standard decision to add the planned shipping handling unit to the handling unit as a reference upon full pallet withdrawal is based on the equality of the handling unit and the planned shipping handling unit, based on packaging material, dimensions, and quantities. It is also possible to optimize these checks according to custom-specific needs in the **Control Planned HU Reference for Full Pallet Withdrawal** Customizing activity, which allows for the deactivation of some of the standard checks.

The important method of this BAdI is CHECK_PSHU_EQUALS_REAL_HU (check if planned handling unit is the same as the real handling unit).

The BAdI is called in method CHECK_PSHU_EQUALS_REAL_HU_BADI of class /SCWM/CL_CORE_PSHU_HU_IDENT.

The relevant Customizing path is **Cross-Process Settings • Warehouse Task • Confirmation of Warehouse Task • BAdI: Control of Planned HU Reference for Full Pallet Withdrawal.**

BAdI /SCWM/EX_CORE_CO_AQUA_UPD

Let's look at the /SCWM/EX_CORE_CO_AQUA_UPD BAdI (Suppression of Update of Cml. Fields in the Available Quantity Table). With this BAdI, you can exclude certain data from the calculation of the available stock datasets, which are created cumulatively from the assigned physical stock. The following fields are no longer updated in table /SCWM/AQUA:

- Shelf-life expiration date
- Goods receipt date
- Inventory active
- Country/region of origin
- Batch in restricted-use stock
- Alternative unit of measure
- Inspection type
- Inspection object
- Certificate number
- Custom-specific fields

When you implement this BAdI, the system no longer reads all physical stock belonging to the available quantity table, which can improve the performance for storage bins with a large number of stock items when calculating the available quantity at the bin level.

> **Caution**
>
> These fields might be relevant for stock-removal strategies, such as the goods receipt date for the first-in, first-out (FIFO) stock-removal rule. Set the export parameter in the BAdI only if the stock-removal strategy does not take any of the listed fields into account and the data is not required for any overviews (e.g., stock overview). All other fields of the available quantity table, such as the quantity, location, and handling unit data, are updated as usual.

The important method of this BAdI is AQUA_NOUPD (no update).

The BAdI is called in function module /SCWM/AQUA_DATA_DETERMINE.

The relevant Customizing path is **Cross-Process Settings • Warehouse Task • Confirmation of Warehouse Task • BAdI: Suppression of Update of Cml. Fields in the Available Quantity Table**.

BAdI /SCWM/EX_CORE_CO_QUAN_UPD

Finally, let's look at the /SCWM/EX_CORE_CO_QUAN_UPD BAdI (Change Attributes of Table /SCWM/QUAN during Warehouse Task Confirmation). With this BAdI, you can change selected attributes of the source and destination quants of the warehouse task. The system executes this BAdI during product warehouse task confirmation. Check the documentation of the BAdI's interface methods for further details.

The important methods of this BAdI are as follows:

- SOURCE_CHANGE (change attributes of source quant)
- DESTINATION_CHANGE (change attributes of destination quant)
- HU_CHANGE (change attributes of all quants that are moved with a handling unit)

The BAdI is called in include /SCWM/LHU_TO_UPDF39, subroutine TO_CONF_SITM.

The relevant Customizing path is **Cross-Process Settings • Warehouse Task • Confirmation of Warehouse Task • BAdI: Changing Quant Attributes during WT Confirmation**.

6.4   Warehouse Orders

Warehouse order creation is a highly configurable application of EWM warehouse logistics that takes care of the grouping of warehouse tasks into executable warehouse orders in an optimal way. Warehouse order creation is called after each warehouse task creation. Various criteria, such as sorting requirements, limit values, and packing algorithms, are considered when grouping and potentially splitting warehouse tasks by warehouse order creation rules. These created warehouse orders will finally be assigned to the appropriate resources for execution. In EWM Customizing, you can find the configuration options of warehouse order creation under the path **Extended Warehouse Management • Cross-Process Settings • Warehouse Order**. Furthermore, you can find the enhancement options for warehouse order creation under the path **Extended Warehouse Management • Business Add-Ins (BAdIs) for Extended Warehouse Management • Cross-Process Settings • Warehouse Order Creation**.

For the warehouse order creation described in this section, we will present each individual BAdI. Figure 6.4 shows the use of enhancement spots within the processing of warehouse order creation. Warehouse task creation starts at the release of a wave. Once the warehouse task creation is done, the warehouse tasks are passed into the warehouse order creation, where they will first be grouped by queue and activity area as these aspects need to be unique for all tasks within an order. For the grouped warehouse tasks, the first applicable warehouse order creation rule will be determined by the activity area of the tasks. The warehouse order creation rule may contain further filtering and limiting criteria to be applied for the task grouping. This means that some warehouse tasks may be removed from the original grouping.

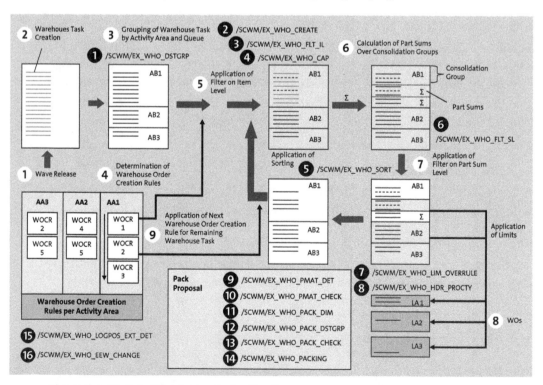

Figure 6.4 BAdIs in Warehouse Order Creation

Once a group of warehouse tasks has been determined, a pack proposal can be created for them. The pack profile in the warehouse order creation rule determines the appropriate procedure of packing, which allows for customization through a high number of BAdIs. The grouped tasks of this first warehouse order will still be sorted by defined sorting rules. For still unprocessed warehouse tasks, the earlier-described logic will be run through using the next available warehouse order creation rule for the activity area. This procedure will be followed until all tasks have been processed. For debugging the warehouse order creation, activation of checkpoint group /SCWM/WHO will be helpful.

6.4.1   Enhancement Spot /SCWM/ES_WHO

For enhancement spot /SCWM/ES_WHO, we will look at 16 different BAdIs in the following sections.

BAdI /SCWM/EX_WHO_DSTGRP

Let's start by looking at the /SCWM/EX_WHO_DSTGRP BAdI (Overwrite Consolidation Group). With this BAdI, you can overwrite the consolidation group in the warehouse task shortly before the warehouse order creation is started. The BAdI is run through for each warehouse task in a group of tasks to be processed for warehouse order creation. You can redetermine the consolidation group and change it if necessary. Changing other fields of the warehouse task is also possible within the BAdI; however, we do not recommend it for standard warehouse task fields as these changes may cause unpredictable side effects to standard processing. Changes to custom-defined fields added as an append to structure /SCWM/INCL_EEW_S_ORDIM_PS (customer-specific fields at the warehouse task level) should be fine.

The important method of this BAdI is DSTGRP (overwrite consolidation group).

The BAdI is called at the beginning of warehouse order creation processing within function module /SCWM/WHO_CREATE.

The relevant Customizing path is **Cross-Process Settings • Warehouse Order Creation • BAdI: Overwrite Consolidation Group.**

BAdI /SCWM/EX_WHO_CREATE

Let's look at the /SCWM/EX_WHO_CREATE BAdI (Full WO Creation Using BAdI). With this BAdI, you can implement complete custom-specific warehouse order creation logic in EWM, including grouping warehouse tasks into warehouse orders and the optional creation of pick handling units. If activated, the BAdI will be run instead of applying any available warehouse order creation rules from Customizing. We recommend that you first exploit the possibilities of the other available BAdIs for warehouse order creation before implementing this BAdI as warehouse order creation is an extensive and complex application and the other available BAdIs in the warehouse order application are normally sufficient to cover most project-specific needs.

The important method of this BAdI is CREATE (user-specific warehouse order creation).

The BAdI is called in include /SCWM/LWHO_MAINF32, subroutine WO_CREATION_BADI.

The relevant Customizing path is **Cross-Process Settings • Warehouse Order Creation • BAdI: Full WO Creation**.

BAdI /SCWM/EX_WHO_FLT_IL

Let's look at the /SCWM/EX_WHO_FLT_IL BAdI (Use Additional Filters at Item Level). With this BAdI, you can add additional filters beside the ones set up in the Customizing of the warehouse order creation rule for filtering at the item level. You need to provide your custom filtering logic in the BAdI method using the CT_TO_SUCCESS return parameter to include items for further processing and CT_TO_FAILED return parameter for items not passing the additional filtering criteria.

The important method of this BAdI is FILTER_IL (use additional filters at the item level).

The BAdI is called in include /SCWM/LWHO_MAINF04, subroutine WHO_FILTER_IL_CHECK.

The relevant Customizing path is **Cross-Process Settings • Warehouse Order Creation • BAdI: Use of Additional Filters on Item Level**.

BAdI /SCWM/EX_WHO_CAP

Let's look at the /SCWM/EX_WHO_CAP BAdI (Filter Planned Shipping HUs). With this BAdI, you can filter the list of planned shipping handling units during the execution of warehouse order creation rules to potentially open up items of planned shipping handling units for packing proposal through warehouse order creation. The assumption is that planned shipping handling units (or shipping handling units more generally) do not need to have further packing proposed. Standard applied fallback class /SCWM/CL_EI_WHO_CAP will delete already existing planned shipping handling units, however.

The important method of this BAdI is FILTER_PSHUS (filter planned shipping handling unit tables).

The BAdI is called in include /SCWM/LWHO_MAINF46, subroutine READ_POHU.

The relevant Customizing path is **Cross-Process Settings • Warehouse Order Creation • BAdI: Filter Planned Shipping HUs**.

BAdI /SCWM/EX_WHO_SORT

Let's look at the /SCWM/EX_WHO_SORT BAdI (Use Additional WT Sorting). This BAdI enables you to perform additional sorting of the warehouse tasks at different times of the warehouse order creation processing:

- Between item and subtotal filtering (inbound sorting, IV_SORTTYPE = A).
- Before packing (IV_SORTTYPE = C).

- At the very end of the warehouse order creation process (outbound sorting, IV_SORT-TYPE = B).
- Without specifying any sorting rule, the default sorting will be applied, which follows the storage bin sorting. The inbound sorting depends on the creation category of the applied warehouse order creation rule.

The important method of this BAdI is SORT (use additional warehouse task sorting).

The BAdI is called in include /SCWM/LWHO_MAINF03, subroutine WHO_TO_SORT.

The relevant Customizing path is **Cross-Process Settings • Warehouse Order Creation • BAdI: Use Additional WT Sorting**.

BAdI /SCWM/EX_WHO_FLT_SL

Let's look at the /SCWM/EX_WHO_FLT_SL BAdI (Use Additional Filters at Subtotal Level). With this BAdI, you can apply additional filter criteria on the subtotal level of the transferred consolidation group next to the filter criteria defined in Customizing for the warehouse order creation rule. Set the CV_FAILED changing parameter to ABAP_TRUE if the given consolidation group has not passed the additional filter. All items that belong to this consolidation group will no longer be processed with the current creation rule.

The important method of this BAdI is FILTER_SL (use additional filters on subtotal level).

The BAdI is called in include /SCWM/LWHO_MAINF05, subroutine WHO_FILTER_SL.

The relevant Customizing path is **Cross-Process Settings • Warehouse Order Creation • BAdI: Use of Additional Filters on Subtotal Level**.

BAdI /SCWM/EX_WHO_LIM_OVERRULE

Let's look at the /SCWM/EX_WHO_LIM_OVERRULE BAdI (Overwrite Limit Values). With this BAdI, you can override values from the limits defined in Customizing of the warehouse order creation rule. To do so, you need to replace the limit values of structure CS_LIMITS in the BAdI method with your own values. These modified limit values are then used in further processing to determine the size of the warehouse order. Note that a maximum of 999 pack proposals can be assigned to a warehouse order.

The important method of this BAdI is LIMIT_OVERRULE (overwrite limit values).

The BAdI is called in include /SCWM/LWHO_MAINF01, subroutine WHO_LIMIT_APPLY.

The relevant Customizing path is **Cross-Process Settings • Warehouse Order Creation • BAdI: Overwrite of Limit Values**.

BAdI /SCWM/EX_WHO_HDR_PROCTY

Let's look at the /SCWM/EX_WHO_HDR_PROCTY BAdI (Overwrite Warehouse Process Type on WO Level). This BAdI enables you to overwrite the warehouse process type of the warehouse order. By default, the warehouse process type of the first warehouse task inside the warehouse order will be used. The warehouse tasks of the warehouse order are passed into the BAdI. You can use this data to perform your own determination of the warehouse process type and return the one found.

The important method of this BAdI is HDR_PROCTY (overwrite warehouse process type on warehouse order level).

The BAdI is called in include /SCWM/LWHO_MAINF26, subroutine WHO_STRUCTURE_CREATE.

The relevant Customizing path is **Cross-Process Settings • Warehouse Order Creation • BAdI: Overwrite Warehouse Process Type on WO Level**.

BAdI /SCWM/EX_WHO_PMAT_DET

Let's look at the /SCWM/EX_WHO_PMAT_DET BAdI (Determine Possible Packaging Materials for Det. the HU). With this BAdI, you can determine available packaging materials for the pack proposal creation. If you return values in table CT_PMAT of the BAdI method, the standard logic for packaging material determination will not be called any more.

The important method of this BAdI is PMAT_DETERMINATION (determine possible packaging materials for determining the handling unit).

The BAdI is called in include /SCWM/LWHO_MAINF28, subroutine PMAT_DETERMINATION.

The relevant Customizing path is **Cross-Process Settings • Warehouse Order Creation • BAdI: Determination of Possible Packaging Materials for HU Determination**.

BAdI /SCWM/EX_WHO_PMAT_CHECK

Let's look at the /SCWM/EX_WHO_PMAT_CHECK BAdI (Check and Sort Found Packaging Materials). With this BAdI, you can implement an additional check and determination of potential packaging materials to be used for the packing proposal. The packaging materials that have been determined by the application are passed into the BAdI method, and you can, for example, apply a custom sorting of the packaging materials by priority.

The important method of this BAdI is PMAT_CHECK (check and sort found packaging materials).

The BAdI is called in include /SCWM/LWHO_MAINF28, subroutine PMAT_DETERMINATION.

The relevant Customizing path is **Cross-Process Settings • Warehouse Order Creation • BAdI: Check and Sorting of Packaging Materials Found**.

BAdI /SCWM/EX_WHO_PACK_DIM

Let's look at the /SCWM/EX_WHO_PACK_DIM BAdI (Check for Length, Width, Height). This BAdI enables you to perform additional checks on the dimensions of a handling unit—or rather, packaging material—in terms of length, width, and height to understand if the packing qualifies for the warehouse task to be packed. The prerequisite for this check to run is to have the dimensional check enabled in the packing profile flag, **Check LWH.**

The important method of this BAdI is PACK_DIMENSION (check for length, width, height).

The BAdI is called in include /SCWM/LWHO_MAINF19, subroutine DIMENSION_CHECK.

The relevant Customizing path is **Cross-Process Settings • Warehouse Order Creation • BAdI: Check of Length, Width, Height.**

BAdI /SCWM/EX_WHO_PACK_DSTGRP

Let's look at the /SCWM/EX_WHO_PACK_DSTGRP BAdI (Check whether WT Is to Be Skipped where DSTGRP Varies). With this BAdI, you can check whether a warehouse task for a deviating consolidation group is to be omitted from the assignment to a pick handling unit. You can use the data passed to perform your own investigation of skipping warehouse tasks. The BAdI is called when the consolidation group of the warehouse task differs from the one of the warehouse tasks already assigned to the pick handling unit and when the maximum number of consolidation groups for the handling unit has already been reached. The assignment of warehouse tasks to the pick handling unit will not stop but will continue with the next warehouse task. The BAdI is linked to the **Skip WT** configuration option of the packing profile.

The important method of this BAdI is PACK_DSTGRP (check whether warehouse task is to be skipped for different consolidation groups).

The BAdI is called in include /SCWM/LWHO_MAINF08, subroutine ADVANCED_PACKING.

The relevant Customizing path is **Cross-Process Settings • Warehouse Order Creation • BAdI: Check Whether WT Is to Be Skipped for Deviating ConsGrp.**

BAdI /SCWM/EX_WHO_PACK_CHECK

Let's look at the /SCWM/EX_WHO_PACK_CHECK BAdI (Check whether WT Is to Be Packed into HU). With this BAdI, you can verify that a certain warehouse task is actually to be packed into the handling unit proposed. Data of the current warehouse task and assigned handling unit are available in the BAdI and allow for an additional check of the warehouse task's assignment.

The important method of this BAdI is PACK_CHECK (check whether warehouse task is to be packed into handling unit).

The BAdI is called in include /SCWM/LWHO_MAINF08, subroutine ADVANCED_PACKING.

The relevant Customizing path is **Cross-Process Settings • Warehouse Order Creation • BAdI: Check Whether WT Is to Be Packed in HU.**

BAdI /SCWM/EX_WHO_PACKING

Let's look at the /SCWM/EX_WHO_PACKING BAdI (HU Determination for Warehouse Order). With this BAdI, you can implement a completely custom packaging logic and handling unit determination for warehouse order creation. You must have selected packing mode **BAdI** in the packing profile of the applied warehouse order creation rule in Customizing. We recommend that you check out the uses of the other available BAdIs of the packing logic before using this more complex BAdI.

The important method of this BAdI is PACKING (handling unit determination for warehouse order).

The BAdI is called in include /SCWM/LWHO_MAINF06, subroutine HU_DETERMINATION.

The relevant Customizing path is **Cross-Process Settings • Warehouse Order Creation • BAdI: HU Determination for Warehouse Order**.

BAdI /SCWM/EX_WHO_LOGPOS_EXT_DET

Let's look at the /SCWM/EX_WHO_LOGPOS_EXT_DET BAdI (Determination of Planned HU Positions for Picking). With this BAdI, you can update the warehouse tasks in a warehouse order with a planned handling unit position (field DLOGPOS_EXT_WT). This field is displayed in the RF picking transaction and helps to choose the correct handling unit position on distribution equipment. The position in the warehouse task can contain the position IDs of several nested handling units if they are used. When working with nested handling units, you can define and use a delimiter (typically /) when concatenating the positions. The system runs this BAdI only if the warehouse order creation category of the warehouse order creation rule is set to I (**Distribution Equipment Picking**).

The important methods of this BAdI are as follows:

- GET_DELIMETER (get the delimiter for concatenated positions)
- LOGPOS_EXT_DETERMINATION (determine planned handling unit positions)

The BAdI is called in include /SCWM/LWHO_MAINF53, subroutine WO_BADI_LOGPOS_EXT of the position determination. It will also be called in RF processing (e.g., function module /SCWM/RF_DDLD_DEST_ENTER_PAI) for delimiter validation.

The relevant Customizing path is **Cross-Process Settings • Warehouse Order Creation • BAdI: Determination of Planned HU Positions for Picking**.

BAdI /SCWM/EX_WHO_EEW_CHANGE

Finally, let's look at the /SCWM/EX_WHO_EEW_CHANGE BAdI (Update of Customer Fields When Creating/Updating WOs). With this BAdI, you can fill your custom-specific fields during warehouse order creation. The prerequisite is to have created beforehand an append that contains your custom fields for enhancement structure /SCWM/INCL_EEW_S_WHO of the warehouse order .

The important method of this BAdI is UPDATE (update customer fields for warehouse orders).

The BAdI is called in include /SCWM/LWHO_MAINF52, subroutine WO_BADI_UPDATE_EEW.

The relevant Customizing path is **Cross-Process Settings • Warehouse Order Creation • BAdI: Update of Customer Fields when Creating/Updating WOs**.

6.5 Exception Handling

The exception handling available in EWM lets you detect abnormal situations in the warehouse processes right at the time that they occur and allows for appropriate reaction and follow-on processing. Thus, inconsistencies of stock and other problem situations can be promptly reported and addressed. The following enhancement spots can be found in checkpoint group /SCWM/EXCEPTION.

6.5.1 Enhancement Spot /SCWM/ES_EXCP_EXC

For enhancement spot /SCWM/ES_EXCP_EXC (Exception Handling), we will look at four different BAdIs in the following sections.

BAdI /SCWM/EX_EXCP_EXC_BLKBINS

Let's start by looking at the /SCWM/EX_EXCP_EXC_BLKBINS BAdI (Control Locking/Unlocking of Storage Bins for Resource). With this BAdI, you can control the locking/unlocking of storage bins for a resource. It is used in the material flow system area. You can filter storage bins to be locked or unlocked by custom logic. In addition, you can determine the locking indicator (putaway and/or removal) for bin determination and set a valid user status for the bin. The BAdI uses the current data of the material flow system, the storage bins affected by the lock, and the user status profile of the storage bins.

The important method of this BAdI is CONTROL_BLKBINS (manage blocking/unblocking of storage bins for resource).

The BAdI is called in method BLCK_REL_BINS_2_RESOURCE of class /SCWM/CL_EXCEPTION_OBJ_MFS.

The relevant Customizing path is **Material Flow System (MFS) • BAdI: Control Locking/Unlocking Storage Bins for Resource**.

BAdI /SCWM/EX_EXCP_EXC_FLT

Let's look at the /SCWM/EX_EXCP_EXC_FLT BAdI (Filter Exception Codes). With this BAdI, you can filter exception codes and potentially remove exception codes that have already been determined by the application.

The important method of this BAdI is FILTER_EXCEPTION_CODES (filter exception codes).

The BAdI is called in method GET_EXCEPTION_CODE of class /SCWM/CL_EXCEPTION_APPL.

The relevant Customizing path is **Cross-Process Settings • Exception Handling • BAdI: Filtering of Exception Codes.**

BAdI /SCWM/EX_EXCP_EXC_FLT_FOLLOUP

Let's look at the /SCWM/EX_EXCP_EXC_FLT_FOLLOUP BAdI (Filter Standard Follow-Up Actions for Exception Handling). This BAdI enables you to filter follow-up actions of the exception handling that have been determined by the application and will allow canceling such follow-up actions in the context of workflows, alerts, and status management.

The important method of this BAdI is FILTER_FOLLOW_UP_ACTIONS (filter standard follow-up actions).

The BAdI is called in method PROCESS_EXCEPTION_CODE of class /SCWM/CL_EXCEPTION_APPL.

The relevant Customizing path is **Cross-Process Settings • Exception Handling • BAdI: Filtering of Standard Follow-Up Actions for Exception Handling.**

BAdI /SCWM/EX_EXCP_EXC_FUNC

Finally, let's look at the /SCWM/EX_EXCP_EXC_FUNC BAdI (Execute Functions). In this BAdI, you can trigger any follow-up actions as a reaction to certain exception codes.

The important method of this BAdI is EXECUTE_FUNCTIONS (execute functions).

The BAdI is called in method PROCESS_EXCEPTION_CODE of class /SCWM/CL_EXCEPTION_APPL.

The relevant Customizing path is **Cross-Process Settings • Exception Handling • BAdI: Execution of Functions.**

6.6   Summary

This final chapter presented a list of selected BAdIs within the core applications of EWM. Use this list as a reference for BAdI determination and extended documentation for custom enhancements to the feature-rich EWM application.

Appendices

Appendix A

Programming Guidelines in Extended Warehouse Management for Enhancements

Uniform nomenclature and structure in programming make the code easier to read and therefore easier to maintain. In this appendix, we describe selected guidelines for programming in EWM. Using these programming guidelines in custom development enables, for example, an application support team to understand your coding faster and eliminate possible errors in custom code.

The guidelines we list here are for your information. It is up to you if you use them in your project (and if so, which ones). We recommend that you agree on guidelines before you start a project, as it's certainly not advisable to switch code just before go-live. Of course, without compliance, you won't be able to develop error-free coding.

[«]

Programming Guidelines within Extended Warehouse Management

Over the past fifteen years, EWM has grown significantly—not only in terms of functionality but also in its number of lines of code. During this period, the programming guidelines have changed and improved so that you will find exceptions in the standard coding for each of the provisions listed here.

A.1 General Guidelines

The general programming guidelines define the very rough level of how programming is done in EWM. They are not project-specific, and we recommend that this be considered during custom development. In the following, we have broken out some of the basic guidelines by category:

- **Language**
  Names for programming elements (variables, routines, etc.) and comments in the code must be in English.

- **Database access**
  For database tables of a new object, it is advisable to provide a new central function group or class for reading and writing, including buffering. Writing database access to standard objects is not allowed; always use the EWM function modules and methods.

- **Messages**
  Use the application log or the /SCWM/CL_LOG class to collect success and error messages. Use the MESSAGE . . . INTO lv_dummy statement to guarantee the reference of messages works.

- **Constants**
  Instead of literals (e.g., PDO), use constants.

- **Checkpoint group**
  Use one checkpoint group per enhancement and the BREAK-POINT ID statement in each function module or method for support reasons.

- **Visibility of variables**
  Local variables are preferred and should be used instead of global ones, if possible. Global variables must be used only for storing data that is relevant for the rest of the logical unit of work (LUW), which is at least longer than the current method call.

- **Interfaces**
  Pass data through well-defined interfaces such as IMPORTING/USING, CHANGING, and so on. Use reference parameters instead of value parameters if possible. Do not use TABLES parameters in function modules (they are only available for historical reasons).

- **Structuring and reusability**
  Use respective classes and methods for better structuring and readability of programs, function groups, and forms.

- **Transparency versus compactness**
  Transparent code is easier to understand than compact code. Avoid compact code if it is not transparent or simple to read.

- **Code inspector and enhanced syntax check**
  Use the code inspector (Transaction SCI) and the enhanced syntax check (Transaction SLIN) after finalizing a program or enhancement.

- **Complex code**
  Avoid overly complex code—for example, three-times-nested IF statements.

- **System variables**
  Do not modify system variables.

- **Macros**
  Avoid macros. Calling positions and interfaces of macros are not transparent.

- **External performs**
  Avoid calls to external form routines

- **Header lines**
  The usage of header lines of internal tables is not very transparent in debugging or reading the code and isn't recommended. The definition of internal tables with table types guarantees that no header lines exist.

- **Obsolete advanced business application programming statements**
  In ABAP Help (Transaction ABAPHELP), you can find a list of obsolete ABAP statements. These should no longer be used.

A.2 Naming Conventions for the Data Dictionary

Data dictionary objects (DDIC objects) in EWM start with namespace /SCWM/ and a prefix, <namespace><prefix>_<name>. The available prefixes are listed in Table A.1. Define your own namespace for your projects (e.g., Z*).

Data Type	Prefix	Example
Domain	DO	/SCWM/DO_TU_NUM
Data element	DE	/SCWM/DE_TU_NUM
Structure	S	/SCWM/S_TU_NUM
Table type	TT	/SCWM/TT_TU_NUM
Search help	SH	/SCWM/SH_LGPLA
Enqueue objects	E	/SCWM/EHU
Views	V	/SCWM/V_LGN_PRES
Database tables	■ No prefix: application table ■ T: Customizing table	/SCWM/HUHDR /SCWM/TPMTYP

Table A.1 Naming Conventions for Data Dictionary Objects

Application tables should be defined by usage of include structures and usage of the GROUP field. Here the table key is one include, and the data part consists of at least one include. Enhanced structuring is useful for bigger tables. For example, the handling unit header database table /SCWM/HUHDR consists of a key structure /SCWM/S_HUHDR_KEY and data include /SCWM/S_HUHDR.

As in internal processing, more fields are necessary than the database fields; almost always, an associated structure exists with the database fields and dynamic fields. This is often signaled by the suffix _INT—for example, /SCWM/S_HUHDR_INT or /SCWM/S_ORDIM_O_INT.

The corresponding table type of such a structure also contains the suffix _INT—for example, /SCWM/TT_HUHDR_INT or /SCWM/TT_ORDIM_O_INT.

In the area of delivery processing (namespace /SCDL/), data elements and domains are indistinguishable; both use the prefix DL. Structures and table types do not use a prefix but a suffix: STR for structures (/SCDL/DM_MESSAGE_STR) and TAB for table types (/SCDL/DM_MESSAGE_TAB).

A.3   Naming Conventions for ABAP Objects

Table A.2 lists the naming conventions for ABAP Objects.

ABAP Object	Naming Convention and Example
Program (report)	<namespace>R<name> /SCWM/RCALL_GWL_UI
Class	<namespace>CL_<object><name> /SCWM/CL_SR_TUDLV
Interface	<namespace>IF_<object><name> /SCWM/IF_TM
Function group	<namespace><name> /SCWM/HUMAIN
Implementing class	<namespace>CL_IM_<object><name> /SCWM/CL_IM_DLV_PPF_SCHED
Enhancement implementation	<namespace>EI_<object><name> /SCWM/EI_CD_OPP_INBOUND
Exception class	<namespace>CX_<object><name> /SCWM/CX_SR_ERROR

Table A.2 Naming Conventions for ABAP Objects

A.4   Naming Conventions for Variables and Parameters

Parameters in interfaces and variables in programs are to be defined in accordance with the pattern <visibility><datatype>_<name>. The possible values for visibility and data type are shown in Table A.3.

Visibility	Datatype				
	V (field/variable)	T (table)	S (structure)	C (constant)	O (object reference)
I (importing parameter)	IV_	IT_	IS_		IO_
E (exporting parameter)	EV_	ET_	ES_		EO_
C (changing parameter)	CV_	CT_	CS_		CO_

Table A.3 Naming Conventions for Parameters and Variables

Visibility	Datatype				
R (returning parameter)	RV_	RT_	RS_		RO_
L (local)	LV_	LT_	LS_	LC_	LO_
G (global)	GV_	GT_	GS_	GC_	GO_
S (static)	SV_	ST_	SS_	SC_	SO_
M (instance attribute of a class)	MV_	MT_	MS_		MO_

Table A.3 Naming Conventions for Parameters and Variables (Cont.)

A.5 Performance Guidelines

The programming guidelines include requirements for performance optimization. We have summarized the principles in the following section. They should help you lose the minimum amount of runtime when working with large amounts of data.

A.5.1 Field Symbols

If possible, use assigning for loops and read statements. Performance will increase, especially on tables with wide or complex structure.

A.5.2 Processing of Internal Tables

If possible, use sorted tables and key accesses—that is, with READ TABLE WITH TABLE KEY or READ TABLE BINARY SEARCH. It is sufficient to sort (ascending) to ensure sorting in a standard table. The use of sorted table types is only meaningful if all accesses are always made via this key. On reading tables with standard functions/methods, check if the result is sorted and access those tables only with BINARY SEARCH.

If only one entry of an internal table is required, reading with binary search as in Listing A.1 is recommended.

```
READ table ASSIGNING <fieldsymbol>
            WITH KEY abs = xyz
            BINARY_SEARCH.
```

Listing A.1 Reading with Binary Search

If multiple records are needed, it's advisable to first position via binary search and perform subsequent processing in a loop, as shown in the example in Listing A.2.

```
READ table TRANSPORTING NO FIELDS
                    WITH KEY abc = xyz
                    BINARY SEARCH.
IF SY-SUBRC is initial.
  LOOP AT table ASSIGNING <fieldsymbol> FROM SY-TABIX.
    IF <fieldsymbol>-abc <> xyz.
        EXIT.
    ENDIF.
Do something
  ENDLOOP.
ENDIF.
```

Listing A.2 Internal Table Access for Multiple Records with Same Table Key

Avoid performing a sort of sorted tables. If you want to insert a new record into a sorted table, use INSERT INTO TABLE.

A.5.3   Database Selections

Avoid your own database selections, especially ones on standard tables.

To make a program performant, you should always read standard data via standard functions. This ensures that any previously read data is taken from the buffer and is not reread. Although only a field of a table may be needed, reading the buffered data is preferable.

To read EWM application data, you'll find reading functions for many objects in Chapter 5. Often you'll find a central reading function available for EWM Customizing tables—for example, /SCWM/T331_READ_SINGLE for table /SCWM/T331.

If you program your own database selection, avoid SELECT – ENDSELECT and use the SELECT INTO TABLE instruction instead.

A.6   Summary

In this appendix, we described the general development guidelines as they are used by the EWM product development team at SAP. You should now have a basic understanding of how to structure and design your own custom coding.

Appendix B
Migrating SAP EWM to EWM in SAP S/4HANA

As SAP EWM, the standalone solution based on SAP NetWeaver, will go out of maintenance in the not too distant future (as of the time of finishing the new edition of this book, mainstream maintenance for SAP EWM 9.5 is slated to be discontinued by the end of 2027), more and more organizations are looking to migrate from SAP EWM. As they might have to migrate a lot of warehouse sites to the new SAP S/4HANA platform, EWM migration initiatives have already started, even ahead of the general SAP S/4HANA transition for, for example, ERP systems.

First and foremost, a decision needs to be made about a deployment option for EWM in SAP S/4HANA: either embedded or decentralized EWM. This decision is quite often easily made, as many customers either do not yet run their ERP system on SAP S/4HANA, so embedded EWM isn't an option, or require connection of multiple ERP systems to their EWM installation, which will require decentralized EWM. Apart from these decisive aspects, a number of strategic, operational risk, operational cost, and hardware cost criteria can be named that should be evaluated to foster the decision process. SAP Note 1606493 introduces EWM deployment options and provides a potential starting point for discussing these decision criteria. We recommend going through the note and potentially seeking your implementation partner's advice in your decision process.

> **EWM Deployment Differences**
>
> Keep in mind that not only performance or cost criteria should be considered in making a decision about the EWM deployment option; there might also be functional requirements and restrictions to be evaluated with your intended SAP S/4HANA release. Study available SAP Notes, like 3218673, and consider your SAP S/4HANA release to include the deployment differences in your deployment decision.

SAP provides detailed documentation on how to migrate from SAP EWM to EWM in SAP S/4HANA. Before we turn to an overview of the procedure and steps, we'd like to introduce the overall migration topic briefly, providing some thoughts about migration strategies.

B.1   Migration Strategies

In general, we see two migration strategies being followed by customers when transitioning from SAP EWM to EWM in SAP S/4HANA. These could be named and shortly described as follows:

- **All at once**
  All warehouses (warehouse numbers) of one SAP EWM system instance are migrated to and set live simultaneously in EWM in SAP S/4HANA. This could also be called a systemwide migration, close to a technical system conversion.

- **One by one**
  Single warehouses (warehouse numbers) of one SAP EWM system instance are migrated and deployed in SAP S/4HANA in sequence, mainly one by one, or n by one, where n is not all warehouses.

You will usually find different situations and limiting factors for customers opting for either migration strategy approach. While some customers will highly value going backward, or more precisely forward, to standard functionality, potentially removing custom enhancements during the transition to SAP S/4HANA, others might be more interested in a mere technical migration or system conversion, accepting and expecting no or very little change in current functionality and running processes.

You can drive the final strategy decision using the following parameters as your decision criteria. We assume the all-at-once approach is more likely (and thus the one-by-one approach is less likely):

- The following criteria will be rated *low*:
  - Number and complexity of custom enhancements
  - Level of potential for new standard functionality, replacing custom enhancements
  - Possibility to close all or most transactional documents at time of go-live
- The following criteria will be rated *high*:
  - Ability to support go-live for all warehouses simultaneously (availability of resources)
  - Number and variation of external interfaces
  - Number of ongoing/planned EWM projects (leaving less time for the migration project)
  - Risk/effort of running two EWM versions in parallel

Applying such criteria in an example, you could say that assuming a low number and complexity of custom enhancements and a high ability to support go-live for all warehouses simultaneously, it appears more likely to apply the all-at-once strategy. However, the decision might also depend on factors other than those listed here, and little bit of gut instinct will certainly play its part at the end as well. Again, you might consider integrating your implementation partner's service for evaluation and determination of potential strategy options.

B.2 Migration Procedure

In this section, we provide a high-level description of potential steps for an EWM migration project, which might not be too far apart from any traditional software migration project as you know it. However, we provide EWM-specific aspects or mention additional sources of information in some of the steps that you might want to consider in your project.

SAP provides two important how-to-guide documents that we strongly recommend that you study and use for your migration projects. We'll refer to these as the Integration Guide and the Migration Guide. Both documents can be found at the SAP Community Wiki, at *https://wiki.scn.sap.com/wiki/display/SCM/How-To+Guides+for+SAP+EWM*.

The Integration Guide is officially called *Integration of SAP ERP or SAP S/4HANA with Decentralized EWM in SAP S/4HANA* and the Migration Guide is *How to Migrate from SAP EWM (Business Suite) to Decentralized EWM Based on SAP S/4HANA*. Both documents contain detailed descriptions of activities to plan for and perform during integration and migration of EWM in SAP S/4HANA following a step-by-step sequence. Where applicable, we will mention the appropriate chapters of the two guides in the corresponding steps of the following procedure, depicted in Figure B.1.

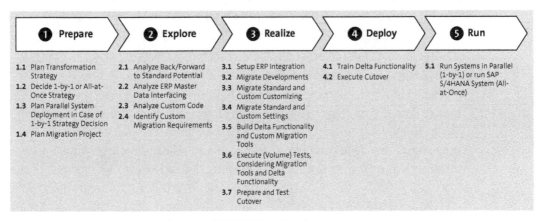

Figure B.1 Possible Phases and Steps of EWM Migration Project

❶ **Prepare**

– **Plan transformation strategy**
Planning a transformation strategy for your EWM installation(s) might get more complicated the more systems you have next to EWM in the overall SAP S/

4HANA transformation and the more warehouses (more precisely, warehouse type clusters) you will need to include. You should develop a clear understanding of the intended SAP S/4HANA architectural landscape to base your EWM transformation strategy on and to decide on EWM deployment options. You will likely also include the development of an instance strategy evaluating, for example, performance requirements or network availability for your warehouse sites to understand how many EWM systems to deploy in which regions of the world.

- **Decide on one-by-one or all-at-once strategy**
  You should select a migration strategy, as outlined in Section B.1.

- **Plan parallel system maintenance for changes**
  You should ensure that you have a plan ready for parallel system maintenance as of the start of the migration project and during the time in which you'll have two EWM systems productively run in parallel until the EWM migration has been completed and all warehouses have moved to the SAP S/4HANA system. The second part will apply only if you opted for the one-by-one strategy. Check Chapter 2, Section 2.3 and Chapter 4 in the Migration Guide for further information.

- **Plan migration project**
  It goes without saying that you should establish a well-detailed project plan for the migration project, potentially following the steps further outlined.

❷ **Explore**

- **Analyze the potential of standard functionality**
  The lower the SAP EWM release you are moving away from, the likelier it will be that the (latest) SAP S/4HANA EWM release you are moving to will provide the potential to eliminate custom enhancements or interfaces by introducing standard functionality. We recommend analyzing this potential in detail and deciding how much of this potential you actually want to realize in the new system.

- **Analyze ERP master data (interfacing)**
  If you've chosen the decentralized EWM deployment option, you'll need to set up master data distribution using ALE (IDoc) interfaces. We recommend analyzing any custom enhancements (custom fields) of transferred master data objects to understand any requirements to take these enhancements over into the new interface processing (basically moving from CIF to ALE). Check Chapter 6 of the Integration Guide for which interfaces to use for master data replication. Even with embedded EWM, you should ensure that you still have EWM-relevant master data enhancements in place in the central SAP S/4HANA system.

- **Analyze custom code**
  As in other SAP S/4HANA transitions, you should run a readiness check on custom code, include an ABAP Test Cockpit check for SAP S/4HANA readiness, and thereby gain an understanding for potential conflicts based on standard code changes. Check Chapter 3, Section 3.2 in the Migration Guide for further information on technical changes between SAP EWM and EWM in SAP S/4HANA, mainly

in the areas of Customizing and master data objects used that are driven by simplification and data redundancy within SAP S/4HANA.

– **Identify custom migration requirements**
Still in the explore phase of the project, you should develop a list of master and transactional data objects that will need to be migrated, including requirements for archived data. We recommend matching each of the objects in the list with a migration tool, standard-provided or custom-built. Consider the migration cockpit, the Change and Transport System, and the comparison and adjustment features of maintenance views as SAP-standard provided tools. Identify required custom tools to be developed and tested in the realization phase of the project for missing migration tools from SAP standard and add them to the backlog list for realization. Such tools may cover custom master data as well as transactional document data migration in case you are unable, for example, to close open transactional documents during cutover, as assumed by the Migration Guide. We highly recommend checking back with your implementation partner on services they might provide centered on additional migration procedures and tools.

[+]

SAP S/4HANA Migration Cockpit for EWM

To get familiar with the features and migration objects to be supported by the migration cockpit, study SAP Note 2976757. It provides an overview of prerequisites for using the migration cockpit for EWM migration and lists further sources of information, such as a link to the SAP Help Portal for an overview of available migration objects for SAP S/4HANA (filter by **Migration Approach: Direct Transfer—EWM**). You can also find the Migration Guide (version 1.7) attached to the note.

❸ **Realize**

– **Set up ERP integration**
One of the first steps in the realization phase of an EWM implementation project is usually the setup of ERP integration, as most EWM processes start and end in connected ERP systems. Follow the steps of the Integration Guide through all chapters.

– **Migrate custom developments**
As the preferred way to migrate custom developments, you can collect changed objects from workbench transports in the production system and include them into one or multiple new transport(s). You can then import these transports into the SAP S/4HANA landscape's development system. Check Chapter 3, Section 3.1 in the Migration Guide for further information.

– **Migrate Customizing**
As before, you can proceed to migrate customizing settings in a similar way, collecting changed objects from customizing transports in the production system and including them into new transports. Again, you can further import these Cus-

tomizing transport(s) into the SAP S/4HANA development system. Check Chapter 4 in the Migration Guide for further detailed information, paying special attention to the recommendations for transporting Customizing for embedded or decentralized EWM.

- **Migrate warehouse-specific master data and settings**
  You can use the migration cockpit for migrating most warehouse-specific master data and settings from SAP EWM to EWM in SAP S/4HANA. From SAP S/4HANA 2022 on, embedded EWM in SAP S/4HANA also supports the direct transfer of migration objects in the migration cockpit. For further information check Chapters 6 and 7 of the Migration Guide.

- **Migrate custom master data and settings**
  As one way to migrate custom master and settings, you could use transport requests with table content for custom master or application data, assuming there will be no changes applied to such custom data objects in the source and destination systems. Another option might be the creation of a custom migration tool.

- **Configure delta functionality and build custom migration tools**
  In this step, you perform the classic activities of a software implementation project's realization phase, implementing earlier identified delta functionality via delta configuration and custom development of backlog items. Custom migration tools might range from small reports, to reading simple data structures from the source system and copying them to identically existing data structures in the destination system, to large reports that might also require more complex remote call–enabled function modules to read data in the source system from multiple tables, mapping this data according to specified rules in the destination system before adding it to defined data structures. The migration cockpit might represent an interesting framework to realize such complex reports with as it offers to create custom migration objects to run with its different transfer methods—mainly direct data transfer or transfer via indirect download and upload using files or staging tables. You can find more detailed information on the migration cockpit in the SAP Help Portal or the SAP Community.

- **Execute tests**
  Ensure that all migration tools and more or less extensively changed process functionality will work properly, performing tool execution and process tests. Make sure to execute the tests with an appropriate amount of data, as close as possible to the data amounts used in the productive environment.

- **Prepare and test cutover**
  Establish a cutover list and keep track of the runtimes of the steps to allow for scheduling activities in deployment and go-live. Use the setup of the quality systems as a first test case for later cutover to the productive system. We recommend checking with your basis team or consultant about options to have these tests

done multiple times—for example, by using defined system states that you can go back to.

❹ **Deploy**

- **Train delta functionality**
  Ensure end users are prepared to work with any new functionality provided.

- **Execute cutover**
  Follow the steps developed in your cutover list for the final deployment in the production system near or at go-live.

  If not defined otherwise, ensure you close all transactional documents. Check Chapter 8 in the Migration Guide for a list of transactional documents to consider for closing. Be aware that SAP does not provide standard any tools for migration of transactional documents. If you have built custom tools for transactional data migration, these should be applied in cutover at go-live.

❺ **Run**

- **Run systems in parallel (one-by-one strategy only)**
  Check Chapter 9 of the Migration Guide for further activities to plan for and execute at the time of go-live, such as migration of stock. Follow the plan developed earlier for running systems in parallel, being aware of transport-based changes to the different landscapes, until the transition has fully been completed. This will not apply to the all-at-once strategy.

B.3 Summary

In this appendix, we described possible migration strategies and procedural steps to bring your EWM implementation from SAP Business Suite to SAP S/4HANA. We hope that the provided information can help you in your migration project.

Appendix C
The Authors

Peter Zoellner joined SAP Consulting in 2001 and has worked for both domestic and international customers from numerous industries, specializing in logistics execution and SAP EWM since its first introduction to the market. He holds a degree in economic studies (Diplom Kaufmann) from the Catholic University of Eichstätt, Germany. Peter is married with children, and he lives in the Kreuzberg district of Berlin.

Robert Halm is the head of portfolio management at prismat, where he focuses on mobile applications and SAP HANA solutions, especially for warehouse processes. Prior to this appointment in 2014, he served the company as a senior consultant and a project manager and has been successfully managing a consulting team since 2011. He has supported companies across numerous industries in the conceptual design, implementation, and optimization of business processes for more than eight years. His focus is on implementation and rollout projects in the field of integrated warehouse and distribution logistics with SAP EWM and workshops on special topics in supply chain management. While collaborating with highly specialized partners from several industries, he continuously drives innovation and go-to-market activities for leading-edge technologies integrated with SAP solutions.

Robert also teaches SAP EWM training courses. He studied logistics at TU University in Dortmund, Germany.

Daniela Schapler is a solution architect at SAP SE. She joined SAP SE in 1996 as a developer in the area of logistics execution, following her study of physics at the Universität Tübingen. In her role as a solution architect, she was involved in the design of SAP EWM from the very beginning. She was instrumental in the development of handling unit management and has supervised several projects for companies running SAP. Since 2010, she has worked as part of the installed maintenance support for SAP EWM.

Karen Schulze has worked as a developer and consultant in the area of SAP EWM for more than 14 years. She is currently a senior consultant at abat, a company focusing on automotive industries and logistics. After finishing her studies in 1998 with a degree in mathematics and computer science from the University of Kaiserslautern, Karen started her professional career as a developer at SAP SE for warehouse management, joining the EWM development team. Starting in 2006, she worked as a consultant for German and international SAP EWM projects across various industries. She is currently working on SAP EWM projects in automotive and furniture industries, where, together with her abat colleagues, she implements SAP EWM standard processes.

Index

- Configure embedded and decentralized EWM in SAP S/4HANA

- Get step-by-step instructions for implementing key warehouse processes, from goods issue and receipt to picking and packing

- Explore your options for integration and reporting on your warehouse

Namita Sachan, Aman Jain

Warehouse Management with SAP S/4HANA

Get your warehouses up and running in SAP S/4HANA! With this implementation guide to extended warehouse management (EWM) in SAP S/4HANA, lay the foundation by setting up your organizational and warehouse structures. Then configure your master data and cross-process settings with step-by-step instructions. Finally, customize your core processes, from inbound and outbound deliveries to value-added services and cartonization. Get the most out of SAP S/4HANA for your warehouses!

925 pages, 3rd edition, pub. 03/2022
E-Book: $84.99 | **Print:** $89.95 | **Bundle:** $99.99

www.sap-press.com/5480

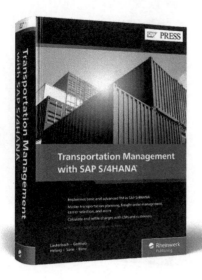

- Implement basic and advanced TM in SAP S/4HANA

- Master transportation planning, freight order management, carrier selection, and more

- Calculate and settle charges with LSPs and customers

Lauterbach, Gottlieb, Helwig, Sürie, Benz

Transportation Management with SAP S/4HANA

The definitive book on TM is back! See how transportation management fits into your SAP S/4HANA landscape and find out what's new for basic and advanced shipping. Walk through master data to get your transportation network up and running. Then follow step-by-step instructions to set up and use embedded TM functionality in SAP S/4HANA for transportation planning, freight order management, transportation execution, charge management, and more. Round out your implementation with detailed integration scenarios, migration tips, and best practices.

1088 pages, 4th edition, pub. 04/2023
E-Book: $94.99 | **Print:** $99.95 | **Bundle:** $109.99

www.sap-press.com/5575

www.sap-press.com

Interested in reading more?

Please visit our website for all new book
and e-book releases from SAP PRESS.

www.sap-press.com